The German path to Israel

The German path
to Israel

A documentation

edited by

Rolf Vogel

with a foreword by

Konrad Adenauer

DUFOUR EDITIONS
1969

© Seewald Verlag Dr. Heinrich Seewald, Stuttgart-Degerloch, 1967. Original German title: ,,Deutschlands Weg nach Israel". © 1969 for the American edition: Dufour Editions, INC. Chester Springs, Pennsylvania 19425. Library of Congress Catalog Card Number: 70 – 88 600. Printed in Germany: Union Druckerei GmbH Stuttgart

Contents

Foreword by Konrad Adenauer — 11

Prefatory note by the editor — 13

The unwritten part of history — 15

The first efforts — 17
Konrad Adenauer's first interview 17 · First meeting with members of the Israeli Parliament 19 · First talk on reparations 20 · An opinion by Hendrik van Dam 21 · Further efforts to establish contacts 26 · The note of the Israeli Government of 12 March 1951 27

The Diet Session of 27 September 1951 — 32

On the way to Wassenaar — 36
Konrad Adenauer's generous offer 36 · Preparations for negotiations 37

Reparations and the London Debt Conference — 39
Between London and Wassenaar 39 · A conversation with Hermann Josef Abs 39

The negotiations for the reparation agreement — 42
Human rapprochement 42 · Complicated negotiations 42 · Arab protests 54

The signing of the reparation agreement at Luxembourg — 55

Ratification by the Diet — 69

The carrying-out of the agreement — 88
Report on the shipments of goods 89 · Appreciation of the agreement by Nahum Goldmann 99 · The extent of German reparations 99

Economic cooperation — 101
German-Israeli tourist travel 104

Help for the living — Remembrance of the dead — 105
Theodor Heuss at Bergen-Belsen 105 · Heinrich Lübke at Bergen-Belsen 108

The meeting in the Waldorf Astoria 115

The situation prior to the meeting 115 · Economic developments 117 · The Adenauer/Ben Gurion conversation 119 · German support for the Israeli development scheme 121

Military Cooperation 122

Franz Josef Strauss on his contacts with Shimon Peres 122 · Interview with Shimon Peres 126

The Eichmann trial in Jerusalem 129

Statements by well-known Germans 129 · David Ben Gurion's viewpoint 132

Prominent Germans in Israel 134

Theodor Heuss on the autogenous nature of democracy 134 · Eugen Gerstenmaier on the change in the German outlook 144

The final phase in the process of establishing diplomatic relations 159

German arms supplies to Israel 159 · Impediments to the establishment of diplomatic relations 159 · Kurt Birrenbach's special mission to Israel 166 · Exchange of ambassadors 175 · Negotiations on the question of German economic aid 176

Konrad Adenauer in Israel 180

Rolf Pauls's first speech in Israel 188

Asher Ben Natan and Abba Eban on German-Jewish Relations 192

Germans and Jews — Discussion during the 5th Plenary Assembly of the Jewish World Congress 197

Abba Eban's speech 197 · Nahum Goldmann opens the Plenary Session 205 · Isaac Remba on behalf of the Heruth-Hatzoar 206 · Statement of MAPAM 207 · Statement of the Achdut Ha'avodah — Poale Zion 208 · Nahum Goldmann's introductory words to the reports 208 · Gershom Sholem's speech 212 · Golo Mann's speech 222 · Salo W. Baron's speech 230 · Eugen Gerstenmaier's speech 240 · The message of Karl Jaspers to the Congress 244 · Comments 249 · Nahum Goldmann's closing speech 255

After the Jewish World Congress in Brussels 258

Conversation with Nahum Goldmann 258

The death of Konrad Adenauer 261

The development of cultural relations 264

Increasing co-operation in the sphere of science 264 · Collaboration with the Weizmann Institute and Israeli scientists 264 · Honorary Fellowship for Ludwig Erhard 266 · Scholarships of the German Academic Exchange Service 271 · Alexander-von-Humboldt Foundation Scholarships 271 · The Friends of the Hebrew University Society 272 · Difficult beginnings 272 · German films in Israel 275 · Depiction of Jewish life 276 · Jewish antiquities of the town of Worms 276 · Axel Springer donates nearly DM 4 million to the Jerusalem Museum 277 · The foundation of the Fritz-Naphtali Institute 281 · German youth in Israel — Israeli youth in Germany 282 · The activities of the German-Israeli Society 282

The Federal Republic and the Middle-East crisis   287

German Policy of peace in the Middle East   290

Statements made by both the Federal Government and the political parties 290 · Agitation against Israel in the Soviet Zone 296 · Memorandum of the Federal Republic to the Plenary Assembly of the United Nations 298 · Kurt Georg Kiesinger on the situation after the Arab-Israeli war 300 · Other German activities 302

Spontaneous reactions among the German people   304

Reports from the various towns 305 · Young people from Germany are helping in Israel 312 · Asher Ben Natan on reactions among the German people 313

Summing-Up   316

Index to documents   317

Index of names appearing in text   323

The German path to Israel has been followed with anxiety and uneasiness by many people there and here. One man towered above the crowd who longed for the moment of reconciliation:
Karl Marx (1897—1966)

As a journalist and German Jew with his *Allgemeine unabhängige jüdische Wochenzeitung* he created a bridge across the abyss between Germany and Israel. To him this book is gratefully dedicated.

Foreword

When I was elected the first Chancellor of the German Federal Republic, in September, 1949, one of the greatest problems calling for political solution was the achievement of a new ordering of the relationship to the Jewish people. The dreadful things that had been done in the name of Germany rested as a heavy burden on all the political problems confronting any German government.

The present book, a description of the most important stages of the German path to Israel up to now, accomplishes a task that cannot be taken seriously enough. It was a great satisfaction that it was vouchsafed to me to see Israel with my own eyes—the peaceful building up of this people and state after everything that the Jewish people had suffered in the diaspora. To us Germans, the most important of political developments, along with all the accomplishments in reconstructing our State and establishing friendly relationships to other peoples after the National Socialist catastrophe, is the fact that we were able to find the path to Israel and the Jewish people.

Rhoendorf, January, 1967

Prefatory note

This book came into being through the years as if of its own accord. The editor, whose own fate has involved him in the most recent history of Germany and Israel, has made 35 visits to Israel. He has observed each step in the evolution of German-Israel relations from close at hand, and has taken an active part in building the bridge between the two peoples. He accompanied Franz Josef Strauss, Eugen Gerstenmaier, Konrad Adenauer, and Ludwig Erhard on their journeys to Israel. He was an eye-witness of the noteworthy encounter between Konrad Adenauer and David Ben Gurion at the Hotel Waldorf Astoria in New York. In the course of years he has had many conversations with the prominent political figures of both countries. As a journalist he has taken a constant part in the German-Jewish dialogue.

The book documents a rapprochement. With protocols, treaties, interviews, statements, speeches, and letters it puts before the reader the stages of the German path to Israel. The documents are shown in the context of events through introductory passages. Where it seemed desirable in order to give a better understanding of this context, special chapters report, for instance, on political and diplomatic relations, or economic and cultural cooperation.

Numerous documents are published here for the first time; protocols, treaties, etc. are given in full for the first time. Many of the interviews and conversations are taken from the editor's tape recordings. A calendar of documents at the end of the volume lists them individually, along with all the other documents. Through the visual indication of type set closely or with space between the lines, the reader can tell immediately whether he is referring to a document or a report (spaced) or a connecting passage by the editor (closely set).

The foreword with which this book begins is the last that Konrad Adenauer wrote for a political publication. He gave it to the editor during the work on the manuscript, (to which he devoted personal interest up to his death) as a *leitmotiv* for the spirit of the book. It is appropriate here to thank all of those who contributed to the success of the compilation and furnished documents for publication.

Bonn, December, 1967   Rolf Vogel

The unwritten part of history

When the gates of the concentration camps opened in the spring of 1945, when the Allied armies deprived the German people of their last illusions that what had been done to the Jews was perhaps not that bad after all, and when the whole world was informed of the full extent of the criminal National Socialist policy towards the Jews, hardly anyone believed it would be possible to create new contacts between the German and the Jewish people.

Yet even in the starving days of the first post-war period something happened that no one who had quite grasped the horror of the barely cold crematories could understand: Jews all over the world were the first do disavow the concept of the "collective guilt of the German people" through their own cation. Victor Gollancz called for concerted aid to the German people; Louis Lochner, the former Berlin correspondent of U. P., discharged his maid in New York so that he would have more money to send Care packages to Germany. These are only two random names to stand for the innumerable "unsung heroes" who had kept their hearts alive during the chaos. Their personal courage and personal involvement made possible the first steps towards Israel and the Jewish people.

Few of the Jews in Germany had survived. In Berlin alone families from all levels of the German population had kept 5,000 Jews hidden. They often lived outside the law for years. In many cases their hiding places were destroyed by bombing, and the Gestapo succeeded in apprehending them. By the end of the war, a scant 1,200 of these 5,000 persons were still alive.

As in Berlin, so all over Germany there had been concerted help: Protestant pastors in Württemberg clearing the way for Jews to get to Switzerland, self-sacrificing individuals like Gertrud Luckner and Margaret Sommer, who did the same with the help of friends in the Catholic church; and then many persons unknown, whose deeds cannot be recounted here.

But it was not only during the Third Reich that these numerous helpers existed. The beginning of the dialogue after the war was also speeded by the confidence placed in those who returned to Germany from emigration. One of these was Karl Marx. All of these, the people who had risen from the ruins and cellars or whom homesickness drove back despite everything that had befallen them in Germany, began to build up a small Jewish community in Germany.

During the early post-war years the first human contacts between individual Germans and the survivors of the former Jewish community in Germany were hesitantly established. Gradually societies for Christian-Jewish cooperation came into being in numerous cities and towns. On the establishment of the Jewish State in 1948, the publicist Erich Lüth started the "Peace with Israel" and "Olive-branch drive" campaigns. In 1952 his "Peace with Israel" activity was combined with the Society for Christian and Jewish Cooperation. The journalist Rudolf Küstermeyer, imprisoned in a penitentiary for more than a decade by the National Socialists, was among the first Germans to initiate the dialogue with the Jewish side; there was also Dean Grüber of Berlin, whose office there conducted a large-scale drive to help the persecuted. In addition there were many young people who had gone through the years of horror as children, and felt a duty to clear away the mountain of German rubble and assist in reconciliation.

All of them jointly took the first steps along a path to the Jewish people that then joined the path of the free German state established in 1949, the German Federal Republic, towards Israel.

The fact that it was possible at all to set up a new, free German state, to find points of contact for a fresh start with us Germans among the political figures, scientists, and journalists in the Western capitals was in no small part the doing of Jews.

And within Germany? Here too there were growing in our people forces that became constantly stronger to gain, out of shame over the past, the courage for a new beginning.

When the Parliamentary Council, the constituent assembly, met in Bonn on September 1, 1948, to draw up the basic law for the Federal Republic of West Germany, it was like a vow in memory of the horrors when the basic rights of men were proclaimed as immediately effective law. Article 1, Par. 1—2, reads: "The dignity of man is sacrosanct. To respect and protect it is the duty of all governmental power. The German people accordingly pledge their allegiance to inviolable and inalienable human rights as the basis of any human society of peace and justice in the world." And Art. 3, Par 3, states: "No-one shall be preferred or discriminated against because of sex, descent, race, language, home and origin, faith, religious or political views." This is a clear profession after everything that had been done to violate the basic right of human dignity.

The first efforts

On 15 September 1949 Konrad Adenauer was elected Federal Chancellor by the first German Diet, which had emerged from the election as the first freely chosen parliament of a new, democratic state. This man, who had had a close personal relationship even during Weimar days to many Jewish friends in Cologne, who understood the Zionists, who, as Lord Mayor, had been a member of the *Pro Palaestina Committee*, knew that any post-war German policy must have "the arrangement of our relationship to the Jews" as its chief subject. In this he agreed with all democratic parties in the first German Federal Diet.

Konrad Adenauer's first interview

On 11th November 1949 the Chancellor gave his first interview. At a reception for Jewish personalities in Germany, he was interviewed by Karl Marx, the editor of the *Allgemeine Wochenzeitung der Juden in Deutschland*. This was the Chancellor's first statement on Jewish questions and on his attitude to the state of Israel, which had been established on 15 May 1948. Here, Konrad Adenauer expressed not only his personal opinion, but the position of the newly formed German government.

Question: "Certain groups still contend that the emphasis on the Christian character of the CDU (Christian Democratic Union) includes an anti-Jewish tendency. Mr. Chancellor, would you care to make a statement in the matter?"

Answer: "In the first government message to the Diet, I emphasized in the name of the government and the political forces behind it, that our work will be founded on the spirit of Christian-occidental civilisation and respect for the rights and dignity of man. In the days of the Hitler regime, respect for the dignity of man was thoroughly destroyed. The degradation of man to an object of governmental purposes was one of the most frightening symptoms of that time. We as Christians mean to restore respect for man without regard to his denominational, racial, or national origin. In the spirit of this tolerance we regard our Jewish fellow-countrymen as fellow-citizens with full rights. We intend that they shall participate with equal rights and duties in the intellectual, political and social building-up of the country. We neither can nor would do without their help. That is what we see as the meaning of the term 'Christian' in this connexion."

Question: "Mr. Chancellor, do you feel that the steps taken against the Germans after the war, for instance in the expulsion from the Eastern regions, can compensate for the wrong done in the name of the German people up to 1945? This is an argument one often hears."

Answer: "Wrongs and sufferings brought upon human beings can never offset wrongs or sufferings brought upon other people. The German people are resolved to make good the wrong done to the Jews in their name by a criminal regime, so far as this is still possible now that millions of human beings have been destroyed beyond recall. This reparation we regard as our duty. Far too little has been done for this reparation since 1945. The Federal Government are determined to take the appropriate steps."

Question: "For us reparation is not only an economic but a moral question. What do the Federal Government propose to do to assist in this reparation?"

Answer: "Moral reparations are part of our reconstruction as a state under the rule of law.

"The Federal Government will exercise their vigilance to assure obedience to the article in the Basic Law that forbids discriminating against anyone because of his origin, race, or faith. I would like to leave no doubt about it that the outrages to Jewish places of worship and the destruction of Jewish cemeteries that have unfortunately continued in recent years will be prosecuted and punished without mercy. It is the duty of the municipalities, in particular, not only to protect the Jewish places of worship but to assist in rebuilding wherever necessary. I have already announced in the first government message that if necessary we shall make vigorous use of the rights that the laws give us against radical tendencies. We shall do this with the utmost severity against anti-Semitic tendencies in the press or in public life if it should prove necessary. We shall combat any anti-Semitism not only because we find it undesirable as a matter of foreign and domestic policy but because we reject it vigorously for reasons of humanity. Through the execution of the articles covering Basic Rights in the Basic Law we have all the legal prerequisites to put our will into effect and protect Jews against all discrimination. We shall secure the Jews against any possibility of fresh persecutions.

"The Federal Government will devote their special attention to an equivalent for the economic wrongs done to Jewish citizens. The existing legislation still requires various improvements and additions. The State of Israel is the outwardly visible concentration of the Jews of all nationalities. The Federal Government intend to put at the disposal of the State of Israel goods to the value of DM 10 million for purposes of reconstruction, as a first direct sign that the wrongs done to Jews all over the world by Germans must be made good. The long persecution of the Jews in Germany during the National Socialist period gave rise to a number of problems about which the Federal Government must keep itself constantly informed. Accordingly a section will be set up in the Federal Ministry of the Interior under the charge of a German Jew to concern itself with these problems. The creation of this section is intended at the same time to give the Jews living in Germany the assurance that the Federal Government will do everything to safeguard their political rights to the full."

Question: "The Jewish victims of National Socialist persecution, particularly the relatives of the Jews killed in concentration camps, are watching with anxiety the tendency to grant amnesty to the political elements responsible for the annihilation, and to discontinue the prosecution of crimes against humanity. Do the Federal Government intend to take steps in this direction?"

Answer: "I have already declared to the Diet that the Federal Government are of opinion that a great deal of harm has been done by the de-Nazification, but that those really guilty of the crimes committed in the National Socialist period and during the war should be punished with all severity. The Federal Government maintain this view unchanged. Criminals guilty of the destruction of human life are not worthy of amnesty, and will be subject in future as in the past to the penalties that are their due."

First meeting with members of the Israeli Parliament

In 1950 when members of the German parliament met an Israeli delegation for the first time at a Congress of the Interparliamentary Union in Istanbul, the first discussion on a political level occurred. Carlo Schmid, who had been the chairman of the steering committee in the first parliamentary council, and was now, as Vice-President of the German Diet, a member of the German delegation, described this encounter to the editor:

"It was in 1950 at Istanbul, where we Germans were admitted to a Congress of the Interparliamentary Union for the first time after the Second World War. The leader of the German delegation was Dr. Ehlers, the president of the Diet. I was his deputy. When the agenda were being drawn up, the spokesman of Israel asked for the floor; it was the subsequent president Ben Zvi. In a terrible and dreadful philippic he protested against the presence of any Germans here. He said it was an affront to any honest and decent person to be obliged to deal here with Germans, as if the Germans were free of everything that had been done in their name to mankind and in particular to the Jewish people. It was really a fearful speech. I have seldom heard anyone speak with such passion as he did at that moment. I immediately took the floor and spoke in two directions: First, I said, I must insist that there be no such talk to people who were guests here like everyone else. And then I asked them not to forget the fact that the ambassadors of various states represented here had still been attending the Party rallies in Nuremberg at a time when several of the Germans present today had already made acquaintance with the prisons of the Third Reich. Germany must never forget what had been done to the Jewish people and other people. We Germans, quite apart from any good or evil that the individual might be responsible for, had to answer collectively for what had been done in the German name. Nothing could ever be offset against those German debts. Even if we were to make restitution for all this to whatever extent was imaginable and possible, it would still not entitle us to expect of the Jewish people that it should forget, or even that it should not regard us Germans with suspicion.

"That was what I said. Other delegates also took the floor, particularly a Swiss, Mr. De Senarclens, from Geneva, who had studied and taken his degree at Breslau. The meeting passed the order of the day, the German delegates took part in the deliberations. The Arabs came to me and said we should tell the Jews what was what, for once, and should denounce the Jews from this platform as enemies of mankind. I told them we were not on their side, and had our own cause to plead, which was not their cause. The reaction of the Arabs to this was extremely hostile. I then sat down with Mr. De Senarclens, talked to him, and got Messrs. von Brentano and Tillmanns of the CDU to join us. De Senarclens told me he believed he would be able to start a talk with the Israelis for the purpose of arranging a meeting between three Germans and three Israelis whom one could talk to. I said if he succeeded he would be doing a fine thing for the good cause. Two days later—or perhaps it was the next day—he told me he could guarantee that the Israelis would delegate three people, but first they would have to get permission in Jerusalem from their party in the Knesseth. The answer came that there was no objection to the talks. We then met; on the German side Messrs. von Brentano, Tillmanns and I, on the Israeli side Mr. Ben Zvi, Mr. Cohen, and the leader of the Liberal Party.

"The conversation began haltingly. French was spoken, although everyone knew that our interlocutors spoke German much better than French. For the time being the Israelis would not speak the language of Hitler's people. I was the spokesman: We regarded it, I said, as a matter in our own German interest, so that we could face ourselves better, if Israel—I put it this way on purpose—would do us the kindness to accept reparation payments. We knew that this could not reduce guilt. But a financial exertion, in order to make good at least something in the material sense, might help to ease the conscience of the Germans.

"The talk was about this problem. On the Jewish side there were voices that vigorously rejected the idea of talking to us at all. The leader of this group was Chief Rabbi Nurok, who was not prepared to exchange a single word with us. He said blood guilt could not be atoned for with money. No material reparation of any kind could pay any of this debt, and it would be a bad thing for the Jews to take blood money. After hours of this conversation with the above-mentioned three Israelis, the leader of the Liberals suddenly started talking German and said to Mr. von Brentano: 'Incidentally, I took my degree with a relative of yours, Prof. von Brentano in Munich. I think it was in 1910 or 1908; Then suddenly all six of us were talking German.

"The agreement was that our interlocutors would inquire of the Knesseth whether an offer from the German government to enter into negotiations about reparation payments to Israel would be entertained. We agreed that we would accept any decision by the Knesseth. We discussed further who might serve as intermediary between the Federal Government and the Knesseth—direct negotiations were not possible, of course—, and we agreed on the Israeli consul at Munich in the American Military Government, Chaim Hoffmann. On the German side the late Jakob Altmaier, the Jewish member of parliament of the SPD, was named.

"I know from Jakob Altmaier that he was then in constant contact with Chaim Hoffmann.

"That was how the thing began, and then there was an offer, and the appointment of a commission that negotiated in Amsterdam. There was also a further decisive factor in the Foreign Affairs Committee of the German Diet. A number of German deputies were not in favour of these restitution payments to Israel. They felt that the individual Jews should be compensated individually. They said there was no legal obligation to the state of Israel. Moral obligations existed only to individuals. These deputies also feared a hostile reaction by the Arabs. The Arabs themselves—particularly the Egyptians—came every day to me and other deputies, trying with threats to argue against such an agreement. I remember very well the Egyptian representative's saying to me that this might lead to a terrible situation, in fact, even wars might be possible. Then there was yet another point. Mr. Abs of the Deutsche Bank was against the intended settlement for financial reasons, and I think he tried to use a good deal of influence in that direction from outside. As chairman of the Foreign Affairs Committe I convened the committee, and succeeded with a speech in getting a vote to the effect that moral obligations took precedence over all legal obligations and legal considerations that might be raised. With that, I believe the last spell was broken and the negotiations were carried to the successful conclusion you know of."

First talk on reparations

By the time Chancellor Konrad Adenauer had taken up the great subject of reparations in his interview with Karl Marx, the various Federal States in the American, British, and French zones of occupation already had restitution and compensation laws that had been passed in concert with the Allied authorities. The problem arose for the Federal Government in a quite new form. At this time neither the Federal Finance Minister nor the Chancellor knew what budget could be expected. Even Ludwig Erhard as Economic Minister could predict nothing about the extent of economic development. Only in view of this can we understand the DM 10 thousand million that Konrad Adenauer mentioned in the interview with Karl Marx as the first visible sign of reparations to the State of Israel.

As to the start of the dialogue with the Jewish representatives all over the world, and through Israeli representatives with Israel, we have the report of Herbert Blankenhorn, at that time one of the closest foreign policy associates on the staff of the new Chancellor, to the editor:

"In the very first weeks of the existence of the Federal Government, around October and November of 1949, there were talks between the Chancellor and me as to the way in which it would be possible to put the relationship of the German people to the Jewish people and to the State of Israel on a new foundation. In these talks it was constantly maintained by me—and the Chancellor fully accepted this reasoning—that the new German state could regain confidence, reputation, and credibility in the world only if the Federal Government and the Diet, in a freely decided act of will, disavowed the past and contributed through impressive reparation payments to the relief of the incredible extent of distress suffered, helping those who had lost everything to build up a new livelihood. We were aware that such an act of will could not undo the unspeakable cruelties committed in the name of the German people and the resulting infinite suffering in the past. Such an act of true reparation was intended to help surmount the unimaginable bitterness that National Socialist crimes had inspired in the Jews the world over and in all right-thinking people. Its purpose was further to make the German people realize the dreadfulness of the past and the necessity of a radical conversion.

"In these discussions the idea soon arose that we should start by making contacts with the appropriate representatives to learn how far Jewry and the State of Israel were interested in such an act of true reparation at all. Thus there were a number of contacts in Bonn and particularly in London with Dr. Nahum Goldmann, the leading personality of the World Jewish Congress and the Jewish Claims Conference, and also with other Jewish personalities, among whom the Englishman Barou distinguished himself."

An opinion by Hendrik van Dam

The discussions with Nahum Goldmann and other Jewish personalities brought it about that the Israelis also began considering how these proclamations of the will of the Federal Government could be transformed into treaty negotiations and later into a treaty. This gave rise to the idea, among others, of asking the Secretary General of the Central Council of the Jews in Germany, Hendrik van Dam, for a professional opinion. He was asked to set forth what problems would arise in arriving at such a treaty.

Hendrik van Dam wrote the opinion after exhaustive studies, particularly in the files of the League of Nations in Geneva. The result of his studies, which he submitted to the Israeli Finance Ministry on July 1, 1950, was as follows:

"*The problems of reparations and restitution for Israel.*

"Preliminary note: 'Reparation' is not merely the sum of possible individual claims resulting from instances of persecution. The mass crime against the Jews was directed at the Jewish people in its entirety, practically destroying its existence in Central Europe and doing immeasurable but also irreparable harm. Just as the distress and the losses of the individual were merely a reflection of the general fate, so today the claims of the small number of surviving Jews (including the claims of heirs) cannot exhaust, let alone replace, the collective claim of the Jewish people.

"I.

"'Reparations'—before it becomes a difficult problem of law—is a problem of morals and politics. This is true for both parties, the German people and the Jewish people.

"a) A Recognition of moral duty, which was felt particularly in the first few years after the capitulation, still exists in a number of leading Germans. The inclination to draw practical conclusions, however, particularly by creating the necessary legislation, grows ever slighter. Time is working against reparations, as it is against the prosecution of criminals against humanity, and against de-Nazification. The sense of moral obligation requiring to be turned into political action is flagging, as is the fear of criticism by the occupying powers. What remains substantially is the realistic reasoning of political and economic expediency. Even now the German governments are interested in a certain clearing up of the reparations situation, from political and economic considerations. Their wish, dictated by political and economic motives, to reach a settlement of the reparation situation and to shake off the disagreeable Nazi heritage, will continue to play a part for a limited time. Laws not enacted within this remaining period will never be enacted later. The same is true of treaties, settlements, and to a certain extent even of making payments.

"b) The moral duty of the German people corresponds to the morally based claim of the Jewish people. The Jewish people in Israel will have to decide whether it will exercise its claims. This decision is by no means a matter of course, and is not even easy. Consistent pursuit of the idea of absolute separation from Germany, along with the impossibility of complete or even adequate reparations, argues for renouncing the claim. Carrying out reparations practically means establishing a contact with Germany. We will refrain here from weighing the arguments for and against this perfectly logical renunciation. We will go on the assumption that the Jewish people in Israel cannot afford this renunciation, and does not wish to. If we reach this conclusion, however, the existing opportunities should be exploited to the full and without delay. This in turn makes it necessary to tackle the problem realistically, i. e. to refrain from burdening it with moral and historical imponderables, and above all to keep demands within the bounds of possibility.

"II.

"The legal claims based on the existing system of law, i. e. in German legislation, in the legislation of the occupying powers and in international law, are of an individual nature so far as they apply to compensation for damage personally suffered. The claims are collective in nature, so far as they are the claims of the community.

"Ordinarily collective claims of this kind following a war are presented by the state as a demand for reparations. The right to reparations is a claim of the state arising out of the damage done it as an organised community and out of the losses inflicted on its citizens so far as the state has made them good or will do so in the future.

"Thus far, Jewish claims have essentially been individual ones, prosecuted on the basis of existing German law, if we except the special case of the restitution of property with heirs to claims against it. (Here a substitute solution has been created in the form of trust companies in which Israel holds a certain participation through the Jewish Agency. This is a special case of the collective claim, but one limited entirely to the property of dead Jews formerly residing in Germany.)

"III.

"The right of the Jewish people to reparations constitutes an exception from reparation claims of other peoples. At the time when the damage was inflicted, there was no Jewish state. The authority of the Israeli government to raise such a claim requires a special justification, which will be but briefly sketched here. The action of Nazi Germany as the *de facto* predecessor at law of the present German states was directed not against Poles, Rumanians, Germans, etc. of the Jewish faith, but against the Jewish people as a whole. That people also suffered disastrous decimation beyond the limits of warfare under international law, a complete spoliation without parallel even in other events of the Second World War. The only organised Jewish community within the meaning of international law is the State of Israel. The state as such was established only after the war, but it existed potentially before its establishment through the Zionist claim. While it was the state doctrine of the German Reich from 1943 to 1945 to carry out collective discrimination against the Jewish people, the task of the State of Israel is the rehabilitation of the Jewish people as a nation. The government of Israel must be regarded as the authority that can successfully prosecute a claim for reparations under international law. In this connexion it should be remembered that any claim for reparations bears a political character, and its recognition rests essentially on political factors, although the determination of the damage inflicted is not a political but a legal act. Here the Israeli reparation claim differs not at all from the claims of other states. Whereas to the other states the necessary prerequisite for a claim is a victory over the adversary in war—an event that often follows the damage by several years—the Israeli claim involves the founding of the state after the event, and the matter of recognition. A precedent may perhaps be found in the reparation payments of Germany to Poland, Yugoslavia, and Czechoslovakia after the first World War—to states, that is, that were founded only after the war ended.

"It is probably of consequence for the recognition of the Israeli claim, so far as it is directed at West Germany, that non-recognition of the Israeli claim would have as an immediate consequence a corresponding recognition of larger claims by the Eastern states, particularly Poland. It seems unjustified to grant reparation claims on account of the mass crime against the Jews in the East to those countries where today only a tiny fraction of the Jewish population survives. It seems far more acceptable for the government of Israel to press the claim for compensation of the Polish-Jewish group than for the claim to be lumped with the Polish reparation claim, and thus lost to the Jewish people.

"After the war, Israel made a substantial contribution to the problem of receiving the Jews persecuted and expelled by Germany: it accepted this particular group without practical restrictions and without regard to the difficulties involved. The IRO is now in the stage of liquidation. There is no further need to call upon an organisation established under international law as the representative of the claims of the Jewish community. The government of Israel is well able to perform this function. The major Jewish aid organisations, especially in America, should welcome all payments from reparation funds to the State of Israel, since this would help reduce their own burdens. But the only possible subject of action under international law is the government of the State of Israel, which could thus come forward as the party authorised to act on behalf of world Jewry.

"IV.

"The Israel government is not only the logical authority to present the reparation claim as a claim of the community. It is also entitled and obligated by the principles of diplomatic intervention to present and prosecute the claims of its citizens.

"It would be nothing unusual for the state of Israel to include these claims in its reparations, as other states have done. This offers an opportunity for compounding, so that the citizens receive the compensation from their own government. With respect to the claims against East Germany it will in fact be necessary to convert individual claims into a single reparation claim. Otherwise, however, the government has the choice of confining itself to supporting its citizens' claims, and making arrangements for transfer. This will be true if adequate German legislation affords a foundation for these individual claims, or will afford it in the near future.

"For West Germany, a study of developments shows the following with regard to the necessity for intervention:

"1. Restitution of identifiable property. Generally speaking there is no need for intervention, since appropriate laws exist in all the zones, and the Western sectors of Berlin. In the matter of transfer upon sale after restitution and the matter of moneys paid by way of compensation, the situation is the same as for other restitution payments. Some of these sums are very substantial.

"In the unclaimed, identifiable property without heirs, Israel has an interest through the participation of the J. A. F. P. in the trust companies. For a number of reasons resulting from what was said in Section I, it would be desirable to arrive at a compounded settlement as soon as possible. It does not seem desirable, in a period when occupation institutions are being abolished, for large Jewish institutions of a semi-official nature to operate in Germany for reparation purposes. This quite aside from the costs that the administrative machinery must necessarily involve.

"2. The damage claims (damages for arrest, health, loss of property, etc.) of claimants living in Israel are most inadequately provided for. The states of West Germany have only a modest interest in the Jews living in their territory. By payments to this comparatively small group they had hoped at least formally to meet their reparation obligations and create a certain reassurance. The laws of the U. S. Zone go further in their provisions, but legislation regarding damages, particularly damages for imprisonment in the British Zone, are conditioned upon residence there on a fixed date. Pensions for persecutees are paid only to residents of the state.

"In Lower Saxony doubts exist whether damages for imprisonment are to be paid to persons who have emigrated even though they were in Lower Saxony on the stated date.

"This covers the large group of persons who passed through the Bergen-Belsen camp. It may therefore be stated as a rule for practical purposes that Jews resident abroad can scarcely collect damage claims. This has extremely unfortunate consequences. It violates the moral principle of restitution when only a small group is privileged. The provisions of the laws encourage false statements, compromise the Jewish reputation, lead to abuses in the presentation of claims through representatives—in short to an undesirable state of affairs. This development is based primarily on the legal position of the German states, which declare themselves as not the legal successors to the Third Reich. Obviously it would be not only legally untenable but impossible for a single state to bear the full burden of reparations for the German Reich. In the matter of damages for imprisonment of the DPs there are also the difficulties of proof. It will therefore be necessary to reach an agreement on a federal level. Securing the damage claims of the DPs who have emigrated from West Germany is a field of great importance. To avoid abuses, too, it will be well to involve the government.

"3. Intervention is also desirable in the field of transferral. So far as Israel is concerned no solution without a transfer agreement seems practicable.

"V.

"For a number of reasons, direct government action now seems desirable, and the intervention of other institutions inappropriate.

"1. The restraint shown by government authorities was necessary in connection with the fear of British quarters that reparation funds would be sent to Israel and used against the British interest. This position is a thing of the past, and thus eliminates one important reason for calling upon other Jewish organisations.

"2. The involvement of several organisations and persons causes confusion. Today a government agency will have the best prospects of success in negotiations.

"3. The general political situation (courting of the Germans) weakens the negotiating position of the organisations of persecutees, including the Jewish groups. The decline of respect for uniforms, the tendency to transfer as many functions as possible to the Germans, the sensitivity towards all intervention not required by the Occupation Statute, reduces the freedom of negotiation for foreign organisations. On the other hand, there is every willingness to deal with representatives of foreign governments and to arrive at results.

"4. The organisations of the Jews within Germany are regarded as the authorised representatives of the Jews resident in Germany. For them to act on behalf of the Jews resident outside Germany is not, indeed, impossible, but lacks convincing authority.

"5. It does not seem appropriate for foreign offices or organisations concerned with the technical settlement of claims to conduct negotiations of fundamental importance. So far as Israel is concerned, such negotiations should be reserved for an Israeli government agency.

"6. The interest of the German governments in a settlement, mentioned under Ia), presupposes a certain economic reciprocal relationship. Hence only an Israeli agency, and only a government agency, can participate in negotiations.

"7. It cannot be overlooked that any indemnification of consequence to Israel would absolutely require a transfer agreement and the acceptance of exports from Germany. The weakness of the legal position (which is not offset in the existing political situation by the moral strength of the claims) requires activity and makes waiting seem dangerous. A realistic restraint in determining the extent of the claims is also essential.

"8. With all due respect to the consequences of the Western powers' policy toward Germany (see 3 above) the United States still has an interest in seeing indemnification carried out, as High Commissioner McCloy has repeatedly mentioned. In addition, a certain alibi is desired for the American policy of giving up denazification and for collaboration. Indemnification, and particularly reparations to Israel, might provide such a counterweight.

"VI.

"Proposal:

"It is proposed that the government dispatch a 'Reparation and Indemnification Mission' with authority to negotiate with German government agencies and to conclude agreements on the indemnification of Jews resident in Israel, transfer, and export of merchandise in this connection; and that will also make preparations for the general reparation claim. The accreditation of this mission cannot be governed by our wishes, but by the situation that the mission finds on arrival. If we are to negotiate in the matter with German government agencies, the proper accreditation should be formally effected if developments require it.

"One possible expedient would be to place the mission under the diplomatic representation of the State of Israel in a neighbouring country, such as Switzerland. Subordinating it to the Swiss mission could then if necessary be explained on the ground of performing international duties.

"VII.

"East Germany. In the Eastern Zone presumably the reparation claim of the Jewish people is the only one with any chance of attention. Individual claims of persons resident in Israel should be transformed into this reparation claim. Here again there is an economic background to the matter. Prospects of success seem not unfavourable if the claims are presented by a suitable mission to the government. No results are to be expected from the intervention of organisations of an international nature. The government unquestionably has a function to fulfil here. It is most important for the claims of the Jewish people that a part of Germany cannot become the exclusive legal successor of the former Reich. Accordingly the presentation of the claims should not be confined to a restricted area of the former Reich."

Further efforts to establish contacts

Like Hendrik van Dam, who jointly with his collegue Liveneh had created links to Israeli agencies, Kurt G. Grossmann of New York, Karl Marx, Robert M. W. Kempner, and others attempted to start conversations for the purpose of arriving at true agreements. In his efforts, Kempner had the advantage over many others of like mind that as the Deputy American Prosecutor at the Nuremberg Trials he was an intermediary subject to no suspicions on the part of Jewish organisations. Kempner had been an official in the Reich Ministry of the Interior, and had been expelled from Germany under the racial laws. Soon after the close of the Nuremberg trials, about the end of 1949, he began talking to friends from Weimar days who were now ministerial directors and secretaries of state in the Federal government or in parliament, urging the creation of individual indemnification for the victims of National Socialism. In his numerous discussions during 1950 he became convinced that the Federal Government regarded the settlement of the reparations problem as the payment of a heavy debt, and as a welcome beginning of reconciliation with the Jewish people. Kempner talked about this in Washington with Counsellor of Embassy Krämer (alias Keren) of the Israeli Embassy.

When Kempner was invited late in 1950 by the Israeli government to deliver political lectures, the opportunity arose in Jerusalem for the first talk about problems of individual indemnification. During this good-will mission, Kempner was able to assure the Israeli government that direct contacts of Israel with the Federal government would be extremely well received.

In late 1950 and early 1951 the *New York Times* and many other papers, in Germany for instance the *Allgemeine Wochenzeitung der Juden in Deutschland*, reported that Kempner had emphatically assured the Israeli government that if it hoped to secure indemnification for victims of National Socialism, it could not do it by way of the Allies or through telepathy. The creditor must deal personally with his debtor. Israel must address itself directly to the Federal government, which had the best of intentions.

Kempner's talks in Jerusalem backed up those groups in Israel and the Jewish organisations that were prepared to negotiate with a democratic Germany. These groups needed strengthening, for there were extremely powerful counter-forces that declined all contact with German agencies.

About this time, too, preparations were being made in Jerusalem for the note of 12 March 1951 to the great powers.

The note of the Israeli Government of 12 March 1951

On 12 March 1951 the Israeli government directed a note to the four allies—the Americans, the British, the French, and the Russians—demanding reparations from the Federal Republic and the Soviet occupied zone of Germany. The payments were to be used for the settlement of Jewish refugees from Europe.

The notes to the four powers were identical in content. The complete text reproduced below is a note that the Israeli Ambassador presented to the French government in Paris.

"The Israeli Ambassador at Paris has the honour, on behalf of his government, to transmit to his Excellency the Foreign Minister the following communication concerning claims of the State of Israel against Germany:

"1. In the note that the Israeli Ambassador had the honour to transmit to his Excellency the Foreign Minister on 16 January 1951 it was stated that the Israeli government reserved the right to deal in a special note with the claims involving Jewish losses, for which Germany must be held responsible, and to which existing laws concerning restitution and personal indemnification do not apply. The purpose of this note is to specify the nature and foundations of these claims and to make specific proposals as to the ways in which these claims can be met.

"2. The harm done to the Jewish people by Germany has no parallel in history. There is no precedent for a massacre and despoliation such as those whose victims the Jews of Europe became through the entire German people. In the course of a few years whole communities more than a thousand years old were systematically annihilated. Over six million Jews were murdered by torture, starvation, exhaustion, and mass executions; many were burned or buried alive. The massacres spared no one. Children were snatched from their mothers' arms and flung into the furnaces of the crematories. Old men and women were hunted and dispatched to the death camps. In Poland and the occupied part of Russia more than 4 million Jews perished. Month after month transports of Jews from Germany and the European countries under German occupation—Norway, Denmark, Holland, Belgium, France, Italy, Greece, Bulgaria, Yugoslavia, Rumania, Hungary, Poland, Czechoslovakia, and Austria—were sent to the annihilation camps. The annihilation of these Jews is one of the saddest chapters in the history of mankind.

"3. Along with the murders, robbery was practised on the same scale. According to moderate estimates, the Nazis in Germany and in other European countries under their domination appropriated Jewish property to the value of some 6 thousand million. This figure includes the collective fine of one thousand million marks imposed on the Jews in Germany the day before the pogrom organised by the government in November 1938, along with the other fines, confiscations, and discriminatory taxes imposed upon them, whence it is apparent that the government of the Federal Republic assumed a liability when it recently proclaimed itself the successor of the Third Reich.

"4. The enormous murder and despoliation of a people shown here formed only the final stage of the persecutions that began on the day when the National Socialist government took power. The judgment pronounced in the war crimes trial at Nuremberg describes these persecutions as 'actions committed on a large scale with consistent and systematic inhumanity'. The following excerpts from the judgment depict the course of this persecution from the start of the Nazi regime to the end of the Second World War:

"'With the seizure of power, the persecution of the Jews was intensified. A series of laws created distinctions and restricted the offices and occupations available to the Jews; restrictions were imposed on their family life and their civil rights. As early as autumn 1938, the Nazi policy towards the Jews had reached a stage aimed at the complete exclusion of the Jews from German life. Pogroms, burning and destruction of synagogues, the looting of Jewish shops, and the arrest of outstanding Jewish businessmen were organised. A collective fine of 1000 million marks was imposed on the Jews, the confiscation of Jewish property was authorised, and the freedom of movement of the Jews was restricted by decree to certain special districts and hours. Ghettos were established to a very large extent, and by order of the security police Jews were forced to wear a yellow star on the chest and on the back.

"'A fine of a thousand million marks was imposed, and the confiscation of Jewish property was decreed at a time when German armament costs had got the German finance ministry into difficulties, and the reduction of armament expenditure was under consideration.

"'The persecution of the Jews in pre-war Germany by the Nazis, harsh and oppressive as it was, cannot be compared to the policy pursued during the war in the occupied territories. Originally the policy was similar to that previously pursued in Germany; the Jews had to register and were forced to live in ghettos, wear the yellow star, and submit to being used as slave labourers. In the summer of 1941, however, plans were drawn up for a ""'final solution'"" of the Jewish question in all Europe. This ""'final solution'"" meant the extirpartion of the Jews, which Hitler had threatened as early as the beginning of 1939 would be one of the results of the outbreak of war. A special division of the Gestapo under Adolf Eichmann, the head of department B IV of the Gestapo, was formed to carry out this policy ...

"'The plan for the extirpation of the Jews was drawn up shortly after the attack on the Soviet Union. The detachments of security police and SD (security service) that had been set up to break the resistance of the population in the rear of the German armies in the East, were assigned to the duty of extirpating the Jews in those areas. The effectiveness of the activity of the detachments is shown by the fact that in February, 1952, Heydrich could already report that Esthonia was free of Jews, and that the number of Jews in Riga had been reduced from 29,500 to 2,500. All told, the detachments operating in the occupied Baltic regions killed over 135,000 Jews in three months.

"'Nor did these special units operate completely independently of the German armed forces. There are definite proofs that leaders of the detachments obtained the cooperation of army commanders …

"'These atrocities all belong to the policy initiated in 1941 …

"'Part of the ''"final solution"'' was the assembling of Jews from German-occupied parts of Europe in concentration camps. Their health was the touchstone of life and death. All those able to work were used for forced labour in concentration camps; all persons unable to work were destroyed in gas chambers and their corpses burnt. Certain concentration camps such as Treblinka and Auschwitz were set aside for this chief purpose. So far as Auschwitz is concerned, the court heard the testimony of camp commandant Höss, who held that position there from 1 May 1940 to 1 December 1943. He estimated that in the Auschwitz camp alone 2,500,000 persons were destroyed during that time while another 500,000 died as a result of disease and hunger. Höss describes the selection for annihilation as follows in his testimony:

"'"Those able to work were sent to the camp. Others were sent straight to the annihilation camps …"

"'The process of killing itself he describes in the following words.

"'"Depending on climatic conditions it took from 3 to 15 minutes to kill the people in the death chamber. We knew when the people were dead because their cries ceased. We usually waited about half an hour before we opened the doors and removed the corpses. When we had dragged out the bodies, our special detachments took the rings off the corpses and pulled the gold out of the teeth of these bodies."'

"'Blows, starvation, torture and killings were the order of the day. The inmates of the Dachau camp were subjected to cruel experiments in August 1942. The victims were plunged into cold water until their body temperature declined to 82°F, when death immediately ensued. Other experiments included altitude tests in pressure chambers, experiments to determine how long human beings survive in icy water; experiments with poisoned bullets, experiments with infectious diseases, and others dealing with the sterilisation of men and women by x-ray and other methods.

"'Witnesses have testified to the treatment of concentration-camp inmates before and after their destruction. It was testified that the hair of female victims was cut off before the killing and sent to Germany to be used in making mattresses. The garments, money, and valuables of the inmates were also seized and transmitted to the appropriate authorities for further use. After the destruction the gold crowns and fillings were removed from the teeth of the corpses, and sent to the Reichsbank.

"'After the cremation the ashes were used as fertiliser, and in some cases experiments were made for the purpose of using the fat of the corpses in industrial soap manufacture. Special details travelled about Europe to uncover Jews and submit them to the ''"final solution"''. German commissions were sent to such vassal states as Hungary and Bulgaria to carry out the transportation of Jews to annihilation camps, and it is known that up the end of 1944 40,000 Hungarian Jews had been murdered in Auschwitz. It was also testified that 100,000 were evacuated from a single part of Rumania for liquidation. Adolf Eichmann, who had been entrusted by Hitler with the execution of the program, estimated that under his policy 6 million Jews were killed, four million of whom lost their lives in annihilation camps.'

"5. A crime so horrifying as this cannot be atoned for by material reparation, no matter of what kind. The Jewish people has been reduced by one-third; three out of every four European Jews were killed. No indemnity can make good the destroyed human lives and cultural values, or pay for the tortures and suffering of the men, women, and children killed by all the means at the disposal of a bestial imagination. Frank, one of the chief defendants in the Nuremberg trial, admitted this: 'A thousand years will pass without erasing this guilt of Germany.' What can be done is: Payment of damages to the heirs of the victims and the reintegration of the survivors under the conditions of normal existence. The Jews have been killed, and the German people continue to enjoy the fruits of the butcheries and plundering of its leaders of yesterday. To quote the Bible, 'Hast thou killed, and also taken possession?' The dead cannot be brought to life. Their suffering cannot be erased. But what can be demanded is that the German people shall be required to return the stolen Jewish property and to bear the expense of reintegrating the survivors.

"6. From the beginning, Israel played a leading part in receiving and integrating these survivors. When the Nazi persecutions in Germany began in the spring of 1933, the Jews in what was then Palestine immediately provided help. A constantly growing flood of German Jews, swelled after the occupation of Austria and Czechoslovakia by the Jews of those countries, made its way to Palestine. In the time between the Nazi seizure of power in Germany and the outbreak of World War II more than 75,000 fugitives from the Central European countries dominated by the Nazis settled in Palestine. Even during the war years, and despite the restrictions imposed, Jewish immigration from Europe never came to a halt. Untiring efforts were made to provide to the Jews the possibility of fleeing from the countries overrun or threatened by the Nazi invasion. After the end of the war the Jews of Palestine took every imaginable risk in order to give the survivors of this immeasurable butchery homes and security. When the State of Israel was established, its first measure was to open its gates wide to the Jewish displaced persons from the vicinity of the former concentration camps. Thus between 1939 and 1950 almost 380,000 Jews from the territories conquered by the Nazis were brought into the country. If we add to this number those Jews who had immigrated from central Europe during the pre-war years of Nazi persecution, we have a total of over 450,000.

"7. Most of these immigrants brought only their own feeble strength with them. They had long since been plundered of their entire property. Many of them were difficult welfare cases, men and women whose health had been irremediably ruined and whom no state but Israel was prepared to admit. In contrast to other countries receiving immigration, where the newcomers can easily be absorbed by a fully developed economic system, Israel had to make considerable exertions and spend substantial public funds to take care of the new-comers and, through investments, to create possibilities of employment for them. The entire economy of the new state was directed to this essential purpose from the very first. It is true that the Jews outside Israel have made a substantial financial contribution, but the fundamental costs arising from the reception and integration of the immigrants has been borne by the population of Israel. Heavy tax burdens and a severe system of economic restrictions had to be decided on in order to procure homes and the means of existence for these immigrants. The population of the country valiantly assumed these burdens. It is certainly not too much to demand that the German people, which is responsible for this predicament, and is still enjoying the use of the property taken from the Jews dead or alive, be called upon to help integrate the survivors.

"8. When the victorious Allies at the end of the war undertook to allot the reparations owed by Germany, the Jewish people as yet had no *locus standi* in the community of sovereign nations. This explains the fact that its claims were neither presented nor defended, although morally they were without doubt even more justified than those of any other nation that had suffered under the Nazis. The time has come to make good this omission.

"Israel is the only state that can speak in the name of the Jewish people—the people for belonging to which 6 million human beings paid by being murdered. Israel was established for the express purpose of offering a refuge to all persecuted and homeless Jews.

"This task was always conceived in a positive fashion: In the war against Nazi Germany the sons and daughters of Israel fought in national units in the Allied forces. A Jewish brigade contributed to the final defeat of the enemy on the Italian front, and played an active part in aid to the surviving Jews in the various parts of Europe and in their rescue. The recognition by the United Nations of the right of the Jewish people to reestablish its state was regarded as an act of reparation for the injustice suffered by that people in the course of history, an injustice most sharply expressed in the Nazis' work of destruction. And thus Israel, since its creation, has assumed responsibility for the reception and reintegration of the survivors of this catastrophe. For all those reasons the State of Israel believes it has the right to demand reparations from Germany as indemnification to the Jewish people.

"9. The amount of these reparations must take into account on the one hand losses suffered by the Jewish people through the Germans and on the other hand the financial burdens involved in integrating in Israel the fugitives or survivors of the Nazi regime. The government of Israel is not in a position to obtain and present a complete statement of all Jewish property taken or looted by the Germans, and said to total more than $6 thousand million. It can only compute its claim on the basis of total expenditures already made and the expenditure still needed for the integration of Jewish immigrants from Nazi-dominated countries. The number of these immigrants is estimated at some 500,000, which means a total expenditure of $1.5 thousand million. This figure corresponds approximately to the total, which will probably be considerably higher on the basis of the economic recovery as of 1951. If the payment of reparations on the basis of the above-mentioned estimate were distributed over several years, and made partly in kind, it would certainly not go beyond the ability of the German people to pay. No settlement of German reparations can be regarded as morally and legally acceptable if it does not meet this minimum demand, presented in the names of those who suffered most under the Nazi regime. The restoration of equal rights to Germany in the concert of nations is unthinkable until this basic measure of reparation is taken.

"10. The government of Israel is convinced that the French government recognises the justice of its demands. It urgently demands that the occupying powers transfer their authority to no German government, whatever it may be, without expressly reserving the question of reparation payments to Israel. The government of Israel would welcome being informed as soon as possible by the French government with regard to its views concerning the concrete measures to be taken in order to realise the plan proposed in this note in the most effective manner possible.

"Paris, 12 March 1951".

The Diet Session of 27 September 1951

Along with the exploratory conversation, which continued after the presentation of the Israeli note to the Allied governments, the question of German reparations to Israel was brought before the public once more on 27 September 1951. On that day Federal Chancellor Konrad Adenauer delivered a government statement on the Jewish question and the problems of reparations before the German Federal Diet. Statements of all the parties represented in the diet followed. Thus 27 September 1951 became a milestone in German-Jewish relations. Konrad Adenauer said:

"I have the honour, on behalf of the Federal Government, to make the following statement before this house.

"Recently world opinion has concerned itself repeatedly with the attitude of the Federal Republic towards the Jews. Doubts have been expressed here and there as to whether the new state has been guided in this momentous question by principles that do justice to the frightful crimes of a past epoch and put the relationship of the Jews to the German people on a new and healthy basis.

"The attitude of the Federal Republic towards its Jewish citizens is unmistakably stated in the Basic Law *(Grundgesetz)*. Article 3 of the Basic Law provides that all human beings are equal before the law, and that none must be discriminated against or preferred because of sex, descent, race, language, birthplace, origin, faith, religious or political views. Furthermore, Article I (§ 1—2) of the Basic Law provides: "'The dignity of man is inviolable. To respect and protect it is the duty of all state authority. The German people therefore proclaims its belief in inviolable and inalienable human rights as the basis of all human society, of peace and justice in the world.'

"These legal principles have the immediate effect of law, requiring every German citizen—and in particular, every official of the state—to reject any form of racial discrimination. In the same spirit the Federal government have also signed the Convention on the Rights of Man drawn up by the Council of Europe, and have undertaken to carry out the legal ideas therein specified.

"These principles, however, can take effect only if the convictions out of which they were born become the common property of the entire people. Justice is primarily a problem of education. The Federal government consider it urgently necessary for the churches and educational administrations of the states to make every effort within their own spheres, so that the spirit of human and religious tolerance in the entire German people, but particularly among German youth, shall not only be formally recognised, but shall become a fact in spiritual attitude and practical action. This is an essential task of the institutions charged with education, but of course it also needs to be complemented by the example of adults.

"To avoid disturbing this educational work and to assure domestic peace in the Federal Republic, the Federal government have resolved to prosecute vigorously those groups that are still carrying on anti-Semitic propaganda. Bills are before the parliament for an amendment to the penal law under which racial propaganda, among other things, is subject to severe penalties. As soon as these provisions are enacted, the Federal Government will apply them with the utmost vigour.

"The Federal Government and with it the great majority of the German people are aware of the immeasurable suffering that was brought upon the Jews in Germany and the occupied territories during the time of National Socialism. The overwhelming majority of the German people abominated the crimes committed against the Jews, and did not participate in them. During the National Socialist time there were many among the German people who showed their readiness to help their Jewish fellow citizens at their own peril for religious reasons, from distress of conscience, out of shame at the disgrace of the German name. But unspeakable crimes have been committed in the name of the German people, calling for moral and material indemnity, both with regard to the individual harm done to Jews and to the Jewish property for which no legitimate individual claimants still exist. In this field the first steps have been taken. Much still remains to be done. The Federal Government will see to it that reparation legislation is soon enacted and justly put into execution. Part of the identifiable Jewish property has been restored; further restitution will follow.

"With regard to the extent of the reparations—a momentous problem in view of the enormous destruction of Jewish values by National Socialism—the limits imposed on German ability to pay through the bitter necessity of caring for the innumerable war victims and the support of refugees and expellees must be considered. The Federal Government are prepared, jointly with representatives of Jewry and the State of Israel, which has admitted so many homeless Jewish fugitives, to bring about a solution of the material indemnity problem, thus easing the way to the spiritual settlement of infinite suffering. They are profoundly convinced that the spirit of true humanity must once again come alive and become fruitful. The Federal Government consider it the chief duty of the German people to serve this spirit with all their strength."

Deputy Paul Löbe spoke for the Social Democrats:

"Germany, in the opinion of the Social Democrats in the Diet, is morally obligated to strive with all its strength for a reconciliation with the State of Israel and the Jews all over the world, and it is up to us Germans to take the first step. We Social Democrats will therefore support the step of the Federal Government just announced with all our hearts, and would have been glad if it had been taken sooner and more decisively.

"The criminal potentates of the National Socialist rule of violence inhumanly persecuted the Jewish Germans and the Jews in Europe and murdered 6 million human beings—men, women, children, and old people—because of their Jewish descent alone. Let us not forget this immeasurable suffering. Every right-thinking person is ashamed of these outrages, committed to the horror of the overwhelming majority of the German people as well as others, and abusing the German name.

"We know that we are indissolubly linked to those Jews who like us were born in Germany, and we cannot imagine our common history without their contribution.

"Germany and Europe owe great things in all fields of intellectual, social, and economic life to men like Felix Mendelssohn, Heinrich Heine, Walther Rathenau, or the numerous German Nobel-prize winners of Jewish descent. Every German is therefore summoned to make good the wrong done to Jews in our midst. And every German is therefore summoned to combat the plague of race hatred and overcome it by reverence for his fellow man. And we are determined to combat without mercy those who have profited from the open and hidden proscription of the Jews.

"The enormity of the injustice to which the Chancellor too has just referred demands sacrifices of us. More than hitherto it must be shown by deeds that this indemnification is also the measure of the renewal of justice in Germany. Out of these feelings we are striving for peace with Israel."

The subsequent Foreign Minister, Heinrich von Brentano, as Chairman of the CDU/CSU group in Parliament, made the following statement:

"In this government message his Excellency the Federal Chancellor has raised a subject that moves us all deeply. For this reason I should like to confine myself to endorsing emphatically what was said in the government message and adopted in part by Mr. Löbe. Each one of us for himself must realise, and each one must try to make the German people realise, that the measure of respect we are prepared to offer our fellow men and also our Jewish fellow-citizens will be the measure of respect that we demand for ourselves."

Deputy Hermann Schäfer for the Free Democrats:

"His Excellency the Chancellor's statement has once again opened one of the darkest chapters in our recent history. I do not believe that further words are calculated to express the determination and the clarity of views that lie behind this government message. I will confine myself to expressing approval in my own name and that of my friends; but I should like to add that it will be one of the decisive tasks for all of us to sweep clean the world of thought and eliminate the remnants of this world that emerges from a completely materialistic view of life, and that led to this madness of an insane biologism. To disavow this and lay the foundations and place the fundamental ideas of practical humanity in the foreground seems to me suitable for the present occasion."

Hans-Joachim von Merkatz, later a cabinet minister, said on behalf of the German Party:

"In the name of my political associates I am to say that in view of the dreadful seriousness of this question we will omit further words of protestation of humanity. We not only approve the statement of the government, we support it with all our hearts, because it is a matter of making good a profanation of divine and human law. In this reparation we will hold to the words: Righteousness lifteth up a nation. We owe it to the earlier history of Germany to take action in this field that will assure the renewal of our state, our national consciousness and our dignity in the world as a whole, and in the deepest spiritual realms."

On behalf of the deputies of the Centre, Bernhard Reismann took the floor:

"The Centre Party welcomes with full conviction and gratitude the statement of His Excellency the Chancellor, which is to represent the first step of the Federal Republic towards the establishment of orderly, peaceful, and, we hope, friendly relations with our Jewish fellow citizens in Germany, in the world, and particulary in the State of Israel. Among the crimes and atrocities of this century, which alas has shown no dearth of them, those committed upon our Jewish fellow citizens in Germany and Europe by the band of criminals that disgraced the German name for a decade occupy a prominent place. We all feel the obligation to do everything in our power to make good the nameless disaster and suffering that has occurred, and also to redress the great material loss to the very best of our ability. Still more important to us, however, is the obligation, also emphasized by the Chancellor, to create an intellectual atmosphere of humanity in which any repetition shall be impossible, indeed the very thought of such things will only arouse loathing in all German fellow-citizens. May the solemn declaration of all the parties here in the Diet and the statement of the Federal Government before the public of the entire world do their part to clear away the natural resentment of those who endured such grievous suffering at the hands of a preceding government of Germany."

The Bavarian Party declared through its deputy Hugo Decker:

"My party feels as follows: Anyone who professes allegiance to the state ruled by law and justice must also accept the Chancellor's statement, welcome it, and support it."

Hermann Ehlers, president of the Diet, concluded this item on the agenda by saying:

"It will be the job of the German Federal Diet, following on the government message, to take the necessary legal measures. I propose that before the German Federal Diet undertakes and carries through this job, it should rise in token of the fact that it is united in sympathy for the victims and is prepared to draw conclusions from what has happened." (The deputies rise.)
"Thank you."

On the way to Wassenaar

Konrad Adenauer's generous offer

In the first days of December 1951, Konrad Adenauer visited the British capital. He took advantage of his stay to continue the German-Jewish discussion. He received Nahum Goldmann at the Claridge Hotel. Today Goldmann tells with a grin how he sneaked into the hotel through a side entrance because it "was still impossible to meet openly with the German Federal Chancellor." The upshot of the conversation was a letter that took on decisive importance for the further evolution of Israeli-German relations. In the letter, Adenauer asked Goldmann to inform the Israeli Government of the willingness of the Federal Republic to negotiate. Indeed he went a step further; he treated the demands made in the note of the Israeli government of 12 March 1951 as the basis of coming discussions. This offer was made against the will of the Allied powers. The text of Konrad Adenauer's letter to Nahum Goldmann was as follows:

"Dr. Nahum Goldmann 6 December 1951
Chairman of the Conference on
Jewish Claims against Germany
London

"With reference to the statements made in parliament on behalf of the Federal Government on 27 September 1951, wherein they expressed their willingness to enter into negotiations with representatives of the Jewish people and of Israel concerning indemnification for the damage done under the Nazi regime, I would inform you that the Federal Government feels the time has come for such negotiations to begin. I ask that you in your capacity of chairman of the Conference on Jewish Claims against Germany inform both the Conference and the government of Israel of this willingness.

"In this connexion I would remark that the Federal Government regard the problem of reparations above all as a moral obligation, and consider it a duty of honour for the German people to do their utmost to make good the wrong done to the Jewish people. In this connexion the Federal Government will welcome the opportunity to contribute to the building-up of the State of Israel through shipments of goods. In these negotiations the Federal Government are prepared to treat the claims advanced by the government of the State of Israel in its note of 12 March 1951 as the basis of discussions.

"With the highest esteem
"Yours sincerely
"(signed) Adenauer."

On 17 February 1952 Konrad Adenauer was again in London. Here Nahum Goldmann informed him that the Israeli Parliament had voted on 9 January 1952 to enter into negotiations with the Federal Government concerning a reparation agreement. The Chancellor arranged with Goldmann for the negotiations to begin in the latter half of March.

At the request of Israel, a small town in Holland, Wassenaar, was chosen because attempts on the life of the Israeli representatives by Israeli radical rightist groups were feared. Only years afterwards did Konrad Adenauer officially connect the attempted murder by means of a bomb parcel, through which bomb expert Karl Reichert lost his life on 27 March 1952, with the reparation negotiations at Wassenaar. Until then only a few people had known that an Israeli radical rightist had made this attempt to assassinate the Chancellor. Adenauer had issued strict instructions not to give publicity to the connexion.

Preparations for negotiations

Ten days after his return from London, on 29 February 1952, Konrad Adenauer wrote a letter to Federal Finance Minister Fritz Schäffer, in which he informed him of his talk with Nahum Goldmann and asked him to prepare for the negotiations with Israel. This letter, a document of the times and a testimony to the spirit in which Adenauer wished the negotiations to be conducted, reads as follows:

"Federal Minister of Finance   Bonn, 29 February 1952
Councillor Fritz Schäffer
Bonn

"Dear Mr. Schäffer:

"As you know, on 27 September 1951 I delivered before the German Diet on behalf of the Federal Government a statement regarding the attitude of the Federal Republic towards the Jews and the State of Israel. In this statement the government touched, among other things, on the obligation of material reparations for the wrong done to the Jews. The last paragraph of the statement begins:

"'The Federal Government are prepared, jointly with representatives of Jewry and the State of Israel, which has admitted so many homeless Jewish fugitives, to bring about a solution of the material indemnity problem, thus easing the way to the spiritual settlement of infinite suffering.'

"In accordance with the principles of this statement, on 6 December 1951 I had a conversation with the chairman of the Conference on Jewish Claims against Germany and delegate of the government of the State of Israel, Dr. Nahum Goldmann. I thereupon informed Dr. Goldmann in a letter of 6 December 1951 that the Federal Government were prepared to treat the claims advanced by the Israeli government in its note of 12 March 1951 to the government of the four occupying powers as the basis of the projected negotiations. I expressed the willingness of the Federal Government to contribute to the building-up of the State of Israel through shipments of goods.

"On 9 January 1952 the parliament of the State of Israel voted to accept the proposal of the Federal Government that negotiations be entered into.

"This decision was communicated to me on 17 February 1952 during a second discussion with Dr. Goldmann in London. During this conversation I emphasized that the Federal Government would welcome an early start of negotiations. It was agreed that if possible the negotiations should begin on 17 March 1952.

"I request you to make the requisite preparations as speedily as possible. The negotiations will be conducted under the auspices of the Foreign Office. It is a matter of course, however, that the other departments will participate to the extent required by their responsibilities. In particular, I would ask you to appoint specially selected gentlemen to the negotiating delegation.

"It is my wish that the hesitations natural under any other circumstances be put aside, and that the negotiations be prepared and conducted in a spirit appropriate to the moral and political weight and the uniqueness of our obligations.

"Sincerely yours
"(signed) Adenauer"

On the recommendation of Secretary of State Walter Hallstein, Professor Franz Böhm of Frankfurt was chosen to lead the German delegation in the negotiations with Israel— a man who was known to see the moral and political involvement with Israel and the Jewish people in the same light as Konrad Adenauer and those who had expressed their assent on behalf of their parties on 27 September 1951 in the German Diet.

Reparations and the London Debt Conference

Between London and Wassenaar

The Debt Conference began in London on February 28, 1952. The Federal Republic of Germany had declared from the first that it regarded itself as the successor state to the entire German Reich. Thus the German delegation was faced with the burden of debts for all Germany. Twenty-three states took part in this conference to settle the German pre-war debts, and at the same time to try to make possible the repayment of the economic aid Germany had received in the post-war years.

Konrad Adenauer saw clearly the financial connexion between the London Debt Conference and the reparation negotiations with Israel. In conversations with the editor, he repeatedly pointed out that the leading bankers, particularly in the United States, would exert their powerful influence on the success or failure of the London Debt Conference if some agreement with Israel were not reached. On the other hand a good settlement with Israel would not have been possible if the London Debt Conference had not had a successful issue. The two simultaneous sets of negotiations were dependent one on the other. For the economy of the Federal Republic a good settlement of the London Debt Conference meant a restoration of credit in the world's eyes. This in turn laid the foundation for the rapidly growing trade with foreign countries. Konrad Adenauer knew that the obligations he had undertaken in the first years of his term as Chancellor, in London and in Wassenaar, on behalf of the Federal Republic could be financed only from an intact and steadily rising economy. In this respect the DM 10 million that he had offered to Israel at his first interview in November, 1949, was an enormous sum, particularly since there were as yet no yardsticks to measure the Federal budget.

The Israeli side was opposed to any such interdependence of the negotiations in London and Wassenaar. The German delegation, on the other hand, resisted granting priority to negotiations with Israel.

A conversation with Hermann Josef Abs

The fact that the negotiations for reparations to Israel and the London conference on German pre- and post-war debts took place at the same time confronted the Federal Government with numerous problems. Chancellor Adenauer consulted Hermann Josef Abs, the chairman of the administrative council of the Credit Institution for Reconstruction, on these questions. Abs became chief of the German delegation at the London Debt Conference. In his conversation with the editor Abs described the difficulties.

"The three main problems were as follows: In a note of 12 March 1951 to the four powers—USA, England, France, Russia,—Israel entered a claim for reparations, and set the amount to be paid by the Federal Republic at one thousand million dollars; Israel reserved the right to present a further claim of $500 million against the Eastern Zone or 'German Democratic Republic'. This note, also mentioned in the well-known letter of Chancellor Adenauer to Nahum Goldmann of 5 December 1951, was the basis for negotiations.

"The decisive factor in the whole matter is a question that cannot be completely answered from the Bonn files, namely how the four powers reacted to the Israeli note. To the best of my knowledge the USSR never answered the note. The other three powers answered it, and so far as I know they declined to support a claim for reparations, because it was in conflict with their policy towards the Federal Republic of Germany. That was the first difficulty.

"The second problem I saw in the open question whether the settlement of pre-war debts, certain debts that arose during the war but did not actually originate in the war, and post-war debts was to be dealt with in London, while reparation claims—this was the object of my negotiations—were to be excluded. Reparation claims were indeed excluded in Article 5 of the London agreement, although Germany—I refer to the appropriate provisions in the German Treaty—was granted assurance that no reparations out of current production would be demanded from the Federal Republic of Germany. In all discussions carried on in London about this Article 5, the objection kept recurring that 'reparation' claims could not be endorsed on behalf of a country that came into being only after 1945 and therefore could not derive any reparation claims from the war itself, like a belligerent country.

"The third difficulty was that the Federal Republic of Germany based its position on the claim of legal identity with the German Reich. This question played a major part. Thus in the Chancellor's statement of 6 March 1951 in preparation for the London Conference we did not agree to undertake a guarantee for the foreign debt of the German Reich as demanded by France, but merely confirmed that the Federal Republic of Germany felt responsible for the debts of Germany and was prepared to negotiate whithin the limits of its capacity for the fulfilment of this obligation. This identity of German Reich and Federal Republic of Germany logically brought it about that all the claims presented against Germany as a whole were settled in London—partly by deferment until reunification, so that reunification would not require new debt negotiations. The creditors gave their receipt for the balance—as in the case of the Swiss clearing thousand million and the mixed claims from America, to mention only a few examples—, or as in other cases, postponed the actual settlement until after reunification. This question has its importance in respect to the double claims of the State of Israel against the Federal Republic on the one hand and the Eastern Zone on the other hand.

"In addition to these problems and difficulties there was the fact that the Federal Government had set me a limit for the London negotiations. In the final settlement, an annual payment of DM 567 million exceeded this top figure by DM 67 million for the first year; only after five years did the annual rate of DM 765 million begin. Only in the light of this limit and the other points I have mentioned can one understand that in conversations taking place probably about March 1952, there was talk of an annual payment of DM 100 million to settle the claim of Israel, although the total amount was never mentioned in my negotiations, originally to be regarded only in the light of London.

"The decisive influence on negotiations with Israel was the consultation with Chancellor Adenauer early in April 1952, in which the sum was to be determined that the

German negotiators, Prof. Böhm and Mr. Küster, regarded as appropriate to cover the expenditure for the integration of 600,000 fugitives in Israel. This figure was set at DM 3000 million and ultimately led to the agreement on the total payments of the Federal Republic of Germany.

"I may claim myself that even then—in early April, 1952,—I declared that any amount we mentioned would at the same time fix the final sum of the obligation we must assume. Actual developments confirmed my belief. In the negotiations with the representatives of Israel at Wassenaar after April, 1952, the main subject was the size of the annual payments, or in other words, the total duration of the agreement.

"In judging the capacity of the Federal Republic to pay, first the matter of capability and second the transfer problem played an important part. The agreement with Israel called for shipments of goods, i. e. payments in kind of various sorts. These wishes were recorded in a list that was re-negotiated from year to year. In that connexion, the Federal Economic Ministry and important members of the government upheld the view that no transfer problem arose for such shipments. I opposed this view from the very first day, because I considered that shipments in the nature of export goods—they had to be charged at valid and ascertainable world-market prices—represented exactly the same kind of payment as an ordinary transfer in currency or any other form. Logically pursuing this view of mine, I successfully used my influence to have part of the German reparations to Israel used in payment of bills for crude oil. Regarded from a transfer standpoint, a payment of this kind was equivalent to the German shipments of goods to Israel, and vice versa."

Question: "You mentioned that the London Debt Agreement practically assumed reunification, a general settlement of German obligations aside from the problem of Israel. So far as I know, Israel never acknowledged any 'general German arrangement' of this kind. The Federal Republic settled its share according to the note of 12 March 1951 with $750 million, and the question of what had happened to the claims of more than $500 million against the Soviet Zone had remained open. It must have recurred ominously in the negotiations at the Waldorf-Astoria Hotel in 1960."

Answer: "I'm not inclined to believe it was mentioned expressly on that occasion. On the basis of many discussions I have had, I do not doubt for a moment that the State of Israel would be willing to recognise that the note of 12 March 1951, addressed to the four powers, referring to payments by the Federal Republic on the one hand and the 'German Democratic Republic' on the other hand, was fully settled by the general agreement between the Federal Republic and Israel; only to the best of my knowledge this was never recorded in statements or documents."

The negotiations for the reparation agreement

Human rapprochement

The negotiations at Wassenaar duly began on 20 March 1952, in a chilly, very formal atmosphere. The leader of the delegation, Franz Böhm, reported:

"You can imagine how we felt at the moment of the first encounter with representatives of Israel. It was a matter of course that the negotiations began with extreme personal reserve. It was the great objectivity and fairness noted by the representatives of the Israeli delegation from the first day forward, that made it possible for the two delegations to begin close, objective collaboration within the first few days."

The Deputy Chairman of the Israeli delegation was the future head of the Israeli mission at Cologne, Felix E. Shinnar. He described to the editor an incident of the first days of negotiations that shows how the men on both sides tried by humanity to bridge the deep gulf created by the recent past:

"At The Hague the language of negotiations during the first few days was English. On the opposite side, Prof. Böhm was the head of the delegation. His deputy was Otto Küster of Stuttgart. On the second day Küster passed me a note that said in substance, 'I think I detect a Swabian accent in your English. Am I right?' In short it turned out that Otto Küster was right. I was born in Stuttgart, went to school there, but more than that it turned out that we had attended the same *Realgymnasium*, now the Dillmann-Gymnasium, and Otto Küster, one year younger than I, attended the same classes, had the same teachers, and a few days later, we wrote a card to a teacher we had highly esteemed, Professor Holl, then still living, and told him of this incident."

Complicated negotiations

Konrad Adenauer's wish to provide Israel with real assistance in integrating the new immigrants from Europe and thus also to prove the will of the German Federal Republic to give true reparations, ran up against the complicated matter of the London Debt Conference, as Abs has already recounted, and the fact that the three victorious Allied powers rejected parallel obligations of the Federal Republic along with payments under the London Debt Agreement. This was the problem.

The Federal Republic could meet financial commitments only within a narrow overall limit. Originally the financial burden upon the Federal budget had been set at DM 500 million. It then expanded, however, to DM 567 million. Hermann Josef Abs remarked in this connexion:

"Only in the light of this limit and the other difficulties I have described can one understand that in discussions taking place about March, 1952, an annual payment of

DM 100 million to settle the claim of Israel was mentioned, yet the total amount was never discussed, even in my earlier negotiations concerned only with London."

With these proposals Abs was soon branded as the exponent of a tendency not to give Israel what had been called for by the spirit of the government's statement of 27 September 1951. The Israeli observer at the London Debt Conference, Embassy Councillor Keren, tried at the conference itself to emphasize the problem of a reparation agreement between the German Federal Republic and Israel and the claims presented in the note of 12 March 1951; he did this in a statement that he made before the London debt conference on 29 February 1952, the second day of negotiations:

"1. The government of Israel are aware that the chief task of this conference is to deal with German pre-war foreign debts and arrive at a procedure for settling them. My government wish every success to the conference and its endeavours to reach this goal.

"2. We have carefully studied the memorandum prepared by the Three-Power Committee, and in particular have noted the substance of Chapter II of the memorandum concerning the extent of the debt settlement and the definition of the term 'pre-war foreign debts'.

"3. My government wish to draw the attention of the conference to the nature of the claims they represent. Although they are aware that these claims go beyond the limits of the present conference, the government of Israel nevertheless consider it essential to inform the conference of the existence of these claims.

"4. The claims presented by the government of Israel derive from the persecution of the Jews that continued from the assumption of power by the Nazi party in 1933 with ever-increasing virulence until the collapse of Nazi rule on 8 May 1945. The special nature of these claims requires a special settlement.

"5. These claims may be summed up under the following main considerations:

"a) The claim of the government of Israel for collective reparations, which Germany must pay on the basis of the crimes committed by the Nazi regime against the Jewish people, as presented in their note of 12 March 1951 to the occupying powers.

"b) Claims for restitution of ascertainable property to persons unrightfully deprived of this property.

"c) Claims arising out of the financial liability of the former German Reich on the basis of deprivation of personal property, including cash, securities, and bank deposits as well as sums of money extorted by discriminatory or compulsory taxation.

"d) Reparation claims of victims of Nazi persecution who suffered damage or losses to person or property.

"6. The general principles on which the claims presented by the Israeli government under the three headings last named are based have already been recognized to a very large extent in the laws on domestic restitution and the legal requirements in force in all or part of the German Federal Republic with respect to general claims.

"7. In addition to the claims of Israeli citizens there are a number of similar claims in possession of individual Jews and Jewish organizations outside the State of Israel.

"8. The Israeli delegation wishes to call the attention of the conference to a statement before the Diet of the Federal Republic of Germany on 27 September 1951, in which Federal Chancellor Adenauer conceded that unspeakable crimes had been committed in the name of the German people, imposing upon Germany the duty of moral and material reparations. In the same statement Chancellor Adenauer confirmed the willingness of the German Federal Government to bring about a settlement of the financial side of the above-mentioned question jointly with representatives of Jewry and the State of Israel. In a communication of 6 December 1951 Chancellor Adenauer confirmed the statement and observed that the Federal Government would accept as a basis for negotiations the claims presented by the Israeli government in their note of 12 March 1951. The Israeli government and a group of representative Jewish organizations have now received an invitation to enter into direct negotiations concerning all questions connected with the satisfaction of Israeli and Jewish claims. Steps have been taken to permit these negotiations to begin at an early date.

"It will also interest the Conference that the governments of the United Kingdom and the United States have expressed a benevolent interest in the results of these negotiations.

"9. As above mentioned, my government are indeed aware that the claims as stated go beyond the limitations of this Conference, but they request the Conference to take note of their existence, since no general settlement of German foreign obligations would be just or realistic that did not duly consider these claims."

It would not be doing justice to the situation in which the Federal Republic then found itself if we did not point out what negotiations were being conducted in addition to the London Debt Conference and the German-Israeli negotiations at Wassenaar.

Negotiations with the three Western Allies were going on concerning the treaty for Germany. This was to end the state of war *de jure*, as well as *de facto*, and to give full sovereignty to the Federal Republic. By this treaty the Federal Republic was to become an equal partner in a European defence community. In addition there were the extremely difficult deliberations concerning the equalization of burdens, i. e. payments to the expellees and victims of bomb damage in the Second World War.

Konrad Adenauer, out for a walk with me during the election campaign, told me what exertions he had to make to keep his head clear for the reparation negotiations at Wassenaar, lest they drown in haggling among the financial experts. Just at that time, he said, mistrust of Germany in Israel had increased again.

This mistrust of Germany could be overcome only by giving concrete assurances to Israel. These assurances in turn depended on the outcome of the London Debt Conference. Concrete assurances must be lived up to without question. Adenauer always emphasized this when referring to that time because—after the years of German political unreliability and dishonesty of National Socialism—he wanted under all circumstances to underline the moral bonds upon the democratic Germany in international treaties. Konrad Adenauer referred again and again to the moral obligation of his country towards Israel, particularly in carrying out the material part of the agreement.

At a period when all the agreements—London Debt Conference, Treaty covering Germany, European Defence Community, Equalization of Burdens, and negotiations with Israel—were still in progress, it was particularly difficult for the Federal Government to emphasize German moral integrity towards the Jewish people.

On 23 April, 1952 the head of the German delegation at Wassenaar, Franz Böhm, wrote to the Chancellor once more, describing the difficult situation:

"His Excellency   Bonn, 23 April 1952
The Chancellor
of the Federal Republic of Germany
Dr. Konrad Adenauer
Bonn

"Dear Mr. Chancellor:

"Discussions having taken place in the last few days with Mr. Abs and Messrs. Goldmann and Barou, I take the liberty of presenting to you a statement of the situation as it appears to me today.

"1. In discussions hitherto it has not been possible for us to make any sort of statement concerning the order of magnitude of possible payments. This can be done only when a general view of the total capacity for transfers by the Federal Republic has been arrived at.

"2. Once this is available, a decision will have to be made as to what share of possible transfers (both transfers proper, in money, and shipments of goods) shall go to pre- and post-war creditors on the one hand, and to the creditors under the reparations to be negotiated at The Hague on the other hand. Although this decision cannot be made as yet, it must inescapably confront us very soon.

"3. This decision cannot be made either in London or The Hague but only by the Federal Government. The success of both conferences is dependent on its outcome.

"4. The Israeli delegation has expressed the fear that the Germans might perhaps proceed in such a fashion that the other creditors would first be satisfied, and Israel (and the organisations) would then have to be content with what remained. Messrs. Goldmann, Shinnar, and Barou indeed expressed this fear to Mr. Abs in the discussion of 19 April 1952. As the memorandum on this discussion shows, Mr. Abs' statements satisfied the Jewish representatives for the time being.

"5. Both the claims of the State of Israel and those of the Jewish organisation, like all other creditors' claims, must submit to a possible restriction through a double consideration: First in view of criticism of the factual justification of the claim presented, secondly with regard to German capacity to pay. Thus far the Hague delegation has studied the claim of the State of Israel with regard to the first point, and has recommended to the Federal government that it be accepted to an amount of DM 3000 million (rather than DM 4.2 thousand million). The consideration of the claims of the Jewish organisations is not yet completed. (This—aside from the payments to be made to the State of Israel—involves a total sum of about DM 3-4 thousand million.)

"6. In examining the second question, namely that of the total amount to which Israeli and Jewish claims can be met, two particularities must be taken account of that do not exist with regard to other creditors. Firstly, the fact that at least the reparation payments to the State of Israel will be made to a considerable extent in goods; and secondly that all reparation payments, if they are to accomplish their purpose, must be made in a considerably shorter period than the other liabilities require.

"7. It must also be taken into account that the reparation payments have an entirely different origin from the indebtedness to be negotiated in London. The situation with the other indebtedness is that on one hand the creditors have a substantial interest in giving every consideration to German capacity to pay. For that reason they will be prepared to make concessions—whether in the form of a reduction of capitalization, or in a lowering of interest and service totals. On the other hand, the Federal Republic is intensely interested in restoring its credit position, and is therefore prepared to give every imaginable proof of its earnest determination to meet its obligations. This situation will benefit the prospect of a favourable outcome for the London negotiations.

"The situation of the reparation payments is different. Here too, indeed, the creditors for these payments are interested in not overburdening German economic capabilities, and in a satisfactory conclusion of the London negotiation. But in their case the fear takes precedence that the Germans have no really serious determination to make restitution, and that accordingly the German tactics in negotiations may consist of depicting German capacity to pay in the darkest colours. They are inclined to suspect that the Germans have nothing like the same readiness to pay that other creditors can count on. On the other hand, the Federal Republic has an interest in making convincing reparations. It is obvious, after all, that German credit depends to a large extent on this. It cannot be denied, however, that the connexion between credit and reparations is nothing like so obvious, and especially is not felt nearly so clearly by wide groups of the population and business, as is the case with the other indebtedness. In addition, the very existence of German reparation obligations is undoubtedly most annoying to a number of creditor groups, since it impairs their chances of obtaining a maximum settlement. Accordingly the Federal Government is confronted with a certain pressure from these creditors' interests, which threatens to conflict with the interest of the reparation creditors in obtaining satisfaction.

"8. This connection makes it necessary to give very special attention to the political and moral weight of the reparation question. If it proves impossible to reach agreements at The Hague that are accepted by those with whom we are negotiating, and by significant world opinion, as proof that Germany has gone to the limits of its capacity to pay, and in addition has exhausted all the possibilities of negotiation available in London to convince the other creditors of the necessity and justification of the reparation claims, the political, moral, and economic value of these agreements will be dubious. The sacrifices that must be required of the German population (and in part from foreign creditor interests) to fulfill these dubious agreements then have no real meaning. Accordingly it seems proper to point out a few facts that are important in judging the importance of the matter with respect to foreign, government, and legal policy and moral considerations and the reparation claims that have been presented.

"9. Both the claims of the State of Israel and the claims of the organisations are high, measured by the capacities of the Federal Republic, but measured by the extent of the damage that has been done, they are undoubtedly more than moderate. Nothing unreasonable has been demanded.

"In my opinion the first consideration should be the constructive aspect for the future. Presumably the most important and urgent task of German policy is to overcome the inconceivable bitterness evoked by the National Socialist crime in the Jews throughout the world and in all right-thinking people, and also to overcome the dreadful blow dealt by this crime to the German reputation.

In addition, at the present moment it is the one German contribution to the rebuilding of a free world that, more than any other decision of domestic or foreign policy, is the result of an independent, purely German act of will; although I recognise that its performance is dependent on the cooperation and decision of Allied authorities. But there can hardly be any doubt that the initiative must come from the German side, and that the outcome of the Allied decision will depend largely, if not exclusively, on the degree of energy of the German iniative. Not only the effect on the State of Israel and the Jews the world over, not only the effect on foreign policy, but—and above all—the domestic effect (to a high degree an effect of political and moral education) depends on the vigour and resolution with which this now imminent decision is taken. Any vacillation, any uncertainty or softness can only benefit the opposing, destructive forces, imperilling the success of the policy that has been and is being pursued by the Federal Government as a long-range objective.

"10. I must not conclude these observations without touching on the important fact that the assessment of German capacity to pay and make transfers can by no means be the result of a scientific computation. It is unquestionably not the case that some objectively calculable German capacity sets inherent limits to German policy. On the contrary, the extent of German capacity depends to a not inconsiderable degree on political decisions. This is true not only of economic policy, but equally for the major outlines of all domestic and foreign policy. Nor is the amount of reparation payments unilaterally determined by the limits of fixed capacity; on the contrary, reparation payments react on the capacity to pay, and not only negatively, but indubitably in a positive way, and this to a degree that purely theoretical thinking is surely inclined to underestimate.

"With the assurance of my most distinguished esteem, I remain,

"Most sincerely yours,
(signed) Böhm."

In consideration of the London Debt Conference, the negotiations at Wassenaar were officially interrupted in April. The Germans did not want to interfere with the debt settlement. This attitude naturally led to a stiffening in the relations between the Federal Republic and Israel; it became apparent again and again even in the official conversations of the two delegations. Uneasiness on this point was expressed particularly in a letter of 19 May 1952 from Nahum Goldmann to Chancellor Konrad Adenauer.

"Dear Mr. Chancellor: London, 19 May, 1952

"On 16 May, immediately on my return from Israel, I sent a telegram from Paris expressing my profound uneasiness about the state of the negotiations between Israel and the German Federal Republic. In that telegram I asked you to inform me when a conversation between us could take place in which a proposal for payment would be submitted to Israel, such a proposal having been promised me by you for May 3, or May 13, or 14 at latest. Unfortunately I have had no answer from you to my telegram.

"On the other hand, a discussion took place today between Mr. Abs and Dr. Shinnar and Dr. Keren in which indeed Mr. Abs emphasized that he was not authorised to present official proposals, but then spoke of an initial annual delivery of goods to the amount of DM 100 million, possibly to be doubled in view of expected American aid, which, however, in our opinion, is completely uncertain. As to the total of the debts to be paid, Mr. Abs said nothing whatever.

"The specific proposals presented by the Israeli delegation in full detail at the various stages were ignored in all substantial points in Mr. Abs' utterances. Of course Dr. Shinnar and Dr. Keren immediately rejected this proposal. I must repeat in all frankness what Dr. Shinnar told Mr. Abs, that his thinking was as completely unexpected as it was disappointing to me and my friends.

"From all our discussions I had gained the impression that you and the German Federal Government were seriously concerned to bring about a true, if partial reparation at least for the material effects of the crimes committed against Jewry. The statements Mr. Abs made to the representatives of the Israeli government today contravened in spirit the statement of the Federal Government of 27 September 1951; still more do they contravene the substance of your letter of 6 December 1951 to me in which you accepted the claim of the State of Israel to the amount of $1 thousand million as a basis of negotiations.

"When I considered Mr. Abs' proposal in the light of the preceding statements, without which there would never have been any negotiations, I am convinced that Jewish public opinion will regard them—forgive the harsh words—as nothing more than an affront. Indeed Dr. Shinnar spontaneously and immediately said this to Mr. Abs. Mr. Abs' views on the solution of the problem show no readiness to make true sacrifices of any kind for reparation. Mr. Abs' thesis concerning the insufficient capacity of the Federal Republic will convince neither the Jewish people nor world public opinion if we consider the constantly rising production power of the German economy, the growing German foreign trade, running into thousands of millions of dollars, and the equalization-of-burdens settlement just concluded. A problem of the moral importance of Jewish reparations cannot be solved by the ordinary methods of commercial negotiations and bargaining. What impressed me most profoundly in my conversations with you, Mr. Chancellor, and induced me to urge Israel and the Jewish people to enter into negotiations with the German Federal Republic, was your view of Germany's moral obligation to make serious restitution at least materially.

"Despite the profound disappointment that Mr. Abs' utterances caused us all, I cannot abandon my conviction that you, Mr. Chancellor, would never endorse such proposals. The contradiction between such proposals and everything you told me during the various conversations is so extreme that I cannot imagine their representing your views in any way.

"If the order of magnitude in which Mr. Abs apparently sees the solution were to represent the official position of the Federal Republic, the Israeli government could not under any circumstances continue the negotiations, and naturally the same would apply to world Jewry. The effects of breaking off negotiations, unfortunately a very real possibility after Mr. Abs' utterances, would be hard to imagine in their extent. The confidence in the honest will of the new German state to make reparations will be profoundly shaken in all those persons who hope to see in you, Mr. Chancellor, the spokesman and exponent of this new Germany. The violent reaction of the whole world, supported by large groups of non-Jews, who sympathised profoundly with the martyrdom of the Jewish people in the Nazi period, would be inevitable and fully justified.

"At this critical moment in our negotiations I appeal to you, Mr. Chancellor, as the German statesman who has made himself the representative and spokesman of the reparation idea, with the plea to restore the negotiations to the high moral level on which you have hitherto regarded them. Do not allow methods customary in truly commercial matters to degrade and imperil these negotiations. The present state of uncertainty, the constant postponing of a specific offer, not consonant with your letter of 6 December 1951, cannot continue.

"The Jewish world and Israel rightly wish to know where they stand. I therefore request you to use all your authority to assure that an offer is promptly submitted that will make it possible to resume official negotiations at an early date.

"In expectation of your reply, on which so much will depend, I subscribe myself with genuine esteem and with salutations,

"Yours sincerely
"(signed) Dr. Nahum Goldmann
"Temporary address: London
"Legation of Israel
"18, Manchester Square, W. 1."

Konrad Adenauer was dismayed at this development in the negotiations, particularly because he had obviously not been informed of the proposal by the Chief of Delegation at the London Debt Conference, Hermann Josef Abs. The Chancellor asked Franz Böhm to get in touch with Nahum Goldmann, since he had a proposal to make in order to get the negotiations moving again. On 23 May Goldmann and Böhm met in Paris. Böhm informed the Chancellor of this discussion in a report on 24 May 1952.

"24 May 1952
"Launitzstrasse 15, Frankfurt am Main

"Report
on the discussion with Dr. Goldmann and the members of the Israeli Delegation in Paris on 23 May 1952.

"The first discussion took place with Dr. Goldmann alone at 11 o'clock and was concluded at 12 noon.

"This was followed by a second discussion, in which Dr. Josephthal, Dr. Shinnar, Dr. Avner, and Dr. Barou of the Israeli Delegation participated on the invitation of Dr. Goldmann. It lasted until 3 p.m.

"*1. Discussion with Dr. Goldmann*

"I informed Dr. Goldmann that I had come on behalf of the Chancellor, but was not authorised to transmit proposals from the Federal Government. I had only been instructed to transmit the substance of a proposal that I myself had made to the Federal Government, believing it might be a suitable basis for further negotiations at The Hague. I said the Federal Government had taken no decision on this proposal. Instead, the Chancellor wished to hear unofficially the views of Mr. Goldmann and the Israeli government on the suggestion before the government transmitted an offer of its own to the Israeli government.

"I said the substance of my proposal was as follows:

"Total amount DM 3 thousand million;

"Duration of performance: not less than 8 or more than 12 years;

"Method of performance: subject to the possibility of a better solution, entirely in goods; the amount and make-up of the year's shipments to be kept flexible, and determined in each case by a mixed commission;

"Alternative methods of performance: as soon as the Federal Republic was able to obtain a foreign loan, the amount of the loan was to be passed on in the given foreign currency and credited to the total indebtedness. The Federal Government considered it quite possible that they would succeed in obtaining such a loan within a few years after the signing of the Hague and London agreements, and felt that they would then be able to meet their entire commitment before the expiration of the proposed minimum repayment term, under favourable circumstances much sooner.

"Initial annual instalment: within the first two years, deliveries of goods to an amount of DM 200 million each. These low initial payments were provided in view of the unusual burdens upon our capacity to pay imposed by the most recent obligations entered into. I said I was quite aware that for the success of the agreement above-average initial payments would have been desirable.

"Dr. Goldmann definitely welcomed this proposal. He said it was undoubtedly a very serious demonstration of the intent to make restitution, and he believed he could say that it might expect a favourable reception from the Israeli government. In any event this conversation today had created an atmosphere that would permit the government of Israel to feel once more that the continuation of the negotiations had some prospect of success, whereas the statements of the previous Monday in London had depressed and embittered the Israeli government. He was impressed above all by the fact that my proposal offered a complete total and final solution, which did in fact provide for substantial reparation payments. This, he felt, was a serious basis.

"From the Israeli standpoint it must be said that my proposal had certain flaws whose elimination should be attempted. He hoped it would be possible for the Federal Government to embody these adjustments in their official proposal; otherwise the matter could be negotiated at The Hague.

"He saw the flaws as the following:

"1. Inadequate initial instalments,

"2. The restriction to payments in kind until the possibility of obtaining a loan became reality,

"3. The excessively prolonged time scheme for performance (8 to 12 years).

"Then Dr. Goldmann took up the total claims of the Jewish organisations represented by him. He said he assumed that this total would be subject to a considerable cut. Assuming the Federal Government granted only 20 to 25% of the sum demanded (e. g. a total of some DM 400 to 500 million) it was to be expected that the Jews, and particularly the American Jews, would react with considerable ill feeling (not only towards the Federal Government, but also towards Israel). He therefore wondered if it would not be advisable for the Federal Republic to add whatever amount it was thinking of granting to the Conference on Jewish Claims against Germany to the total being offered to Israel, leaving it to Israel to reach an agreement with the world organisations on the distribution of total reparations. Israel would then be the sole creditor of the Federal Republic and the recipient of German payments in kind, but would, under the agreement, assume an indebtedness to the organisations payable in money to the amount of the agreed proportion of the annual German payments to Israel. In this way, both parties would profit. Israel would receive the goods it needed, and the organisations would receive money for the support of needy Jews.

"Dr. Goldmann emphasized that he was making this proposal without having consulted and without authorization. He believed, however, that both the Israeli and the Claims Delegation would accept such a solution if it were offered by the Federal Government. In any case he would personally endeavour to win over these parties in our negotiations.

"I said I was willing to discuss this suggestion at Bonn, but emphasized that a money payment to the organisations could be offered only in the form of a blocked-mark balance, whereas the total amount to be negotiated with Israel would have to be paid in goods or, in the event of a loan, in foreign currency. If we accepted Dr. Goldmann's proposal we would have an additional transfer problem. Dr. Goldmann conceded that this was so.

"Finally Dr. Goldmann asked me to report to the Federal Chancellor that in his opinion a great deal depended on an *extremely quick* decision by the Federal Government. He would be highly gratified if the Chancellor could give him certain *binding statements* covering the total figure of the proposed agreement, during his stay in Paris at the beginning of the next week. If the Chancellor found it possible to concede these points, the discussion could be immediately followed by a *press communiqué*, in which a date for the *resumption of the Hague negotiations* could be set. This communiqué would then be the first foreign-policy decision of the sovereign Federal Republic, and as such would go down in history. This gesture would make a deep impression on Israel and the Jews.

"*2. Discussion with Dr. Goldmann, Dr. Josephthal, Dr. Shinnar, Dr. Avner, and Dr. Barou*

"The gentlemen of the Israeli Delegation also expressed themselves favourably with regard to my proposal, but were more disturbed than Dr. Goldmann by the fact that *no payments* in *foreign exchange* were provided aside from the possible loan. The very detailed discussions dealt primarily with this point.

"Dr. Avner pointed out that Israel could cover its vital needs for oil only from English suppliers, but was absolutely denuded of sterling. Here Israel was confronted with a bottleneck that might endanger the entire development programme. Since the Federal Republic had sterling balances, the Israeli government were much concerned to obtain German help on this point in particular.

"Dr. Shinnar once again explained the previously discussed Israeli proposal concerning *payments in foreign exchange*.

"Monthly payments: total: $3 million
"Payable: $1.4 million in British currency = £500 thousand
"Payable: $1.6 million in American currency
"This makes an annual payment of $36 million or DM 151.2 million;
"Payable: $16.8 million in British currency = £6 million,
    $19.2 million in American currency

"In reply to my question whether these payments were to be credited against the annual deliveries of goods Dr. Shinnar said it depended how large the payments in kind during the first four years were to be. If the Federal Republic could offer only DM 200 million in goods he felt that the annual payment of DM 150 million should be *additional*. If, however, the German intention was to fulfil the entire agreement in eight years, i. e. to pay annual instalments averaging DM 375 million, Israel would of course agree to credit the amount in foreign exchange fully against the annual instalment. In this case only DM 225 million need be paid in kind.

"Dr. Shinnar emphasized that according to the by-laws of the European Payments Union balances of one member state with another member state could be ceded by the creditor state to a non-member state, and that in this case only the consent of the debtor, not of the Union, was required. Thus the Federal Republic could cede its sterling balances to Israel, requiring only the agreement of Israel. England would presumably make its consent dependent on Israel's promise to place orders in England. Israel was prepared to do this.

"I said I was willing to report to the Federal Government that Israel attached great importance to payments in foreign exchange, but emphasized that in my view the Federal Republic was not capable of foreign-exchange payments to this amount. The proposed sum would absorb about half of all the foreign-exchange reserves available for debt service over a period of four years. Even considering that the German payments under the London Agreement would begin only 18 months after the signing, it was to be feared that such a promise to Israel would wreck the London Agreement, benefitting nobody, Israel included. If my proposal, aside from the possible loan, included only payments in kind, it was because in that case the rivalry in currency transfers with the other creditors of the Federal Republic would be eliminated. The German payments would then be substantially a purely German effort, a sacrifice by the population, whereas in the case of foreign exchange payments other nations and groups of creditors would have to make the sacrifice.

"Dr. Shinnar conceded this, but once again pointed out the difficult position of his country.

"In addition I pointed out the large dollar gap, a source of grave concern to the Federal Economic Minister in particular.

"Dr. Josephthal then submitted my proposal to summary criticism. He said the proposal left *four points* open, which he would arrange in order of importance:

"*1. The share of foreign exchange.* Through approaches in London his delegation had ascertained that an agreement to make payments in foreign exchange would not encounter insuperable resistance. While it was not an actual matter of life and death for Israel, it was a question of great importance.

"*2. The smallness of the first annual payment.* He said his delegation had always emphasized the importance of specially large *initial payments*. In the first stage of building up the country, the hunger for goods and the requirements for investment were particularly large. For Israel it was a matter of getting started. Psychologically, too, it was of great importance that the Federal Republic should make impressive payments in the early years, particularly. Since the beginning of the Hague negotiations the belief on the part of Israel in a serious German will to make good had grown ever fainter. This belief urgently needed revival.

"*3. The prolonged duration of fulfilment* (8-12 years). Eight years might be accepted. Twelve, however, was too long.

"*4. The total amount.* Thus far, the German delegation had offered no explanation of its proposal to the Federal Government that the amount be reduced to DM 3 thousand million. But this question stood in last place for Israel. He would not revert to it.

"In reply to my enquiry whether Israel would resume negotiations if the Federal Government embodied the proposal communicated by me in an *offer to the Israeli government*, Dr. Josephthal replied that he feared the consultations at The Hague would soon come to a halt again unless the offer of the Federal Government made concessions from the start at least in the first two wishes of Israel.

"Dr. Goldmann asked me not to take this last reply of Dr. Josephthal as meaning that acceptance of the Israeli wishes for changes here discussed was in any way a condition for the continuance of the negotiations or that a German offer in accordance with my proposal would evoke a reaction of annoyance on the part of the Israeli government. If the Chancellor told him in Paris that the Federal Government could not go beyond my proposal, the Israeli government would perhaps attempt unofficially, outside the Hague negotiations, to obtain an improvement of the German offer, so that the negotiations at The Hague could be concluded without tension. Anxiety about the renewed setbacks was seen in the Israeli government. At worst, the negotiations would then start somewhat later. But the substance of my proposal offered no grounds for apodictic declarations or objections.

"Dr. Goldmann finally emphasized once more his request *for all possible speed*, and repeated his suggestion that the Chancellor might specially consecrate the offer by making it the first act of foreign policy by the sovereign Federal Republic.

"After the end of the consultation Dr. Goldmann seized an opportunity to talk to me alone. He asked me to transmit his greetings to the Chancellor, and to convey his belief that the government of Israel valued my mission to Paris and the substance of my communications as he himself did. He would be in Paris the first part of the week, and would be available at any time if the Chancellor intended to receive him.

"*3. Discussion with Dr. Josephthal*

"On my departure from Paris Dr. Josephthal was waiting for me on the platform, and made the following statement:

"He felt impelled to explain to me why the desire of the Israeli government for foreign exchange had grown so urgent. In recent weeks Israel had attempted to obtain a *loan* in London, and had failed. Mr. Abs was informed of this. The embarrassment that this caused Israel led him to declare to me that Israel would be prepared to agree to a reduction of the total amount if the Federal Republic could promise to make some of the annual payments for the next few years in foreign exchange.

"He said that Dr. Shinnar was prepared to discuss this question with the Federal Economic Minister if desired. In that case he requested that we notify him of the date at his London address."

When the Chancellor was in Paris a few days later, on 28 May, 1952, to sign the treaty on the European Defence Community, he met Nahum Goldmann again. In this difficult situation Goldmann once more showed deep understanding for the anxieties of German foreign policy and for the fact that Abs could not yet propose any final decision. At all events, a communiqué was drawn up on this occasion with promising aspects for the future. It read as follows:

"On 28 May, 1952, Chancellor Adenauer received the Chairman of the Conference on Jewish Claims against Germany, Dr. Nahum Goldmann, for a discussion. During this talk the Chancellor expressed his and the Federal Government's determination and confidence that the negotiations with Israel and the Jewish organisations should be brought to a favourable conclusion. The Chancellor and Dr. Goldmann were in agreement that it would be desirable to resume the official negotiations as soon as possible. To accomplish this, another discussion was planned for the near future, in which a specific proposal to satisfy the claims of Israel and the Jewish organisations is to be presented."

As early as 10 June 1952 the decisive conversation in Bonn took place. For Israel, Goldmann and the subsequent Ambassador Shinnar took part; for Germany, Secretary of State Walter Hallstein and Hermann Josef Abs. This discussion was decisive because it proved possible here to set the final amounts for the treaty, with the Federal Government undertaking to put German treaty payments at DM 3.4 to 3.5 thousand million. The individual annual instalments were also set. It was agreed that by 31 March 1954 shipments of goods to a value of DM 400 million would go from the Federal Republic to Israel, and that there were to be ten subsequent annual instalments of DM 250 million each.

A week later the Federal Cabinet agreed to all the details of the discussion of 10 June. Accordingly it was possible to begin the final round of negotiations on 28 June, 1952, at Wassenaar with the technical and administrative questions being decided as well.

Difficulties arising in this part of the discussions were soon settled, so that the treaty was ready for signature at the beginning of September.

Arab protests

The Arab states protested against any reparations by the German Federal Republic to Israel, since in their view they were still in a state of war with Israel and therefore regarded payments to a belligerent state as a violation of neutrality. The governing consideration for the Federal Government was that the Security Council of the United Nations had declared that no state of war existed. Accordingly the Germans rejected the allegation of a violation of neutrality, pointing out that the shipments of goods promised to Israel served peaceful purposes alone. Offers of guarantees to the Arab states were made, emphasizing that under this agreement no munitions or material of war would be supplied. Nevertheless suspicion and indignation were great in the Arab states, largely because it was believed that by re-exporting the German shipments Israel could obtain possession of foreign exchange for the purchase of armaments. But according to the reparation agreement all re-exports were out of the question.

The Arab League also spoke of the upsetting of the economic equilibrium in the Near East by the building-up of the Israeli economy. The Federal Economic Ministry dispatched Secretary of State Westrick to Cairo to offer to the Arab states assistance by German engineers and experts and expansion of German-Arab trade and a fixing of this in trade treaties. The boycott of German goods threatened by the Arab League in case of a German-Israeli treaty did not take place, mainly because the Germans had taken pains to explain the agreement with Israel in the Arab capitals.

Konrad Adenauer always saw German-Arab relations in a realistic light. In particular, he was aware that in view of divided Germany a boycott by the Arab states would cause political and not merely economic losses. Nevertheless, Konrad Adenauer was never diverted from his attitude towards Israel by the threats of the Arab states and the office of the Arab League in Bonn. The evolution of a good relationship to the Jewish state and the Jewish people was for him a moral obligation, and he always refused to have the commitment to Israel compared to anything else in politics. For him this question stood above any political or economic considerations.

The confidence of the Jewish people was not to be won by declarations alone; it also required material sacrifices. After everything that had been said and written on the question in Germany, he knew that the German people, German business, and the unions were agreed on his view of the matter. The German Federal Republic could not and would not submit to extortion by the Arab states. It was believed in the Federal Chancellor's office that the time up to the ratification of the German-Israeli agreement would suffice to obtain understanding for the German attitude on the part of the Arab states.

The signing of the reparation agreement at Luxembourg

The moment for the signature of the German-Israeli reparation agreement had been set in all secrecy for 8 a.m., 10 September 1952. Israeli quarters feared outrages by extreme rightists of their own nation. Only a few journalists were present on the historic occasion; there were no film cameras; only a few photographers were present. When a photographer's flash bulb exploded with a loud bang, people thought an assassination was in progress. The atmosphere was extremely tense.

Kontad Adenauer had been anxious to have the treaty signed on 10 September. That very day, only a few hours later, the groups of the newly founded European Coal and Steel Community met for the first time. Adenauer did not want Germany to enter the community of free European peoples without offering clear evidence of reconciliation and of assistance for the victims of Hitler's Jewish policy.

The Israeli Foreign Minister, Moshe Sharett, had come to Luxembourg to sign the treaty. Felix E. Shinnar, who together with the subsequent Minister Josephthal had borne the chief burden of negotiations on the Israeli side, said of this occasion:

"I remember very well how we met at 8 o'clock in the morning of 10 September in the Maison de Ville, the city hall of Luxembourg City; the Israeli delegation, to meet shortly after 8 with the German delegation led by Chancellor Dr. Adenauer. The signature of the treaty followed, an act that all the participants will always remember. A treaty was signed that I believe will belong, in historic perspective, to the most memorable in human history. Although it was the settlement of a matter of material damages, the subject of discussion, so to speak the caption over the meeting, was the renewed encounter of the German and the Israeli people after the days of injustice and violence under Hitler."

Moshe Sharett, who had sat opposite the German Chancellor at the signing of the agreement in Luxembourg, putting his signature under the treaty on behalf of his people, later said to the editor in Paris:

"The signing of the reparation treaty between Israel and Germany, which gave me my first opportunity to meet Chancellor Adenauer personally, has remained an unforgettable event to me. It was a political fact of enormous international significance, something quite unprecedented, which has taken a most momentous place in the history of Israel and of Germany. This was a historic act that brought honour to free post-war Germany, and became for Israel a force of most important constructive aid. The moral credit that the Federal Republic thus earned is owed primarily to Dr. Adenauer, who had suggested this agreement on the German side and brought it to a conclusion. I should also like to mention the share of the Social Democratic Party, and I personally do this with great satisfaction. Its vigorous support played a decisive part in the final ratification of the treaty."

How the two great problems, the rapprochement of the two peoples and material reparations, complemented each other is plain from the text of the treaty between the German Federal Republic and Israel.

Agreement

between

the Federal Republic of Germany

and the

State of Israel

Whereas

unspeakable criminal acts were perpetrated against the Jewish people during the National-Socialist régime of terror

and whereas

by a declaration in the Bundestag on 27th September, 1951, the Government of the Federal Republic of Germany made known their determination, within the limits of their capacity, to make good the material damage caused by these acts

and whereas

the State of Israel has assumed the heavy burden of resettling so great a number of uprooted and destitute Jewish refugees from Germany and from territories formerly under German rule and has on this basis advanced a claim against the Federal Republic of Germany for global recompense for the cost of the integration of these refugees

now therefore

the Federal Republic of Germany and the State of Israel have agreed as follows: —

Article 1

(a) The Federal Republic of Germany shall, in view of the considerations hereinbefore recited, pay to the State of Israel the sum of 3,000 million Deutsche Mark.

(b) In addition, the Federal Republic of Germany shall, in compliance with the obligation undertaken in Article 1 of Protocol No. 2 this day drawn up and signed between the Government of the Federal Republic of Germany and the *Conference on Jewish Material Claims against Germany*, pay to Israel for the benefit of the said *Conference* the sum of 450 million Deutsche Mark; the said sum of 450 million Deutsche Mark shall be used for the purposes set out in Article 2 of the said Protocol.

(c) The provisions hereinafter contained in the present Agreement shall apply to the total sum of 3,450 million Deutsche Mark so arising, subject, however, to the provisions of Article 3, paragraph (c), and of Article 15.

Article 2

The Federal Republic of Germany will make available the amount referred to in Article 1, paragraph (c) of the present Agreement for the purchase, in pursuance of Articles 6, 7 and 8, of such commodities and services as shall serve the purpose of expanding opportunities for the settlement and rehabilitation of Jewish refugees in Israel. The Government of the Federal Republic of Germany shall, in order to facilitate the purchase of such commodities and the provision of such services, take the measures and accord the facilities as set out in Articles 5, 6 and 8.

Article 3

(a) The obligation undertaken in Article 1 of the present Agreement shall, without prejudice to the provisions of Article 4, be discharged by the payment of annual instalments, as follows: —

(i) As from the coming into force of the present Agreement until 31st March, 1954, an amount of 200 million Deutsche Mark for each financial year. The first financial year shall be deemed to be the period commencing on the date of the coming into force of the present Agreement and ending on 31st March, 1953; thereafter, each financial year shall be the period commencing on the first day of April of one year and ending on the thirty-first day of March of the following year;

(ii) As from 1st April 1954, nine annual instalments of 310 million Deutsche Mark each and a tenth annual instalment of 260 million Deutsche Mark, subject to the provisions of subparagraph (iii) hereof;

(iii) Should the Government of the Federal Republic of Germany be of opinion that they cannot comply with the terms of sub-paragraph (ii) hereof, they shall, three months before the beginning of the third financial year, give notice in writing to the Israel Mission referred to in Article 12, of a reduction of the annual instalments payable under subparagraph (ii) hereof, provided, however, that the said annual instalments shall in no circumstances be allowed to fall below the sum of 250 million Deutsche Mark.

(b) The annual instalments hereinbefore referred to shall become due in equal amounts on the fifteenth day of April and on the fifteenth day of August of each year.

The first annual instalment shall be paid as follows: —

60 million Deutsche Mark on the day of the coming into force of the present Agreement, and 140 million Deutsche Mark three months thereafter, or on 31st March, 1953, whichever date may be the earlier.

(c) Any annual instalments paid in pursuance of the provisions of this Article shall, when paid, diminish the obligation undertaken by the Federal Republic of Germany in Article 1, paragraph (b) in the proportion which that obligation bears to the total sum payable, and referred to in Article 1, paragraph (c).

The Government of Israel shall, when such annual instalments have been received, pay to the *Conference on Jewish Material Claims against Germany*, or to its successor or successors, an amount in the proportion hereinbefore referred to, within one year from the receipt of such instalments.

(d) The annual instalments shall, in accordance with Article 9, be paid into the Account of the Israel Mission with the *Bank deutscher Länder* or with any central bank of issue which may take its place.

Article 4

(a) The Federal Republic of Germany will endeavour, by increasing the annual instalments, to pay the sum payable in pursuance of Article 1 of the present Agreement, within a period of time shorter than that which would result from all or any of the provisions of Article 3, paragraph (a).

(b) In the event of the Government of the Federal Republic of Germany obtaining an external loan or any other financial relief from external sources in a currency generally and freely convertible and destined exclusively for the purpose of financing the obligation undertaken in Article 1, the entire proceeds of such loan or relief shall be used for such purpose, and shall be applied to the last annual instalments payable under the present Agreement.

(c) In the event of the Government of the Federal Republic of Germany obtaining an external loan or other financial relief from external sources in a currency generally and freely convertible and not destined for a specific purpose unconnected with the present Agreement, the Government of the Federal Republic of Germany shall, if and inasfar as they consider themselves capable of so doing, apply an appropriate portion of such loan or relief to financing the obligation undertaken in Article 1; in that event such portion shall be applied to the last two annual instalments, or to any part thereof, unless the amounts due in respect of such instalments shall have been previously redeemed.

(d) The proceeds referred to in paragraphs (b) and (c) hereof shall be made available to Israel in the currency in which, and at the time when, such loan or relief is obtained.

(e) Any redemption, whether premature or not, may be effected by the Government of the Federal Republic of Germany at any time in any currency generally and freely convertible, or in Deutsche Mark if and when the Deutsche Mark becomes generally and freely convertible, or in any other currency agreed upon.

(f) Whenever premature redemption of the whole or part of the sum still payable is offered in Deutsche Mark at a time when the Deutsche Mark is not generally and freely convertible, such redemption shall be accepted by Israel, provided that the proceeds thereof can be used for the purchase of commodities and services falling within the Schedule referred to in Article 6, paragraph (a), which may then be applicable, subject, however, to the provisions of Article 6, paragraph (e); the proceeds of such redemption shall be applied to the last annual instalment or instalments then payable.

(g) In the event of the obligation of the Federal Republic of Germany being prematurely redeemed, the Mixed Commission referred to in Article 13 shall decide whether, and if so, to what extent, having regard to all the relevant circumstances, a cash discount shall be granted to the Federal Republic of Germany in consideration of such premature redemption.

Article 5

(a) The delivery of commodities falling within the Groups comprised in the Schedule, shall in every respect be subject to the general conditions applicable at the time to the export from the Federal Republic of Germany of commodities of the same kind. There shall be no discrimination as compared with exports to any third country, in particular, also, insofar as prices are concerned which are now or may in future be subject to the effects of governmental action.

(b) Deliveries of commodities to Israel shall, in regard to taxation, be subject to the following treatment: —

(i) Commodities delivered by suppliers in the Federal Republic of Germany under a contract of delivery with the Israel Mission shall, upon proof that they have been consigned to Israel in compliance with the terms of such contract of delivery, be deemed to be export deliveries *(Ausfuhrlieferungen)* within the meaning of that term in the *Umsatzsteuergesetz in der Fassung vom 1. September 1951* (BGBl. I 791) and in the *Durchführungsbestimmungen zum Umsatzsteuergesetz in der Fassung vom 1. September 1951* (BGBl. I 796). The provisions of sections 23, 25 and 26 of the said *Durchführungsbestimmungen* shall be applied accordingly;

(ii) Deliveries of commodities effected on or after 1st April, 1953, shall be accorded the export traders' refund and the export refund *(Ausfuhrhändlervergütung und Ausfuhr-*

vergütung), and the provisions of sections 70—80 of the *Durchführungsbestimmungen zum Umsatzsteuergesetz in der Fassung vom 1. September 1951* shall be applied accordingly;

(iii) The provisions of the *Gesetz über steuerliche Maßnahmen zur Förderung der Ausfuhr vom 28. Juni 1951* (BGBl. I 405) relating to taxation on income and profits and the implementary provisions enacted or to be enacted thereunder shall not apply to deliveries of commodities under the terms of the present Agreement;

(iv) If any of the tax provisions referred to in sub-paragraphs (i) and (ii) hereof are amended, or repealed and replaced by tax provisions of a similar nature, such tax provisions shall, insofar as they are of general application, apply to deliveries of commodities to Israel.

(c) The Government of the Federal Republic of Germany shall take all necessary administrative measures for the carrying into effect of deliveries of commodities to Israel, in particular insofar as the same may be required in connection with any internal economic measures, such as allocation of export quotas and the like, which now apply or which may in future apply to commodities of a kind to be delivered to Israel.

(d) Any internal restrictions imposed on the export of commodities from the Federal Republic of Germany shall apply to commodities to be exported to Israel only insofar as they are oguneral application to countries or groups of countries maintaining foreign trade relatios ʝwith the Federal Republic of Germany.

(e) The coumodities exported to Israel under the terms of the present Agreement shall not be re-exported to any third country, unless otherwise agreed by the Mixed Commission. This prohibition shall not apply to commodities which have undergone their final, substantial and economically justified transformation in Israel.

(f) In the event of such commodities being re-exported in a manner contrary to the provisions contained in paragraph (e) hereof, the Arbitral Commission referred to in Article 14 of the present Agreement, on finding that such export has taken place, shall be entitled to impose on Israel a penalty equivalent in amount to the value of such commodities at the time when the same were re-exported as aforesaid. The said penalty, if found to be due, shall be deducted from the annual instalment next payable.

Article 6

(a) The commodities and services to be purchased by the Israel Mission shall be comprised in Schedules.

(b) In laying down such Schedules account shall be taken especially of capital goods.

(c) Commodities delivered under the terms of the present Agreement may also be of non-German origin.

(d) The commodities and services included in the Schedule for the first two financial years shall be comprised in the following Groups: —

    Group I   — Ferrous and non-ferrous metals;
    Group II   — Products of the steel-manufacturing industry;
    Group III — Products of the chemical industry and of other industries;
    Group IV — Agricultural products;
    Group V   — Services.

(e) The amounts by which the annual instalments under the present Agreement may increase shall be apportioned as follows among the Groups mentioned in paragraph (d) hereof: —

13% of the increase to go to Group I;
30% of the increase to go to Group II;
45% of the increase to go to Groups III and IV;
12% of the increase to go to Group V.

(f) The Schedules shall, as from 1st April, 1954, be laid down by the Mixed Commission on the basis of lists to be submitted by the Israel Mission for an agreed period of not less than one year, in accordance with the following provisions: —

(i) The Israel Mission will submit to the Mixed Commission its list for deliveries not later than six months before the expiration of the Schedule then current;
(ii) The Mixed Commission shall meet not later than three months after receipt of the list referred to in sub-paragraph (i) hereof, in order to lay down, in accordance with the terms of this Article, the Schedule then following.

(g) Each Schedule laid down for a period subsequent to 31st March, 1954, shall, in principle, be based in its composition on the Schedule immediately preceding it. The Mixed Commission shall, however, be entitled to introduce modifications in such Schedule when laying down the same in accordance with the terms of paragraph (f) hereof. In considering modifications in the composition of each such Schedule the Mixed Commission shall take into account, in an appropriate manner, the requirements of Israel and the possibilities of the economy of the Federal Republic of Germany to carry into effect deliveries of commodities.

(h) In the event of the Mixed Commission failing to reach agreement on modifications, each such Schedule shall, subject to the provisions of paragraph (e) hereof, be based in its composition on the Schedule immediately preceding it, provided, however, that the foregoing shall not apply to modifications which have been agreed expressly as applying to a fixed period of time.

Article 7

(a) Purchases of commodities and services under the terms of the present Agreement shall be carried out solely and exclusively by the Israel Mission.

(b) Contracts for the delivery of commodities or the provision of services, in accordance with the Schedule in force for the time being, shall be concluded between the Israel Mission of the one part and German suppliers of the other part.

The procedure for the purchase of commodities of non-German origin shall be regulated by the Mixed Commission.

(c) The legal relations of the Israel Mission arising in connection with the delivery of commodities and the provision of services which fall within the ambit of private law shall be subject to German law.

(d) The procedure relating to the examination of orders placed by the Israel Mission with German suppliers is set out in the Annex to the present Article.

Article 8

(a) The amounts to be set aside for the provision of services under any Schedule in force for the time being shall be used for the payment by the Israel Mission of insurance and transport charges, of administrative expenses, including wages, salaries, rent and the like, and of any other expenses incurred by the Israel Mission in connection with the implementation of the present Agreement. In the event of any such amounts having remained unspent at the expiration of any of the periods referred to in Article 6, paragraphs (e) and (f), such amounts shall be used for the purchase of commodities during the period then commencing; they shall be apportioned among the Groups of commodities contained in the Schedule then coming into operation, and in the proportion therein laid down.

(b) The Israel Mission will, in principle, cover with German insurance companies, risks concerning commodities under the present Agreement. Contracts of insurance shall be expressed and insurance premiums paid in Deutsche Mark. Claims arising under such contracts shall be satisfied in Deutsche Mark and the proceeds used for the purpose of providing replacements. Such replacements shall be subject in every respect to the provisions of the present Agreement.

(c) If the Government of Israel employ German shipping lines for the transport of commodities, the freight required shall be paid in Deutsche Mark and shall be charged against the amount set aside for services under the present Agreement. Sea-freight payable in any currency other than Deutsche Mark shall be paid by the Government of Israel out of funds other than funds obtained under the present Agreement.

(d) Where transport by way of a German sea-port involves expenditure or arrangements which, having regard to all the circumstances, are economically unreasonable, the Israel Mission shall be entitled to use sea-ports outside the Federal Republic of Germany; the question whether such expenditure or arrangements are economically unreasonable shall be determined by reference, principally, to the normal method of transport which would be used in cases of a similar nature.

The Government of Israel shall not be entitled to use funds obtained under the present Agreement for the purpose of defraying charges for transport operations or for other services beyond the German frontier.

Article 9

(a) The Israel Mission shall, upon the coming into force of the present Agreement, apply to the *Bank deutscher Länder*, or to any central bank of issue which may take its place, for an Account in Deutsche Mark to be opened in its name. Without prejudice to the right of the Government of the Federal Republic of Germany to pay, upon their falling due, the annual instalments payable under the terms of Article 3, paragraph (b), into the Account of the Israel Mission, the Government of the Federal Republic of Germany shall, upon the request of the Israel Mission, pay into the said Account such annual instalments as have fallen due, in the amounts indicated in each case by the Israel Mission, in order to meet its financial requirements as they arise.

(b) Any balances, the transfer of which to the above Account has not been requested by the Israel Mission by the end of any one financial year shall be brought forward to the credit of the Israel Mission with the Government of the Federal Republic of Germany for the following financial year.

(c) The provisions relating to the implementation of the present Article are contained in the Annex thereto.

Article 10

(a) If, during the currency of the present Agreement, the economic or the financial capacity of the Federal Republic of Germany shall be adversely affected in a fundamental and lasting manner, the Contracting Parties shall consult with a view to adjusting to the changed circumstances resulting therefrom the further discharge by the Federal Republic of Germany of the obligations under the present Agreement.

(b) Such adjustment shall not cause the total sum payable by the Federal Republic of

Germany in pursuance of Article 1 of the present Agreement to be reduced, but shall merely result in a temporary suspension or a temporary reduction of the annual instalments payable in pursuance of Article 3.

(c) If, in the event of the financial capacity of the Federal Republic of Germany being adversely affected in a fundamental and lasting manner, negotiations fail to lead to an agreement, and if thereupon application is made to the Arbitral Commission, the Government of the Federal Republic of Germany shall be entitled, pending an award of the Arbitral Commission, to reduce the amount of the annual instalment next due, provided that they give such notice as is appropriate in the circumstances, of their intention so to redue such instalment.

Article 11

If, during the currency of the present Agreement, circumstances change in such a manner as to result in an essential reduction of the substance of the obligation undertaken by the Federal Republic of Germany under the present Agreement, the Contracting Parties shall consult with a view to adjusting to such changed circumstances the annual instalments still payable.

Article 12

(a) The Government of Israel will send to the Federal Republic of Germany as their sole and exclusive agent a Mission which shall be charged on their behalf with the implementation of the present Agreement. The name of the Mission shall be "Israel Mission", or such other name as may be agreed upon between the Contracting Parties.

b) The Israel Mission shall be entitled to engage in all activities which may be required in the Federal Republic of Germany in connection with the expeditious and effective implementation of the present Agreement, and shall, in particular, be entitled: —
(i) To place orders and to conclude and execute contracts for the delivery of commodities and the provision of services under the terms of the present Agreement and to incur expenditure therefore;
(ii) To consult with governmental or non-governmental bodies or organizations on any question relating to the implementation of the present Agreement;
(iii) To deal with all other matters incidental to the activities hereinbefore referred to.

(c) The Israel Mission shall be deemed to be a juristic person within the meaning of German Law. The Israel Mission shall not be required to be registered in the *Handelsregister*. The names of the persons authorized to represent the Israel Mission shall be published by the Israel Mission in the *Bundesanzeiger* from time to time and shall, in addition, be given notoriety by other means. In relation to third parties such persons shall be deemed to be entitled to represent the Israel Mission as long as the withdrawal of their authority has not been published in the *Bundesanzeiger*.

The Israel Mission shall be subject to the jurisdiction of the German courts in regard to legal relations arising out of and in connection with its commercial activities. The Israel Mission shall be exempt from the obligation to give security for the costs of legal proceedings. The Account of the Israel Mission with the *Bank deutscher Länder*, or with any central bank of issue which may take its place, and its accounts with banking institutions authorized to engage in foreign trade transactions shall be liable for all obligations arising out of or in connection with such activities, and in particular, to attachment and execution.

(d) The Head of the Israel Mission requires the consent of the Government of the Federal Republic of Germany for the admission to the performance of his activities. Such consent may be withdrawn by the Government of the Federal Republic of Germany. The names of all personnel of the Israel Mission, with special indication of its senior officials, shall be communicated by the Head of the Israel Mission to the Government of the Federal Republic of Germany.

(e) The Israel Mission shall be entitled to establish offices in the Federal Republic of Germany as may appear necessary for the effective performance of its activities, provided, however, that the places where such offices shall be located shall be agreed between the Israel Mission and the appropriate authorities of the Government of the Federal Republic of Germany.

(f) The Israel Mission, its personnel of Israel nationality and its premises shall be entitled to the following rights, privileges, immunities and courtesies: —

- (i) Such administrative assistance as is usually accorded to foreign missions in the Federal Republic of Germany and as is required for the effective performance of the activities of the Israel Mission and of its personnel of Israel nationality;
- (ii) Exemption of the income of the Israel Mission derived from the performance of all or any of the activities referred to in paragraph (b) hereof, and of the property of the Israel Mission serving such activities from all taxes imposed in the Federal Republic of Germany on income, profit or capital *(Steuern vom Einkommen und Ertrag und Vermögensteuer);*
- (iii) Exemption of real estate owned by the Israel Mission in the Federal Republic of Germany and used directly for the performance of the activities of the Israel Mission or for the accommodation of its members of Israel nationality from real estate tax;
- (iv) Exemption of the salaries and emoluments of the Head of the Israel Mission and of its permanent officials of Israel nationality derived from the performance of their activities as members of the Israel Mission from all taxation imposed in the Federal Republic of Germany on income;
- (v) Exemption of all articles destined for the official purposes of the Israel Mission and the personal use of the Head and of the senior officials of the said Mission of Israel nationality from customs duties, irrespective of whether such articles have been imported on first arrival of such officials in the Federal Republic of Germany or at any time thereafter during their term of office, provided, however, that no articles the importation of which into the territory of the Federal Republic of Germany is prohibited under the laws or regulations in force at the time of importation shall be brought into that territory; exemption of all articles imported into the territory of the Federal Republic of Germany by virtue of this sub-paragraph from all economic restrictions on their importation into or their exportation from the said territory.

    The granting of the privileges herein referred to may be made contingent upon an assurance in writing by the Head or by a senior official of the Israel Mission authorized by him for this purpose that the consignments concerned, which the said Head or official shall identify by quantity, kind, markings, numbers and contents, are destined solely for one of the purposes herein referred to;
- (vi) Exemption of the Head and of the senior officials of the Israel Mission of Israel nationality from German civil and criminal jurisdiction in all that pertains to any acts carried out by them within the framework of their official functions, subject, however, to the provisions of paragraph (c) hereof; exemption of the said Head

and of the said senior officials of the Israel Mission from arrest, except for such infringements of the laws of the Federal Republic of Germany as are therein defined as *Verbrechen;*

(vii) Exemption of the office premises of the Israel Mission from any acts of the authorities of the Federal Republic of Germany, and in particular exemption of the archives from inspection, impounding or seizure, subject, however, to the right of the said authorities to serve process;

(viii) Exemption of the Head and of the members of the Israel Mission from any obligation to produce in court or elsewhere documents from the archives of the Israel Mission, or to testify to their contents, unless such documents relate to the commercial activities of the Israel Mission;

(ix) The right of the Israel Mission to use cipher and to receive and despatch diplomatic couriers.

Article 13

(a) The Contracting Parties shall set up a Mixed Commission composed of representatives of the Government of the Federal Republic of Germany and of the Government of Israel, respectively.

(b) The Mixed Commission shall meet at the request of the representatives of either Party.

(c) The Mixed Commission shall have the following functions: —

(i) To deal with all questions arising between the Contracting Parties out of or in connection with the implementation of the present Agreement, to review the progress of such implementation, to examine any difficulties that may arise, and to take decisions in order to resolve such difficulties;

(ii) To lay down Schedules in accordance with the provisions of Article 6.

Article 14

(a) All disputes between the Contracting Parties arising out of the interpretation or application of the present Agreement not settled by negotiation shall be submitted, at the request of either Party, to an Arbitral Commission, constituted in accordance with the provisions here following: —

(i) Each Contracting Party shall notify the other Party of the appointment of an arbitrator within a period of two months from the coming into force of the present Agreement;

(ii) The Contracting Party shall, within a period of two months subsequent to the appointment of the two arbitrators, by agreement, appoint the umpire of the Arbitral Commission;

(iii) If, within the periods respectively referred to in sub-paragraphs (i) and (ii), either Contracting Party fails to appoint an arbitrator, or if the Contracting Parties fail to agree upon the appointment of an umpire, such arbitrator or umpire, as the case may be, shall be appointed, upon the request of one or other of the Contracting Parties, by the President of the International Court of Justice;

(iv) The umpire shall not be a national of either of the Contracting Parties, or ordinarily resident within their respective territories, or in the service of either of them.

(b) The members of the Arbitral Commission shall be appointed for a period of five years. The Arbitral Commission shall be reconstituted in accordance with the provisions of paragraph (a) hereof, three months before the expiration of the said period of five years. The members of the Arbitral Commission are re-eligible.

(c) A member whose term of office has expired shall continue to discharge his duties until his successor is appointed. After such appointment he shall, unless the umpire directs otherwise, continue to discharge his duties respecting pending cases in which he has participated, until such cases have been finally decided.

(d) If an arbitrator, or the umpire, during his term of office, dies or retires, the vacancy shall be filled in accordance with the provisions of paragraph (a) hereof.

(e) The Arbitral Commission shall meet at a place to be designated by the umpire.

(f) The Arbitral Commission shall lay down its own rules of procedure; in particular, it shall have power to request the attendance of witnesses and experts and the submission of advisory expert opinions in writing.

If the Contracting Parties agree, the Arbitral Commission may dispense with oral proceedings.

(g) The Contracting Parties shall cause their courts of law to execute letters of request for the examination of witnesses and the service of documents issued by the Arbitral Commission in connection with any case pending before it.

(h) The Arbitral Commission, and in case of urgency and subject to confirmation by the Arbitral Commission, the umpire, shall have power to issue orders for provisional measures to preserve the rights of either Party. Such orders, when issued by the umpire, shall lapse after one month, unless confirmed by the Arbitral Commission.

The Contracting Parties shall comply with such orders.

(i) Each Party shall bear its own costs, including the costs of the arbitrator appointed by it. All costs of the Arbitral Commission shall be apportioned equally between the Contracting Parties. The fees of the umpire for each case and the apportionment thereof between the Parties shall be fixed by the Arbitral Commission.

(k) The awards of the Arbitral Commission shall not be subject to appeal and shall be binding upon the Parties.

The Arbitral Commission may set a time limit for the execution of its awards.

(l) Unless the Contracting Parties agree upon another solution, any dispute which may arise between them as to the interpretation or execution of any award of the Arbitral Commission may, at the request of either Party, be submitted to the Arbitral Commission.

If, for any reason, the Arbitral Commission does not accept the submission within a period of one month, and if the Parties have not agreed upon another solution, the dispute shall be referred to an ad hoc Arbitral Commission constituted in accordance with the provisions of paragraph (a) hereof.

(m) The Arbitral Commission shall not be competent to deal with disputes between the Contracting Parties arising out of the legal relations referred to in Article 12, paragraph (c) until all local remedies have been exhausted.

Article 15

(a) The Arbitral Commission referred to in Article 14 of the present Agreement shall be competent to deal also with disputes arising out of the interpretation or application of Protocol No. 2 this day drawn up and signed between the Government of the Federal Republic of Germany and the *Conference on Jewish Material Claims against Germany*, in the cases here following and subject to the provisions hereinafter set out: —

(i) If the Government of the Federal Republic of Germany are of opinion that the said *Conference* has failed to comply with the terms of Article 2 of the said Protocol, they shall be entitled to invoke the Arbitral Commission within a period of one year from the date fixed for the making of the communication referred to in the said Article.

If the Arbitral Commission finds that the said *Conference* has used any sum for purposes other than those referred to in the said Protocol, or has without adequate reason failed to use such sum or has failed to make the communication provided for in Article 2 thereof, the Federal Republic of Germany shall be entitled to withhold an amount equal in value to the sum the use of which has been in dispute. Such amount may be withheld from the annual instalments next due, to the extent that such annual instalments are in excess of 250 million Deutsche Mark. In the event of an annual instalment not exceeding the amount of 250 million Deutsche Mark, the sum to be withheld may be deducted from the last annual instalment payable under the present Agreement;

(ii) Application may be made to the Arbitral Commission requesting it to find that subsequent to its award under the terms of sub-paragraph (i) hereof the said *Conference* has used for the purposes referred to in Article 2 of the said Protocol moneys derived from independent sources, or has subsequently spent an unused sum for such purposes, or has subsequently made the communication referred to in the said Protocol. In the event of the Arbitral Commission finding in favour of such application, the Government of the Federal Republic of Germany shall have lost its right to withhold or deduct such sum under the terms of the award previously made, and shall pay any sum that may have been withheld previously;

(iii) In the event of any doubt arising as to the continued existence of the *Conference on Jewish Material Claims against Germany* or as to its successor, the Government of the Federal Republic of Germany shall be entitled to request an award of the Arbitral Commission to resolve such doubt;

(iv) The Government of the Federal Republic of Germany shall be entitled, within three months after receipt of the notification referred to in Article 3 of the said Protocol, to request a finding of the Arbitral Commission as to whether the assignment or intended assignment of the rights and obligations of the said *Conference* to a successor may be regarded as fulfilling the purposes referred to in Article 2 of the said Protocol.

(b) The *Conference on Jewish Material Claims against Germany* shall be entitled to intervene in any proceeding instituted under the terms of this Article.

Article 16

(a) The following Annexes and Letters shall form an integral part of the present Agreement: —

(i) Schedule;

Annex to Article 7;

Annex to Article 9;

(ii) Letter No. 1a: Letter from the Minister for Foreign Affairs, State of Israel, on the settlement of the Israel claim and the rights of Israel nationals under legislation in the Federal Republic of Germany on restitution, compensation or other redress for National-Socialist wrongs;

Letter No. 1b: Reply of the Chancellor and Minister for Foreign Affairs of the Federal Republic of Germany to Letter No. 1a;

Letter No. 2a: Letter from the Head of the German Delegation concerning Article 5;

Letter No. 2b: Reply of the Joint Heads of the Israel Delegation to Letter No. 2a;

Letter No. 3a: Letter from the Chancellor and Minister for Foreign Affairs of the Federal Republic of Germany concerning Article 6;

Letter No. 3b: Reply of the Minister for Foreign Affairs, State of Israel, to Letter No. 3a;

Letter No. 4a: Letter from the Minister for Foreign Affairs, State of Israel, concerning Article 6;

Letter No. 4b: Reply of the Chancellor and Minister for Foreign Affairs of the Federal Republic of Germany to Letter No. 4a;

Letter No. 5a: Letter from the Joint Heads of the Israel Delegation concerning Article 7;

Letter No. 5b: Reply of the Head of the German Delegation to Letter No. 5a;

Letter No. 6a: Letter from the Joint Heads of the Israel Delegation concerning Article 8;

Letter No. 6b: Reply of the Head of the German Delegation to Letter No. 6a;

Letter No. 7a: Letter from the Head of the German Delegation concerning Article 8;

Letter No. 7b: Reply of the Joint Heads of the Israel Delegation to Letter No. 7a;

Letter No. 8a: Letter from the Minister for Foreign Affairs, State of Israel, concerning Article 12;

Letter No. 8b: Reply of the Chancellor and Minister for Foreign Affairs of the Federal Republic of Germany to Letter No. 8a;

Letter No. 9a: Letter from the Joint Heads of the Israel Delegation concerning Article 12;

Letter No. 9b: Reply of the Head of the German Delegation to Letter No. 9a.

(b) Copies of Protocol No. 1 and of Protocol No. 2 this day drawn up and signed between the Government of the Federal Republic of Germany and the *Conference on Jewish Material Claims against Germany* are appended for reference only.

Article 17

(a) The present Agreement shall be ratified with the least possible delay in accordance with the constitutional procedures of the Contracting Parties.

(b) The instruments of ratification shall be exchanged as soon as possible by accredited representatives of the Contracting Parties, at the Secretariat of the United Nations in New York.

A procès-verbal shall be drawn up by the Secretary-General of the United Nations, who is hereby requested to furnish each Contracting Party with certified copies thereof.

(c) The present Agreement shall come into force upon the exchange of the instruments of ratification.

In faith whereof the undersigned representatives duly authorized thereto have signed the present Agreement.

Done at Luxembourg this tenth day of September, 1952, in two originals in the English language, one copy of which shall be furnished to each one of the Governments of the Contracting Parties.

For the Federal Republic of Germany
s/ Adenauer

For the State of Israel
s/ M. Sharett

Luxembourg, 10th September, 1952

Attached to the agreement were several letters, interpreting many details. The most important politically was a letter from the Israeli Foreign Minister Sharett, confirmed by an almost identical letter from the Federal Chancellor. The letter of the Israeli Foreign Minister read as follows:

His Excellency,
The Chancellor and Minister for
Foreign Affairs of the Federal
Republic of Germany

Mr. Chancellor,

I have the honour to convey to Your Excellency the following on behalf of the Government of Israel: —

1. Considering that the Federal Republic of Germany has in the Agreement signed today undertaken the obligation to pay recompense for the expenditure already incurred or to be incurred by the State of Israel in the resettlement of Jewish refugees, the claim of the State of Israel for such recompense shall, insofar as it has been put forward against the Federal Republic of Germany, be regarded by the Government of Israel as having been settled with the coming into force of the said Agreement. The State of Israel will advance no further claims against the Federal Republic of Germany arising out of or in connection with losses which have resulted from National-Socialist persecution.

2. The Government of Israel are here proceeding on the assumption that claims of Israel nationals under legislation in force in the Federal Republic of Germany on internal restitution, compensation, or other redress for National-Socialist wrongs, and the automatic accrual of rights to Israel nationals from any future legislation of this nature, will not be prejudiced by reason of the conclusion of the Agreement, provided, however, that the provisions of No. 14 of Protocol No. 1 this day drawn up and signed between the Government of the Federal Republic of Germany and the *Conference on Jewish Material Claims against Germany*, shall apply to Israel nationals only insofar as the said provisions concern the payment of compensation for deprivation of liberty and the payment of annuities to survivors of persecutees.

I shall be obliged if you will confirm receipt of this letter, and if you will also confirm that the assumption of the Government of Israel referred to in paragraph 2 hereof is correct.

I avail myself of this opportunity to express to Your Excellency the assurance of my highest consideration.

(signed) M. Sharett

Ratification by the Diet

On 4 March 1953, Chancellor Konrad Adenauer personally presented the reparation treaty signed on 10 September 1952 at Luxembourg to the German Diet for the first reading. On this occasion the Chancellor once more made an inclusive statement before the Parliament, describing the background and substance of the treaty. The statement was as follows:

"The treaty with the State of Israel that the Diet is treating today has been a matter of great concern to the German and the world public ever since the start of the Hague negotiations and more particularly since it was signed in Luxembourg on 10 September 1952 by me and the Israeli Foreign Minister, Mr. Sharett. And very rightly; for with this treaty, together with the restitution law that is shortly to be presented to the diet, the Federal government now confirm by action the solemnly promised termination of what is for every German the saddest chapter of our history. Such an action is a necessity if only for moral reasons. Certainly not all Germans by far were National Socialists, and there were also some National Socialists who did not approve of the atrocities committed. Nevertheless this act of restitution by the German people is necessary. The outrages began, after all, with the misuse of the name of the German people.

"So far as our strength can accomplish anything to eliminate the results—I am thinking of the material damage done by National Socialism to those it persecuted—, the German people has a grave and sacred duty to help, even though sacrifices be demanded, perhaps heavy sacrifices from those of us who do not feel personally guilty. Ever since it was established, the Federal government has always recognised this duty. By fulfilling it we want to make good the damage, so far as possible, so far as it is within our power. The name of our fatherland must regain the esteem appropriate to the historic accomplishment of the German people in culture and economic matters. The treaty now before you, covering reparations to the Jews, represents a section of the field of reparations, though perhaps the most important. The Jews, not only in Germany but wherever the arm of National Socialism reached—for a long time during the war this was the greater part of Europe—had to undergo the cruelest of persecutions. The extent of this persecution, the sacrifice of human and material values that it brought, not only justifies but demands a special treatment of the reparation to the Jewish persecutees. In the name of the Federal government I made a statement on 27 September 1951 before this House on the subject of Jewish reparations, of which I would like to repeat a few sentences here:

"'But unspeakable crimes have been committed in the name of the German people, calling for moral and material indemnity, both with regard to the individual harm done to Jews and to the Jewish property for which no legitimate individual claimants still exist. In this field the first steps have been taken. Much still remains to be done. The Federal government will see to it that reparation legislation is soon enacted and justly put into execution; further restitution will follow ... With regard to the extent of the reparations—a momentous problem in view of the enormous destruction of Jewish values by National Socialism—the limits imposed on German ability to pay through the bitter necessity of caring for the innumerable war victims and the support of refugees and expellees must be considered. The Federal Government are prepared, jointly with representatives of Jewry and the State of Israel, which has admitted so many homeless Jewish fugitives, to bring about a solution of the material indemnity problem, thus easing the way to the spiritual settlement of infinite suffering.'

"This House then voted unanimous approval of the statement. With this the Federal Government received from you, ladies and gentlemen, a mandate to enter into negotiations with the State of Israel and the Jewish world organisations, whose result is the treaty before you.

"Let me take up briefly its basis and its most important provisions. The payments of the Federal Republic to the State of Israel are not reparations. The German Reich committed no acts of war against this state (which, as we know, came into being only in 1948) that would have obligated the Federal Republic to reparations. The payments promised in the treaty are intended rather to compensate the State of Israel, within the limits of our capability, for the burdens imposed on it by the integration of hundreds of thousands of Jewish fugitives from Germany and the territories formerly under German rule and for burdens yet to come. These burdens are a direct or indirect consequence of the measures of extermination carried out against Jewry by the National Socialist regime of violence. The persecution of the Jews began in Germany with the National Socialists' seizure of power in 1933. It increased steadily, and during hostilities, without becoming an act of war as defined in international law, it reached that ghastly level whose full extent became known to us all only afterward.

"While the persecutions until 1939 could be directed only at Jews with German citizenship, during the war it also affected—something sometimes forgotten here—almost all the Jews of foreign citizenship who came within reach of Hitler's power. For the survivors the results meant an uprooting that was not finished with the end of the war. On the contrary, this uprooting then forced the Jews from Eastern European regions in particular to emigrate. Hundreds of thousands of them have, as I said, been received in Israel. Accordingly the agreement with Israel takes its places in the great field of reparation of National Socialist injustice. In one important point it supplements the legal measures already enacted or projected on behalf of those who were persecuted by the National Socialist regime of violence because of their political convictions or reasons of race, faith, or world-view.

"As you know, in this field of individual indemnity there are already a large number of laws and decrees; to mention only the most important: Even before the establishment of the Federal Republic the three Western occupying powers, each in its own zone, regulated the restitution of ascertainable property. This field of individual restitution is the core of all reparation for National Socialist injustice. The payments for individual restitution, benefitting not only Jews but all those persecuted by National Socialism, will —something often overlooked—considerably exceed in value the blanket payments to Israel and the Jewish organisations.

"The extension of legislation on individual restitution was very thoroughly discussed in the Hague with the Jewish world organisations forming the Claims Conference. The result of these negotiations is recorded in Protocol No. 1; you have it before you in printed form, since it had to be attached to the agreement with Israel for reference purposes. The programme of legislation envisioned in this protocol is not, however, for the benefit of persecuted Jews alone, but for all persecuted persons alike. As I mentioned at the beginning, a draft bill of the Federal Government, embodying both the commitments in Part 4 of the Transition Agreement and the points agreed on in Protocol No. 1, is in preparation and will be presented to this house before the end of the present session.

"When, pursuant to my statement before this house in December, 1951, already cited, I met the delegate of the State of Israel and the leader of the world Jewish organisations, Dr. Nahum Goldmann, in London, I told him in the name of the Federal government that the time had now arrived to begin negotiations with representatives of the Jewish people and of Israel for reparation of the damage done by National Socialist persecution. In the negotiations with Dr. Goldmann I pointed out the most important considerations, which also govern the agreement now before you.

"The Federal Government have concluded the agreement in order to meet a compelling moral obligation of the German people represented by the Federal Republic; not, however, to satisfy a claim of the State of Israel under international law. This is assured by the text of the preamble and Article 1 of the agreement. The treaty makes of the moral obligation a legal obligation. In the field of individual restitution, legal claims can arise only through domestic German laws.

"The calculation of the payments to Israel is based on the Israeli note of 12 March 1951 to the four occupying powers. In the negotiations at the Hague, the Israeli delegation pointed out that Palestine and later the State of Israel had received more than 500,000 Jewish fugitives, most of them without funds, who had lost their homelands through National Socialist persecution. Taking account of the sum regarded by the experts of the Federal government as appropriate for the costs of integration of fugitives in Israel, as well as taking account of the capacity of the Federal Republic to pay, a sum totalling DM 3 thousand million has been agreed on as a payment to Israel. In view of the interest of Israel in the shortest possible maturity of the agreement, the amount of the annual instalments has been adjusted to the economic capacity of the Federal Republic, making allowances for its other obligations. In the opinion of the Federal government, a sum of DM 200 million for the first two fiscal years and (assuming normal economic development) DM 250 million for subsequent fiscal years seems feasible. The DM 310 million provisionally set at the request of Israel from 1 April 1954 as an annual instalment can be provided only if economic developments are unexpectedly favourable. On the other hand, the reduction in the capacity to pay of the Federal Republic in consequence of unforeseen unfavourable economic of financial developments can be allowed for by appeal to Article 10.

"Transfer of the payments to Israel in foreign currency is not feasible for economic reasons. Even in my first negotiations with Dr. Goldmann in London, therefore, payments in kind were envisioned. Under the agreement, the state of Israel is entitled to buy goods with the D-mark funds made available in Germany, and to export them to Israel. It would take us too far afield to detail these provisions here. They will be found in the text of the agreement before you, and are explained at length in the preamble.

"One thing I would like to emphasize. Care has been taken in two different ways to prevent abuse of the agreement, for instance, by the shipment of arms, munitions or other military equipment. Israel does not enjoy full freedom of choice in buying goods; she is restricted to the categories listed in the agreement. But even within the list of goods, Article 2 of the agreement permits only those goods to be bought that will serve to extend the opportunities for settlement and reintegration of Jewish refugees in Israel. Compliance with these provisions, which are particularly important because of the conflict of Israel with the states of the Arab League, will be supervised by a government agency. As I had expected from the time of my meeting with Dr. Goldmann in London, negotiations were conducted not only with the state of Israel but with representatives of the Jewish world organisations; these have undertaken to care for those Jewish refugees from National Socialist persecution who emigrated not to Israel but to other parts of the world. I have already pointed out that a considerable part of these negotiations with the representatives of Jewry dealt with individual restitution, and that the results are recorded in Protocol No. 1. In addition the Jewish world organisations demanded a lump sum for restitution and reparation claims without surviving heirs, where the claims had not been prosecuted by the so-called successor organisations. They pointed out that they had had to support the Jewish victims of National Socialist persecution for decades. To relieve the distress still undoubtedly prevailing among Jewish refugees from National Socialist persecution all over the world outside of Israel, the Federal Government have decided to provide DM 500 million; to avoid repetition, let me refer to the preamble of the agreement with Israel before you for the various considerations in detail. Since the Claim Conference represents only interests of Jews by faith, whereas the National Socialists persecutions were equally directed against non-professing Jews regarded as full-blooded Jews under the Nuremberg laws, the Federal Government will set up, out of the total DM 500 million, a fund of DM 50 million to be administered by the government for the assistance of non-professing Jews.

"As you will see in the printed document, for reasons of currency transfer the DM 450 million due to the Claims Conference will also be put at the disposal of Israel for purchases in the Federal Republic. Israel will then transmit corresponding sums to the Claims Conference. Detailed provisions assure that the money passed on by Israel to the Claims Conference shall be impartially used by the latter for the support, integration, and settlement of Jewish victims of National Socialist persecution.

"As you know, the Arab League and its member states have protested against the payments to the State of Israel. Even threats of boycott have been uttered. The objections of the Arab states may be summed up under two main headings.

"Firstly the Arabs point to the matter of the Arab refugees from Palestine; they maintain that the State of Israel is not entitled to demand compensations for Jewish refugees admitted, so long as it has not in turn met its liabilities regarding the Arab fugitives from Palestine. On that point that following should be noted: These are two different problems that must be kept separate. The question of compensating the Jewish refugees who escaped from National Socialist persecution must be settled between the Federal Republic and the Jewish people. As to the question of the Arab refugees from Palestine, the Federal Republic has neither the right nor the opportunity to take any position. Let me add one thing: We have too much experience of the distress and cares of refugees not to wish with all our hearts for swift and generally satisfactory settlement of this refugee problem as well.

"The second group of objections by the Arab states may be summed up as follows: They pointed out that they were still in a state of war with Israel, and that therefore a payment by the Federal Republic to one of the belligerents would constitute a violation of neutrality. The question of whether one can really speak of a continuing state of war is not for me to discuss here. The Security Council of the United Nations has rendered a contrary decision. But be that as it may, no possible violation of neutrality is involved. In addition, as I said before, precautions have been taken to see that the agreements shall not be used for the shipments of arms, munitions, or other military equipment to Israel.

Theodor Heuss with Karl Marx, editor of the "Allgemeine Wochenzeitung der Juden in Deutschland", as it was then called, in 1953

ARTICLE 17

(a) The present Agreement shall be ratified with the least possible delay in accordance with the constitutional procedures of the Contracting Parties.

(b) The instruments of ratification shall be exchanged as soon as possible by accredited representatives of the Contracting Parties, at the Secretariat of the United Nations in New York.

A procès-verbal shall be drawn up by the Secretary-General of the United Nations, who is hereby requested to furnish each Contracting Party with certified copies thereof.

(c) The present Agreement shall come into force upon the exchange of the instruments of ratification.

IN FAITH WHEREOF the undersigned representatives duly authorized thereto have signed the present Agreement.

DONE at Luxembourg this tenth day of September, 1952, in two originals in the English language, one copy of which shall be furnished to each one of the Governments of the Contracting Parties.

For the Federal Republic of Germany

For the State of Israel

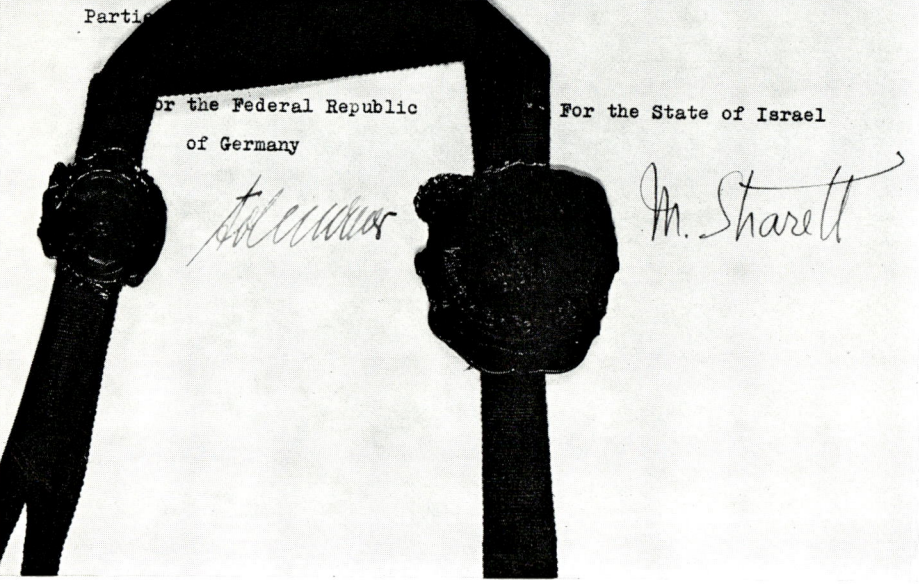

The last page of the German-Israeli Reparation Agreement of 10 September 1952

The signing of the German-Israeli Reparation Agreement in the Town Hall of Luxembourg. German delegation, right to left, Abraham Frowein, Franz Böhm, Konrad Adenauer, Walter Hallstein, Herbert Blankenhorn (hidden), Jakob Altmaier (SPD)

The signing of the German-Israeli Reparation Agreement in the Town Hall of Luxembourg. Israeli delegation, left to right, Felix Shinnar, Giora Josephthal, Moshe Sharett, Nahum Goldmann

Heinrich Lübke deposits the wreath
at Bergen-Belsen

"In addition the Federal Government have taken pains to inform the Arab countries of the background and limitations of the agreement with Israel, and thus to eliminate the anxiety that has arisen. They have also proclaimed their readiness to cultivate and intensify the traditional friendly relations of Germany with the Arab world. They have declared their willingness to contribute so far as possible to the building up of the economy of the Arab states. As you know, a representative German economic delegation led by Secretary of State Westrick conducted negotiations on the subject at Cairo. The delegation has returned to Bonn in order to give the Federal Government an opportunity to study the Egyptian wishes in detail. We are also prepared to send commercial delegations to the other Arab capitals in order to consult, if desired, on the economic needs of each individual country and the possibilities of strengthening the relations with German business. I need hardly add that such negotiations can be brought to a successful conclusion only if conducted in a friendly spirit on both sides and not impaired from the first by threats.

"World public opinion vigorously applauded the signing of the Luxembourg agreement between the Federal Republic and Israel. The Jewish people in Israel and elsewhere has recognized these agreements as a detailed settlement (making allowance for the capacity of the Federal Republic) of the indemnification question, as regard compensation for the material damages that the Federal Republic, for the reasons above mentioned, feels morally obligated to make good. We therefore have a well-founded hope that the conclusion of these agreements will ultimately head to an entirely new relationship between the German and the Jewish people, as well as to a restoration of normal relationships between the Federal Republic and the State of Israel. After all that has happened we have to show patience and put our trust in the effectiveness of our will to make reparations, and finally in the healing power of time. It is already plain that the conclusion of the agreement has brought a clear relaxation of the tension between the Federal Republic and the State of Israel. As you know, there is property of German nationals to a not inconsiderable value within the territory of the state of Israel. I may point out here in particular the group of some 2000 German nationals belonging to the Society of Templars, who own valuable buildings and estates in Israel. By a law of 1950 the State of Israel sequestered all German property to secure the claims of Israeli citizens against the German Reich and its successor states and against German nationals. The German delegation at the Hague succeeded in preparing an agreement with the Israeli delegation that was signed simultaneously with this other agreement as a government treaty at Luxembourg on 10 September 1952. This agreement provides that negotiations between the Federal Republic and the State of Israel are to be conducted at stated intervals after the effective date of the Israel agreement in order to ascertain this German property. In the government treaty—and I consider this extremely significant—Israel has definitely committed herself to pay compensation for the sequestered property. In case no agreement is reached in the negotiations between the Federal Republic and Israel on the value of the property to be compensated, the two signatories have already undertaken to accept the decision of a neutral arbitrator as binding. I believe that this treatment of German property in Israel represents the very most that could possibly have been attained.

"A considerable easing has also occurred in the question of displaying the German flag. The text of the treaty agreed on at The Hague assumed that the law against displaying the German flag then still in force in Israel would not be indefinitely maintained, although it was not then possible to obtain, before the signing of the agreement, any firm promise from Israel to repeal the law withing a definite period of time. Since then the Israeli government have undertaken on the basis of renewed representations by the Federal government, to do away with this ban as of the date of ratification of the agreement. The arrival of the first shipments of goods in Israel will considerably accelerate the evolution, already becoming apparent, toward a fundamental change in the German-Israeli relationship.

"In conclusion, let me once again emphasize the importance of the agreement in the more general context of the development of the human coexistence of nations. In recent weeks race hatred and race persecution have once again been made use of as political weapons within the sphere of the Communist regime of violence. You are all familiar with the Slansky trial in Prague. Following that trial, the Jews also began to be subject to threats and persecution in other satellite states. One world-famous Jewish welfare organisation, whose great accomplishments in relieving human distress are beyond question, was pilloried as a sabotage and espionage center. German nationals of the Jewish faith have also had to flee from the Soviet occupied zone and East Berlin. The free world observed these occurences with detestation and alarm.

"At the present time we want to make our standpoint clear and quite unmistakable by ratifying the agreement before you. No doubt we ourselves must bear heavy burdens to relieve the distress of our own refugees. Nevertheless we must stand by our moral duty to combat within the limits of our capacity, the misery and distress of refugees who suffered through the guilt of a former government. The Federal government hope that the acceptance of this agreement at the present moment will take effect as a German contribution towards strengthening the spirit of human and religious tolerance in the world."

This statement by the Federal Chancellor was received with lively applause by government parties and the Social Democratic opposition. The bill was referred for further deliberation to the Committee on the Occupation Statute and Foreign Affairs of the German Diet.

As early as 18 March the debate in the full assembly of the diet preparatory to final ratification of the agreement was resumed. As the reporter of the Committee on the Occupation Statute and Foreign Affairs, the CSU Deputy Count von Spreti gave a summary of the discussion in that committee.

"The Committee on the Occupation Statute and Foreign Affairs has appointed me to report on the second and third deliberations on the bill for an agreement between the German Federal Republic and the State of Israel. Let me begin by saying that the task here set me is extremely difficult in view of the characterisation of the bill, since it requires a rectrospective view.

"I cannot but take a backward look to draw attention to that which took place in the years from 1933 to 1945, bringing dishonour to the German name. You will permit me to remind you briefly, almost stenographically, of the outburst of anti-Semitism in 1933, of the provocation on 1 April, when the Storm Troop sentries were posted before Jewish places of business, to remind you of the Jewish legislation of Nuremberg and everything connected with it, down at last to the arrests, extortions, and expropriations. Perhaps one or the other of you may remember how on some nights a married couple would commit suicide or others were arrested by the Gestapo late at night and carried off. I must also recall that in those days concentration camps, ghettos, and annihilation camps existed that were crammed with thousands of human beings, and served for systematic experiments in destruction. In this retrospect of the past I am to quote a sentence that recently appeared in a newspaper criticism of a book:

"'If I shut my eyes today, I hear once more the screams of my companions being tortured, the shots under which they collapsed, the click of the guillotine under which their heroism was sealed.'

"I therefore felt called upon, following the statement of the Federal Government, to make a survey of the press, and I could not but find that after the statement and the signing in Luxembourg the domestic and foreign press was unanimous in its acceptance of this act of reparation. Only the *Manchester Guardian* made the statement, 'The sum is not large in comparison to the crimes', and went on to say, 'Fifty pounds per dead Jew'.

"Here, I believe, a person must try to call a halt, and so I should like to quote a remark of Guardini's to the effect that this injustice burdening Germany must be dealt with in some form or other. He must, he continues, point out that 'there is in the history of our last 20 years a monstrosity that has not yet been worked out at all'. Explaining this working-out, he says, 'Incidentally, it must take place in the realm of morals'. This attempt was made by the German Federal Government, with the result that the government made a statement in this place on 27 September 1951. Perhaps I may remind you—and I would also like to say it to those who do not know—that a member of this house who had experienced the most dreadful things within his family was prepared to be the first to engage in a dialogue with the Chancellor, since he felt it was his duty as a member of this house to bring the German people upon a peaceful level with the Jewish people. These attempts began, and it took some time before the representatives of the State of Israel agreed to give a sign that they were prepared to enter into discussions.

"And perhaps I may remind some of my colleagues in this house of the Convention at Istanbul, where the representatives of the Israeli people refused to sit down at the same table with the German deputies. Upon the return of the delegates of this house, a conversation took place with the Chancellor, and perhaps, I might say here, this very experience then led the Federal Government to make their statement even sooner than they had intended.

"In the statement the Chancellor said: 'During the National Socialist time there were many among the German people who showed their readiness to help their Jewish fellow citizens at their own peril for religious reasons, from distress of conscience, out of shame at the disgrace of the German name.'

"That is true. But in those days too much happened for it to be covered and shielded behind those acts of courage and inner decency. Hence the Chancellor declared here that 'The limits imposed on German ability to pay through the bitter necessity of caring for the innumerable war victims and the support of refugees and expellees must be considered', but he continued, 'The Federal Government are prepared, jointly with the representatives of Jewry and the State of Israel, which has admitted so many homeless Jewish fugitives, to bring about a solution of the material indemnity problem, thus easing the way to the spiritual settlement of infinite suffering'.

"With the permission of the President I may perhaps quote a few sentences spoken by the representatives of the various parties following the government statement.

"The Senior Deputy, *Mr. Löbe*, said in part in the name of the Social Democratic Party: 'Every right-thinking person is ashamed of these outrages, committed to the horror of the overwhelming majority of the German people as well as others, and abusing the German name', and continued, 'The enormity of the injustice to which the Chancellor too has just referred demands sacrifices of us.'

"*Dr. von Brentano* spoke for the CDU: 'The measure of respect we are prepared to offer our fellow men and also our Jewish fellow citizens will be the measure of respect that we demand for ourselves.'

"For the FDP *Dr. Schäfer* said, 'I do not believe that further words are calculated to express the determination and the clarity of views that lie behind this government message', and went on, 'I will confine myself to expressing approval in my own name and that of my friends.'

"*Dr. von Merkatz* said on behalf of the Deutsche Partei, 'We not only approve the statement of the government, we support it with all our hearts, because it is a matter of making good a profanation of divine and human law.'

"For the Centre, *Dr. Reismann* said, 'May the solemn declaration of all the parties here in the Diet and the statement of the Federal government before the public of the entire world do their part to clear away the natural resentment of those who endured such grievous suffering at the hands of a preceding government of Germany. In that spirit we thank the Federal government for its statement.'

"Finally *Dr. Decker* spoke for the Bavarian Party; he characterised the position of his group with the words, 'Anyone who professes allegiance to the state ruled by law and justice must also accept the Chancellor's statement, welcome it, and support it.'

"Recently there has been a great deal of talk and criticism, and it is therefore necessary when discussing the problem to make an effort to understand the feelings that are perceptible, perhaps indeed alive, in a group belonging to a denomination, the Jewish denomination, at the thought of entering into discourse with those who—at least under the name of 'Germans'—somehow took part in or are guilty of this disaster.

"There is no sense in playing down the word 'guilty'. We must try to understand that Europeans and Israelis, that is, the inhabitant of the State of Israel, think altogether differently. On the one side, with us, secular thinking prevails; on the other side, completely theocratic and sometimes mixed theocratic and secular thinking. This is he great problem in Palestine. Here two sides are face to face, perhaps in some danger of talking at cross purposes. That this secular and theocratic thinking conflict in Palestine itself is apparent everywhere to anyone who tries to study destinies and psychological factors. Thus in Palestine large complexes of problems have grown up, perhaps even bringing the possibility that Palestine may be spoken of as a stricken area. It is a mistake to think there is no resistance in Palestine to our 'attempt' to make a contribution to so-called moral indemnity; on the contrary, the vote in the Israeli parliament showed that the opportunity to commission delegates on behalf of the government to establish any sort of contact with Bonn was created only by a very slight majority. Accordingly the groups designated here for the assignment needed a keen ear for this theocratic-biblical thinking, and they also had to respect this thinking.

"As you know, at the same time that the negotiations were beginning, attempted assassinations played a part both here in Germany and in The Hague. In Munich there was an explosion, the public generally was much exercised, and it is almost a miracle that the attempt on the life of the head of the delegation in The Hague was not fatal.

"Now for the question whether the figure of 500,000 emigrés, refugee emigrants of the Jewish faith, is in accordance with the facts or derives from imaginary statistics. Here I must ask you to show some understanding and to cast a backward look at a time whose guilt we cannot deny. Some of these people began systematically emigrating from 1933 on. We may perhaps remember the big packing cases on which the places were marked where these persecutees or refugees hoped to find a resting place. Some of us may remember that in those days, along with the direction 'London' or 'South America' or 'North America' we often found the name 'Tel Aviv'.

"The further question whether all 500,000 really came from Germany must be anwered in the negative. In order to understand this, we must remember that it was actually National Socialism that pushed the wave of anti-Semitism before it as the war advanced, and these people were either arrested and destroyed or compelled by psychological pressure to emigrate again. In Czechoslovakia, in Rumania, in Hungary the most awful things were recorded. After 1945, however, we discovered that these Jewish emigrants, hoping to return from the concentration camps or the ghettos, made an attempt to settle again somehow in their old homelands, but owing to the dissolution of their community they no longer had an opportunity to remain, since a certain anti-Semitism had grown up there as well. They then passed on to Israel. This group is the subject in dispute, and we must recognise—as indeed the delegation recognised in its report to the Foreign Affairs Committee—that we cannot get away from this fact.

"The next question is the question of cover, and this naturally causes headaches to many who are anxiously following the budget of the Federal Government. We must not dismiss the matter of cover as a trifle. The question is only—and here I would like to recur to the words of Mr. Löbe—whether the word 'sacrifice' would not be appropriate here. We must show public opinion all over the world that the German people is ready to offer the hand of peace and also to accept the hand of peace.

"The Foreign Affairs Committee was unpleasantly surprised, in discussing this agreement and its background, to find that while we were in a state of spiritual distress, from which we are trying to escape, at that very moment a certain counter-movement arose in the Arab countries calculated to interfere with our effort at indemnity. I believe I may say—and I would emphasize this—that the Arab nations in general, and especially the Islamic people have proved by their history that Islam in particular has a very strong sense of justice. I assume that with this sense the Arab countries will show understanding for the attempt of the German Federal Government to make restitution. But it can only be noted with a certain amount of surprise that at the very moment the German delegation was in Cairo a delegation from the Eastern Zone was also received.

"Permit me after this introduction to get down to the agreement itself. But I must ask you to realise that in the statement of the Conference on Jewish Material Claims Against Germany the sentence occurs: 'We are prepared to negotiate about certain claims of a material nature. It is, however, our duty to make clear from the start that no negotiation of moral claims can take place.' It is further stated that this is possible only through spiritual purification. This was the premiss of the Federal Government, and the attempt was made to find a common denominator for the various interests in this agreement.

"Article 1 states that this is not an act of international law, and fixes the sum of 3 thousand million. This sum was computed on the basis of the experience provided to us by the Refugee Ministry, from which, and particularly from the Sonne Plan, we found that the costs of integrating a refugee lie between DM 7,000 and 10,000, and the figure of DM 7,000 was agreed on. The sum for integrating the fugitives in Palestine is DM 1,000 less. A second item is the DM 450 million demanded by the Conference on Jewish Material Claims Against Germany. This sum is earmarked for restitution to the Jews not resident in Palestine.

"Art. 2 fixes the goods that are to be supplied. When I use the word 'goods', I must mention here that there was a discussion of the 'goods' concept, that there was a debate about currency versus goods. Here it was Mr. Abs in particular who espoused the opinion that goods and currency must be equated, and that if we were to speak of goods as a matter of payment we must do it quite consciously and not surreptitiously.

"Art. 3 covers the annual payments.

"Art. 4 was included at the request of Israel; it provides that account is to be taken of a possible economic boom in Germany. This provision also mentions a loan that Germany might obtain. It may perhaps be in the interest of the entire German Federal Diet if I express the request that foreign powers may show understanding for us in this connection.

"Art. 5 governs payments and is to be regarded in connexion with Note No. 2. This is intended to provide an incentive for business. It is specified that no discrimination may be shown as against exports to third countries; this applies particularly to prices subject to official regulation now or in future. This article also deals with taxation.

"Art. 6 gives the list of goods, and Article 7 states that there is no German Central Office, and that the Israeli Mission may purchase here independently. A Federal agency is, however, envisioned; these duties are to be assigned to the 'Federal Agency for Goods Traffic'.

"Art. 9 governs the banking procedure, and includes an annex on the subject.

"If I may skip at this point, I will draw your attention to the two protocols. Protocol No. 1 establishes the basic principles for individual restitution with respect to the future Restitution Act. Protocol No. 2 applies to the Jewish Claims Conference and regulates the use of these funds, and also makes reporting mandatory.

"This concludes my remarks, and I would like to leave you with one request. It is a matter of fact that in Jerusalem we find a dividing line between Old and New Testament. May it be granted to us with this dividing line to create peace between the two, between the Old and the New Testament, and may good will help to show the others that with this good will great abuses and great psychological differences can be bridged over."

This report was followed by the discussion among the spokesmen of the various parties. The subsequent president of the diet, Eugen Gerstenmaier, spoke on behalf of the Christian Democrats:

"I have the honour to deliver the following statement in the name of my political associates:

"Among the most incomprehensible phenomena of recent history will allways be the outburst of madness to which an estimated six million German, French, Belgian, Polish, Russian, Hungarian, Danish, and other European citizens fell victims. Systematically, and with almost perfect technique they were shot, gassed, annihilated, from infant to ancient, for no other reason than that they were ostensibly or really persons 'of different blood', persons of the Jewish race. The order went out to render Germany, 'greater Germany', indeed Europe 'Jew-free'. He who did not flee fell to the hangman. He who issued the order and those who carried it out were base murderers. But they had the power in Germany, and they spoke in the name or at least at the expense of Germany. There were hundreds of thousands in Germany who shuddered at this. There were thousands who, in torment, tried to give help. And there were not a few who risked their necks in this help, and lost. It is to these martyrs of humanity, representatives of the German people, that Germany chiefly owes its ability to reject the doctrine of the collective guilt of all Germans.

"But their number is far from large enough to permit the other doctrine of collective innocence. No matter how guilt and innocence may be blended here, one thing is certain: it was in the name and at the charge of Germany that the citizens of the Jewish race within the sphere of power of the Third Reich were sent to the ghettos and thence into exile or to the gas ovens. The result was the counter-blow of history that we have witnessed. The result was that Germany, all Germany, was transformed into one great ghetto. More insuperable than the wall of an Oriental ghetto for us Germans were the walls of hatred, contempt, and hostility, built around us even before the war, to hold us captive after the war.

"It is true that breaches have been made in these walls around Germany—wide breaches in fact. We regard it as one of the greatest accomplishments of German policy since the war, particularly of the foreign policy of the Federal Government, that it has been able through persistence and a straightforwardness that inspires confidence to guide Germany largely out of this ghetto. But only a touching unworldliness or an impudent forgetfulness could act as if we had turned the corner in this matter, as if hostility to Germany, as if moral and political condemnation of Germany were finally overcome or forgotten in this world. That calls for more than a naive spirit or casual forgetfulness. This is a matter not merely of well-meant words; this is a matter of documenting a new attitude in a way to win respect. We believe that this is the intellectual position in general and the political position in particular form which this first treaty of the German Federal Republic with the State of Israel must be understood and judged.

"So far as Germany is concerned, this treaty arises from the fixed determination to give material expression to a clearly and precisely perceived moral obligation according to the measure of our national strength. And this treaty has the purpose of delivering Germany fully and forever from the ghetto. I cannot see why both points should not be freely stated. In this matter Germany has an inescapable double duty, firstly to the victims of tyranny, secondly to herself, her name, and her outraged honour. We are not prepared to start discussing this. But we are aware that in connexion with the treaty certain questions remain to be settled:

"1. The question of individual restitution. Before the present treaty was negotiated and signed—permit me to call your attention to this—, this house considered a reparation law, and on 3 July 1952 approved the motion of the Committee for Judicature and Consitutional Law. The motion required the Federal government 'to submit a bill governing indemnity to the victims of National Socialism through a Federal supplementary and skeleton law'. We insist that this law be submitted as quickly as possible according to the principle here already decided upon; because we insist on individual reparation to all victims of National Socialism without regard to race or denomination.

"2. We know that beyond all individual indemnity there will be an unsettled remainder. We know that even the material sacrifices of European Jewry through the mass murders are so immeasurable that individual restitution cannot encompass them. Who is to represent families, groups, and villages murdered to the last man? We know, too, that the overflowing measure of suffering and of those done to death cannot be paid for with three and a half thousand million marks. We therefore think it fitting to give that amount on behalf of half a million persons living in Israel, persons in Israel whom the 'Third Reich' once robbed of their livelihood. We know that even then an impalpable balance that we cannot repay will remain; it can only be left to the hope of funtre reconciliation.

"3. We regret that this treaty has brought about a temporary impairment of the German-Arab relationship. We value the old-established friendship of Germany for the Arab states, and anything that can be done on our part to give moral and political support to the Arab efforts on behalf of refugees should be done. But the bridge that we

Germans must walk in the present matter leads from the Jews driven out and murdered in the name of Germany, not to the Arabs, but to Israel. We welcome the efforts of the Federal government to live in close friendship and fruitful economic relationship with the Arab states. But we can and will not let even the Arab friends of Germany prevent us from doing as conscience and honour bid us. Let the Arabs see by this how trustworthy the friendship of such a Germany can be in critical situations.

"A servant of the Prussian state, grown old in honour, an elderly Berlin member of the Board of Health, was taken away with his family during those iniquitous years and sent to the crematories of Theresienstadt. The son escaped to Sweden. He came back in the winter of 1945-46. He worked devotedly and unreservedly for the rebuilding of Germany. He was probably the only German to deliver a memorial address (at a Bavarian university last year) to Prussia as to the dear departed. The speech was dedicated to his murdered father, and entitled, 'The honour of Prussia'. It seems to me that it is time, high time that we ceased letting ourselves be put to shame. The honour of Germany commands it. That is why we say yes to this treaty."

Carlo Schmidt took the floor on behalf of the Social Democrats:

"In the name of the Social Democratic deputies I have the following statement to make:

"The reign of terror set up by the authorities of the National Socialist regime in Germany and the countries occupied by her was responsible for crimes without number. Millions of innocent persons were shut up in the concentration camps, murdered, or driven from their homelands. This barbarism fell most dreadfully upon the people of Jewish faith and Jewish descent. Millions of them were murdered, hundreds of thousands driven or displaced from their homes, hundreds of thousands later had to leave their country, grown uninhabitable through the consequences of the National Socialist terror.

"The Social Democratic Party has always demanded the making good of this injustice to millions of Germans and foreigners. Particularly the late Dr. Kurt Schumacher never wearied of pointing out the primary duty of indemnity towards the Jewish people.

"In accordance with this conviction, the Social Democratic deputies declared through their spokesman on 22 February 1951 that the German people must acknowledge a special moral obligation for restitution to the Jews, and that therefore a special right to the indemnity payments of which the German people were capable must be granted to the Jewish victims of National Socialism.

"Moral obligations, however, call for greater efforts than the payment of a debt based only on standards of written law. Accordingly for the sake of justice it is necessary to go to the utmost limit of German capacity to pay. The Social Democratic deputies reject the thesis of the collective guilt of the German people as they do the other, equally false thesis of collective innocence. But even without collective guilt, the totality of Germans must stand good, within the limits of the capacity of our people; for indemnity for the injustice that was committed, outraging our name in the process.

"The Social Democratic deputies, through their spokesman, on 22 February 1951, further declared that they considered the State of Israel entitled to represent collective claims of the Jewish people, because the State of Israel is regarded even by the great mass of those Jews who wish to remain citizens of other states as authorised, above and beyond mere moral authority, to act for all Jews who do not feel otherwise bound. Our party will remain true to this attitude.

"The treaty concluded with the State of Israel must in no way limit the fulfilment of the obligations owed individually to all victims of National Socialist persecution. The Social Democratic deputies expect the restitution law to grant prompt and adequate indemnity to all those who suffered loss of property, life, freedom, for political, religious, or racial reasons, regardless of whether they are living abroad or in Germany. The deputies regard it as highly deplorable that so many claims have not yet been met or not adequately met.

"The party further expresses its regret that the negotiations with the State of Israel were conducted without adequate simultaneous information to the Arab states. If this information had been properly given, the difficulties that have now arisen in the relationship to the Arab states would have been more easily avoided. The Social Democratic deputies expect the Federal Government to do everything that can legitimately be required in order to restore the former relations to the Arab states by economic agreements in line with the traditional friendship of our peoples. They most emphatically condemn the participation of German circles in the efforts to prevent the treaty with Israel from being concluded and ratified.

"The Social Democratic Party hopes that the conclusion and implementation of the treaty with the State of Israel may be understood by the whole world as a sign of the earnest determination of the German people to make good at least some of the awful disaster that the National Socialist rule of violence brought upon the German people and the other people ravaged by it. It is aware that even this treaty cannot alleviate, let alone undo, the suffering inflicted on millions of people, so many of whom were faithful citizens of the German state and highly valuable members of our people, whose names will stand for all time on the fairest pages of the book of honour of our nation, that German nation struck to the core by the murder or expulsion of our Jewish fellow citizens at every level of their existence.

"We do not want the conclusion of this treaty to be misunderstood as meaning that the German people believe it can thus cause these crimes to be forgotten. We summon the German people to do everything that may serve to make good National Socialist injustice, and to wait with patience and without demands to see whether one day the descendants and companions of the victims of that barbarism that disgraced the German name will offer it the hand of reconciliation. The deputies of the Social Democratic Party of Germany will vote for the treaty, and move for a roll-call vote."

Deputy Hasemann declared on behalf of the Free Democrats:

"The present agreement between the German Federal Republic and the State of Israel is intended to put a period to one of the darkest chapters of German history, a chapter that has covered the German name with shame and disgrace. This agreement is based on the statement of the Federal Government of 27 September 1951 on the problem of reparation in relation to the State of Israel, which the Federal Diet unanimously approved at the time. For years the Federal Government has made consistent and strenuous efforts to restore the moral reputation of the Federal Republic in the world and to give convincing evidence that the German people, even though rejecting a collective guilt, have been jointly summoned and are also minded to make good injustice and damage done. I may say of my party that it has fully supported the Federal Government in every way in this effort, both for humane and for political reasons. We know that it is very hard to make just recompense even for the material harm done to Jewry and all other victims of Nazism. We know, too, that it is even harder to make indemnity for the spiritual agony suffered, and finally we know that there is no compensation for death. We shall always be ready to recognise the just claim of every victim, and to fulfil it within the limits of existing possibilities, and there can be no hair-splitting about this legal claim of the victims of the Nazi regime.

"The agreement with the State of Israel is not material indemnity based on a claim at law; this agreement is an act that asks to be morally evaluated and that is intended to cleanse the German reputation and the German name in the world of the blemishes that still inhere.

"Whether the present agreement is calculated to accomplish the necessary and desired end is a subject of debate not only in public opinion but within my party. Some of my associates feel that this treaty is not a particularly successful structure. It is idle to dissect the treaty, as it were, isolating its inadequacies and ambiguities and making predictions as to its consequences. It does not seem to me useful to debate here in the full session whether and how individual restitution, say, may be impaired as a matter of time and financially by this treaty; whether the figure of 500,000 expelled Jews, taken as a basis for the reintegration costs of the State of Israel, is accurate; or how it was possible for the treaty to be signed despite the so-called flag clause, which was cancelled only through the reaction of the public and through the intervention of the Upper House. There can and must be no haggling in public over this treaty if the moral effect is not to be wasted. Nevertheless it ought perhaps to be said that all these questions should more properly have been discussed with the appropriate committee of the Federal Diet before signature, as Mr. Abs, for instance, did in settling the German foreign debts.

"And though I said that I did not consider it useful to dissect the treaty here, a problem must nevertheless be mentioned in this connexion that my predecessors on the floor have already touched upon: The effect of the agreement on the Arab States, and beyond this perhaps upon the whole Mohammedan world. My party does not share the unconcern of the Federal Government in this respect. We are of opinion that the diplomatic screening off of the States of the Arab League was inadequate. It is not merely considerations of a material nature, derived from export or import figures with the Arab area; it is rather considerations of a political nature that cause us uneasiness. We do not want the great measure of trust and friendship that Germany has long enjoyed in the Mohammedan world to be hastily squandered; our true friends in this world are few and far between. We feel that the Federal Government should have taken account of and allowed for the legitimate interests and views both of the State of Israel and of the Arab League at an early stage of the negotiations—views resulting from the fact that the State of Israel is still in a latent state of war with the Arab states. I would like to express here the hope the Arab states may be able to understand our obligation to make indemnity for the injustice done to Jewry through this act of restitution. At the same time we request the Federal Government by means of further and, we hope, most intensive negotiations with the Arab states to preserve the honest feelings of friendship for our people and country on the part of these states. On the other hand it is to be hoped that the act of good will manifested in this treaty will find in the State and people of Israel and beyond this throughout the world the echo that we expect. This treaty is an integral whole and it has been signed by the Federal Republic. There can only be a yes or no. The yes for some people will not be joyful. A no will not be possible for some because despite certain misgivings the moral effect inherent in this agreement is recognised, and must not be impaired. Accordingly the position of my party on this treaty is not uniform. A free decision is left to each individual conscience.

"In this connexion I am to present to this House in the name of my party a resolution that has been distributed as Reprint No. 795. This resolution makes reference to Printed Document No. 3583. In the 229th session, of 11 September 1952, the Federal Diet, with only a few abstentions, passed a motion of the Committee for Judicature and Constitutional Law'. Item 2 of which requires the Federal government to submit forthwith a bill 'on the liabilities of the German Reich under reparation law and the elimination of the patent hardships arising from the regulation of restitution by the occupying power'. The resolution presented by my party would call upon the Federal Government to present this bill by 1 May of this year.

"The reparation law enacted by the occupying powers had beyond doubt in many cases worked undue hardship upon persons who acquired Jewish property in good faith and indeed with good will. Every one of you will know of cases——they are by no means few—in which the purchaser acquired the property of a Jewish emigrant with his full consent and indeed often at his desire. The hardships arising in such cases are to be eliminated at the almost unanimously expressed wish of the Diet. It is therefore only logical for you to concur with our motion, which I request you to do in the name of my party."

In the name of the German Party, Deputy Hans-Joachim von Merkatz said:

"In the name of the deputies of the German Party I have the following statement to make: The Deputies of the German Party have examined the treaty submitted with a lively sense of responsibility. Pledged as we are to the values of honourable German tradition, we welcome the effort implied in the treaty to give a visible symbol in order to overcome a disastrous past, with fair realisation of the magnitude of the injustice done, so that trust in our people may be restored, the future deprived of its poison, and that any similar event may be prevented by all decent Germans. We decline a collective guilt, but are jointly liable for the restoration of honour of our people. This means reparation so far as it lies within our power and ability.

"In view of grave concern and well-founded doubts as to whether the road chosen by the treaty is a proper one in its foundations and effects, part of our party, in a justifiable conflict of conscience, has felt unable to answer in the affirmative. The members of the party who have made this decision did so not because they wanted to haggle about the payment, but because their sense of justice brought them to this conclusion. They regard individual indemnity to the Germans of the Jewish faith and to the European Jews as endangered by an assent to this treaty. This conclusion was also influenced by the fact that unfortunately new injustice is being done in carrying out restitution. What we miss, however, is any real sign of readiness to make good the injustice done in Germany, in Europe, and in the world by all concerned to the expellees; this injustice goes back to the same totalitarian perversion of state power, and should be indemnified with the same insight, responsibility, international honour, and joint liability; right and justice are indivisible and their validity is absolute."

The present chairman of the National Democratic Party of Germany (NPD), Deputy von Thadden, at that time representing no party because the Deutsche Reichspartei had been banned, declared:

"The fact that we are concerning ourselves today with the treaty of the Federal Government with the State of Israel directs the attention of us all once more to one of the gloomiest chapters of recent times. That persecution by German authorities killed over a million of the approximately 5.6 million Jews who lived in Europe before the war, cannot be extenuated by anyone or made good by any human being. Murder is murder whether committed upon one or upon millions of human beings.

"When we rigorously reject the injustice done since 1945 to Germans, and affirm our belief in the state governed by law and justice, it is a matter of course that we accept and demand the complete return of all property values that were taken from Jews or that they had to sell under pressure. Appropriate legislation exists or is in the process of being enacted. But the state should also take note, before it is too late, that in the process much new injustice has been done to the innocent.

"This treaty, however, does not involve the return of property. This is an agreement with the State of Israel, founded on 15 May 1948. According to the preamble of the treaty, along with the payments to the world Jewish organisations we are to pay DM 3 thousand million for the integration of 540,000 Jews who emigrated from Europe to Israel. Only part of these, however—125,000 according to the figures I have seen—, came from Germany. For direct assistance in integrating these people, a different treaty would have been needed in our opinion. So far as the emigration from Eastern Europe goes, which this treaty also calls on us to pay for, the question arises: Did no liberation take place there after 1945?

"Accordingly we accept the payments to German Jews as part of restitution to Israel as well, but not to those from the 'liberated' regions in the East and West.

"The signing of the treaty with the State of Israel, which continues in a state of war with the States of the Arab League, has called forth violent protests from the Arab countries, with which we are linked by century-old friendship that goes far beyond business relations. The Arabs are not opposed to help and indemnification on our part, they are opposed to Germany's one-sidedly taking the part of Israel in its quarrel with them. We believe it was wrong to negotiate directly with the State of Israel, which is at war with countries friendly to us. The route by way of the United Nations would have been better. The Arab countries can neither understand nor approve nor excuse our partisanship here. They fear the economic rearmament of Israel supplied by us will be followed by new expansion and aggression. We should not forget that more than a million Arabs had to surrender to the Jewish immigrants not a desert but all that was valuable in a thriving country, without any compensation whatever. The Federal Government have behaved in the way that usually comes of 'lonely' decisions. Through the SPD and the CDU the acceptance of the present treaty seems assured. Nevertheless, the French are trying to change, may upset the EEC treaty by amendments. Accordingly we believe that a simple supplementary protocol should name the U. N. as trustee, through whose hands all payments are to pass. This could change much that threatens to do grave harm to our relationship to the Near East. In view of the fact, once admitted by a Federal Minister, that this treaty came into being under heavy pressure from the Americans, the appointment of the U.N. here could provide a solution satisfying to all concerned. Until something is done in this direction, we of the DRP shall reject the treaty."

At that time the Communist Party of Germany was still represented in the German Federal Diet. Its deputy Müller took the floor with the following statement:

"The deaths and the murder of 6 million Jews are one long indictment of a fearful system of barbarism and contempt for mankind. A good many emotional words have been spoken here about this. But we protest against people's taking the floor here, who, when it was a matter of preventing these crimes, either stood aside or assisted.

"And I say today with the same emphasis that this agreement between the Federal Republic and the State of Israel does not serve to make restitution for the unbounded and bestial crimes of Hitler barbarism against the persecuted Jews. For the moment, I will let the facts of the agreement speak for themselves:

"1. The Federal government undertake to pay DM 3 thousand million to the State of Israel.

"2. In addition to this sum there is a figure of DM 450 million to a Federation of Zionist Organisations.

"The payment of the entire sum is to take place in the form of shipments of goods to the State of Israel. According to the list of goods attached to the agreement, the shipments are to consist of pig iron, rolling-mill products, castings, iron and steel products, of the steelworking and chemical industries, and a few others. In addition, the English shipment of oil to Israel in the amount of DM 75 million annually is to be paid for.

"It is worth noting that the shipments of agricultural products make up only 1.5% of the annual total. Under the name of indemnity, therefore, the industrialists of Israel will receive from West Germany everything they need to build up their basic industries. The fact proves that this agreement has nothing whatever to do with reparation. This is confirmed by the statement in the agreement under which these payments to Israel are not to be affected by the payments to the individual Jews under the domestic German reparation laws. In plain words this means that the persecuted individuals in Israel will not receive a single penny of the three thousand million, whereas the industrialists will do a splendid stroke of business. Not only they, however, are the beneficiaries of this agreement, but above all the gentlemen in the American armament industry and high finance. It is they who are behind the agreement and brought it about; not for reasons of humanity and philanthropy. Very concrete reasons underlie this policy. The American imperialists are creating a strong strategic and military base in the Near East, partly against the English, but also against the peoples of the Near East and North Africa. With the help of the industrial equipment of West Germany, then, the Americans wish to build up the State of Israel, which is in their hands, into an armament and operating base for their aggressive policy.

"Those who gain from this agreement are not only the masters of industry in Israel and the Americans, they are also the industrialists of West Germany, who are thus assured sales and giant profits for several years ahead. Is it not a downright disgusting mockery of the racially persecuted that those who share in the responsibility for the mass murder, who made huge profits under Hitler and on his massacres of the Jews, today once more wish to pocket giant profits under the cloak of this sort of 'reparation', while those racially persecuted and all others in the Federal Republic must wait years for adequate restitution and pensions? Is it not a bloody mockery that here in the Federal Diet people are working for this sort of 'restitution' who, like Mr. Pferdmenges, once helped to finance the S.S., to whose special account we must post the murder of millions of Jews, or an economic warfare official, Dr. Frowein, of whom the following was written in a document of 31 May 1940:

"'Mr. Frowein has learnt that any desired number of Jewesses can be supplied to us. They will have to be definitely employed on the night shift and quartered, if possible, in huts, or in apartments as poor as possible. Mr. Frowein suggests 500 Jewesses.'

"Or a certain Dr. Lehr who gave instructions as Lord Mayor in 1933 to eliminate Jewish shops, lawyers and doctors. These names alone are proof enough that this agreement can never be a matter of reparation. I know that most of the racially persecuted persons living in the Federal Republic reject this agreement. We Communists reject it. We demand that funds be provided at long last here in the Federal Republic to satisfy the claims of all those persecuted by the Nazi regime, the claims to which they are entitled as reparation."

Deputy Decker spoke for the Federalist Union, a predecessor of the later Bavarian Party:

"In his statement on the attitude of the Federal Republic towards the Jews, the Chancellor said: 'Unspeakable crimes have been committed in the name of the German people, calling for moral and material indemnity, both with regard to the individual harm done to Jews and to the Jewish property for which no legitimate individual claimants still exist.'

"On behalf of my party I made the following rejoinder: 'Anyone who professes allegiance to the state ruled by law and justice must also accept the Chancellor's statement, welcome it, and support it.'

"I am glad this sentence has already been quoted today; there has been no change in the attitude of my party towards this question. Now as in the past my party accepts the duty to make reparations for the injustice, and so far as humanly possible, for the inhumanities committed against the Jews by those in power in the Third Reich and their unscrupulous tools. My party is also gratified that steps in this direction have been taken in the form of an agreement, but has objections to this particular agreement and has warned against it from the first. We are of the opinion that this agreement does not take the best and most favourable path possible to close the still gaping wounds, to heal them, and to initiate a reconciliation between the Jews and the German people. It is our impression that the Foreign Office handled the question of restitution far too much in isolation, in a vacuum—independent of the inter-connexions of world politics.

"The German people very rightly reject collective guilt in this matter. On the other hand, the German people are willing collectively, that is as a whole, to make reparations. This does not necessarily mean that the reparations as such should go primarily to the sufferers collectively. The first necessity, for simple reasons of humanity, is individual restitution and assistance. First the immediately persecuted and harmed members of the Jewish people must be helped. Many of them are so aged, and in the most difficult economic circumstances, that any delay of individual aid will no longer permit them to enjoy it. The consequence of the present bill, however, will be that individual assistance is delayed for years in favour of a collective measure, namely a measure in favour of the State of Israel, simply because the funds of the Federal Republic do not suffice for both at the same time. A solution preferring individual assistance to any other kinds and giving consideration to Jewry as a whole without regard to its internal levels and cleavages would have received our approval at once. This agreement, however, which has no effect on all the Jews who suffered, but will involve perfectly senseless damage to the foreign relations of the Federal Republic, is not one we consider calculated to solve the question before us. Let me sum up. Reparation? Yes, with all our hearts.

"*This* agreement, however, we must decline and say no to. We shall abstain from voting not because we are undecided or indifferent in the question, but because we wish to express that we must unfortunately say no to the agreement, but affirm reparations as a deep duty of conscience."

After the second reading of the bill, the Social Democrats moved a roll-call vote. Hermann Ehlers, president of the Diet, announced the result of the ballot count in the following words:

"I announce the provisional results of the roll-call vote. Participating were 358 deputies entitled to vote and 19 Berlin deputies. Of deputies entitled to vote, 238 voted for, 34 against, with 86 abstentions. Of the Berlin deputies 16 voted for, with 3 abstentions. The bill for the agreement of 10 September 1952 between the Federal Republic and the State of Israel is accordingly passed on its third reading. I believe I should express my feeling that the vote on this treaty moves us all most deeply regardless of the individual decision. I have no doubt that this decision will have a mighty echo not only in Germany and in the State of Israel, but throughout the world. That is true not only of the immediate payments that the treaty provides. This decision must tell all those who are persecuted everywhere that violence and crime must not be the ultimate in the world.

"I understand the decision of the Diet to mean that it wished to bear witness at this moment that policy within our own people and in the relationships of human beings and people amongst one another must not be determined merely by questions of tactics and utility. We wish thus to demonstrate to ourselves and others that there are principles of right and morality that are the real foundations of living together on earth. No sacrifice must be too great for us in helping to make this principle a reality."

With that, the agreement was ratified by the German Federal Diet. On the German side it was now legally valid. Acceptance of the agreement in Israel was not easy. On this subject Felix E. Shinnar said to the editor:

"I believe one may say that public opinion and the prevailing opinion in parliament welcome this treaty and the arrangement it brought about as a serious contribution to reparations for the material wrong done and the resulting damage; at least a clear difference was apparent as against the reception by public opinion at the beginning of the negotiations. You know that public opinion was very much divided as to whether the State of Israel should conduct these negotiations with the Federal Republic or not. This difference was evident in the question of whether the agreement negotiated should be accepted and ratified. Here it has been realised that both sides had a duty to do so. On the side of the State of Israel because Israel, as a state in which the victims of the National Socialist regime found a home, had the duty to require indemnification for the damage done by that regime, in order thus to master the enormous task of building up this homeland and creating a basis for the livelihood of these victims. On the other side, it was a duty of the Federal Republic, which entered upon it with a voluntary readiness based on a sense of responsibility, and thus demonstrated that the Federal Republic as a community under the rule of law and justice intended to return as an equal member to the family of peoples."

The carrying-out of the agreement

Four and a half months after the ratification of the Luxembourg agreement by the German Federal Diet, the first shipment—iron components—was taken aboard the Israeli freighter *Haifa* on 30 July 1953. This event was of real importance for the further history of the two nations.

Felix E. Shinnar tried to give a solemn touch to this first step after the difficult negotiations and discussions of the agreement; he invited public figures of the Hanseatic city to a dinner on board the *Haifa*. He told the editor the following anecdote:

"We met aboard the *Haifa* for a lunch attended by Mayor Kaisen, the head of the Municipal Port Department, the head of the Economic and Finance Department, and a few other public figures in the city of Bremen, about 25 all told. At lunch it was mentioned that Mayor Kaisen did not come from Bremen, and the question arose in conversation who of those present was Bremen born. In short, neither the Mayor or the head of the Port Department, nor the other public figures of the city of Bremen, had been born there; the only one of the party of 25 born in Bremen, it turned out, was the Israeli captain of our Israeli freighter, the *Haifa*."

The Israeli mission in Cologne under Felix E. Shinnar was expanded to become a dynamic institution for the economic building-up of Israel. In a retrospect of the work done by his agency and the importance of the agreement for Israeli development, Shinnar said:

"For Israel the necessity of receiving goods was important because thus she had the opportunity, putting aside the urgent needs for daily consumption, to obtain substantially only those goods that served the peaceful, industrial, or agricultural upbuilding of Israel. Some 80 per cent of the agreement was accepted in shipments of capital goods of all kinds, and accordingly the shipments under the agreement (and I believe that this does justice to the meaning, the inner meaning of the agreement) were a visible, lasting constituent of the building-up of industry in Israel in those first years, so decisive for the economic consolidation of Israel. Shipments under the agreement constituted 12% of all annual Israeli imports. An important and thoroughly constructive contribution to this process of industrialisation in Israel, still in its first though fairly advanced stage. Under the agreement some 50 vessels, almost all freighters, were acquired; the copper smelters in King Solomon's copper mines in the south of our country, the ironworks in the north were built entirely from German shipments; in addition, about 2000 individual enterprises, from a largish workshop to a medium-sized factory, received machinery and equipment from the shipments under the agreement, which allowed them to rationalise and modernise the operation. These few hints show that shipments under the agreement were to be found all over Israel and certainly in all the regions of industrial importance, making plain the contribution of which I spoke, whose effect was particularly constructive and effective beyond the mere amount of the figures at that particular time."

Report on the shipments of goods

The agreement was fulfilled in full by the end of 1965. The Mixed Commission of representatives of Israel and the Federal Republic, called for in the treaty, went to work immediately after ratification. Between 17 June 1953 and 16 March 1965 the lists of goods were drawn up in 18 protocols, and instructions for carrying out the shipments were given.

A concluding report of March 1966, presented by Regierungsdirektor (ret.) Joachim Ebeling on behalf of the chairman of the German delegation in the German-Israeli Mixed Commission on the carrying-out of the agreement, contained an exact survey of the carrying-out of the treaty in every detail. Among other points, the report says of the shipments of goods and the services under the agreement:

"For the purchase of goods and services there was an expenditure totalling
DM 2400 million
and for the oil shipments from the United Kingdom
DM 1050 million
total DM 3450 million

"The goods and services are broken down into the following groups and items

Group	Item	Type of goods	Amount in thousands of DM	%
I	1	Products of the iron and steel industry	274,292	11.5
	2	Foundry products	20,814	0.8
	3	Cold-rolled and drawn products	28,866	1.2
	4	Products of the non-ferrous metal industry	66,815	2.8
		Group I	390,787	16.3
II	1	Machinery	315,894	13.2
	2	Automotive industry	24,582	1.0
	3	Steel construction	129,949	5.4
	4	Shipbuilding	585,572	24.4
	5	Electrical industry	223,125	9.3
	6	Precision mechanics and optics	20,321	0.9
	7	Metalwares	27,501	1.1
		Group II	1,326,944	55.3
III	1	Rubber and asbestos	18,106	0.7
	2	Chemical and pharmaceutical products	159,629	6.7
	3	Textiles	74,766	3.1
	4	Wood products	35,766	1.5
	5	Leather	12,583	0.5
	6	Quarry products	13,877	0.6
	7	Ceramic and glass products	14,000	0.6
	8	Petroleum and mining	8,198	0.3
		Group III	336,925	14.0
IV	1	Agricultural products	91,217	3.8
V		Services	254,127	10.6
		Groups I to V	2,4000,000	100.0

"On looking at the calls made upon the various groups and items we find that under Group I the most extensive purchases were made for item 1 (Products of the iron and steel industry). This involved chiefly the procurement of structural steel for the large facilities that were later to house the manufacturing plants of varied industries. But pig iron (billets) for the iron and steel industry in Israel was also supplied as a raw material under this item. Shipments of structural steel covered chiefly the first nine years of the total period, declining sharply in the last four years, since the major projects were concluded by 1962. The demand for castings, shown under item 2, was of no great importance. It appears to a larger extent only in 1957 and 1958, at a time when products of this industry were needed on a large scale in Israel for the Negev Desert irrigation project.

"The purchases of cold-rolled and drawn products, item 3, were made largely in the first six years, up to 1958. By then the Israeli facilities had been expanded to a point where purchases from third countries could be substantially reduced. On the other hand the shipments of semi-finished non-ferrous metals and alloys, item 4, were higher. These shipments of semi-finished materials were processed in Israel to build industrial plants.

"The largest orders in proportion to the other groups of goods came under Group II, capital goods industries, with some DM 1327 million. From the first drafting of the agreement the parties both felt that the need for investment goods should be given primary consideration in order to set up an efficient economy in Israel; as already mentioned, the Mixed Commission took account of this fact in drawing up the annual lists of goods. The supplying of capital goods was also of special importance to the economy of the Federal Republic and the various suppliers, since these were products whose manufacture, in contrast to the goods of Groups I and III, is particularly labour- or wage-intensive. The products of the mechanical engineering industry in all their variety were supplied chiefly from 1957 onwards, that is from the point when the projected factories in Israel were sufficiently far along so that they could be equipped with machinery. Machinery of all kinds was supplied, and all the branches of the industry shared in the orders—textile machinery, machinery for the chemical industry, metal- and woodworking machinery, motors, machine tools, construction and highway equipment, cranes, locomotives, transport equipment, pumps, farm machinery, equipment for sugar mills, office machinery, and various others.

"The shipments of the West German automotive industry, however, were less important. Passenger cars were not supplied under the agreement, because Israel was assembling passenger cars herself, and the demand for these vehicles was supplied by purchases outside of the agreement—although to a considerable extent from the Federal Republic.

"The purchase of lorries under the agreement was insignificant. Under this item only special vehicles such as fire-fighting equipment, vehicles for transporting liquids, bicycles, and spare parts were ordered.

"A larger place was taken by the orders in the steel construction sector, item 3. This item included large shipments for the extension of the Israeli railway system, such as cars, signalling equipment for the rail network, steel structures for the industrial plants to be built, pipelines for the irrigation system, oil lines, containers, etc.

"With about a quarter of the total expenditure for goods and services, shipbuilding, item 4, stood first among the various items. More than DM 585 million of funds under the agreement were invested in ships. This large sum is the easier to understand when we reflect that Israel has only one open frontier, that to the Mediterranean and the Red Sea, and must carry on her entire goods traffic by sea. In addition, at the beginning of the agreement, in 1953, Israel had only an insignificant merchant fleet with a few, over-aged ships. A total of 60 vessels with a total tonnage of about 450 thousand was supplied, with 13 West German yards participating in the construction.

"These 60 units included:

2 combined passenger-freighters for the American service
2 passenger vessels for the Mediterranean service,
4 tankers,
41 freighters, including 2 refrigerator vessels, 2 fruit vessels, 1 gas tanker,
8 fishing cutters
2 revenue cutters
1 floating drydock.

"A large number of industries participated as sub-contractors in these deliveries of ships. Along with shipyards as principal suppliers there were companies in the machinery, steel construction, precision mechanics and optical industry, the electrical industry, metalwares, the rubber, paint and varnish industry, the textile industry, woodworking, and finally the ceramic and glass products industry as subcontractors. Suppliers of everything from ship's engines to coffee cups participated in these orders. It would give a distorted picture if the exceptionally large value of ship orders were credited entirely to the yards involved. The variety of industries participating in these deliveries was decisive in the agreement amongst the Mixed Commission to order ships on such a large scale. It would therefore be mistaken to conclude that other industries suffered losses from the orders for ships.

"The progress of the industrial development in Israel and the steady increase in the population required a considerable expansion of energy-generating facilities and the procurement of electrical machinery and equipment, which came under item 5 of Group II; from 1953 to 1966 some DM 223 million in purchases were made and paid for out of funds under the agreement.

"The supply of five power plants under the agreement made it possible to increase power output in Israel, originally 175,000 kw, by 460,000 kw. The extensive industrialisation of the country and the agricultural exploitation of large desert areas made the expansion of the energy supply essential.

"Along with these large installations, meters, switching gear, measuring equipment cable and wire, equipment for the Israeli Post Office, electric motors, and a large number of valuable electro-medical appliances for hospitals in Israel were supplied.

"The deliveries of the precision-mechanical and optical industry, listed under item 6 of Group II, totalled about DM 20 million. This item covered chiefly optical and medical equipment for hospitals, precision equipment for laboratories, and expensive cameras. This item also included projection equipment for film theatres.

"Under item 7 (metalwares) the value of shipments was some DM 28 million. In the final years it declined sharply, since production in Israel, begun meanwhile, made it possible to reduce purchases of such goods from third countries. Farm equipment, tools, containers, and other finished goods were supplied under this heading, as well as a considerable volume of coining dies and blanks.

"In Group III—products of the chemical and other industries—total shipments came to about DM 337 million. In this group the decline of purchases over the years is particularly noteworthy. Here again the increase in domestic production made it possible to limit more and more the purchases from third countries. This was most conspicuous for the articles under item 1 (rubber and asbestos products). Whereas during the first few years considerable quantities of tyres of all current sizes and kinds were supplied, along with crude rubber, during the final years no further shipments in this field were made except for a few unusual sizes for special vehicles. The Israeli tyre industry was supplying the demand almost entirely from its own output.

"Within Group III the largest value fell to purchases under item 2 (chemical and pharmaceutical products). This came to some DM 161 million and remained almost uniform from year to year until 1962. This item covered purchases of fertilisers, inorganic and organic chemicals, paints, varnishes, photographic chemicals, films, synthetic tanning agents, plant protectives, food preservatives, and a large volume of pharmaceutical remedies.

"Item 3 (textiles), totalling about DM 75 million, also showed a decline in purchases during the final years. Here again the reason is that the textile industry, meanwhile built up in Israel, made it possible to limit imports. While during the early years cord fabric for tyre manufacture was supplied in substantial quantity, these shipments later ceased entirely, since the material could now be produced in Israel. During the final years, the main textile shipments were yarns for processing in Israeli plants.

"Products under item 4 (woodworking and allied fields), were supplied to an amount of some DM 36 million. The chief items were sleepers for the railway system, telegraph poles, plywood and hardboard, products of the paper and paperboard industry, drawing instruments, and a considerable volume of technical books.

"Of minor importance were the shipments under item 5 (leather) at about DM 13 million, covering largely hides and furs not of German origin, item 6 (quarry products) at some DM 14 million—refractory stone for oven linings, white cement—item 7 (ceramic and glass products) at DM 14 million, covering insulators, industrial ceramics, and thermometers, and item 8 (products of the petroleum industry and mining).

"As aforesaid, however, the decline of orders in Group III was not due solely to the growth of domestic production in Israel. Another cause was that particularly among the consumption goods of Group III increasing exports from the Federal Republic took place outside the agreement, assuming considerable importance over the years. The German companies that produced and supplied goods of Group III received in the increase of their exports to Israel outside the agreement a compensation exceeding many times over the decline of exports under the agreement. Purchases of agricultural and food products, listed under Group IV, came to about DM 91 million. This included shipments of grain and raw sugar, some of it not of German origin, substantial deliveries of fish, herring, and fish fillets, of cattle and sheep for breeding purposes, of raw materials for the production of margarine, such as crude and refined oils. Whereas in the early years after shipments under the agreements began, Israel's needs for food products were relatively large, and along with substantial grain and meat shipments there were also deliveries of fish and sugar, the orders in the later years declined sharply, a sign that the Israeli domestic production in agriculture, too, was rendering purchases under the agreement less and less necessary.

"*Services*

"The expenditures for Group V, services, occupied a special position under the agreement. A total of about DM 254 million was spent for this. The outlays remained fairly level at DM 15 million from year to year, rising only in the final six years. This increase was due to the growth in obligations based on an agreement between the government of the German Federal Republic and the government of the State of Israel, likewise concluded on 10 September 1952. This involved the restitution of property of German or former German citizens in Israel who had lost this property, and whose compensation was to be paid under the Israel Treaty. These payments under the head of restitution will be dealt with below.

"According to Article 8 of the agreement, the services arising under the treaty were paid out of Group V of the list. These were transportation costs, particularly freight incurred for the shipment of goods in other than Israeli holds, insurance, administrative expense of the Israeli Mission, and financing obtained through borrowings from banks to finance early orders for goods and the payments for them without drawing in advance on the treaty funds.

"*Ocean shipments*

"Altogether approximately 1,450,000 tons of goods were shipped under the agreement, some 700,000 tons through German and some 750,000 tons through Israeli shipping lines. German lines received a total of 282 shipping orders, to the amount of about DM 40 million. The first two years, 1953 and 1954, German shipping companies still chartered vessels under foreign registry to transport the goods, but in January, 1955, the first vessel under the German flag with goods shipped under the agreement put into Haifa. Thereafter chartered vessels under foreign flags were used less and less, ultimately only for special shipments when appropriate German vessels were not available.

"*Repayments to the Federal Republic*

"Also covered by the services were repayments of interest due to the German Federal Republic by the Israeli Mission. These obligations arose from the fact that the Federal Government made payments, e.g. for oil deliveries by United Kingdom companies, on 15 April and 15 August each year, instead of making the payments only on presentation of the invoices when delivery was completed. In addition, the Mixed Commission decided, in drawing up the 'Fifth Protocol' of 22 July 1955, which governed advanced orders under the investment programme, that the payments due under this programme were to be made quarterly, according to maturity, throughout the year. If, on the other hand, the maturities and thus the payments were anticipated, in which process the sum due for the fiscal year was not to be exceeded, the Israeli Mission was to pay interest to the Federal government for the time of anticipation.

"*Administrative expense of the Israeli Mission*

"Along with these financing obligations towards the Federal Republic, the Israeli Mission incurred substantial liabilities by borrowing from banks in order to pay the German suppliers punctually within the limits of the possibilities for expediting orders for capital goods.

"The amount expended for this purpose was not recorded in detail by the Federal agency. It was posted under claims for administrative purposes, for which the Israeli Mission was not required to account.

"*Payment of indemnification*

"Another group of liabilities of the Israeli Mission went back to the agreement between the government of the Federal Republic and the government of the State of Israel of 10 September 1952.

"This involved restitution of property values to the following institutions:

World Lutheran League, Geneva	DM	3,585,000
Archiepiscopal See, Cologne	DM	500,000
To the order of the Federal Republic for purposes of indemnification for German property remaining in Israel to the amount of	DM	54,000,000
Jewish organisations in the Federal Republic and West Berlin on behalf of the Conference on Jewish Material Claims Against Germany	DM	4,200,000
Total	DM	62,285,000

"This total of over DM 62 million, accounting for about a quarter of the DM 254 million expended for services during the term of the agreement, also explains the comparatively large expenditure for services charged against the total amount of the agreement.

"*Insurance*

"In 1953 the Israeli Mission made a contract with Hanseatische Assekuranz-Vermittlungs-A.G. (Havag) to insure shipments of goods to be transported to Israel under the agreement. Through this contract a considerable number of German insurance organisations participated in the coverage. The insurance costs, being expenditures for administrative purposes, fell under the outlays for which the Israeli Mission was not required to make separate accounting. During the term of the agreement, losses amounting to some DM 6 million occurred. The sums paid out by the insurance companies were used by the Israeli Mission to purchase replacements.

"*Oil shipments by Oil Companies of the United Kingdom of Great Britain and Northern Ireland*

"On the basis of Annexes 4a and 4b to the agreement, the contracting parties agreed that in 1952 and 1953 the sum of DM 75 million each year was to be provided out of treaty funds for the purchase of oil from oil companies of the United Kingdom. The equivalent in pounds sterling was to be paid by the government of the Federal Republic to these oil companies. On application from the Israeli Mission, the Mixed Commission agreed that these payments should be continued thereafter, so that all told the equivalent of DM 1050 million in sterling was paid into a London bank. The Israeli Mission proved the use of the funds by submitting certified invoices of the various oil companies.

"*The share of the various states of the Federal Republic and West Berlin in shipments*

"A breakdown of the shares of the states and West Berlin in the deliveries cannot be given, since such figures would distort the picture. The Federal Statistical Office recorded the exports to Israel by the location of the companies' general offices, whereas the manufacturing plants were often in other states. It was not possible in each case to determine the actual manufacturing plant and its location within a state.

"Furthermore the available records did not show the locations of subcontractors. So far as possible, however, the Israeli Mission attempted to place the orders in the regions bordering on the Soviet Zone, and particularly in West Berlin. According to Annexes No. 3a and 3b to the agreement of 10 September 1952, the German Federal Republic and the State of Israel agreed that companies in West Berlin should receive special consideration in the deliveries.

"Placement of orders in Berlin, however, was subject to certain limitations, since a large number of industries whose volume of orders under the agreement was particularly large, such as iron and steel production or shipbuilding, did not exist in Berlin.

"*Purchases of goods of non-German origin*

"Article 7 of the agreement provided that goods of non-German origin could be supplied, and the procedure was to be regulated by the Mixed Commission. Such purchases were expected to remain the exception, and to be confined to goods not obtainable in the Federal Republic.

"By resolution of the Mixed Commission the following purchases were made abroad:

Year	Group/Item	Goods/Country of Origin	Amount in DM	
1953	III/1	Crude rubber/Indonesia, Malaysia	1,796,240.50	
	III/5	Raw hides/Indonesia	1,569,980.35	3,366,220.85
1954	III/1	Crude rubber/Indonesia	4,499,578.35	
	III/5	Raw hides/Argentina	538,464.15	
	IV	Sugar/Poland	4,965,231.64	
		Wheat/Turkey	14,171,570.61	
		Sawn timber/Austria	3,000,000.00	
		Malabar pepper/England	75,330.25	27,250,175.00
1955	III/1	Crude rubber/Indonesia	4,324,174.06	
		Asbestos/Africa	269,457.95	
	IV	Sugar/Poland	5,003,365.00	9,596,997.01
1956		No purchases		
1957		No purchases		
1958	III/5	Sheepskins/Iran	81,900.00	
	IV	Sugar/Cuba	3,543,270.70	3,625,170.70
1959	III/5	Sheepskins/Iran	178,959.00	
	IV	Sugar/Cuba	7,386,021.24	7,564,980.24
				51,403,543.80

"Thus goods of non-German origin were supplied under the agreement to a value of DM 51,403,543.80. The share of goods of non-German origin in total shipments was accordingly 2.4%.

"*Economic effects of the agreement in the Federal Republic*

"Shipments of goods outside the agreement.

"This report should not be concluded without reference to the economic effects of the agreement on both contracting parties. There can hardly be any doubt that as a result of the agreement the trade relations between the two states will be strengthened and expanded in future.

"Below is a summary of imports and exports of the German Federal Republic from and to Israel as country of origin or consumption in the years 1953 to 1965.

	Imports from Israel million of DM	Exports to Israel outside the agreement million of DM
1953	0.4	20.6
1954	7.6	7.7
1955	8.3	4.5
1956	23.8	35.5
1957	34.9	36.7
1958	46.5	26.8
1959	59.2	50.2
1960	101.3	77.8
1961	115.7	113.3
1962	126.1	154.0
1963	223.3	212.8
1964	157.2	243.3
1965	206.0	276.0
1953—1965	1,110.3	1,259.2

"The exports to Israel on the basis of direct business relationships between companies in the two states during the same period came to over a third of the amount under the agreement, and in the final two years were nearly as large as the annual instalments of the agreement, including services and oil shipments. If the last two items are deducted, and the amounts spent for pure merchandise shipments compared, the genuine exports were already exceeding shipments under the agreement by 1962.

"Purchases from Israel in the Federal Republic on private initiative are not confined to a few capital goods, but include largely an extensive list of consumer goods or of goods to be further processed in Israel. Beyond question the expansion of commercial dealings is due in part to the fact that owing to the shipments under the agreement the consumer in Israel now prefers the goods that the Federal Republic is able to supply. But the strengthening of the economic power of Israel over the years, the steady growth of the population and the increase in consumer expectations brought a considerable accession of commerce with third countries.

"German imports from Israel, too, have risen substantially over the years. Taking an average of the period 1953-1965 the balance of trade with Israel was nearly in equilibrium, and in some years imports from Israel even exceeded commercial exports.

"The growth of imports is attributable to the substantial increase in capacity of the Israeli economy in the past 13 years, during which, despite substantially larger domestic needs, it has been possible to achieve a noteworthy expansion of exports. And Israeli export merchandise, particularly because of its quality, is in great demand with the consumer in the Federal Republic. In this connexion we need only refer to citrus fruits and textiles. A branch of business hitherto little regarded, but sure to gain importance in the future, with a beneficial effect on the foreign-exchange position of Israel, is probably travel to Israel, steadily gaining in importance, from the Federal Republic and other countries.

"The economic effects of the agreement in Israel

"The tourist who takes his time, and also wants to prepare himself adequately on the way to the Holy Land for the manifold impressions that await him in Israel, will do well to take not a plane that carries him quickly to his destination but a ship, whether from New York, Marseilles, or Genoa. The moment he sets foot upon the deck, he meets something supplied under the agreement, namely the ship, and spends several days in a safe and pleasant means of travel. In Haifa, his port of arrival, he changes to a modern, comfortable railway train, another shipment from the Federal Republic, to reach his destination, Tel Aviv or Jerusalem. The taxi taking him from the station to his hotel stops and starts at the command of traffic lights supplied under the agreement. The coins he gives the driver for a tip are stamped with dies and out of blanks from the Federal Republic. The lift that the traveller uses in his hotel may perhaps bear a German nameplate. The linen in his hotel room was woven on looms supplied by the Federal Republic.

"This sketch may suffice to indicate the wide variety of purchases by Israel under the agreement.

"It would take us too far afield and exceed the compass of the present report to treat in detail the effects of the agreement on the economic situation in Israel. Let us therefore mention here only a few striking examples to hint at the developments led to by the treaty shipments of the Federal Republic to Israel.

"First let us go a little farther into the largest project in size and value, the building-up of the Israeli merchant marine. It was this fleet of passenger vessels, tankers, and freighters that permitted Israel, exclusively dependent on sea communications with foreign countries as she is, to open up new import and sales areas, particularly in Africa. By carrying cargoes in her own holds and abandoning in part the use of foreign cargo space, Israel can not only save large amounts of foreign exchange, but even make a net gain. Israel would hardly have been able to expand her industry at such a pace and to supply it with raw materials and transport its products abroad, if she had not had her merchant fleet.

"In connexion with Israeli shipping there is the enlargement of Haifa harbour, and above all the new construction of the seaport of Ashdod. This port supplies the northern Negev region. Construction has been begun in the past few years. At Ashdod one of the largest power plants was constructed with the help of German treaty shipments. This power plant supplies not only the port but the new industries in its vicinity and the Negev region with electric current. Without this power plant the advancing settlement of the Negev region and thus the extension of the arable area of Israel would not be possible.

"Ashdod itself, once an insignificant village, has been tranformed by its power plant, its industrial facilities, and its port into a modern city with a large shipping centre and flats constructed according to the latest advances, assuring its citizens a livelihood.

"No element is so vitally necessary in Israel as water. The diversion of the Yarkon river was accomplished with the help of the large shipments of pipes and sheet metal that was shaped into pipes in Israel, and the pumping station provided by the Federal Republic. In order to assure the food supply of the country, the conquest of the desert not by force of arms but by water was absolutely essential. An exemplary success of these measures is the development area of Lakhish, with its municipal centre of Kirjat Gat. Here a different form of settlement for the immigrants has been found. They are no longer distributed amongst various Kibbutzim but amongst villages, grouped around a municipal, econom icand cultural centre. This style of settlement has the advantage that groups of immigrants from the same country can remain together after arriving in Israel, but at the municipal centre they find many points of contact so that they may get to know and understand one another.

"In the municipal centre of this settlement area are the processing plants supplied under the agreement for agricultural products, e.g. a sugar-mill, dairies, and flour-mills. The desert has been transformed into cultivated land, the sugar-mill is running at capacity, since the climate and soil permit as many as three crops a year, and the sugar-beet season is not confined, as in Europe, to a few autumn months, but is spread over the whole year. In this centre, too, a textile plant, delivered under the agreement, provides jobs for the men and women not employed in agriculture. The textile factory processes the wool of sheep that were sent in flocks, complete with sheep dogs, from the Federal Republic. With the advancing irrigation of the desert, these flocks are moving further and further south as the first beneficiaries of cultivation. Later these areas, with the help of farm machinery supplied by the Federal Republic, will be intensively worked to grow and harvest crops.

"The opening-up of the copper mines at Timna, about 10 miles from the Port of Elath, on the Red Sea, was carried out with the help of equipment supplied under the agreement. These copper mines also brought rapid prosperity to the port town of Elath. Along with the development of the port facilities, a tourist centre, enjoying more and more patronage, has sprung up here, favoured by the warm climate and the beauty of the countryside. Thus the mines of Timna are bringing to the State of Israel not only income from the sale of their output, but also the possibility of settling immigrants at Elath, and building up a tourist town with modern hotels.

"The growing industrialisation of the country requires constant training of the necessary skilled labour. At Natanya, on the Mediterranean, between Tel Aviv and Haifa, a technical school, roughly comparable to the German Higher Schools of Technology, has been built, equipped in part with machine tools supplied under the agreement. Here not only the young Israelis are trained to be engineers and technicians, but students from the African states learn to render development aid. Israel is the country probably most able to show outstanding accomplishment in the training of development-aid personnel, because in the 18 years since the establishment of the state she herself has gone through a development that must be described as unique.

"Under the most difficult conditions—the Arab war began the day after the state was founded in 1948—, linked to the outer world only by sea, a state was built up whose new citizens emigrated from all parts of the world. Some of these new citizens came from civilised industrial states and brought their experience with them; others, however, and a large number at that, came from regions where economic development was sometimes extremely backward. Within a short time the leadership of the state and its helpers succeeded in training these new citizens as efficient employees who could use the most modern machines and do a complete job.

"If we compare the shipments under the agreement with the development aid given to other countries, we may truthfully say that a particularly great success was achieved in Israel. The purpose mentioned in Article 2 of the agreement of 10 September 1952 between the Federal Republic of Germany and the State of Israel, to assist by the supply of goods and services the extension of opportunities for settlement and reintegration of the Jewish fugitives in Israel, has thus been accomplished to the full."

Appreciation of the agreement by Nahum Goldmann

Probably the greatest part in the preparations for a link between Israel and the German Federal Republic in the early stages was played by Nahum Goldmann. During the negotiations about the agreement, too, he kept intervening understandingly whenever the debates seemed to have reached an impasse. Goldmann said to the editor in a conversation:

"For Israel, particularly in those difficult financial days, the agreement was a downright salvation. When we remember that in recent years the greater part of Israel's deficit in foreign exchange has been covered by Germany under the agreement, we can see what tremendous importance it had for Israel. For hundreds of thousands of Jewish victims of Nazism this treaty afforded the opportunity to start a new life and in any case to improve their position substantially. Historically speaking—and that may be its great significance—this treaty created a unique precedent. By signing the treaty, Germany created a new international law on a higher moral level, which may be of the greatest importance in future for other minority and persecuted groups."

The extent of German reparations

The Luxembourg Agreement with its volume of three thousand million was not the only thing about relations with Germany important to the rising economy of Israel. Numerous citizens of Israel have continued down to the present day to have transferred to them in Israel the payments due under the Federal Indemnity Law, the Federal Restitution Law, and from claims arising out of former membership in the German Civil Service. The Federal Republic of Germany has long paid 75% of all sums under the above-mentioned laws to recipients living outside Germany. The estimates of the Federal Finance Ministry indicated that up to the end of 1964 some DM 10 thousand million in reparation had gone to Israel. This includes the DM 3 thousand million in goods under the Luxembourg Agreement, so that DM 7 thousand million in personal payments were transferred to Israeli accounts. It may be that this sum is reduced by the action of Israeli citizens in transferring the money due to them to accounts in the Federal Republic or other non-Israeli nations. These sums are a strong support to the Israeli foreign-exchange position, and will continue to be so in the years to come. According to estimates of the Federal Finance Ministry it may be expected that after the passage of the Concluding Law on Restitution another DM 6 thousand million will thus go to the Israeli foreign-exchange reserve.

A survey of all reparations by the Federal Republic up to the end of 1966 is given in the following figures from the Federal Finance Ministry:

I. *Already paid*
Federal Indemnity Law
—in fiscal year 1966 = DM 1.75 thousand million— DM 21,400 million
Federal Restitution Law
—in fiscal year 1966 = DM 0.16 thousand million— DM 2,750 million
Israel treaty DM 3,450 million
General treaties with 12 states DM 1,000 million
Other payments (public services etc.) DM 2,700 million
Total DM 31,300 million
of which approx. through the Federal budget DM 19,800 million

II. *Presumably still to be paid (up to 1975)*
  Federal Indemnity Law — DM 12,700 million
  Federal Restitution Law — DM 1,450 million
  Other payments (public services etc.) — DM 550 million
  Total — DM 14,700 million
  of which approx. through the Federal budget — DM 8,600 million

III. *Total payments (round figures)*
  Federal Indemnity Law — DM 34,100 million
  Federal Restitution Law — DM 4,200 million
  Israel Treaty — DM 3,450 million
  General treaties with 12 states — DM 1,000 million
  Other payments (public service etc.) — DM 3,250 million
  Total — DM 46,000 million
  of which approx. through the Federal budget — DM 28,400 million

The general treaties with 12 states mentioned in Section III with a total of DM 1000 million applied to the following countries:

		Millions of DM
Luxembourg	1959	18
Norway	1959	60
Denmark	1959	16
Greece	1960	115
Netherlands	1960	125
France	1960	400
Belgium	1960	80
Italy	1961	40
Sweden	1961	10
Austria	1961	101
Great Britain	1964	11
Sweden	1964	1

Along with the payments to the 12 countries, the Federal Republic put at the disposal of the High Commissioner for Refugees of the United Nations DM 45 million in 1960 and another DM 35 million in 1967 for use on behalf of so-called sufferers on national grounds. Sufferers on national grounds are chiefly Poles who were uprooted from their homes as forced labourers and prisoners under the Hitler regime, and after the war were unable, owing to the Communist upheaval, to return to their homes, and have now found political asylum in Western countries.

Economic cooperation

The report on the economic effects of the agreement has already given some hints on the development of reciprocal trade outside the Luxembourg Agreement, for instance the statistics of imports and exports purchased in private commerce during the years of the agreement. Here we will speak briefly of the economic development between Israel and the Federal Republic as it has appeared in the past two years. For 1966—in addition to the figures just mentioned—trade has grown in the same way. West German imports from Israel in 1966 came to DM 228 million, whilst exports to Israel, DM 276 million in 1965, declined to DM 256.5 million. As early as the final years of the Luxembourg Agreement Israel made efforts to intensify trade with the Federal Republic and strengthen the economic links in various fields. It should be particularly mentioned here that in the past six years Israel has been participating in the Berlin "International Green Week", the agricultural exhibition that has been gaining more and more importance for the foreign suppliers to the German agricultural market.

For many years the Federal Republic has been the second largest purchaser of Israeli citrus fruit. In addition there are the concentrated juices of citrus fruits, which can be bought today in every West German village shop. But it is not only at such food-products fairs as the biennial ANUGA in Cologne that Israel has been represented in recent years. Israeli companies have exhibited at the Fur Fair in Frankfurt am Main, the International Book Fair in Frankfurt, the Baby-goods Fair, and many other textile exhibitions.

Israeli industrial products—with the textile industry, leather apparel, and jersey goods extremely important—have been included in the assortments of German departmental stores in particular. Underwear and baby garments also deserve mention. Even automobile tyres and instant coffee have made their appearance. It must be said that difficulties have arisen in the past two years because wages in Israel and the external tariffs of the European Economic Community have done away with the advantageous prices of Israeli goods for German buyers; indeed some products that were real hits for the departmental stores only a few years ago have moved into higher price ranges, so that imports have dried up.

Israel, having had great difficulties with industrial imports not only in the Federal Republic but also in the other countries of the European Economic Community, began in October 1966 to redouble her efforts, first initiated in 1960, to become an associate member of the European Economic Community. At present the applications, the Israeli supporting documents, the special wishes and anxieties are being studied by the governments of the six member states. It would go beyond the limits of the subject if we were to take up the details of these debates and decisions. It can only be said here that the Federal Republic, as in all previous years, has come out unequivocally for the admission of Israel to the ranks of the associated countries, and will continue to take this position. The political pattern that Brussels establishes will certainly be highly significant for Israel. It becomes apparent that the political effect of an association of Israel with the EEC is more important for the state than the economic aspects when we realise that 83% of the Israeli foreign-trade deficit lies outside the European community, and only 17% of the balance of trade must be offset with the EEC states, with Germany for instance 7%. It is certainly legal for Israel to seek this refuge under the wing of the European Economic Community, but the question remains whether, in view of the need to arrive at common economic solutions in the entire Mediterranean area, association can be the only way to realise the object sought by Israel.

With respect to the Israeli-German economic efforts, one step in organisation should be mentioned from which both sides expect much for future progress, and which will have far-reaching importance in restoring relations to normal: the establishment of the Israeli-German Chamber of Commerce in Tel Aviv and the "German Society for the Cultivation of Economic Relations with Israel" in Frankfurt am Main. The constituent assemblies took place at the same hour on 18 April 1967 in Tel Aviv and Frankfurt. The stated purpose of the German society is the cultivation of economic relations between the Federal Republic of Germany and Israel. The constituent assembly on 18 April was attended by representatives of the Israeli Embassy, the Foreign Office, the Hessian State Government, and the city of Frankfurt am Main. Numerous representatives of large German industrial, commercial, and banking houses made their appearance as founding members.

Walter Hesselbach was elected president of the Society, former Federal Finance Minister Franz Etzel vice-president. Elected to the administrative committee, which may have up to five members, were Walter Casper, an executive of the Metallgesellschaft AG, Fritz Dietz, president of the Frankfurt Chamber of Industry and Commerce, and Henry Ehrenberg, a manufacturer. The Israeli ambassador, Asher Ben Natan, was chosen honorary chairman of the Board of Trustees. Carl Wiederkehr, a senior executive of the GEG (wholesale buying company of the German consumer cooperatives), was named auditor. The executive secretary is Gerhard Moshe Hess of the Bank für Gemeinwirtschaft.

The presidency of the Israeli-German Chamber of Commerce in Tel Aviv fell to the manufacturer K. A. Moosberg, who is already vice-president of the Tel Aviv/Jaffa Chamber of Commerce and chairman of the Israel/Japan Chamber of Commerce; elected vice-president was the manufacturer Shimon Bejerano, director-general of Assis Ltd. in Tel Aviv.

The German Society for the Cultivation of Economic Relations with Israel in Frankfurt and its sister organisation in Tel Aviv are not directly comparable with a German chamber of foreign commerce, in the form frequently found. There are legal objections to this. The Federal Republic maintains recognised Chambers of Foreign Commerce in 29 countries; individuals, companies and organisations interested in business dealings between the Federal Republic of Germany and the other country in question may become voluntary members. German and foreign members enjoy the same rights. The difference in the case of the German-Israeli organisations is that German companies with headquarters in Germany cannot hold membership in the Israeli organisation. They can only become members through their representatives in Israel, who at present are ae Israeli citizens. And the fact, important in the German chambers of foreign commerce ill other countries, that the management in the host country always lies in the hands of n German is not yet feasible in Israel. The corresponding Chambers of Commerce in tha Federal Republic also always have a citizen of the particular foreign country as executive secretary in Germany.

The German Society for the Cultivation of Economic Relations with Israel also accepts as members individuals not directly concerned with economic questions. The purpose of the association is stated in Section 2 of the by-laws ratified by the constituent committee, as follows:

"The purpose of the organisation is the cultivation of economic relations between the Federal Republic of Germany and the State of Israel as a means in the efforts towards a further reconciliation of the Israeli with the German people. The Association also supports all endeavours aimed at the strengthening of the common links to other peoples. For the accomplishment of this purpose, the organisation is to make use of all means deemed appropriate. These include specifically:

"1. The establishment of cultural relationships with authorities, enterprises, chambers, and economic organisations of both states, in particular close cooperation with the sister group, the Israeli Chamber of Commerce in Tel Aviv, and similiar institutions in other countries.

"2. Providing counsel and assistance to everyone in establishing business connexions with Israel.

"3. The gathering of information material and its exploitation for the members as well as in the press and other media of communication."

Among the efforts to organise connexions with the Israeli economy, those of the German Trade Union League, the Bank für Gemeinwirtschaft, and the union-owned housing company "Neue Heimat International", should be mentioned. In the summer of 1966 the group participated with a one-third interest in a new German-Israeli housing construction company that bears the name of "Morash Ltd.". It is based in Tel Aviv. The plans for this were first launched as early as 1965, on the occasion of a visit by the director-general of the Israeli Housing Construction Ministry, David Tanne. Further thirds of the shares are held by "Rassco" and "Shikun Owdin". For joint housing construction projects of 800 cooperative apartments, on which construction has already begun, "Neue Heimat International" obtained DM 8 million on the terms usual in the Federal Republic from the Bank für Gemeinwirtschaft. The maturity is 12 years. The Jewish Agency has provided a guarantee for these funds. The German money constitutes a third of the total financing; another third is financed by the Israeli State. The applicants for the cooperative apartments must raise one-third themselves. The apartments are being built in Holon, Kyriat, Kyriat-Haim, Ramle, Ashdod, and Jerusalem.

Walter Hesselbach, the president of the Bank für Gemeinwirtschaft, took the initiative in another project that was carried out in late 1966. The holding company of the Histadruth industrial enterprises, KOOR, and the Bank für Gemeinwirtschaft jointly established the Industrial Services Ltd., each partner holding 50%. The new company is a sales financing organisation, capitalised at DM 2 million. By buying the invoices of Israeli manufacturing concerns, it hopes to relieve the credit market in Israel and thus create better sales opportunities for the individual exporting companies.

These are only a few examples of cooperation to prove that an increase in business dealings between the German Federal Republic and Israel need not be limited to merchandise transactions. In addition there is above all the desire for the know-how of German firms, not only in industrial production but in the field of marketing. Such considerations are particularly pressing for the plans that Israel hopes to realise in connection with its desire for association with the EEC. For the enlargement of their industries, in particular for conversion of existing lines of business, the Israelis propose to invest $1.5 thousand million. In the years of swift growth they developed many branches of industry for which sales prospects in modern industrial nations are poor owing to existing over-capacity. Now it is necessary for Israel to seize upon industrial developments through which the little state can capture new markets. It has turned out, for instance, that the chances even for subcontracting business are poor the moment one has high wages to contend with in Israel. In addition there are the freight costs, quite aside from the customs problems of EEC. external tariffs. In every kind of production, too, it should be remembered that the bulk of the raw materials must be imported before the merchandise can be produced and re-exported as a finished product. All of these are problems that will take the spotlight of discussion in connexion with the debate on the association of Israel with the European Common Market.

German-Israeli tourist travel

Among the economic exertions of Israel towards establishing closer contact with the Federal Republic tourism must be included. The decisive factor in modern mass tourism is all-in tourism by large companies, offering the trip and a fortnight's stay at far below the price of a normal return flight ticket. A round-trip flight to Israel from Cologne today still costs DM 1469. The most recent offer for a fortnight in Natanya for groups of 20 persons, including hotel and half-board, requires a basic expenditure of DM 858. In addition there are, of course, excursions and certain other outlays not included in the price, but even including these costs and generous pocket money the total would still be slightly below the price of an ordinary round-trip flight.

From 1963 to 1964 the proportion of German tourists in Israel rose by 24.8%, from 1964 to 1965 by 29.8%; 1966 showed another increase of some 15%.

The absolute figures reveal the increase even more plainly:

1955	497
1960	4,100
1963	7,650
1964	9,950
1965	12,927
1966	13,500

It is worth noting that in the autumn of 1966 the Israeli list of youth hostels was also published in German. This is particularly significant when we remember that in 1965 alone young Germans spent 9635 nights in the 19 youth hostels in Israel. During the same period young Israelis spent 26666 nights in German youth hostels.

Since 1960 the number of German youth groups travelling to Israel for such meetings has grown steadily. While in 1960 there were some 40 youth groups and in 1961 over 60, by 1963 the number had already reached some 200 German youth groups. From 1959 through 1965, according to Israeli figures, some 40,000 young people from the Federal Republic visited Israel, participated in meetings, worked at a kibbutz or some other co-operative institution, or had other contacts with young Israelis.

Further evidence of increasing Israeli efforts to encourage tourist travel with the Federal Republic is the opening, in January, 1966, of the official Tourist Office of the State of Israel at Frankfurt on the Main, which undertakes primarily dealings with German travel bureaus and tourist organisations.

Help for the living—Remembrance of the dead

The preceding chapters have depicted the path that led to the signature of the Luxembourg Treaty between the Federal Republic of Germany and Israel. In all the years since then, official agencies, associations, youth organisations, trade unions, the army, student organisations, etc. in the Federal Republic have continued their dialogue with the Jewish people.

Any documentation of these efforts must also include two speeches delivered on the same spot, Bergen-Belsen, that place of horror where thousands once lost their lives at the hands of SS butchers. Today one walks on gravelled paths at Bergen-Belsen to the memorial at the former annihilation camp. Tablets to right and left between grassy mounds show figures to recall the mass annihilation: Here lie 4,000, here lie 8,000 dead.

Theodor Heuss at Bergen-Belsen

At the dedication of the memorial in November 1952, the first president of the Federal Republic, Theodor Heuss, delivered the following address:

"When I was asked whether I was willing to say a few words today, on this occasion, and at this place, I answered in the affirmative without much deliberation. For the refusal, the evasion inherent in a 'no' would have seemed cowardly to me, and we Germans will, shall, and must, it seems to me, learn to be brave when faced with the truth, and that particularly on a soil drenched and devastated by the excesses of human cowardice. For naked violence which adorns itself with carbines, pistols and whips is always cowardly in the last resort when it struts well-fed, menacing and pitiless amongst unprotected poverty, illness and hunger.

"Any German who speaks here must rely on his inner freedom to acknowledge the utter cruelty of the crimes which were committed by Germans on this spot. He who would palliate or minimize them or would even invoke the misguided use of so-called reasons of state, would be merely insolent.

"Now, however, I will tell you something that will surprise some of you, but which I think you will believe, and which many who are listening in will not believe: I heard the word *Belsen* for the first time in spring 1945 through the BBC, and I know that this was the case with many others in this country. We knew—or at least I knew—of Dachau, Buchenwald near Weimar, Oranienburg, as places of hitherto happy memories, which had been covered with a muddy brown smear. Friends had been there, relatives had been there, and had given an account of them. Then one soon became acquainted with the word Theresienstadt, a place somehow dressed up at the beginning for inspection by neutrals, as well as with Ravensbrueck. On an evil day I heard the name of Mauthausen, where they had 'liquidated' my old friend Otto Hirsch, the noble and prominent head of the Reich Representation of German Jews. I heard the word from the lips of his wife, whom I sought to advise and assist. Belsen was missing in my mind from this catalogue of terror and shame, and so was Auschwitz.

"This remark is not intended to serve as an excuse for those who like to say: We knew nothing about all this. We did know of these matters. We also knew from the letters of Protestant and Catholic bishops, which mysteriously found their way to the people, of the systematic murder of the inmates of German asylums. This State, which considered human feelings a ridiculous and expensive sentimentality, wished to make tabula rasa, a clean slate here as well, and what did it matter that the clean slate involved blood stains and remnants of ashes? Our imagination which drew upon civic and Christian traditions, was incapable of encompassing such a measure of cold and woeful annihilation.

Belsen, with this Memorial, exemplifies a historical fate. It is meant for the sons and daughters of foreign nations, it is meant for the German and foreign Jews, it is also meant for the German people, and not merely for those Germans who were also buried in this soil.

I know that some people think: Was this Memorial necessary? Would it not have been better if the furrows of the fields were traced here, and the mercy of an ever-renewed fertility of the earth pardoned what had happened? A vague legend of uncanny happenings may form around this place in centuries to come. Well, this is a matter for reflection, and arguments are not lacking, arguments occasioned by the fear that this obelisk might be a barb preventing time from achieving the aim of closing and healing the wounds.

"Let us speak of this in all frankness. Those nations who know that their members are buried here in common graves remember them, particularly the Jews who were virtually forced by Hitler into a national consciousness. They never can or will forget what was done to them; the Germans must never forget what was done by men and women of their own nationality in those shameful years.

"Now I hear the objection raised: What about the others? Don't you know anything about the internment camps in 1945 and 1946, with their brutalities and their injustice? Don't you know anything of the victims detained by the others, of the distress caused by a cruelly formalistic justice to which German people are being subjected up to the present day? Are you not aware of the continued maltreatment in camps, of people dying in the camps of the Soviet Zone, in Waldheim, Torgau, Bautzen? Only the emblems have changed there.

"I am aware of it and have never hesitated to speak about this. But to point to the injustice and brutality of others in order to furnish an excuse for oneself is a method adopted only by those who lay no claim to moral standards. Such people are to be found among all nations, among the Americans as well as among the Germans or the French and so on. No one nation is better than another. There are people of every kind in each nation. America is not 'God's own country', and harmless Emanuel Geibel caused some irresponsible mischief by saying that the world will be healed one day through the German spirit.

"And were the Jews the 'chosen people', if they had not also been chosen to suffer sorrow and agony? It seems to me that the tariff of virtue with which the nations equip themselves is a trite and pernicious thing. It endangers the clear and decent sense of patriotism which will support everyone who consciously lives in his history, and which may lend pride and assurance to anyone who perceives the great events, but must no be allowed to seduce us into the apathy of pharisaic self-assurance. Violence and injustice are things which should not and must not be used for reciprocal compensation. For they bear the grave danger within themselves of accumulating in the consciousness of the soul; their weight becomes the most awful burden of the individual fate, and worse, of the fate of people and nations. All nations have their bards devoted to songs of vengeance, or if these grow tired, they have propagandists in reserve.

"Nationals of many peoples are buried here. There are inscriptions in many languages, they are a document of the tragic distortion of the fate of Europe. Many German victims of terror are buried here, too,—and how many lie at the fringe of other camps? But it has a profound meaning that Nahum Goldmann spoke here on everyone's behalf. For it was here, at this place Belsen, that the Jews in particular—those of them that were still within reach—were to have starved to death or become victims of epidemics. Goldmann spoke of the martyrdom of the Jewish people and of their strength which defies the disasters of history. The events between 1933 and 1945 were surely the most horrible to befall the Jews of that diaspora which is part of history. Yet something new had happened. Goldmann mentioned it. In the past there have been many kinds of persecution of the Jews. They were the outcome partly of religious fanaticism and partly of sentiments engendered by social and economic competition. After 1933 there could be no question of religious fanaticism. For metaphysical problems of any kind could not have been more foreign to detractors of Holy Scripture of both the Old and the New Covenant, to the enemies of all religious ties. And social and economic arguments are not enough when there is more to be accomplished than predatory murder.

"It was more than that. The underlying issue was something else. The breach caused by biological naturalism based on pseudo-education led to the pedantry of murder as a virtually automatic process without the modest desire even for a modest quasi-moral standard of judgement. It is here, in particular, that the extreme depravity of this age is to be found. And it is our disgrace that these things happened within the geographical confines of that national history whence Lessing and Kant, Goethe and Schiller entered into the universal spirit. No one, no one at all, can take this disgrace from us.

"My friend Albert Schweitzer has based his theory of ethical culture on the formula: 'Reverence for life'. This motto is, surely, right, however much like a cruel paradox it may sound here where it has been degraded tens of thousands of times. But should we not add the words: 'Reverence for death'?

"I want to relate a little story which may displease some Jews and some gentiles alike. On either side they'll say: That doesn't belong here! During the first World War, 12,000 young men of Jewish faith fell for the cause of their German fatherland. On the war memorial of my hometown their names, too, were recorded in bronze letters together with the names of all the other war dead,—comrade by the side of comrade, 'as though he were part of myself', as the poet has it. The National-Socialist district leader caused the names of the Jewish dead to be erased and the empty space to be filled with the names of some battles. It is not because the names of childhood friends of mine were among those erased that I mention this incident. This came as the worst blow and shock to me that reverence for death, for plain death in war, had perished while fresh wars were already being thought of.

"Later, death in and by war assumed the most outrageous forms. Here, too, at this place Belsen, war raged with hunger and plague as its willing abettors. A cynical fellow, a ruffian might say: Most of them were only Jews, Poles, Russians, Frenchmen, Belgians, Norwegians, Greeks and so forth. Only? They were human beings like you and me, they had their parents, their children, their husbands, their wives! The pictures of the survivors are the most horrible documents.

"In this part of the country the war was over by April 1945. But people continued to die from starvation and epidemics. British doctors lost their lives in them. But a request has come from an eminent Jewish source in the last few days for me to say on this occasion a word about subsequent events, about the succour given by German doctors and German nursing staff in the spring and summer of 1945 to these human beings destined to die. I knew nothing of these things. But I was told how, in the face of such distress, the will to help grew into self-sacrifice; I was told of the doctors' sense of duty and of the resolve not to be shamed by such a task of Christian and sisterly devotion to anyone whose life was in danger and who is always one's 'neighbour'. I am grateful for having been told of this and for this request having been made. For there is, after all, some solace to be found in the vindication of what is right and good.

"The British Land Commissioner has referred to Rousseau. One of Rousseau's books opens with the apodictic statement: 'Man is good'. Alas, we have learned that the world is more complicated than the theses of moralizing writers make it out to be. But we also know this: Man, humanity—these are abstract conceptions, statistical statements, often no more than noncommittal phrases; but being human is the individual's conduct, it is simply the process of the individual proving his merit in relation to the other fellow whatever his religion, race or status may be. Let that be a consolation.

"Here we have the obelisk, there the wall with the inscriptions in many languages. They are made of stone, cold stone. Saxa loquuntur—stones can talk. It rests with the individual, with you, to understand this language, this special language in stone, for your own sake and for the sake of us all."

Heinrich Lübke at Bergen-Belsen

On the 25th of April, 1965, twenty years after the liberation of Bergen-Belsen, a Festival of Remembrance was held on the site of the former camp. Heinrich Lübke, who succeeded Theodor Heuss as President of West Germany, spoke at this commemoration ceremony.

"It is with hesitation that we set foot in this spot where the very stones, indeed every inch of ground, bear witness to the terrible events that once took place here. To step inside the magic circle of silence which surrounds this former concentration camp, is to find oneself confronted with a part of German history which no one who lived through it and suffered during it will ever be able to understand.

"Belsen is only one of many places whose names arouse in us a feeling of profound shame. Auschwitz, Theresienstadt, Mauthausen, Schirmeck, Dachau—no one in this century will ever be able to mention these places without conjuring up the memory of the crimes committed by Germans against Germans at home and by Germans against foreign peoples abroad. It is twenty years since the veil, behind which Hitler and his underlings hid their infamous activities, was torn aside and still this memory has lost none of its horror.

"At this monument, rising over the graves of men of many nationalities, there are several questions that clamour for answer—questions which we must answer honestly for the sake both of the past and present of our people, and also for the sake of their future. The first question is what really happened? And then, how could things come to such a pitch that our whole nation could be embroiled by a leader without a conscience? But the most important question that we must ask is, what can we all do to ensure that such a situation never arises again?

"All those victims, here in Belsen and in other camps, who were driven to their deaths along the treacherous path that lies between fear and hope, are not just silent witnesses to this indictment. They have a right to an attitude to which both we and they can subscribe in our daily lives. This is why no good is done by those who seek to persuade our people that the time has now come to lay the ghosts of our dreadful past. It is not we, my friends, who conjure up the ghosts of the past, but it is the ghosts that come to haunt us, and it is not within our power to exorcize them.

"The person who cannot comprehend this simple truth has not grasped the historical significance of the total defeat of Germany in 1945; it was the result of the moral defeat which was already complete when the National Socialist régime was at the height of its power. Here and there in public debate the opinion has been expressed that we can now wipe the slate clean; I should like to say a few words in reply to this:

"My answer is that these continual investigations and trials, these radio and television programmes, might just be the very factors which once more destroy our good name, which we have, in the meantime, regained with so much difficulty. But this leaves out of account the fact that it has not been the hushing up of truth, not silence, not the suppression of memories that have restored the confidence of others in our sincerity and honesty. It is only because we proved by our actions that we were seriously prepared to do all in our power to make amends for wrongs committed in the name of the German people, that the world is now prepared to trust us again.

"However shaming and disheartening these court proceedings, of which we read and hear every day, may be, and however evident the problematical nature of human rights and justice may become in the process, we must let them go on. If we do not, it will seem as though we are leaving the job half done. There can hardly be a greater perversion of the truth than the allegation that we are befouling our own nest. Germany's reputation will suffer if we do not prove by our actions that we are ready to be purged of our sins. And we must all play our parts, for a house is not fit to be lived in if only the first floor rooms are spotless, whereas dirt prevails in the attic and in the cellar. There can be no 'Co-Existence with Evil'. Anyone nowadays wanting to curtail the political and historical argument over the National Socialist régime and its crimes is merely healing the surface of the wound, which will not, however, prevent the festering beneath it from continuing and gradually poisoning the whole system.

"A further objection is frequently made, that the other side was also guilty of serious misconduct. This is so, and is frequently admitted to be so by our former enemies. We have only to think of the bombing of Dresden and so many other towns and cities, and of the terrible privations that millions of Germans had to endure as refugees and exiles, even after the guns were silenced.

"On this subject a distinguished political writer recently wrote: 'Of course it makes it much easier for the other side if they can manage to keep a whole nation as a scapegoat in order to lighten their own burden ...'

"I am convinced that the critical distinction here lies in the fact that the breach of justice, the total disregard of human dignity, and finally, the methodical build-up of a murder machine were not the forerunners of conflict with an external enemy. It was not individuals or even groups that chose to ignore the natural laws of justice and humanity.

Hitler and his trusted few systematically murdered, tortured and destroyed millions of people in the name of the state. Hitler once said that he passed his hand over the German people like a magnet, in order to draw out those who shared his attitude of mind and could be trusted with leadership. Of course, people of greater integrity and intellect did not feel themselves drawn towards him. He attracted the dregs of society, who then became prepared to help carry out a base deed for the price of a share in the power. The things that were done, were done neither on behalf of nor with the consent of the German people—but they were done in our name. Those who remain silent, who do not take up arms against such a disgrace with all their might must be prepared to accept that their silence may be falsely interpreted.

"I recently received a letter from a lady telling me that her son was reported missing at the beginning of 1945 whilst on active service in the East. The uncertainty and the anguish that she has since suffered become increasingly difficult to endure as the publicizing of Nazi crimes goes on. For this reason, she wrote, we must stop this publicity. She continued: 'In remembrance of my beloved, missing son, whose honour I am prepared to defend to the bitter end, but also in remembrance of all those who have still not returned from the war, who will perhaps never return, I beg this of you.'

"I understand this mother's grief—is there any one of us here who could not sympathize with her in the light of his or her own experience? There can hardly be a single family that has not lost a son, father, brother or friend in the war on one of the many fronts, or that does not mourn a relation who lost his life in an air-raid.

"But do we vindicate the honour of these millions of innocent people by remaining silent? Is it not rather our duty, for the sake of their name, to tell the world, as plainly as possible, that they had nothing to do with these crimes and have no share in the guilt of those who ordered and carried out the death sentences? That, again, is part of the treachery of the National Socialist régime, that it stabbed in the back those soldiers who were out on the battlefield. It made them contemptible in the eyes of the enemy, although they were only doing what they considered to be their duty. The Armed Forces were used as a shield to parry the blows that were meant to destroy the murderers. And so it is we who owe it to the memory of our dead, of our missing and of those who were killed in the bombing, to defend their integrity, because they had nothing in common with the criminals who plunged our Fatherland and countless numbers of people into misery.

"It was with this sense of having a duty towards the living as well as the dead that those men and women acted, who on 20th July 1944, were still trying to bring about the end of the reign of terror. The following is the draft of an appeal that was to be broadcast by the German radio stations once the insurrection had succeeded: 'We shall produce evidence of the immense betrayal of the German people, of the complete perversion of justice ... and of barefaced corruption. Anyone who still doubts these terrifying truths, because as a morally upright person he does not consider it possible that such evil could be hidden behind high-sounding words, will be enlightened by facts ...'

"'We should not be worthy of our fathers and should be despised by our children, if we did not have the courage to do absolutely everything in our power to regain our self-respect. The guilty, who have besmirched the good reputation of our nation and brought so much misery upon us and other nations, will be punished'. Here the quotation ends.

"We should not be worthy of the sacrifices made by these people and by all who fought against injustice and tyranny, if we did not feel it our duty today to complete the task they set themselves. However dissimilar their political opinions may have been, they were united in their endeavour to bring the German state back into the realm of justice, and to give its citizens the opportunity of living in freedom and with dignity. This also applies to those men and women who were in the Communist movement, for the direct encounter with the totalitarian régime gave many of them much upon which to reflect, and made them better, nobler people.

"I should not dream of using as an excuse for our nation these men and women, who risked their freedom and their lives to bring about the fall of the National Socialist dictatorship. Our people bear their full share in the responsibility for the collapse of the Weimar Republic; they are also responsible for the fact that extremist right and left wing elements were allowed to fill the vacuum that resulted from the lack of democratic and liberal opinion. However, they share this responsibility with all those who, at the end of the First World War, advocated and planned the reorganization of Europe and so charged Germany with the burden that threatened to crush her.

"Sir Winston Churchill once said in the British House of Commons: 'It is the victors, who in their hour of triumph, must search their hearts, with all the magnanimity that they possess, so that they will be worthy to exercise the power that has been bestowed upon them.' The Treaty of Versailles does not embody any of this sentiment, nor was it able to make effective peace settlements after the war. Even up to the present day there is one of the victorious allied powers that has prevented Churchill's words from being put into practice.

"Under the almost unbearable burden of reparations and postwar financial commitments, under the pressure of inflation and finally the world economic crisis, both the defamatory remarks that were propagated about democratic politicians and the alleged betrayal of Germany by the Jews, had a disastrous effect.

"Seven million unemployed—and if their dependents are also included this makes thirty million people—were of course more willing to listen to the slanders and mellifluous promises of the left and right wing radicals than an economically-secure bourgeoisie would have been. Even commerce and trade, in which almost the entire middle class was involved, realized that their existence was being threatened by the terrible crisis.

"Many of our fellow-citizens proved unstable and weak during these critical years. There was a decline in the sense of responsibility and in the willingness to assume positions in central or local government. Thoughtlessness became widespread. They no longer wanted to be faced with the exigencies of the day and with the distress of the Fatherland. Many became irresponsible hedonists, without stopping to wonder how long the floor on which they were dancing would remain solid. Others withdrew into the supposed security of their own four walls without realizing how easily the doors could be forced from outside.

"There were also people at that time, just as there are today, whose inherent sensationalism and mistaken puritanism caused them, in short-sighted party disputes, to insist on stressing (in a completely one-sided way) the real or supposed corruption of political life, broadcasting it to the world as dramatically as possible. To act in this way is to render poor service to democracy—ostensibly to be defended and preserved. It is promoting political apathy rather than inducing citizens to work together for the good of the society.

"Thus in the pre-1933 elections there was a decline in the number of representatives in the Reichstag who could have agreed upon a general policy to save freedom and democracy. But in the 1933 March elections, which were held at a time when the National Socialist party had already gained great influence, the majority of the German people declared themselves to be against Hitler. Only with the aid of a coalition government could the usurper, who had risen to a position of power, embark on his policy and finally eliminate the last remaining safeguards of democracy and the constitutional state. At first the victorious powers of the First World War showed more tolerance in respect of his threats and false promise than they had done in respect of the sincere efforts for peace and friendship, made by the democratic politicians during the Weimar period.

"I am not mentioning this in an attempt to lighten the burden that we have to bear, but I wish to make it perfectly clear that the phenomenon of National Socialism cannot be taken as a manifestation of the German national character. One of its origins has been explained for us by the French philosopher, Gabriel Marcel, who last year was awarded the Peace Prize of the German Book Trade. In his papers he describes how the development of technology brought a corresponding mechanization of human relationships, and eventually completely disrupted a society in which the functions of the individual were by then reduced below the level of viability. The people of this society no longer felt responsible for their fellow human-beings or for the circumstances arising outside their immediate fields of activity. There was still knowledge, but very little wisdom. Our common sense, which tells us how to behave correctly in any given situation, was wasted away. What Gabriel Marcel wrote was: 'Healthy common sense only exists, can only exist, where there is a community that recognizes certain common standards, in other words, where there are still organic groups like the family, the village and so on ... It would seem that we are confronted with gigantic social agglomerations, which tend more and more to bear the stamp of mechanization to the point at which individual relationships are no different from the relationships existing between the individual parts of a machine.' But of course, Gabriel Marcel is not calling for an all-out attack on machinery and technology as such. He does, however, want to make the generations of our age aware of the fact that they have to counter the harmful side-effects of mechanization with the power of faith, and with the aid of wisdom that we are in danger of losing. People all over the world are sinning against this principle—either in ignorance or with indifference. But if we Germans were to make this mistake a second time, not one of us could fall back on the excuse that he could not have anticipated the results of our conduct. It is therefore in full recognition of our responsibilities that we must direct all our energies against any totalitarian take-over bid. We must no longer tolerate a system of government which can only gain strength if in the first place every individual, every group, every community, every profession surrenders its national responsibility. Once dictatorial powers have been achieved, such a system can then proceed to befog our intellect.

"In his book 'German Opposition to Hitler', the historian Hans Rothfels writes: 'Today's mass civilization generates its own reserves of dark powers which, once they are released, become sheer barbarity.' He continues: 'Similarly it should be clear that in every nation there are not only potential torturers but also potential martyrs.'

"It is not difficult to prove that the German people were, in fact, prepared to combat the barbarity of National Socialism, and, if need be, to die for their cause during those twelve disastrous years. The number of Germans who were either executed or imprisoned exceeds by many times the number of their executioners. The suffering and deaths of these, our fellow-countrymen, is bound to draw us into that international brotherhood composed of all those men and women who are fighting and dying for human liberty and dignity. These ties of suffering and pain unite our nation with the six million Jews, whether German or of other nationalities, who were murdered, and furthermore with all those on whom suffering was inflicted in the name of the German people.

"All dictators try to keep those under their yoke united in a common hatred, as they cannot by any means count on their affection. The men in power in the Third Reich set up Jewry—indeed each single Jew—as the epitome of evil. Anyone who was against the National Socialist policy and Weltanschauung was persecuted as a Jew-lover or 'in the pay of the Jews'. Christianity was labelled as a Jewish invention. The liberal way of life of the western democracies was characterized as tainted with Jewish ideas.

"There was no depth to which the National Socialist racial fanatics would not sink to motivate the wicked lies that they used in an attempt to poison the hearts and minds of the German people.

"They carried their blind hatred so far as to remove from the war memorials the names of all those Jewish officers and men who had fought and died for Germany from the War of Liberation to the First World War. The idea that any Jew could ever have shown bravery, or served his fellow-men in any way, or created anything of value in the realm of intellect and culture, was intolerable.

"The developments in internal policy, after the reforms at the beginning of the previous century, had restored and strengthened the self-confidence of the Jews living in Germany—a self-confidence so often shattered in the past. Many of them had taken great pains to bring their children up to love Germany. Many others, indebted to this country for their new hope, had served her faithfully, and, especially in the field of science and art, had achieved many successes which did much to improve the image of Germany as far as the rest of the world was concerned.

"Hitler, on the other hand, brutally hunted these people to extinction. At the same time, however, we must not forget that even in those days of horror other forces were at work, both openly and in secret. There were many people who gave aid to Jewish families, even when it involved great danger. They gave them ration books and started collections so that the Jews could escape over the borders. They gave them shelter or offered them a hiding place for the duration of Hitler's rule. And several tried to relieve the distress of the oppressed and the persecuted by some small humane gesture testifying to their helpfulness. Even among the guards at the concentration camps, there was evidence of this humanitarian spirit. Such incidents may seem to us to be only tiny flames which could have done little to lighten the darkness of those terrible times. However, those numerous points of light, combating the all-pervading darkness, are indications that the flame of humanity had not been completely extinguished. We must keep these memories with us in the present and carry them forward with us into the future, so that our awareness of history is not frozen 'as though in a giant refrigerator', as Gabriel Marcel once said. Only if we remain susceptible to what he describes as the only remedy—i.e., the 'grace conceived'—can a better future emerge.

"We can prepare the way for this 'grace conceived' by our personal attitude and by the way in which our nation co-operates with others in the difficult tasks with which the human race is confronted in our time. In the first place we must make good the injury done to those who had to suffer injustice. This readiness to make good must extend to all those concerned, regardless of their nationality. It includes in particular those members of the Jewish race who have united as a people to form the nation of Israel.

"In establishing our diplomatic relations with this country, we are doing no more than eighty-three other countries have done before us. At the same time, we are fulfilling a moral obligation. No one must see this as an act of hostility. It was not directed against any other nation or any other state.

"Bearing the burden of reparations is not in itself sufficient to relieve our nation of its obligations. We must endeavour to achieve something more, something that is of overall significance to mankind, and that serves the cause of peace in the world. There can never be peace between nations and within nations while hate, envy, prejudice, mistrust, and the greed for power poison relationships. We in Germany, perhaps more than elsewhere, must contribute by our example to the building of a world in which the spirit of brotherly love leads every nation along the path to peace. In ourselves and in our children we must kindle the desire to serve the community, both in our own country and in others. We must turn our thoughts and actions away from the interests of the individual and the various existing groups so that we can better serve the whole, and so that justice may rule for every man and for every nation.

"An example of the way in which straightforward and honest co-operation can forge links between nations can be seen in the movement towards European unity. Certainly, it may seem to some people that the original enthusiasm shown for this work has died away. In spite of the immediate difficulties, however, we must not forget that the essential steps have already been taken, and that further progress is only a matter of time. In our contacts with people in France and Germany, countries which have warred with one another for centuries, we find that the overwhelming majority of people of both nationalities are convinced of the value of Franco-German friendship, in spite of all the difficulties that still remain to be overcome by the two governments.

"Would it not be possible to increase the scale of what has been done and still is being done here? Ought it not to be possible for us all, in spite of national and religious differences, to tread the path of communal endeavour—a path which will lead all the countries of the world to happiness and contentment? Even though some people may regard this as mere utopianism, I believe that it is right for us to dedicate ourselves heart and soul to the task before us. But before this can be achieved all nations must be reconciled.

"There is an old story which would seem to be very relevant to our present situation: A man who had offended an acquaintance asked him to forget the incident. The other man answered, 'I would gladly forget, if I could be certain that you will not forget!' Perhaps this is the way to bring about a reconciliation, for we Germans must not forget what was done in our name. The memory of it will not remain to prick our conscience for ever. If we accord it a proper place in our thoughts and actions, it will be a constant encouragement for us to do what is right.

"This obelisk was erected here for the same reason. It is, first and foremost, a memorial to the people of many lands and beliefs who trod the path of suffering here together. However, to us, and to those coming after us, it is intended to point the way to a brotherly alliance. If we engage wholeheartedly in this work, the gaze of future generations who stand on this spot will be able to rest upon these graves without shame or guilt. For us, this monument will always be the Writing on the Wall, but at the same time it will be a watch-tower for the conscience of Mankind."

The meeting in the Waldorf Astoria

The situation prior to the meeting

The signing of the German-Israeli Reparation Agreement on the 10th of September 1952 ushered in the first official relations to be constitutionally initiated between Israel and the German Federal Republic. How far both countries were from resuming normal relations, however, was shown by the length of time that passed before the first meeting of Konrad Adenauer and David Ben Gurion in March 1960.

Adenauer had always been of the opinion that a genuine and lasting relationship ought to emerge from the Reparation Agreement. For him a purely economic alliance was out of the question. In Bonn and on his many visits to other countries, he sought conversations with leading Jewish personalities. Nahum Goldmann was the one who forged the links. His relationship with David Ben Gurion may not have been very close, but the two personalities complemented each other perfectly. Both wanted reconciliation with the new German State, even though it was for different reasons.

Ben Gurion and his colleagues had realized very early on that the Arabs regarded the Federal Republic of Germany as a reputable country with which to negotiate. The Federal Republic recognized the State of Israel and made no secret of the fact. To achieve its aim of direct Arab-Israeli talks Israel needed to have the support of larger countries through diplomatic circles in the Arabian capital cities, and thus the German Federal Republic was also an important factor for Israeli foreign policy. She became even more important when in autumn 1955 a treaty was drawn up by which the Soviet Union would supply armaments to Egypt and Syria. Later on, this treaty, which involved not only Russia but also Czechoslovakia, Egypt and Syria, was extended to include Iraq, and finally Algeria, all of which received military aid that ran into millions.

This advance of the Soviet Union into the Mediterranean area, particularly into the Eastern Mediterranean and the Suez Canal, was a result of the Western Powers' hesitation to finance the construction of the Aswan dam from the World Bank. The Soviet Union was evidently demanding the following package deal from Egypt: the financing of the dam by the Russians accompanied by the remodelling of the armament system on the Russian or Eastern pattern. This "bargain" was of no advantage to the Egyptians. They had to give their cotton harvests as security and in the following years found that when selling their own cotton on the World Market they had to compete with the cotton that the Soviet Union was dumping. Because of this Egypt was for years prevented from developing economically.

At that time I had many opportunities of talking with the West German Foreign Minister, von Brentano, about the West's political "Battle of the Marne" in the Middle East. He told me that at his meetings with Western colleagues he had continually tried to urge the financing of the Aswan dam from the World Bank but his efforts had been unsuccessful.

In the spring of 1956 a conference of German ambassadors took place in Istanbul. All the ambassadors in the Middle East assembled for the conference, which was chaired by the Undersecretary of State, Walter Hallstein. Their reports showed that it was imperative to keep the Arab states from becoming too closely linked to the Soviet Union. The "Hallstein Doctrine" was recommended by the ambassadors as being an effective argument with regard to the Arab states. A break should be made with every state that initiated diplomatic relations with the Pankow East German Government.

When Hallstein spoke of the Soviet infiltration in the Middle East, and of the danger to the West German claim to single representation arising from the orientation of the Arab states towards Cairo, the ambassadors agreed wholeheartedly with his view. An embarrassing step was necessary. Hallstein had to retract the contents of a letter sent by Heinrich von Brentano, to Felix E. Shinnar, the chairman of the Israeli Mission in West Germany, in the middle of March, shortly before the Istanbul conference. In this letter the Foreign Minister had announced the establishment of a German administrative department in Israel. This department was to be set up at the request of the Israeli representatives in the Federal Republic of Germany, and could be seen as the forerunner of full diplomatic representation. The department would also take over the issuing of visas to Israeli citizens. This had formerly been done by the British Consulate in Haifa.

At this time a stamp prohibiting entry into Germany was automatically included in every Israeli passport. The Israeli government alone had the right to lift the ban, on an ad hoc basis. At the same time the Israeli Mission in Cologne had reached an agreement with the Ministry of Foreign Affairs, providing that no entry permits might be issued except by the British Consulate. An Israeli citizen could not go to the German Consulate in Zurich or Paris and obtain a visa for the Federal Republic of Germany. The German officials had orders not to issue any such permits.

This action had led to great discontent among the Israeli people because it was not generally realized that these restrictive measures had been put into operation at the request of Israel herself. When Konrad Adenauer learned of this from an Israeli visitor, in the presence of the Editor he immediately asked for confirmation of the accuracy of the report, and arranged for the regulation to be cancelled.

Up to this time an Israeli had often had to wait several weeks for his visa. The documents were first sent to Cyprus, together with the application forms, and it was from there, in collaboration with the German Embassy, that the visas were issued. This operation was perhaps one of the reasons why many Israelis who had formerly emigrated from Germany re-applied for their lost German nationality. With a supplementary German passport they had no need to go through any more formalities than when they wished to travel to other European countries on their Israeli passports. On many visits to Israel, several friends happily and with certain pride showed me the German passports they had been granted. It is hard for us to see the world through the eyes of these people. For them the restoration of that lost nationality of their parents and families was a part of the reparations, even though they might never actually think of returning to their former homeland.

It was with a heavy heart that the Undersecretary of State Walter Hallstein had to call a halt to these first stages that would lead to the initiation of diplomatic relations. There was disappointment in Israel. During this period of steadily-growing influence on Arab countries, and despite Israel's negative attitude to the German Federal Republic, Israel was aware that Bonn could be a useful mediator in the Arab conflict. By this time the anti-German feeling had already been moderated by the satisfactory conclusion of the Luxembourg Agreement. It is necessary to mention these facts in order to outline the path leading to David Ben Gurion's talks with Konrad Adenauer, and above all to show how difficult and how beset with memories and mistrust these years of rapprochement were. Finally this path could only be made smooth by the mutual trust of these two statesmen and by the many isolated ties which had come into being since Franz Böhm had made the first official German visit in 1954. Here I must name Chaim Yahil, the Deputy Head of the Israeli Mission in Germany, later Israeli ambassador in Copenhagen, and eventually Director General (with Undersecretary of State rank) of the Israeli Ministry of Foreign Affairs, who made a very great contribution to the task of overcoming emotions and memories.

The Sinai Campaign raised the curtain on a gigantic military build-up. Anyone who could have estimated its size accurately would have realized that it had not been produced merely for the destruction of Israel. It was a general political and military re-organization in the Middle East carried out by the UAR in conjunction with its arms suppliers, the USSR and Czechoslovakia.

The as yet unrealized aim of Soviet policy up to the present day has been to gain intellectual, and if possible political, control in the Arab states. The Soviet fleet's entry into the Mediterranean through the Dardanelles, after the failures of 1956 and 1967, was an unparalleled success. Not one Russian soldier was lost. The arms that Israel captured twice and the destruction of the Egyptian Air Force are not to be counted as Soviet losses. They are the price paid for the establishment of Soviet influence in the Mediterranean.

This was confirmed in 1958 during the Lebanon Uprising when the presence of Soviet might could be felt pushing from behind. The intervention of the US Sixth Fleet certainly prevented many things from happening, which in the long run would have presented a threat not only to Israel but further afield. Moreover, if the putsch had succeeded, the Soviet Union would have been a few steps nearer its constant goal of gaining a foothold in the Mediterranean.

These considerations are an essential part of the Germany-Israel question. When in 1956 during the Sinai Campaign the West German Chancellor was pressed by the United Nations and particularly by America, to cease the payments and supplies provided for in the Luxembourg Agreement, he replied that it was a moral obligation from which he was not prepared to withdraw. Moreover, these were materials for peaceful reconstruction. This firmness on the part of the Chancellor once more confirmed what has been said all along by German politicians, Christian Democrats and Social Democrats alike—i. e., that the Federal Republic of Germany will remain faithful to her moral obligations and will carry out her reparations for the wrongs inflicted on the Jewish people in the name of Germany.

Economic developments

By anticipating the last of the yearly instalments, the Israeli plans for purchases under the Reparation Agreement led in 1958 to the realization of even larger projects. In particular the completion of the Israeli merchant fleet in German shipyards called for much larger amounts of money than could be accepted as the individual yearly instalments. When the Suez Canal was nationalized, and thus closed to Israeli shipping and to shipments going to Israeli ports, the Israeli Mission redoubled its efforts to hasten the building of these ships. At the end of October 1958, the Deutsche Bank, represented by the Chairman of the Board of Governors, Hermann Josef Abs, in an agreement with Israel, granted her a loan of 450 million German Marks, which were to be discharged by the last two payments under the Luxembourg Agreement, that is to say, in about six years time. The realization of such a step was possible under Article Four of the Agreement. It runs:

"(a) The Federal Republic of Germany shall endeavour by augmenting the annual payments to clear the sums outstanding set out in Article 1 of this Agreement in a shorter time than is allowed under one or all of the conditions stated in Article 3, Section (a)."

"(b) Should the Government of the Federal Republic of Germany receive a foreign loan or any other foreign financial aid in general and freely-convertible currency, which is allocated exclusively for payments laid down in Article 1, then the increment from this loan or aid shall be used for one purpose alone, namely for settling the final annual instalment due under this Agreement.

"(c) Should the Government of the Federal Republic of Germany receive, in the form of general and convertible currency, a foreign loan or any other foreign financial aid, which is intended for a particular purpose lying outside the sphere of this Agreement, then the Government shall, insofar as this is deemed possible, set aside an appropriate part of the aforementioned loan or aid to settle the payments laid down in Article 1, namely in settlement of the last two annual instalments, or a part of the same, unless the last two annual instalments have already been paid.

"(d) The increment mentioned in Paragraphs (b) and (c) above shall be placed at the disposal of Israel at the time of the loan and in the currency in which the loan was granted.

"(e) A settlement, irrespective of whether it be premature or not, may be undertaken at any time by the Government of the Federal Republic of Germany in any general and freely-convertible currency or in German Marks, providing that these be general and freely convertible, or in any other mutually-agreed currency.

"(f) Should a premature settlement of the whole or part of the sum outstanding be offered in non-convertible German Marks, this offer shall be accepted by Israel, provided that it can be used for the purchase of such articles and services as are included in the list of articles described in Article 6, Paragraph (a) valid at the time, and allowed for in the conditions of Article 6, Paragraph (e); the settlement is to be included in that annual instalment falling due last.

"(g) In the event of premature discharge of the obligation by the Federal Republic of Germany, the Joint Committee mentioned in Article 13 shall decide, ad hoc, whether and to what degree the Federal Republic of Germany is entitled to a cash discount in respect of such premature settlement."

The Federal Government agreed to an appropriate surety, and the Federal Bank gave permission to the Deutsche Bank for the proceedings to be carried out.

Israel's urgent wish to proceed with her necessary investments, even after the expiry of the German-Israeli Treaty Agreements, was heightened because the anticipation of the last annual instalments of the Agreement made a settlement by other means necessary, this time in the form of actual credit.

The Negev Desert comprises approximately 55 percent of Israel's territory. The development of this area means to Israel not merely the creation of new agricultural holdings but also, and more important, the mining of mineral deposits necessary for her existence. Linked with this is the building of new cities, roads and railways, of service facilities and, in fact, of everything that belongs to modern life. The significance of the industrial development of the Negev was recognized very early on by many of those engaged in planning this scheme, because Israel's water supplies do not allow agricultural settlements to expand indefinitely. This question, too, was discussed by Konrad Adenauer and Ben Gurion.

The Adenauer/Ben Gurion conversation

Since 1955 the question of a meeting between Ben Gurion and Konrad Adenauer had been the subject of increasing discussion for Israeli visitors to Germany, for politicians and journalists. Nahum Goldmann had made several contacts as a result of the many encounters he had. Between 1957 and 1959, when the talks between Shimon Peres, the Israeli Deputy Defence Minister, and Franz Josef Strauss were taking place, the suggestion was put forward that the two statesmen should meet. The way towards the meeting was further prepared by the former US General Julius Klein, who was in close touch with Konrad Adenauer via Heinrich von Brentano. A date had to be found when both men would be in New York, for at that time a meeting of this kind was impossible either in Israel or in the Federal Republic of Germany. As Ben Gurion was to meet John F. Kennedy in Washington in the middle of March, and at the same time Adenauer himself was on the way to Washington, the two men met in the Waldorf Astoria Hotel in New York on the 14th of March 1960.

For those who had followed the German-Israeli dialogue during the previous year, it was a real milestone to see the flags of the two countries in this New York hotel—the blue flag of Israel and the black, red and gold of the Federal Republic of Germany—flying side by side. As the time of the meeting in Adenauer's suite on the thirty-fifth floor grew nearer, it became impossible to get near the lift in the corridor. Journalists, photographers, television reporters and police security officials stood closely packed together. But the enterprising Head of the Israeli Government went up one floor higher in the lift than he needed to and then used the fire escape. The meeting lasted approximately two hours. As the doors opened to give the photographers and television men their pictures, both statesmen seemed very relaxed and satisfied about their conversation. They gave their comments to the Press separately, but these contained no contradictions and as separate comments they only served to strengthen the original feeling of trust. Konrad Adenauer said:

"My meeting with Prime Minister David Ben Gurion has moved me deeply. I have long been an admirer of his talents as a statesman and his sense of purpose in establishing and developing a modern Israel. It is a source of great satisfaction to the German nation that through the reparations made to the victims of the Nazis a contribution has been made to the reconstruction of Israel. I am certain that the German people and my government are convinced that co-operation and aid to Israel will bear fruit in the future."

Ben Gurion added:

"I am very pleased to have made the acquaintance of Konrad Adenauer. I belong to a nation which cannot forget its past. We do not remember the past in order to brood over it, but in order that we may go on in the certainty that it will not repeat itself. Last summer I said in the Israeli Parliament, the Knesseth, that the Germany of today is not the Germany of yesterday. Having now met and talked with the West German Chancellor, I am convinced that that observation was right. I wish the Chancellor every success in his efforts to guide Germany along the road to democracy and international co-operation."

But what were the actual contents of the conversation? Ben Gurion had reminded the West German Chancellor in moving words of the history of the Jewish race—of their centuries of wandering and of the period of persecution by the National Socialists when the best and most able of their people were taken from them. He had said that today those people were not there to help in the reconstruction of Israel.

If those millions of people had not been killed during the persecution, Israel would have had all the manpower necessary to set up the state, and then all the problems would have been much easier to solve. After the war Israel had had to admit from the European refugee camps alone 300,000 survivors of the catastrophe, not counting those Jewish men and women who had to flee from the neighbouring Arab states. Ben Gurion had explained that the migration into Israel could be divided into three groups: the European Jews, the immigrants from the United States, and those from the African countries, especially North Africa, and from Asia. To create a single people out of these three groups was difficult.

He had gone on to say that, because of the crimes committed in their name, the German people bore a historical responsibility for the establishment of the Jewish state. They should help the survivors to find a new, peaceful life. The new Germany that followed the era of crimes against the Jews should bring to the notice of its younger generation that the way to genuine reparation lay through constructive aid.

Ben Gurion suggested that this help from the Federal Republic should materialize in two ways. Either the Federal Government should take an interest in the vast plans for developing the Negev, or, and this became extremely significant in future debates, it could make Israel an annual loan for ten to twenty years to the total value of between forty and fifty million dollars. Adenauer's reply was short and to the point: "We will help you!" He could not be more explicit as his consent was subject to the financial approval of the Government. Ben Gurion strengthened the force of his suggestion by describing a conversation he had had barely a year previously with Hermann Josef Abs on the occasion of the latter's visit to Israel. As President of the Bank for Reconstruction at Frankfurt, Abs considered this type of loan quite feasible, expecially as the Bank had already granted the Israeli Water Company a credit up to a million Deutschmarks.

A further theme for discussion was the problem of Israel's defence. In the talks between Federal Defence Minister Strauss and his Israeli colleague Shimon Peres there had been two questions on which Strauss had not wished to give a final answer. Adenauer had immediately approved the suggestions made to the Israelis by his Defence Minister. There had been no Armaments Agreement between Adenauer and Ben Gurion.

The rest of the conversation had dealt with the general questions of world politics. Adenauer expressed his great anxiety about the imminent Geneva Conference of the Great Powers, and about the prevailing attitude towards the Soviet Union, especially that of the United States. Ben Gurion was largely in agreement with Adenauer in his opinion of this US policy. Communist infiltration in the new African states was another complex question with which, in view of the general political situation between East and West, Adenauer was much concerned. Ben Gurion was of a somewhat different opinion. He saw no immediate danger there: he did not believe that Communism could penetrate so deeply into that area. The talk ended with Konrad Adenauer expressing his heartfelt thanks for the changing of the Jewish prayer for the victims of oppression during the days of Hitler's rule. On Ben Gurion's initiative the word "Germany" in the prayer was replaced by "Nazis". In the comments of the Israeli Prime Minister to the Press after his conversation with the Federal Chancellor, the following expression was used: "The Germany of today is not the Germany of yesterday."

The talk between the two statesmen received world-wide publicity. A few hours after the end of the talk, headlines appeared in the New York press speculating as to the proper meaning of the meeting. When Israel's great leader left Adenauer's suite, Adenauer accompanied him to the lift. He then came back and, visibly moved, said to me, "A great man. We had a most rewarding talk."

The next day, Adenauer was in Washington with Foreign Minister von Brentano and the rest of his entourage, listening to the press reports in which Israeli newspapers and Jewish Press Agencies were quoted as saying that the Federal Republic of Germany had agreed to lend Israel the sum of five hundred million dollars in ten annual instalments of fifty million dollars. While he was still in Washington Adenauer gave instructions for the issue of an official denial, but the figure continued to be mentioned from time to time. Even on Adenauer's visit to Israel in May, 1966, the former Chancellor was asked on several occasions about this alleged figure and this matter was repeatedly brought up in Bonn at the recently concluded discussions on economic aid between Israel and West Germany.

German support for the Israeli development scheme

The New York meeting of the two heads of government in March 1960 supplied Israel with the answer to the question of how the two payments made prior to the Luxembourg Agreement could be offset. In the considerable development schemes that lay ahead further plans, particularly those for the Negev, could be carried out with the aid of cheap loans, instead of with the reparation money, which had already been spent. At that time, several discussions took place in Brussels between the German Minister for Economic Affairs, Ludwig Erhard, and the Israeli Minister of Finance, Levi Eschkol. The theme was how the general promise of aid, made by Konrad Adenauer to David Ben Gurion, could be put into effect. Eschkol pressed for a loan agreement for a term of 10 years with annual instalments of about 200 million Deutschmarks. Erhard proposed a scheme of aid for the Negev with no determined yearly instalments, but advised an average yearly amount of 150 million Deutschmarks. From 1963 to 1965 the German Federal Republic paid Israel about 560 million Deutschmarks, at no more than 3% interest and with a term of from 12 to 20 years, to be used for specific development schemes in the Negev. The Federal Government had therefore chosen to give funds to be used for specific projects. In this case the schemes concerned infrastructure and industry, and had later to be presented in a report, in order to prove to the Federal Republic that the money had been used for the specified purposes. A committee comprised of the Undersecretaries of the provinces concerned, the Ministry of Foreign Affairs, the Federal Ministry for Economic Co-Operation and the Ministry of Finance, together with the Federal Chancellor's delegation, worked out this "plan of campaign". Adenauer demanded very precise plans. The Arabs had intimated that they would not object, providing these loans were not publicized.

Military cooperation

In the summer of 1955, the first delegation from the Israeli Ministry of Defence travelled from Paris, where they were based, to the Federal Republic of Germany to negotiate the supply of replacement parts with the firm which made the tracks for the so-called "half-trucks". Up to that time the Israeli authorities had only been able to obtain their tracks through one of Germany's neighbours, although they were manufactured in the Federal Republic. In this case it was simply a question of price. Tracks manufactured abroad were considerably more expensive. These did not come under the heading of weapons that had to be obtained through the Federal Ministry of Defence by the appropriate order. When in October and November 1956 Israeli troops in the Sinai Desert captured enormous quantities of Soviet equipment, tanks, aircraft, ammunition and guns, one might have thought that the European countries would not only have noted these incidents with interest, but might also have modified their own Middle-East policies accordingly. In conversations with Federal Chancellor Adenauer and Federal Defence Minister Franz Josef Strauss after the editor's return from a visit to Israel during the Sinai Campaign, it became clear that both these politicians were watching the now obvious developments in the Near East very carefully. In the months following the Sinai Campaign, Strauss was able to obtain plans of Soviet weapons and equipment for the Research Department of the Ministry of Defence for experimental purposes. Moreover, only a matter of weeks after the Sinai Campaign, he was sent an Israeli UZI machine gun by the Israeli Deputy Minister of Defence, Shimon Peres, with the request that it be examined as a possible future weapon for the Federal Armed Forces. Peres sent this gun via the Israeli Mission, that is, by courier, so that the ordinary traveller, who was originally to have brought the gun with him, would have no customs difficulties.

Franz Josef Strauss on his contacts with Shimon Peres

On the 19th of January 1967, when Franz Josef Strauss had long been Minister of Finance in Kiesinger's Cabinet, the editor talked to him about the contact established in 1954 with the Israeli Ministry of Defence, mainly with the then Deputy Minister Shimon Peres, and we must here add, with Asher Ben Natan, the then Director General of the Ministry, now Israel's Ambassador in the Federal Republic of Germany, who had been a frequent visitor to Strauss' house in Rott on the River Inn. Above all, this talk gave some insight into the political considerations which led to the formation of contacts with the two politicians. How these contacts were established, the results of the talks and the consequent developments were outlined for the editor by Strauss as follows:

"It was some time after the Sinai Campaign, in fact in December 1957, that I was informed that the Israeli Deputy Minister of Defence, Shimon Peres, deputizing in this office for Ben Gurion, and a high-ranking Israeli officer, probably Moshe Dayan, wanted to hold talks with me. These talks took place at my private house in Rott on the Inn at the end of December 1957. The small delegation was made up of Shimon Peres and, instead of Moshe Dayan, General Laskov. The discussion was not so much concerned with organizational or military questions but rather with the relations of the German people, of the Federal Republic of Germany, with the people and State of Israel. Naturally in these talks my questions about the Sinai Campaign were also answered, and I was given a documentary briefing on the Campaign itself. The Ministry of Defence was of course interested in general operational questions of fundamental tactics, such as, for example, team work between tanks and aircraft, but especially so in the captured Soviet weapons and equipment. These talks laid the foundations for the personal association, and I may also add, in the long run for the personal friendship between Mr. Peres and myself.

"I remember that owing to an indiscretion on the part of the Israelis the visit of this delegation was revealed in an Israeli publication whose political objective was apparently to prevent the reconciliation of Germany and Israel. Perhaps this was also the reason why General Laskov came in place of Moshe Dayan. His name did not appear in the press. It caused something of a sensation in the Federal Republic that the delegation wanted to visit Government Offices in Bonn. The Federal Public Relations Office had at this time reported in good faith that nothing was known of a projected visit to a Bonn Government Office by any such delegation. I then informed the Foreign Secretary, Professor Hallstein, of this, and requested that he would let Minister von Brentano know, and I myself subsequently gave Chancellor Adenauer a detailed survey of the talks. We agreed, notwithstanding our mutual desire to continue normal and friendly relations with the Arab states, that the Germany-Israel relationship was of a special type with special meaning—a matter of *sui generis*. I was of the opinion that effective cooperation between the Federal Republic of Germany and Israel would be a significant contribution towards the task of leaving the past behind us. I meant this in the sense, not only of the reacceptance of Germany in the world, but acceptance of the Federal Republic of Germany as a state with equal rights in the field of present-day world politics. I saw in this not only financial and moral but also historical reparation. Under the stress of urgent present-day affairs we are too easily inclined to overlook the need for giving due consideration to these things."

The Editor: "From these talks there emerged a very concrete and practical system of co-operation between the Defence Ministries of the two countries, which was made possible by the trust that you had established."

Strauss: "Some time later Shimon Peres came to see me again and told me in detail about Israel's security problem. It was clear from the start that under the Government of Ben Gurion there was no question of expansion, that is of aggression against and conquest of the Arab states, but only of Israel's self-preservation. In these talks I formed an opinion to the effect that, in a conflict with the Arabs, Israel might win every battle and still lose the war within a short time. This opinion is paradoxical only on the surface. All the known geostrategic and geomilitary facts confirm it. With the purely defensive object of mere self-preservation in mind, I said I was prepared to introduce Mr. Peres to Chancellor Adenauer. I had no intention of making any arrangements or taking any steps behind the Chancellor's back. I was aware that this would have to be a matter of general government policy, and that it challenged mainly the Federal Chancellor's competence as a leader. Without going into detail I may say that Dr. Adenauer empowered me to work with the Israeli Government on certain of the questions being considered by Mr. Peres. This was not a matter of any vast military aid of a scale that has been given by the Soviet Union to the United Arab Republic, but a matter of education, technical co-operation and the supply of small quantities of military equipment. In principle, Adenauer and I were agreed that where lives were concerned aid to Israel was more than a matter of obligatory reparation; it was of especial moral and political consequence to us all. I came to this conclusion with the fact in mind that millions of Jews were murdered as a result of criminal German policy and with German weapons. It is not for us to criticize the setting up of the State of Israel, or the decision of the United Nations, or the correct implementation of this decision, by our German standards. It is an established fact that some of the Jews of the world have found a new home and accomplished a marvellous task of reconstruction. Many threats have been uttered against this country and its people; threats from a hostile world that it will be conquered and its people wiped out. If therefore the Federal Republic of Germany can make a modest contribution to keeping the peace in the Middle East—a critical factor for us too—then this goes some way towards reparation in the very sphere in which Germany committed some of her worst crimes.

"A further consideration was that in the case of an Arab-Israeli conflict the World powers would not and indeed could not intervene in time. Above all, in such a case, there would be the danger of a confrontation between Russia and America. That would also be the immediate consequence in the German Federal Republic, this latter being the bone of contention between America and Russia in any case. I would not go so far as to say that the German Federal Republic has a direct responsibility for the safety of the Middle East. We do not have a policy that comprises the whole world, as America must have. But in all emergencies and in all possible disturbances and crises we must consider what repercussions there may be in our affairs. From this point of view it seemed advisable to make some contribution towards preventing military action, apart from the inevitable border clashes. My aim was to ensure that military action could not be taken either by the Israelis—who could not have carried out a policy of this kind without risking their own self-destruction—or by the Arabs. So this policy seemed to Adenauer and to myself to be a contribution towards reparation and towards safeguarding peace."

The Editor: "Sir, the political talks developed out of the trust that you had fostered between yourself, Ben Gurion and Shimon Peres. I recall the time of the Eichmann Trial in which the German image was decidedly better than it often is today in Jewish circles throughout the world. The presentday German State became divorced from what had happened in the Third Reich. The many talks between yourself and Shimon Peres contributed towards this."

Strauss: "Since that time I have enjoyed the personal friendship of Mr. Peres and also of Ben Gurion. Perhaps I may also take this opportunity to say that I once had a three hours' conversation with Ben Gurion in Paris that so far has not been made publicly known. No nefarious plots were hatched, but the German-Israeli relationship was discussed in detail, and from those standpoints already mentioned. This conversation was also the beginning of the personal relationship between Ben Gurion and myself—a relationship that later, on my visit to Israel after my retirement, developed into a most agreeable friendship. It was a very cordial meeting. This friendship continued in the succeeding years and was deepened by the exchange of messages of goodwill and letters. I took it for granted that my partners in the talks, considering that Germany had defended Israel's safety in such a way as easily to incur international criticism—criticism which was, indeed, forthcoming—in connection with the Eichmann Trial, would not hold the German Federal Republic morally, politically and publicly responsible and collectively guilty for the crimes of a previous generation. In this regard, I also encountered an understanding and co-operative attitude among my partners in the talks. If I am not mistaken, Ben Gurion made a very definite statement at that time. I am not, however, betraying any secret by saying that the German Government, with the Federal Chancellor, Dr. Adenauer, as its head, was at that time very concerned about the possible consequences that the disclosures at the Eichmann Trial might have on world opinion about Germany, and about how far the foreign policy of the German Government might be affected by it."

I broke in: "Particularly by propaganda from the East Bloc?"

"This propaganda is always an important factor here. From the very start Ben Gurion's statement stole the thunder of those who wanted to use the Eichmann Trial and its disclosures as political dynamite; and this not for moral, but for political and tactical reasons and out of ulterior motives. At that time I was often surprised that so little understanding was shown in other countries for this form of co-operation, which had brought us such great political success in Israel, and for which the Federal Government in general and Adenauer and myself in particular were most violently attacked. It is my belief that in our genuine and sincere attempts to pursue a policy of peace, we must regard military co-operation as a part of this policy, just as we did at that time."

The Editor: "Sir, Shimon Peres was not the only person with whom you co-operated in these matters. Very early on you introduced Israeli sub-machine-guns into the Federal Armed Forces, and I believe that it was not only for technical reasons that you decided to do so."

Strauss: "For a considerable time we tested all models and examined the various possibilities with the aim of introducing a sub-machine-gun into the German Armed Forces military equipment. There was a Swedish, a German-Finnish, a French, an English and an Italian model; there was also an exclusively German model and finally the Israeli weapon, the UZI. A comparative survey of all these models showed that the UZI cost almost the same as the Swedish, and as far as licencing conditions were concerned, it proved to be the most suitable one for manufacture in Germany. Moreover, it had proved a success under the conditions of desert warfare during the Sinai Campaign. For these reasons I decided to introduce the UZI into the Federal Army. Up to now there has been no reason to regret or to reverse this decision. The UZI has also proved to be the best standard sub-machine-gun in the Federal Armed Forces arsenal. Moreover, certain defence contracts have been placed with Israel. In particular, ammunition for mortars and for infantry has been bought. We were always very satisfied with the quality and the price of the Israeli consignments. This point, too—supplies from Israel—comes into the overall category of political considerations as mentioned above."

When the Ministry of Defence got Israeli textile firms to produce uniforms and suchlike, the first reaction of the Israeli workers was to stage strikes that were easily broken by internal exchange schemes. It had been generally established from talks with Israelis that the foremost of German considerations was to provide economic help by means of these orders placed with Israeli industries by the Federal Ministry of Defence. This did not only apply to these sections, but also to orders for tyres and similar pieces of equipment for the Federal Armed Forces.

Interview with Shimon Peres

This account would be incomplete if we were only to hear Franz Josef Strauss's words on this difficult, complex question of German-Israeli co-operation. At the beginning of 1967, the editor had a conversation with Shimon Peres. Since 1956 he had frequently had the opportunity of talking to him, and Peres' friendship with Franz Josef Strauss had become very evident to the Editor, mainly because the latter had accompanied the former German Defence Minister on his visit to Israel. It was therefore natural for the question of when the two politicians had first met to be raised at the very outset. Peres answered:

"I think that it must have been in 1957 or at the beginning of 1958 that we met for the first time."

The Editor: "In your first meeting did you discuss direct aid for your armed forces or the sale of your UZI and other armaments to the Federal Armed Forces?"

Peres: "Our first talk lasted five hours and we touched on every possible subject. At first we analyzed the basic problems of Israeli-German relations. After that I tried to explain that in my opinion Germany should contribute in every possible way to Israel's safety and we therefore discussed the two questions: the supply of German weapons to Israel and the sale of our weapons to the Federal Armed Forces.

The Editor: "Did you visit Dr. Adenauer immediately after this meeting or at a later date?'

Peres: "I met Dr. Adenauer much later. I believe I visited him before he had his meeting with Ben Gurion."

The Editor: "What agreement was made between yourself and Mr. Strauss?"

Peres: "So much is being said about an agreement, but in fact we worked out nothing that can be described as a formal agreement. However, we reached a considerable degree of understanding. It was not long before we put everything in writing. In Germany I had the same experience which I had previously had in France: during this meeting a mutual trust developed and was the dominant factor from beginning to end. Most of our agreements were verbal and were carried out in a way that was true to the letter and the spirit of our talks."

The Editor: "Could you tell me something about the type of weapons for which you negotiated with Mr. Strauss? Were they offensive or defensive weapons?"

Peres: "At first we spoke about equipment that could increase the mobility of our forces and then about weapons for our own defence, such as anti-aircraft guns and similar armaments."

The Editor: "Was this meeting with Herr Strauss of significance as far as co-operation with Germany was concerned?"

Peres: "In my view it brought about political contact between ourselves and Germany, because we did not deal mainly with financial problems, nor solely with the past. Germany undertook to make reparations to Israel in a broader sense, that is, she made a contribution towards protecting Israel against the dangers of the future."

The Editor: "Would you say that Herr Strauss gave this aid because the Middle East is being freely supplied with Russian weapons and Communist influence is strong there?"

Peres: "My assessment of Herr Strauss is based on different standards from those of most people. It is my opinion that he fully realized the importance of forging the links of a relationship between Israel and Germany. It was precisely on this point that we achieved perfect harmony of opinion. It was more than a mere question of the mathematics and finance; as I said earlier we had a general political discussion of the problems that existed at that time, as indeed they still do today, between the German and the Israeli peoples."

The Editor: "Did you then visit Dr. Adenauer and discuss the problems of Israeli-German relations?"

Peres: "Yes. I met Dr. Adenauer later; I think we met, on the suggestion of Herr Strauss, in order to modify our agreement to include greater aid from the German Government. I talked with Dr. Adenauer about all types of problems in the Middle East, about the possibilities of peace between the Arabs and ourselves and about the balance of arms between the Israelis and the Arabs; we no doubt touched in general upon the present situation as regards Germany and Israel."

The Editor: "And then there was the Eichmann Trial. The news of former crimes, which reached the public during the trial, shocked the Jewish world. I have heard that you were very much in favour of spreading Ben Gurion's ideas among Jewish communities in America—that the new Germany should not be identified with the Germany of Hitler and Eichmann—and that before you went to the USA you had talks with Herr Strauss."

Peres: "We met frequently and had discussions lasting many hours. As far as I can remember, we made no settlements concerning this matter; however, I was in fact one of those who endeavoured to explain to the Israelis, and to the Jews in the United States, the importance of the new relations between ourselves and Germany. Of course I also mentioned the action that Herr Strauss was taking to help Israel."

The Editor: "When you look back today on that great period of German-Israeli relations, does it seem to you to be one in which the foundations were laid for the new contacts that we can now establish as the scope of diplomatic relations develops?"

Peres: "Yes, it was indeed the beginning of diplomatic relations between ourselves and the Federal Republic. I do not think that diplomatic relations would have been established otherwise; moreover, it was not only from Adenauer and Strauss that we received support. The Social Democratic Party was also in favour of diplomatic relations, and thus mirrored the general German policy, for which Strauss had paved the way. I personally believe that diplomatic relations, which are a pure formality, prosper best if facts are recognized—facts that arise long before relations are established."

The Editor: "Is it true that the Social Democratic politician, Fritz Erler, was once one of the strongest S.P.D. champions of co-operation with Strauss and the Federal Armed Forces?"

Peres: "I was in continual contact with Fritz Erler on the subject and there were numerous occasions on which I found him to be understanding and willing to give his support."

The Editor: "Mr. Peres, at that time many Israeli soldiers and officers came to our training camps. What was the experience of these young people who stayed in our country and met our young soldiers?"

Peres: "Of course it is very difficult for me to generalize. It was doubtless a strange experience for them at first. However, it seems to me that they were given a very friendly reception. They all gained the impression that they were seeing a new Germany and a new German Army."

Franz Josef Strauss's visit to Israel at a time when German public opinion had hardly a good word for him, convinced even the sceptics that his relations with Israel were sincere.

Moshe Dayan, who at that time was the Minister of Food in Ben Gurion's Government, personally went to the airport. "I have come to thank this man, who has stood by our Nation in its most difficult hours." These were his words to the eagerly waiting journalists. Franz Josef Strauss's visit lasted five days. Wherever he and his wife appeared in restaurants and in other public places he was shown no hostility by the people. More than once he was personally welcomed by Israeli citizens who had previously lived in Germany and many even wanted his autograph. The right-wing radical Heruth Party, which had at first demonstrated, stopped doing so when their leader, Begin, was informed by Peres about the help that would be given to the Israeli forces on Strauss's initiative. How it came about that in later years, when Strauss was no longer in charge, this cooperation ceased, will be explained elsewhere in this book.

The Eichmann trial in Jerusalem

On the 11th of April 1961, exactly one year after Adolf Eichmann had been seized in Argentina by the Israeli Secret Service, the trial of the man in charge of the "Movement for the Final Solution of the Jewish Problem" began in Jerusalem. Among the hundreds of pressmen from all over the world there were more than fifty German journalists at the trial. The Israeli public was impressed by the size of this contingent of radio, television and press reporters from Germany. During the months of the trial, as well as having the job of reporting the proceedings, these journalists were privileged to witness the positive attitude of the Israeli people and Government to the Federal Republic of Germany. This trial, which once more exposed all the horror of the mass extermination of the Jews under Hitler as if it were a ghastly world-wide history lesson, was not charged to the account of the present-day German state and its people.

Statements by well-known Germans

President Lübke:

"A few days ago in Jerusalem there began a trial the name of which has become at once symbol and stigma of the terrible crimes committed by Hitler and his supporters in the name of Germany. Even today we Germans, including former resistance-workers and those who opposed Hitler, are still filled with deep shame that some of our fellow-countrymen were accessories to such crimes. In spite of this we must establish, for the sake of that same justice that has brought Eichmann to trial today, that it is fundamentally incorrect to equate the term "National Socialist" with "German"."

Federal Chancellor Adenauer:

"It is our wish that in this trial the whole truth should be brought to light and that justice should be done. After Germany's collapse, all those who undertook the task of rebuilding her were filled with shame and concern. We were filled with shame because we then became clearly aware, for the first time, of the terrifying abyss of National Socialism. We were concerned—for how, we asked ourselves, would it be possible to remove this poison from the memories and the thinking of large sections of our community?

"Our anxiety proved to be not so justified as we had feared. In the German people, in their ethics, there is no longer any trace of National Socialism; we are no longer sensitive to Nationalist ideas. We have a constitutional government.

"President Ben Gurion said a few days ago that today's young Germans cannot be made to bear the responsibility for the crimes committed by some members of a previous generation. He stressed his country's concern that its relationship with the new Germany should be a friendly one. We are sincerely grateful to him for these words, spoken before the institution of proceedings against Eichmann."

The President of the Bundestag, Eugen Gerstenmaier:

"... It is my guess that the Eichmann Trial will do quite a lot of harm to Germany's reputation abroad, and that it will once more raise the burning question that is a part of everyone's conscience: how could it have happened? I believe that no one who has not himself experienced the terrible power and hypnotism of a totalitarian police state, can provide us with an answer. The monstrous crimes connected with the name of Eichmann will also continue to torment and be a burden to us for as long as we live ..."

The Vice-President of the Bundestag, Carlo Schmid:

"... What can be done? Is there anything we can do that can bring back what we have lost? Can we replace the Jews? There is little we can do, because we cannot bring back to life the people murdered in the gas-chambers; the exiles will never return—or at least only very few of them. And who can blame them? However, there is something we can and must do: whatever can be made good, we must make good. Whatever we do, it cannot buy our innocence, and we are all guilty, all of us who called ourselves Germans at that time without averting the evil—or perhaps without being able to do so. Even those who are innocent in law must share the blame for everything that was done in their name ..."

The Mayor of Berlin, Willy Brandt (now Foreign Minister):

"... The start of the Eichmann Trial triggered off a strong world-wide reaction. However painful this trial may be at many of its stages, we should not fear the judgement of the world. We should not gloss over any of the questions that are raised, but must tackle them openly and honestly. Criminals must be brought to justice, and Eichmann is a criminal. The world judges us today by what we do today, by our present behaviour, and naturally also by our attitude to the past. No responsible German can help being ashamed of what was done in the dishonoured name of Germany ..."

The Vice-President of the Bundestag, Thomas Dehler:

"... I regard it as simply a matter of our political responsibility. Because after the First World War we failed to give the German people the right political constitution or to make them aware of the tasks they had inherited from their own past, because we failed to show them the value of liberal democratic, constitutional government, all that was most base and vile became exalted, and found slaves to serve its ends. In Jerusalem we are trying one of these slaves—one who bears a particularly heavy burden of guilt; we are not trying the German people. But for us Germans it cannot but be a period of torture, involving as it does deliberating upon the causes of the German political catastrophe and its outcome for us and the world, and asking ourselves: have we learnt from our experiences? Are we politically more astute and wiser? Do we now know how easily freedom and justice can be thrown away? Do we realize that every authoritarian state harbours the danger that human rights will be disregarded, and the most terrible injustices committed ...?"

Professor Franz Böhm:

"It is a tragic fact that the schools of thought that were opposed to totalitarianism began far too late to take notice of this theory of government, and to study not only the doctrine but the whole practice of totalitarianism. This is indeed one of the reasons why it must be in the interests of the civilized world, and above all, of this nation, to see this terrible business of the Nazi annihilation of the Jews thoroughly investigated and explained down to the last detail. Although during this terrible affair old wounds may be opened up, emotions revived, our reputation damaged a second time, although our feelings refuse to concentrate on this blot on the escutcheon of our history, still we may not falter ... I should like to be able to believe that these feelings are shared by every right-thinking and responsible man, who is not necessarily seeking political understanding of the past, but whose heart bleeds when he thinks of all the horror and the immeasurable suffering inflicted; the man who believes that every right-thinking German will naturally be ashamed and will offer ready sympathy to the victims of this great crime. He will know reparation to be a matter of the heart. Simple honesty is the shortest way to political understanding in this, the greatest-ever problem to face mankind."

Minister Bruno Heck:

"As I have already said, this trial could be made easy, not only for the rest of the world but for us too. I should like to repeat that it would be unjust to try the German nation in the person of Eichmann. However, it would also be wrong to evade the issue with Cain's question: 'Am I my brother's keeper?' We tolerated the SA and SS, the 'yellow star', and the public degradation and slander of innocent people, and we should not now be able to look back on this without remorse and regret, without feeling determined that we must not allow such a thing to happen again, that we should not let ourselves be led astray a second time ... It may be very unpleasant for us in the coming weeks to be reminded of much about which we are partially or totally ignorant. But it all belongs to our past, and we want to know the truth. Adolf Eichmann's trial must serve to hand down the truth to the world of the future. Both our generation and generations to come may learn something from it."

The Archbishop of München-Freising, Julius, Cardinal Döpfner:

"... And this is the origin of the terrible guilt that the people of our nation bear. They tried to overthrow the creation of the Lord, who creates all human beings with love and offers them eternal salvation. They took it upon themselves to exalt or abase human beings according to the standards arbitrarily chosen by their party to suit their theories of racialism. This is what made it possible for human beings to inflict such cruelty on others, cruelty which once more assails conscience at a trial in Jerusalem ... In Jerusalem we are trying a man who wanted to destroy the Jewish race. The plan to wipe out the people of Israel—'The Ultimate Solution of the Jewish Problem', as it was so cynically and unemotionally called—was full of pagan arrogance. And we are ashamed that such heathen crimes should be thought out by people brought up in a Christian world. They certainly did not live and work in the spirit of Christ. We reverently salute God's Chosen People who, and here again I am quoting St. Paul, 'are loved because they are the Chosen Ones'."

Provost Heinrich Grüber:

"... I sincerely hope that this trial will not only settle the Israel-German relationship, but will also help humanity as a race—or as a cause. I may say to my many friends from Israel that at the time when I felt as though I was completely surrounded by the bodies of the slaughtered, the words of Ephraim were as a banner before me: 'God let me grow in the land of my misery', and this is my heartfelt plea to all those on whom some new suffering has been inflicted, or for whom painful memories have been revived, that they might all realize ... that God provides for growth in the land of our misery. My dearest wish is that love and forgiveness shall come to us—love which forgives here on earth, and forgiveness for our sins in the hereafter, that we may all meet before God's throne ... This is my plea and it will remain my wish ... for all—even for those accused."

David Ben Gurion's viewpoint

During the months of the Eichmann Trial, Israel's Prime Minister David Ben Gurion indicated clearly to his people that he disassociated this trial in ever-increasing measure from today's free Germany.

The attempts made by the propaganda apparatus of the Eastern Bloc and by the lawyer Kaul from East Berlin, who appeared as co-plaintiff and who continually tried to establish some kind of connection between Eichmann and Bonn—these attempts were frustrated by Ben Gurion through his dramatic speeches and actions. Ben Gurion said in a number of interviews what he first expressed to the Editor in a talk for the "Deutsche Zeitung und Wirtschafts-Zeitung".

The Editor: "Long before the start of the Eichmann Trial, you laid particular emphasis on the fact that it was the main task of these proceedings to put before the youth of Israel and the world the annihilation of the Jews in its historical context. Today, now that the hearing of evidence in these proceedings is over, I should like to ask you if this has been achieved."

Ben Gurion: "I think that the trial has achieved its object even though the verdict, which I do not consider to be so important, will not be announced for some time. The main thing was to show the young people of our country the terrible tragedy which overtook this scattered nation, dependent as it was on the mercy of other people, when a brutal régime without a trace of human conscience decided to annihilate our Jewish people for the simple reason that they were Jews. Moreover, the trial demonstrated to world opinion the great dangers of anti-semitism and racialism."

The Editor: "Do you think that this trial, which without doubt aroused in the Jewish people terrible memories of the atrocities they had suffered, has influenced Jewish feelings towards the Federal Republic of Germany or to the German people?"

Ben Gurion: "My opinion of the present-day Germany remains unchanged. Nazi Germany no longer exists. Our Scriptures tell us: 'The fathers shall not be put to death for the children, neither shall the children be put to death for the fathers; every man shall be put to death for his own sin.' (Deuteronomy, Chapter 24, Verse 16) and the prophet Ezekiel devotes a whole chapter to this humane problem (Chapter 18). The development of our relations with Germany today depends on the intentions and the policy of the German Government. For our part, we are ready to take up normal and close relations and to co-operate to the fullest extent."

The Editor: "For some time your Government has been intensifying its efforts to have Israel accepted as a member of the European Economic Community. Surely such efforts will raise new problems for Israel's economy; what advantages do you expect for your country if she joins the Community?"

Ben Gurion: "Although our integration into the European Common Market may possibly bring hardships for some sections of our economy, the overall advantages of being a member would make up for these hardships. I set great store by the elimination of barriers between countries—not only customs barriers, but other kinds of barriers too. It is vitally important to strengthen co-operation between nations in the spheres of economics, culture and politics, but at the same time the complete independence of all free nations must be guaranteed."

The Editor: "The Reparation Agreement between the Federal Republic of Germany and the State of Israel expires in a short time. Do you envisage the possibility of continuing and extending the co-operation between the Israeli and the German economies?"

Ben Gurion: "In my opinion, there are far-reaching opportunities for co-operation, particularly in connection with German investments in Israel, in the development of industry, in building houses, and in transport, especially in the Negev. I am convinced that Dr. Adenauer's declaration was no mere formality, and that he will certainly carry it through. I trust and believe in the moral obligations under which Dr. Adenauer and other leading personalities in modern Germany have placed themselves."

The Editor: "For several years now, there have been regular delegations visiting Israel from the new African and Asian states. What is, in your opinion, the best way for your country to help these new nations to establish themselves?"

Ben Gurion: "Israel is a young country with an old tradition. The re-establishment of our country involved building up an economy and a social order from scratch. Israel is not bound to the same rigid economic and social traditions that prevail in countries that have led a normal life for centuries. For this reason, our experiences in starting from scratch in the fields of education, the creation of the armed forces and the national economy, and the development of the co-operative system and the workers' movements—all these experiences can be of great value to the new countries in Africa and Asia. Moreover, the fact that we are only a small country means that these nations need have no fears of domination or neo-colonialism on our part, as the Communists and their adherents call it. Israel welcomes the young men and women from these countries who wish to study our methods and at their request we are willing to send specialists to their countries."

The Editor: "The main concern of future Israeli policy is surely her relationship with the neighbouring Arab states. Would you be so kind as to explain the trend of your policy in this sphere?"

Ben Gurion: "Ever since the day Israel was founded, she has always remained constant in her desire for peace, exactly as explained in the text of our Declaration of Independence. We are confident that the time will come when the Arab rulers see the uselessness of their hate, and when a peaceful alliance will come about. Israel will then collaborate with her Arab neighbours in the fields of economics, culture and politics, on a basis of equality and mutual respect. We will gladly make available to our neighbours, for the development of the Arab countries, all the experience and knowledge that we have available."

Ben Gurion did not want to endanger the forging of the links between the new democratic German state and Israel through the past deeds of the National Socialist party. The majority of the people of Israel and also those of the Jewish race throughout the whole world have understood his attitude.

Prominent Germans in Israel

Any rapprochement between the two peoples is inconceivable without regular visits by leading German politicians of all political factions. Members of Parliament, leading trade unionists, burgomasters and mayors of German towns, delegations from the Laender parliaments, high-ranking officers of the Federal Armed Forces, leading men and women in the field of political education have been paving the way for a deeper mutual understanding. Every single one of them has made his own individual contribution to bridging gaps, has aided the process of gradually getting rid of what are quite understandable negative feelings towards the Germans on the part of the Jewish people and enabling them to see present-day Germany in a different light.

Some of these visitors deserve special mention; there is, for example, Franz Böhm, who visited Israel in 1954 at Easter-time and was given a conducted tour of the country with full-scale security precautions and sometimes travelling incognito. What a difference compared with his visit in 1963 on the occasion of the 10th anniversary of the Luxembourg Agreement when grand public receptions were given in his honour! Mention should also be made of the visits of Ludwig Rosenberg, Chairman of the German Association of Trade Unions, of the occasion when Carlo Schmid visited a Hebrew university and gave a lecture on a European subject and of Willy Brandt who, in his capacity of Chairman of the German Social Democratic Party, revived former close contacts—in the same way as his predecessor Erich Ollenhauer—with many Israelis through his earlier acquaintance with their German social democratic friends.

Theodor Heuss on the autogenous nature of democracy

In the abundance of visits there are two that have assumed particular importance: The visit of the first President of the Federal Republic of Germany, Theodor Heuss, who, early in May 1960, paid a visit to Israel and gave a lecture in German at the Hebrew University—at this time this was by no means an established practice—and the visit of the President of the German Parliament, Eugen Gerstenmaier, two and a half years later. Theodor Heuss lectured on the autogenous nature of democracy. Martin Buber's introduction to this lecture in the Hebrew University was one of the great moments of German-Jewish dialogue:

"Dear Professor Heuss,

"In welcoming you with all our hearts it is not the former President of the Federal Republic of Germany we welcome, but Theodor Heuss, the historian and constitutional scholar, the man whose ideas and words are alive today. And yet it is essential at this juncture to point out that whenever your name is mentioned over here the first association we have is that of the man 'who came after Hitler'. Of course, this does not suggest that you had established 'another' Germany in place of Hitler's Germany—the Germany that spelt death by torture for millions of our people; things like that do not even happen in cases of less moment—and this one was certainly the most momentous in world history. You did not establish the other Germany then but you have now represented her in the re-established freedom of the peoples and presented her to the peoples of the world with the same personal integrity, the same constancy and steadfastness of purpose that were always associated with you in the days of the self-abasement of the German people and the subjection of other peoples.

"When I addressed you just now, I came close to using the expression, 'Dear Colleague' because I have in mind that we are colleagues in connection with the Peace Prize of the German Book Trade, a prize that I received in 1953 and you last year—in fact at the very moment when you were no longer the President of the German Federal Republic but once more the man and citizen Heuss. I recall seeing you sitting in front of me in the first row next to my late wife when I was standing on the rostrum to thank that other Germany that had bestowed this prize on me, and in my heart I recall that, before I started to speak, I looked across at my wife, who imbued my life with the permanent presence of a real and free Germany, but then I looked at you, the man who, for me, was the undeniable embodiment of German integrity, an integrity that had overcome the betrayal of the past. It struck me as a symbolic and a logical act for the Germans to have elected a man of such simple honesty of purpose and deep-rooted humour to be their first representative after the era of pathos, after the gross desecration and deception of the past. Even before this I had well understood that after the end of this destructive, sub-human creature that called itself the 'Fuehrer' it had to be a humanitarian that assumed the leading position; but now it became demonstrably clear to me that this was humanism in the true sense of the word and not that second-best variety summed up in the word 'virtuous'.

"The wave of anti-human feeling that surged up in history together with Hitler is rooted in the increased mutual distrust of the peoples of our time; it is from this that has arisen the mutual distrust between peoples that prevails at the present hour throughout the world. What can we find to combat this? When you, Herr Heuss, thanked the German book trade some months ago for bestowing the peace prize on you you said: 'All my life I have had a natural dislike for the word *tolerance*' and in saying this you did indeed take the very words right out of my mouth. Nothing is achieved if people merely try to tolerate each other for the simple reason that evolution is the sole panacea—not something that has to be aimed at—like the coexistence we talk of today. But what is there that has 'evolved' in this way? At the end of another speech, in which you also offered thanks for a prize awarded you last year, namely the Hanseatic Goethe Prize, you Professor Heuss, talked about 'human trustfulness' that is deeply rooted in mankind and you called it the basis of the democratic way of life. But it must also be the basis of any communication between the champions of democracy. We, the sons of a young democracy that, though itself young, recognizes that it is the laws and the promises of yesteryear that are inherent in it today—we gladly listen to your words about the autogenous nature of democracy, knowing that they usher in an age in which this communication is possible."

Theodor Heuss was the next speaker:

"My friends,

"I wish to express my sincere appreciation of the honour which has been done me in being invited to lecture in this noble centre of learning. You will realize that it is not without some slight degree of embarrassment that I take up the invitation. However, the fact that my friend Professor Carlo Schmid created something like a precedent in the use of the German language in this same room some months ago has made my undertaking easier.

"Quite some time ago, when I discussed the selection of an appropriate subject for this lecture with Israel's representative in the Federal Republic of Germany, Ambassador Dr. Shinnar, he suggested—probably in order not to take up too much of my time—that I should talk about the same problem about which I was asked to propound a theory by the Freiherr-vom-Stein Foundation in Hamburg last November, namely, 'The Autogenous Nature of Democracy'. This was all very well, but there is a difference between using municipal self-government as an example that for centuries has been the sphere of power of an exclusive line of patrician families, to give an interpretation of this system that just 100 years ago had taken the first steps towards the democracy of limited franchise, and to speak here and today, in an environment that is rich in historical associations—both good and bad—as only very few places are. Because it was here that 12 years ago, after passing through the intermediate stages of an uncertain legal position, a state was audaciously—one might almost say improvised—and then properly planned; this state was faced with the task of forming a nation out of a populace of multifarious origin, using the instruments provided by democracy, in fact having none other.

"But rest assured, I am not presuming to talk wisely about the problems of Israeli democracy in a place where I am a guest, even though my many friendships and associations have rendered me not altogether unfamiliar with the historical background including as it does Zionism with its underlying yearning for return to the 'Land of the Fathers' and also the so-called 'assimilation' to the way of living, thinking and orientation of a variegated environment. On the one hand the accent on religion, with the features of theocracy, and on the other, a pure personal retreat from the pattern of the Mosaic Law—implied and not discussed, an extension of Jewish origin into the national aspects of the historically-conditioned environment—or into the field of human affairs as such.

"In my capacity as Federal President I have been able to accumulate a certain amount of experience in these fields. I do not propose to go into great detail here but one letter remained in my memory: It was written by an artist who survived the period of shame and crime in Germany going underground with friends. This man, whom I do not know, asked me in my speeches not to talk about 'German Jews' but of 'Jewish Germans' because this would be the correct designation for him and certainly for many many others. This sounds as though I want to tell anecdotes because this has little to do with the 'Autogenous Nature of Democracy'. But on the other hand I do not feel to be overstepping the bounds of correctness in preparing the way for my lecture with a few impressions taken from the vast store of ideas and events.

"As I now come to the actual subject—which will be concerned more with historical than abstract variations on the relations existing between state and people, I propose to start with a few brief propositions that sound almost rough-hewn but that have been used by me on occasions in the past: 'Every state pattern is based on the power to give orders and the right to exact obedience.' The question remains open whether and to what extent this proposition is safeguarded by an adequate and recognized legal system that binds both the party giving orders and the party called upon to obey them. Where are the boundaries set up for authority by the elementary demands and duties of humanity? When does the right to exact obedience dwindle to insignificance? You feel that this touches upon the so-called 'right to resistance'. The austere expression: 'power to give orders' should not, however, be given the connotation of the attributive: 'by force' and should not, in line with the purely semantic association, be thought of in exclusively military terms. It comprises definitely civilian sectors, such as, for example, compulsory general education which itself was once the subject of 'orders' and sometimes even had to be enforced with no little difficulty by penalties. Another example would be the regulations concerning the protection of workers in firms, social insurances and public finances etc. etc. which take a legal form. The second axiom that I like to use is: 'Democracy is the order to rule for a *certain limited period of time.*' This involves a little comparative philology because the simple translation of 'government by the people' does not say anything about the institutions. Obviously 'the people' are thought of in terms of giving the 'order' but in a way that restricts the order, the execution of the order, i.e. the 'ruling' to a certain period of time and renews it according to a fixed time schedule. Adherence to dates, however, such as, for example, the duration of the period for which a state parliament, local government, a head of state has been elected has frequently been a philosophical issue and one of practical politics; it will probably remain so. Is the 'people's sovereignty' upset if it sacrifices its potential daily activities? After 1918 we had a violent discussion of the so-called 'council system' in Germany; this system probably originated in Michael Bakunin's French Revolution technique of 1871 and comprises the enduring possibility of recalling a 'council' or some of its members. Both in theory and in practice this method has lost its immediate topicality as far as I can tell. This applies also to the Anglo-Saxon sphere where this 'recall' procedure has been discussed but the vital aspects of it never got beyond the discussion stage.

"There is, however, a certain reservation here. Democracy, which allocates tasks (afterwards we shall have to deal briefly with the way in which it does so) is probably the element of will in a *republic*. Bismarck starts his 'Reflections and Reminiscences' with the somewhat ironical statement that when he left school he thought that the republic was the 'most reasonable form of a state'. Later, however, he disassociated himself to a large extent from this 'conviction'. But the historical situation is different. It is true that during the last 50 years very old monarchies and dynasties of great historical tradition have fallen to the sword of war and revolution—these include the Romanovs, the Habsburgs, the Hohenzollerns, the Osmans and the House of Savoy; in Britain and Scandinavia, however, in the Benelux countries and Greece, as also in a few important states in Asia and Africa, they survived because—and this is true particularly of Europe—the vicissitudes of history had already achieved something of a counter-balance in the shape of rationalized flexibility. Wherever the house rules of the dynasties prevail this 'task to rule for a certain limited period of time' becomes invalid. Death is the immediate and legitimate historical force, or may at least act as such, without, however, ensuring the worth of the successors. It remains a somewhat uncanny commentary on the closing of the Hohenzollern dynasty that the last two German emperors, Frederic III and William II—the one tactfully and the other tactlessly—were impatiently waiting for their fathers' death.

"The existence of the 'will of the people', taking the form of Rousseau's 'volonté générale' or Hegel's 'Volksgeist'—a somewhat uncertain quantity—has to be taken for granted because it is the ideological and practical reserve from which to create a *new* legitimate system when the historical form of state breaks down. But whereas this will requires a) a legal form of order, a technical procedure to establish it, we are faced with the fact that b) all these technical procedures can be manipulated. For example, when some months ago the Russian President of the Council of Ministers, Khrushchev, informed the German Federal Chancellor that rather more than 98% of the population in East and

Central Germany had affirmed, confirmed and consequently 'legitimized' the state of affairs in the so-called GDR in the previous people's elections he was either ill-informed or ill-advised. For a long time this figure of 98% had been too familiar to Germans and, for that matter, to the world at large; Hitler had certainly quoted it to Germany and the whole world in connection with his elections. Apart from everything else, he, too, allotted a small distinction: to elect means to select. The monopoly of a single party, even when it is not masked in a 'standardized list' lumped together with the so-called 'permitted' factions, is the end of all democracy; democracy is only viable when its core contains an elementary liberalism, i.e. freedom of thought and the free right of individual decision.

"But now who is it that constitutes this 'nation' that allocates 'tasks to rule'—the word 'rule' also comprising simple municipal administration work—every two, four, five or seven years? The 'terms' differ among the states as a result of very different conventions, but this is a matter of secondary importance. Does the term 'nation' refer to the 'population' living within a well-defined state area? Obviously not, because the statistics also include women and minors in the population figures. It was not before the 20th century that the female contingent was democratically officially recognized and became a legally-accepted part of the political 'will'. The tradition of monarchy had given Elizabeth I and Victoria of England, the Russian Catherines and Habsburg's Maria Theresa the chance to make their mark on their epochs. And then this strange thing: In Europe's model democracy, in the Swiss Federation that I very much love and respect with its legislative plebiscites and canton civil servant elections, democracy is still a predominantly masculine business. If I have followed the news correctly there are no more than two or three cantons in which women have been given the right of co-determination within the cantonal sphere of influence.

"Perhaps I may be allowed just one incidental remark here—in connection with a completely different frame of reference: The executive of criminal law is entitled to deprive the guilty party of the 'honorary rights of a citizen' in very serious criminal offences. Is this point worth bringing up at all? I think it is, because the underlying tenor is: If a citizen destroys his own integrity he has, even though usually only for a limited period of time, undermined his citizenship, consisting as it does of honour, duty and fate. Democracy cannot do without ethical premises.

"History, and the ideologies embedded in it, provides a very variegated answer to the question: What constitutes 'the nation' that, in an orderly and legal way, allocates time-limited tasks to rule in order to ensure definite settlement of its community life and the safeguarding of it. The *nation*, as a result of the sequence of generations, is a *lasting* element whereas the states, in their internal structure and their external spheres of influence, are subject to never-ending change. But do we not talk of nations or peoples that have 'declined'? The period of migration supplies many illustrations of this: we find the Vandals in North Africa, the West Goths in Spain, the East Goths in the Balcans and in Italy etc. and they have submerged in the original population or have been absorbed by it. But then again, what does this little word 'ancient' (in the historical sense) imply when studying what we refer to as pre-history or early history?

"Of course it is an exaggeration to say that the 'people' as a self-existent phenomenon that can be objectively considered and assessed is a discovery that belongs in the second half of the 18th century—indeed, 'belongs', one might say from two different points of view: In his Contrat Social of 1762, J. J. Rousseau creates the state entity out of the will of the people and 16 years later we have J. G. Herder editing the collection which is given the title 'Voices of the Peoples in Songs'. The two are highly effective in the way in which the forces of enlightenment on the one hand and of the coming romantic age on the other meet. Rousseau releases the desire for a system of properly laid down public order that is not inherited by the traditional rights of a leader but is vested in the 'volonté générale'. Herder stresses the capacity for linguistic manifestation—and that is the use of the word 'voices'—he notes the conditions of the various strata of a population whose inherent value he describes and interprets in a human, christian spirit. A uniform language is, of course, a definite and most important constituent element in the creation of any definite identity of a people. But that it is not the final factor in the assumption of a state identity is shown by such examples as the Swiss Confederacy and the political status of Canada, where a state of equilibrium and national consciousness was achieved by the combination of history, tradition and discernment. Unfortunately, the attempts made to achieve the same result within the framework of the League of Nations by the creation of so-called 'rights of minorities' were not attended with success. The achievement of the First World War, after all, designated the 'self-determination of peoples' without any definition being given of what actually constitutes a 'people'. Then the war had a dichotomous aftermath with, on the one hand, the over-enthusiastic claims of the so-called 'young' nations and on the other, the distressing feeling of injured national pride on the part of the defeated party. This has now become an odd paradox and is a lesson we have to learn from the past: Democracy, having become a highly demanding confession of faith as the result of such events as the American Wars of Independence and the defensive wars of the French Revolution, has achieved at the same time both negative and positive values, born of passionate nationalism. To take an easy example, it is only the fact that we have become accustomed to the delightfully lilting melody of the French national anthem, the Marseillaise, that we have tended to forget the super-abundantly militant message of the text.

"And in addition to this, let us consider a popular feeling without authoritative regulation of the gathering pathos—an example that has excited little notice in the historical stream of consciousness: When in 1906 the Austrian President, von Beck—going deep down into popular feelings—substituted for the right to elect members of Parliament based on the various strata of the population a uniform right to vote for everybody, this put a sudden end to the Social-Democratic Party, which, properly considered according to its programme of internationalism, had actually found the right vehicle for its ideology in this polyethnic state. From that moment on, there was a Polish, a Czech, a German and an Italian party group. Many of you may think that this has really nothing—or very little—to do with the development of the subject. Perhaps you have been expecting something about the nature of franchise, about relative or absolute majority in parliamentary elections, about rank and settlement of self-government in the communities/municipalities and about the rights and wrongs of parties—which I once referred to as 'stages on the way to active patriotism', with two-party systems, three-party systems, multi-party systems etc. And indeed, something of all this may perhaps still be touched upon. All of it applies to the protean structure of a '-cracy' (if I may coin a word) which regulates itself outside the framework of a dynastic and monarchical world of emotions or in a traditional feudal system inasmuch as the system itself has not yet got as far as the stage of sociological decay. But the 'client'—i.e. the 'people' must be present in the picture.

"But I did not come here to Israel in order to *teach* others but to *learn* from them and I certainly have succeeded in learning a number of things from others—including those who, a couple of generations ago, were my own students at the Berlin 'Deutsche Hochschule für Politik'. But there is something spiritually exciting about it, particularly for historically inclined persons like myself—I should point out right away that I do not stand before you now in the capacity of a retired politician—to be a contemporary and a witness of the undertaking, that *both* these things, a state and a nation, are being recreated on soil that bears the imprint of history.

"We were aware of the tragedy of the Jewish people in this country, which we sometimes knew as 'Palestine' and sometimes as the 'Holy Land', and the political trials and tribulations of a folk in constant exile. All this was known to us in our school days and was reflected in the most peculiar mixture of theocracy, monarchism and both the moral and practical leadership of seers and prophets. When the Roman Titus destroyed the temple the race lost what one might refer to as its spiritual centre. Indeed, if I may use this expression, it became a 'Mosaic Diaspora', true to its legitimacy, as handed down by tradition, bound by it and maintained by it—and, at the same time, separated from it—a most peculiar situation if we can see the spiritual significance in the structural organization. The 'old schools', the Jewish synagogues in Prague and Cracow—the ones that I know—are Gothic, as was normal in the days in which they were built. Yet the dome architecture of many of the German synagogues of the 19th and 20th century is 'oriental' in effect although the so-called 'emancipation process' was already a thing of the distant past. There is a strange contrast between the naturally naïve attitude of taking the general order of things for granted that existed right up to the time of the ghettos and the conscious expression of separation in a time which seems largely ready to cancel this separation ...

"When we in Germany were going through the shocking process of reversion to the primitive, when Hitler's 'biological naturalism', as I called it a couple of generations ago, oversimplified with convenient interpretations the racial theory of the Frenchman Gobineau, *all* wicked things, without exception, were inventions of the Jews, particularly from his point of view the internationally-styled socialism of the rabbi's son Karl Marx. I have already had the opportunity, both at home and in America where I was visiting the Leo-Baeck Institute in New York, of mentioning the fact that in the Frankfurt National Assembly of 1848 a Jew, Gabriel Riesser, most impressively and eloquently advocated a German imperial dynasty of the Prussian Hohenzollerns and that Eduard Simson, in 1849 as the Head of the Paulskirche and in 1870 as Speaker of the North German Reichstag, again offered this to a Hohenzollern. But then there is also this side of the picture: The man who offered the Prussian type of national conservatism an ideology—in a period that had not yet lost its capacity for national philosophy—was Friedrich Julius Stahl who, although he was converted in faith, was nevertheless of Jewish origin. All this is, of course, as viewed in the German perspective.

"But this expression 'German perspective' may be an irritant to some people. The 'German perspective' must include not only what individuals of Jewish origin have achieved on the stage of German history—politically, philosophically, artistically etc.—but also the suffering that countless myriads have had to undergo just because of this racial background. And it is not for me to understate the matter in rhetorical abstractions. Some ten years ago, a few weeks after I took office, I dealt with these matters for the first time, and I opposed the idea of 'collective guilt' which was still in vogue at that time and which world opinion had laid at Germany's door. I did go so far as to use the words 'collective shame'—of which we, the contemporaries of such shocking crimes, could never, ever rid ourselves—and we must be the very last to try and shrug off this moral incubus; however terrible both the intention and the execution may have been it is not merely a question of the attempted liquidation of the Jews and all that they stood for but—and here we have something of the 'German perspective'—the defilement that can hardly be eliminated. In addition to the Jewish martyrs and witnesses there are also German martyrs.

"But here in Israel the deeply-moving—indeed, the soul-stirring idea of a *'people'* that was forced to flee its ancient settlements and had lost its national and constitutional 'raison d'être' had to be recreated. Human beings of dozens of different origins who were driven here either by their faith or by the desperation of their circumstances had to be integrated into a newly-created, homogeneous whole with its own, conscious, ethnic identity. The word 'homestead', which appeared in the Balfour Declaration, had emotional overtones suggesting 'comfortable rehabilitation' in the promised land of the forefathers; the idea is—at least for the children and the grandchildren—for it to replace the 'origins' of a scattered race by a *'homeland'* imbued with real affection. But the new homeland has become a *state* in the true sense of the word, a democratic state, a sovereign state with all the qualities that I attempted to sum up in telegraphic style at the beginning of this lecture. But again this is exaggerated, for here again the political groups and parties, without which no democracy can be viable, are more important in building up the personality of a people than are the purely physical advantages; thus this state is inevitably faced with the primary task of forming a people—*its* people, so to speak. And in doing so—and in sober consciousness of its duty—it is obliged, whatever be the recognition of its religious genius which remained a fertile and viable entity in the Mosaic Diaspora, to allow for the process of spiritual secularization which for two centuries has permeated West European Jewry in particular. And now, at the risk of being misunderstood, I will venture to repeat something that I once said many years ago. In the poly-ethnic empire of the Habsburg monarchy the German language of commands used by the army was an element—in fact, it was *the* element—able to preserve the state in the midst of the chaos of warfare. In Israel the Hebraic language of commands has become one of the most important methods by which *a people can be imbued with an identity* in the course of peaceable compulsion to military service—where the basic forces of *any* democracy, quite irrespective of the danger of national and nationalist hubris that may be added, are present at the same time.

"It is not necessary for me to go into the question of their remarkable achievement of rendering a language that had developed primarily in the service of cult and ritual flexible enough for daily use in a changed world. I do know that the creative power of one individual person became the starting point and I was told how this evolutionary process gradually became something of a state function in the introduction of which the traditional and the imaginative were able to potentiate each other mutually. Another matter on which I shall not venture to touch in a context of this kind is the socio-economic and the ethno-psychological project of the kibbuzim. In the weeks that are to come I shall be able to learn something of these by personal experience but it seems to me that the Israeli army, that is to be the guarantee of the greatly-desired feeling of 'sheltered security' constitutes the melting pot in this process of creating a people—and this by virtue of the numerous personal contacts made and certainly not merely by virtue of the language of command.

"Now of course in the meantime I have digressed considerably from the proposed subject of my lecture 'The Autogenous Nature of Democracy' and have said something of the structure of the 'demos'—in fact, of a people. But I must no longer trespass upon the patience that you have so kindly vouchsafed me and shall have to leave the question of constituent party matters, of the ideology of class representation and so on and also the essentially centralized nature of the independent examination by impartial judges of political decisions. This is the heritage of the great French political philosopher Montesquieu, who with his theory of 'sharing of powers' has attached a special value to the 'right' of decision by judges on what is legally correct in matters affecting the constitution. This subsequently became of such paramount importance in history and tradition on its being incorporated in the constitution of the USA. Owing to the fact that the struggle for 'power and ultimate responsibility', whether for great or modest power, is an essential feature of any political activity, this theory is not always without embarrassment for a member of the executive—and also for a Parliament—and complaints are then heard that the system is a jurisdictional system of politics; even I myself have had reason to complain about this during my own period of office. But from the overall impression gained from our experiences in Germany, and also from what I personally know of America, a system of this kind constitutes a regulative force, constantly warning against the impending danger of misuse of power.

"And now that, I think, should be my closing word. I have little talent for passionate appeals and personal confessions of faith; in any case there are a number of political matters that have to be touched upon—we are, after all, in an academic community and not in a political arena; and so perhaps the best thing for me to do is simply to close with an expression of thanks for being allowed to speak to you in a place which itself bears such promise for the future."

The closing speech was given by Professor Simon of the Hebrew University:

"My colleagues have honoured me by choosing me to express to you our sincere and cordial thanks for appearing here and for giving us this lecture today.

"In your charming youth memoirs 'Prelude to Life' (Vorspiele des Lebens) you recount an episode from your school days. For students of philology it has the special charm of containing references to 'descriptive names'; the teacher is called Herr Gutermann and the schoolboy Richard Faul ('good man' and 'lazy'—Tr.). You had written Faul's essay for him and when Herr Gutermann returned it after marking he said: 'Very good, but the essay is written by Heuss.'

"Today we can repeat this verdict 'Very good' in all sincere gratitude and without having to make reference to Herr Gutermann and the boy Faul. What was it that gave us such a pleasing feeling every time we heard from you—a feeling that we have today when we have again had the privilege of listening to you. You will doubtless be tired of having your own—so very aptly chosen—expression 'collective shame' mentioned to you. But in coining this expression you have not only enriched our vocabulary but added to the stock of ethical and cultural capital of your people and indeed of humanity as a whole. It is always those who personally have no need for individual shame who are capable of feeling and expressing collective shame. Those not directly involved in misdeed are ashamed for the active miscreants and may conceivably prevent similar mischief in the future and in this way the world makes a little progress.

"In your speech you referred to the problem of resistance to the unjustly exercised authority of a state. But in you, spiritual resistance, that kind of resistance that was the only kind left to many of us—particularly the Jews in National-Socialist Germany, has been carried to the point of active patriotism. It is the very fact that it does not share the moral decay afflicting country and people that enables it to serve that country and people. Your published work during that period of terror is a living testimony to this.

"In 1936 you published a great work about your teacher Friedrich Naumann. Naumann was born 100 years ago, in 1860, the same year as our Theodor Herzl. These two men have one feature in common that links them with each other and with their own time: They aimed at bridging the gap between purely national and purely social ideas. It is with a shudder that we all recall the bestial caricature that National Socialism succeeded in making of this constructive technique. But that should not stop us from continuing to work for its ultimate achievement.

"In this book you speak in a frank and open manner of Jews with whom Naumann came into contact. You characterized, for instance, the great-hearted philanthropist Charles Hallgarten as a 'consciously proud member of the Jewish race' but at the same time added that he was not a Zionist. At that time this remark had a special overtone. Those having 'eyes to see' could not take it as drawing a line between Jews and Zionists whom you have always approached with the most sympathetic consideration but as a statement of a historical fact that, to the people in power, implied that there must be room for a conscious and proud Jew, even in Germany. You carried your spiritual resistance even further and spoke with breath-taking frankness of the 'destruction of the life of a people' (Page 312) which was going on while you were actually writing those very words. This frankness at a time like that certainly put you in a position of some danger of which you must have been aware and must be thankful—as we are today—that you were spared the worst consequences of your courage. This meant that in the second edition of your book, which was published *after* the downfall of the Tyrant, you did not need to alter a single word. There are very few political books written at that time of which the same can be said.

"Your Naumann book was the last that you were able to produce under your own name; later you were largely condemned to remain anonymous. Your articles in the 'Frankfurter Zeitung', that have now been collected and published in your excellent book 'Deutsche Gestalten' ('Personalities of Germany') strengthened the attentive reader in his convictions of moral and spiritual resistance and put in his hand an instrument of moral rehabilitation that was not a crusade—an affair of clanging armour but that conveyed a gentle, and in the long run unmistakable, warning. Two examples will suffice to illustrate this:

"You describe Leopold von Ranke and point out that his warning against national arrogance unfortunately fell on deaf ears. Another of your articles is devoted to an appreciation of his great opponent Hegel and you say that his delayed impact was veiled in a peculiar sort of anonymity. Even at that time it must have been obvious to the reader that the unknown author was referring to the particular conditions which forced him to adopt the cloak of anonymity but at the same time all this could do was to limit his range of efficacy; but it could not stop him functioning as a social force. In these articles you developed the language to a stage that one could call the 'style of the soothsayer', since it was on the forum of the publicity that this style created a secret sphere of agreement between the writer and his readers. In his book 'Persecution and the Art of Writing', Professor Leo Strauss in Chicago has gone into this phenomenon in some detail.

"Your open-mindedness in your contact with the world and your appreciation of human values has brought you not only closer to many Jewish people but to Jewish affairs as such. We read how on a visit to Prague you are struck by the fact that the main synagogue, the ancient 'Alt-Neuschul', was built in the Gothic style of its age instead of in the exotic oriental style of many other synagogues. A statement like this may perhaps be compared to the bold insight of Nicolaus von Cues: 'Una est religio in ritum varietate'.

"Whatever may be the—conceivably justified—differences in faith and whatever may be the necessity felt by all faiths to retain the material amplitude of form and ritual peculiar to them, we—both Jew and Gentile alike—must never lose sight of the common ground of our faith that makes it possible for this amplitude to have one uniform point of reference. And here I might perhaps add a final touch to my illustration of this point with an example from the Talmud. In your speech you stressed that the majority of 98%, of which the National Socialists were so proud, is exactly the same as the figure given in the results of communist elections. Our rabbis of old laid it down that a person guilty of a capital crime and condemned to death by a completely unanimous vote shall go free because everyone has the right to at least one voice raised in his defence. And it is from this original idea that the special function of the champion developed; formerly it was one of the judges who had to undertake this himself; it is now one of the essential principles of spiritual and temporal democracy.

"You are with us at a special period of the Jewish year—during the seven weeks betwen our Passover and the Second Feast of the Reaping—Shawuoth as we call it, corresponding to your Easter and Whitsuntide. At Shawuoth—and only at Shawuoth do we decorate our synagogues with flowers.

"I thought of this when I had the privilege of reading a poem by your late wife Dr. Elly Heuss-Knapp, the illustrious daughter of the great Strasbourg financier; this poem speaks of decorating an altar, so let the poem itself decorate the altar of our thanks to you and let the expression of the welcome we bid you be conveyed by means of those verses which, here in the holy city of Jerusalem, in the Hebrew University, can perhaps express what we feel at this moment far better than any words of our own:

> 'Vases and bowls for the altar
> The prayers, the prayers and the gifts:
> Empty bowls are there—and empty hands
> Waiting, waiting to be filled
> And to take the offered blessing;
> The seasons of the year have given to us,
> The speeding change, the steady, silent, passing.
> And then there comes the offering
> Of what we have received—
> Bowls filled to overflowing
> Give thanks that prayers are answered!'"

Eugen Gerstenmaier on the change in the German outlook

Writing in the "Süddeutsche Zeitung" of 4th December 1962, the Israeli correspondent of the newspaper, M. Y. Ben-gavriêl, made the following statement in connection with the visit of the President of the Bundestag, Eugen Gerstenmaier:

"The number of German visitors to Israel is very small compared with the number from other countries but despite this fact a change in the attitude of Israel towards Germany is becoming noticeable—a change that is symptomatic of the attitude of the average Israeli citizen. All these visits—private, demi-semi-official and semi-official (there are no official ones so far)—have one thing in common: they are all good-will visits."

Konrad Adenauer and David Ben Gurion in 1960 at the Waldorf-Astoria Hotel in New York. This was a meeting which made history as well as making the headlines.

Carlo Schmid in a workshop for trainees of the ORT School in Natanya, Israel (1959)

Hendrik van Dam, the Secretary-General of the Central Council of Jewish Affairs in Germany (1966)

Hermann Josef Abs, leader of the delegation to the Debts Conference in London, and Financial Adviser on Reparations to Konrad Adenauer (1966)

The visit of Eugen Gerstenmaier, which presumably would not have been possible at this formality-level a few years earlier, constituted something of a touchstone for those groups who were interested in a political rapprochement between Germany and Israel and those who were definitely against it. It was not, of course, possible for Gerstenmaier to be received by the President of the Israeli Parliament in parliament itself but he was certainly received with the utmost cordiality at the President's private residence at the Kvutsah Deganyah. His visit to the President of the state was "almost official" and he talked for a very long time with President Ben Gurion about most current political matters, without, however, a joint communiqué being issued; he was treated, not only by people at all government levels but by the general public, as though Germany had an ambassador in Israel who had officially introduced the visitor.

This fact, quite inconceivable a few years earlier, is indicative of the change in the attitude of the Israeli public to Germany. The attitude of the Israeli government was already known. It was ready to take up normal diplomatic relations with Germany. At that time Bonn was still not willing to accept diplomatic relations. Despite this attitude on the part of the Federal Government, from which Israel had definitely expected a different approach to this matter, in Israel the man in the street had gradually got used to the idea of making no distinction in the treatment of German visitors and tourists from any other country. The tone of the Israeli press also reflected the public attitude. Like almost all the other newspapers the government-oriented *Jerusalem Post*, in addition to publishing a daily *reportage* of Gerstenmaier's travels through the country, printed benevolent articles, biographical notes and, indeed, finally wrote: "If ever relations with Germany should be taken up this visit will be remembered as one of the most important stages in the process of their resumption."

This appreciation, given by Ben-gavriêl, reflected the thoughts that accompanied the representative of the German Parliament on his visit. In contrast to the visit of Theodor Heuss, Gerstenmaier's visit took place in the atmosphere of the Eichmann trial that had ended in the summer of 1962 and that affected the entire Israeli population so deeply. One of the most moving moments of the entire visit—and one which the editor of this book was personally privileged to witness was when Gerstenmaier—the same Gerstenmaier who, on 20th July 1944, on the occasion of the tragic attempt to get rid of Hitler and what Gerstenmaier referred to as his "gang of murderers", was himself arrested by the SS-Führer Skorzceny in the headquarters of the German Wehrmacht in Berlin and had miraculously survived the trial by Freisler's Special Court—laid a wreath with a black-red-gold ribbon down in Yad Washem. When we left the memorial at the foot of the hills of Jerusalem we were met by a group of young German "Evangelical" Protestants who were also visiting the memorial. Gerstenmaier followed the group with his eyes and said: "I wonder whether they will ever realize what exactly did happen to the Jewish people? No—that is probably too much to expect!"

In the evening of that same day the President of the Bundestag responded to a request of the Israeli Political Science Society by speaking on the difficult subject "The Change in the German Outlook". The audience numbered 400 and the text of the speech was as follows:

"After all that lies behind us and all that has been between us I am bound to say that I am conscious in equal measure of the honour on the one hand and the risk on the other that is attached to speaking in public in what is, to me, the most highly-revered city in the whole world. Perhaps from our point of view—and certainly from mine—it would be simpler if I were to speak of the Germans and their changes in outlook in something like the same way as we spoke in the darkest years of Germany in the company of those who were conspiring to kill the monster holding us in thrall, or again as we spoke later with our companions in misfortune in Gestapo prisons and penitentiaries. But meanwhile the passage of time has brought changes affecting us all. This really became clear to me for the first time in the April days of 1945 when American troops appeared amid the smoke of Bayreuth. They released the four or five thousand political prisoners who had been herded together in the neighbourhood of Richard Wagner's opera house. Up to this time there had been something like a solidarity of common suffering between us, without regard to nation and origin. But the moment we were released that was the end of that. We had the choice of severing our ties with Germany or, on the other hand, embracing the idea of holding the entire German people collectively responsible for what had been happening. The majority of us accepted this and that was the change, the change that I referred to above.

"The bankruptcy of the Weimar Republic and the so-called seizure of power by Hitler, his maniacal racial theories and the war unleashed by him have cost altogether 50 million lives, of which 6 million were Jews and 7 million were Germans; Germany has been divided into three and the dominion of Communism has been extended from the old Eastern border of Poland to the very centre of Germany. Germany has ceased to be a great power—let alone a world power. She is not even capable of ensuring the continued existence of her capital city without outside aid. It was, of course, possible to give a new life and livelihood to 12 or 13 million refugees and expellees but there are 17 million German citizens in East Germany for whom she cannot obtain decent living conditions and cannot even begin to think of having them join in a common existence with common social and civil rights and privileges.

"That Hitler was bound to lose the war in the end is, I believe, an intellectual—if not a moral—conclusion which the majority of the German people have succeeded in reaching today. But that the free world should have ended up by losing the peace—that is certainly beyond the capacity of the majority of Germans to grasp. This constituted one of the greatest subliminal difficulties in the realization of the Adenauer scheme of foreign policy and the plan for ensuring the security of the country. The creation of the German armed forces, conscription, entry into the NATO—all these encountered strong resistance because they involved being drawn into the orbit of those powers of whom many Germans were inclined to be critical—not so much because they were their opponents in war as because they had allowed themselves to be so easily deceived by Soviet Russia.

"Feelings of this kind often went hand in hand with unqualified resignation of the 'Little man, what now?' variety. Indeed, that had already been the unspoken question in the minds of many Germans witnessing the brutal force of a totalitarian régime during the pre-war sabre-rattling of Nazism. During the war this feeling of being a pawn of fate became potentiated to the point of utter helplessness, even in the case of those who in the beginning had enthusiastically dedicated themselves to the 'cause'. The subsequent unconditional surrender was finally seen by the majority as nothing more than confirmation of the situation by the action of other absolute powers. The system of 're-education' introduced into Germany by the Americans was unable to dispel this belief and moreover, political developments throughout the world, which resulted in the formation of two gigantic world blocs confronting each other in armed preparedness on German soil, was not calculated to dispel from the minds of the Germans the idea that they were no more than the passive object of world politics. Passive pawn of fate under Hitler, passive pawn of fate afterwards—this feeling constitutes a potential mental danger that has not been completely overcome, even today.

"For although it contributed to dispelling quite a number of illusions in that the constant feeling of being nothing more than a passive object in the hands of superior powers produces the two-fold effect of eliminating residual traces of National Socialism and of 19th century nationalism—although all this may seem very impressive yet the attitudes and feelings arising out of this process are not, in themselves, enough. However much real life may prove the Germans to be right, their factual denial of any ultimate action worthy of the name does not do justice to the situation. Indeed, the practical release from the critical faculty, from personal and national involvement in respect of the rights, privileges and duties of life associated with the foregoing, is distinctly unethical from the citizenship point of view. Admittedly, the terrible superior force of unscrupulous state powers produces a mentally crippling effect but it is decidedly unethical simply to abandon all personal responsibility in advance on the excuse of being overwhelmed. The effect is to produce that very vacuum which renders the individual—and in the same way an entire people—powerless to deal soberly and dutifully with the situation created by his or their own actions, good or bad, or by his or its attitude and way of life in general. Thus the main question with which I am concerned here, in developing my subject, is not whether there has ever been any change at all in the outlook in Germany—of course there has—but first, whether such change of heart has been brought about by the earnest and critical self-appraisal of the Germans, second, what were the forces directing it and finally, what is to be its future function.

"The political change that has taken place in Germany since World War II is essentially associated with the programmatic renunciation, in German politics, of the policy of sovereignty of nation-states. I have no doubt at all that this renunciation is also approved by the majority of Germans behind the Iron Curtain. One of the reasons why it is so important is that it also includes the abandonment by Germany of a Great-Power policy of her own, deployed between East and West. It constitutes, at the same time, the abandonment of a German solo policy, directed towards the East. Even today there is still a certain amount of controversy in Germany about this but the reason is not that the archaic prefabricated patterns of thought belonging to the Bismarck era are still particularly active but that there are still some people who cherish the illusion that it is possible for a neutral Germany to achieve her unity and to maintain her continued existence in freedom while still retaining her neutrality. But any serious political viability that this neutralism may once have had in Germany has disappeared since the advent of Social-Democrat opposition to the line of foreign policy laid down by Adenauer.

"One of the major reasons for this is the emergence of Soviet Russia and its satellites as a power bloc and the threat that this presents to Western Germany. But one might go so far as to say that even without this threat there would have been a fundamental change in German thinking in the planning of foreign policy which would have been reflected in the action taken by the government. The recent visit of the French Head of State to the Federal Republic presented a most impressive example of this. The reception given to General de Gaulle in Germany was so cordial, in fact, so rousing as to exceed the wildest forecasts. There was no shortage of voices saying that this was a manifestation of the German tendency to leader-worship but this interpretation of the situation misses the whole point. Anyone who has trodden the blood-soaked soil of the Franco-German battlefields of two or three wars and has opened his eyes to the need for peace of the two peoples will know better than anyone else the deep-rooted feelings that were responsible for the welcome given to de Gaulle in Germany. The keynote was: Let war between Germany and France be a thing of the past and let us make an end to this long, catastrophic saga of strife between us and our neighbours.

"It was this expression of will that burst upon the French Head of State when he arrived in Germany. It was this will that rallied a solid phalanx of Germans to the banner of European unity. In the Kreisau circle we had already made up our minds as long ago as the beginning of the second World War that Germany's future could only be assured under circumstances of long-lasting state-federative community in partnership with our European neighbours. And there were others who also saw these things in the same light. But obviously there had to be the battles of World War II and the emergence of such political super-powers as the USA and the Soviet Union to bring home to us in Germany—and not only in Germany—that no other way was possible. The unification of Europe and the forming of the Atlantic Community was seen by the Germans not only as a way of making a political virtue of the necessity arising out of defeat but as the positive aspect—viewed in a world context—of a horrible series of events. German policy had to be governed by this interpretation, namely the pattern of a new and lasting system of peace and freedom in Europe.

"This constituted a union of political common sense and open-minded ethical self-appraisal. German foreign policy was nothing more than a rehearsal for this; it was in no way abandoned even when it was unavoidably endangered in the name of national unity. The re-creation of national unity is recognized by the Germans as an obligation. But this does not alter the fact that German post-war foreign policy is determined by a soberly conceived order of priorities in which freedom—and thus solidarity with the free world—is the first desideratum, peace (together with the implicit renunciation of aggression or armed force for the re-establishment of vanished frontiers) the second and, as a logical corollary, national unity in the third place. It is, of course, a pattern of politics which brings its own problems. But it is one that has been accepted and confirmed by the vast majority of Germans and I believe that this attitude in the motives underlying it may be considered as the true expression of a genuine readjustment of the German way of thinking.

"It is clear enough that a readjustment of this kind involves not only changing the structure of military policy and foreign policy but reassessing traditional national feeling and the corporate consciousness of the state entity. There is, of course, a considerable amount of controversy today about the exact nature of German national feeling, indeed, about the fact of whether there still is such a thing, whether one can really speak of German national feeling at all. Of one thing, however, I am certain—this national feeling—whatever it may be called—is constantly stimulated by the desire for the reunification of Germany and kept very much alive by the permanent state of near-crisis in Berlin. But there can be no doubt in my mind that this national feeling and consciousness of a state entity not only has a real existence but is today expressed in terms of the readjusted German way of thinking.

"This not only applies to the forms in which it is outwardly expressed. Anyone wanting to appeal to his audience today on the lines of the traditional patriotic speech or the traditional repertoire of national songs in Germany would be simply inviting ridicule. This is not only a consequence of the general changes in style—changes that have been taking place in the language and in the national image—but is connected with something like the wholesale rejection of the ideas of entire epochs of German history and their associated values. Of course, it cannot be said that everything emerging from this change in a way of thinking is clear and convincing. Here again, it is often no more than a negation of what has gone before, the mere rejection of something without putting something else in its place—a process that inevitably causes a vacuum. The conformism that was forced upon the people by the levelling effect of national socialism has been to a large extent replaced by habitual non-conformism which is frequently less concerned with the aim towards which it is directed than with making a demonstration of non-conformism. Perhaps it is sufficient to satisfy certain of its champions but it seldom takes a productive form. It is often denounced as nihilism and this reproach not infrequently turns out to be quite justified. It may be that all the peoples in the civilized system of the world are aware of similar symptoms but I doubt if they can be as 'conformist-non-conformist' in nature as here in Germany.

"Perhaps the most positive thing that can be said about the situation is that it still bears all the symptoms of an instinctive and violent reaction against the contamination of the German people with the ideas of National Socialism. In the Germany of the present day, for example, it is necessary to have seen the spontaneous reactions of university students and seniors in schools to the gramophone records of Hitler's speeches. I shall never forget that it was ever possible for more or less rational beings to be led astray by that hysterical bawling. The ensuing discussions are rendered profitless by the fact that it is completely impossible to give the young people of today even the vaguest idea of the subjective and objective atmosphere in which Hitler and his followers uttered the cries that we now hear under sterilized recording conditions. With all due reserve it can really be said that in such discussions it is not Hitler and his gang that were in the dock but practically the whole of the two upper age-groups in Germany.

"It is quite clear to everyone that Hitler and his followers were out-and-out criminals of the first order. But there is no answer to the question that is now put to the older generation: How could you possibly bow down to and follow something like that? In fact, the question does not even have to be formulated in this way, it carries its own implied reproach; however it is put and however much is said on the subject one way or the other the element of reproach cannot be eliminated. The result is that this kind of discussion is frequently avoided in the pious hope that the practical problems of the present day displace the theoretical ones of yesterday and cause these awkward questions to be forgotten. And the majority of even those who reject the expression 'collective guilt' as inapplicable know that a question like this can only be answered by frank and open self-humiliation.

"An expression has been coined for this attitude which, though it may not be universal, is very wide-spread; it is the expression: an uneasy past—a past with which people were unable to come to terms. This expression is not exactly false but it is futile. For who could simply 'come to terms' with the kind of past that is referred to here anyway? Could the matter be settled by those collectively-responsible survivors of Nazi days publicly recanting and confessing their misdeeds? Many have, of course, done it and the others ought to. But if I myself, for example, were to do this I would lose nothing, either in my conscience or my thought-processes, of the mark of Cain that was branded on the foreheads of the German people in those days. Since the end of the war we Germans have intimately experienced the transforming power of reconciliation. But this is a miracle that we ourselves have not wrought. It has determined our thinking more radically than can be seen from an outside standpoint but this miracle would be the last thing that might be supposed to release us from the shame of what was undeniably done in the name of Germany and the Germans, even if there were quite a number of Germans who did not give their sanction, or indeed, who actively opposed it. I only need to leaf through the evidence—evidence such as that of Poliakov-Wulf—in order to be confirmed in my belief that for us Germans—i.e. for my own generation—there is simply no way of 'coming to terms' with this past for the rest of our lives. It is simply impossible for people of any conscience at all to conveniently 'settle' the past in this way.

"But perhaps it would at least be possible to restore the much-distorted German sense of history. This sense of history has been so dislocated as a result of the happenings of the past thirty years, has become so uncertain and so diffused that it seems to me to be an even more problematical affair than our present feeling of nationhood. It is true that we can point to a number of honourable efforts which include the complete revision of our school-books, the conscientious work of the Institut für Zeitgeschichte (Institute of Current Affairs) in Munich and the scientific overall pictures of considerable value. But as far as our history is concerned—our history at least from the Seven Years' War up to the Treaty of Rapallo—all this is for many Germans—perhaps indeed for most of them— still shrouded in obscurity. As a German writer put it recently, the German of today lives among the ruins of his history—and there are quite a number of people who feel the same. Of course, there are others that are little or not at all concerned to account for this state of affairs. But judged at its most favourable, the situation is such that many people are conscious of a vacuum which nothing had been able to fill and in the presence of which true nationhood and national feeling cannot be properly directed and coordinated.

"National Socialism was not the first political system in which conscious German nationhood was exaggerated to the dimensions of monstrosity. In the 19th century, German national feeling degenerated, as did that of some other peoples—at least temporarily—into an exaggerated form of nationalism. German conservatism (and German liberalism in any case!) was not powerful enough to prevent this exaggeration and corruption of nationalism. The restoration and normalization of the German feeling of nationhood after 1918 were certainly not assisted—in fact, actively impeded—by the loss of World War I and the subsequent attempt at Versailles to hold Germany solely and exclusively responsible for the war. But it was not until the advent of National Socialism with its maniacal racial theory and shameless ambitions that the feverish German national identity of the Weimar days became completely contaminated with the nationalist poison. Nationalism, hysterical nationalism, had existed before and has existed since in other peoples as well. But the maniacal racial theories of National Socialism poisoned the German idea of nationalism sufficiently to create the background conditions for the committing of large-scale crime in the name of Germany—and then the technical conditions for executing it; and there are few comparable examples of this in recent history. I personally am convinced that it was not exclusively the compulsory orders of a totalitarian state that rendered possible this ruthless extinction of millions of people. It was also necessary to have the utterly mortal poison of an ideology, the maniacal atmosphere of which was alone sufficient to conjure forth a large enough group of hangmen and their assistants to carry out such an operation.

"I think there can be no doubt that this maniacal racial theory of National Socialism, the perverted national opportunism and the cynicism of national-socialist methods, have been completely eliminated from the German national consciousness. What remained after this process, however, was a German national consciousness that, if not actually destroyed, was at least radically disturbed. In its place many Germans are conscious of that vacuum to which reference has been made above. One of the vital questions with which the minds of Germans are today occupied is whether (and if so, how) they can achieve a healthy state of national consciousness and can see German history in its true perspective. In the long run it is in these factors that the true patterns of past events will be found—a pattern that is not, incidentally, confined to a consideration of Hitler and his epoch—and a philosophical foundation laid for our actions in the future.

"And of no less importance than the ultimate designation of traditional nationalism is the exact definition of the sense of loyalties in the consciousness of a people—which follows as an indispensable corollary.

"When I was a boy the growing nationalism in my honest and straight-forward Württemberg home country frequently reminded me of the fact that it was necessary to learn thought and action in the same way as the British on a 'My country, right or wrong!' basis. Later, the Nazis used the expression: 'The people is always right'. Today, in the free part of Germany, this attitude of mind can no longer be publicly sold or lauded under any circumstance, the reason being not that there would then be a court case but that the public has become allergic to anything even remotely smacking of National Socialism or reminding them of the nationalism of earlier days and its total meaning in terms of the state entity as they see it.

"The latest conflict that we have had to cope with in Germany—the so-called 'Spiegel' affair—is an interesting example of this if not, in fact, of more than this. The real or presumed mistakes made by the authorities in this matter have called forth such a storm of protest in Germany against anything that is even remotely reminiscent of opportunist abuse of power and restrictions of freedom that the 'Spiegel', suspected as it was of treason, was not only out of the line of fire but also even enjoys the publicly-proclaimed favour of many of its erstwhile opponents and critics.

"This example is intended as no more than a slight indication of the extent to which the national consciousness of the Germans has changed since—at the very latest—the downfall of Hitler. The many exaggerated nervous and disproportionate reactions in Germany to potential formal trespasses of the authorities on citizens' rights or against certain political decisions can only be properly understood if we see the situation as reflecting an exaggerated positive swing corresponding to an equally exaggerated negative swing during the Hitler days. Not only did Hitler and his gang disregard the law of property but, with unparalleled cynicism, they had no hesitation whatsoever in perverting the ends of formal justice for whatever purpose they felt to be desirable. When we hear references to Gestapo methods in the Germany of today this is either gross slander against the Federal Republic or a cynical minimizing of the crimes of the Hitler days. But the overall picture of public discussion—unfortunately by no means free of stiff-necked pomposity—cannot be understood without the realization that these exaggerated and desperate reactions are seen in a country in which today we still have terrible memories of the Gestapo and in which we still have the haunting spectre of the 'political police' in the communist East Zone of Germany.

"The reaction of a large proportion of the German public to the 'Spiegel' case is interesting in respect of the point I would like to make here about loyalties. A national state—or at least a nationalistically-inclined state—will always tend to regard treason as the most 'capital' of all crimes. It seems to me that today Germany is in the opposite state—i.e. the absolute antithesis of nationalism, so to speak; this becomes evident from the fact that in the 'Spiegel' case, for example, many people of otherwise sound judgment—although not, of course, regarding treason as no more than a misdemeanour—nevertheless tend to take what may be nothing more than procedural errors on the part of the authorities as jeopardizing the constitutional state and as such are liable to condemn it with disproportionate harshness. Opinions may differ on the political aspect of the 'Spiegel' case but public reaction, as far as it can be analyzed up to now, seems to me to suggest beyond all doubt that there is no further likelihood of the German public conscience proclaiming the idea of the 'right or wrong' or 'that which serves the people must be right'.

"The marks of a guilty past are so strongly branded in the German national consciousness that if the authority of the state is not as a whole a doubtful proposition from the very start it is nevertheless only its morally-acceptable authority that has a real chance of succeeding. But there are difficulties attending the exercise of even this legitimate authority in the Germany of today, particularly because the moral value of decisions made by the state is often prejudiced in advance. A case in point was the introduction of conscription a few years ago when the government of the German Federal Republic had to overcome considerable resistance from a number of citizens, the resistance in some cases being made on ethical grounds. Examples of resistance to an emergency law show that it is a matter of great difficulty—or even impossibility—to convince everyone in Germany that the legal rights of the citizen, as safeguarded by the Basic Law, have, from time to time, to take second place to the stern necessities of the continued existence and the security of the country. These borderline cases of legal responsibility, in which it is not a clear matter of right and wrong—of a positive against a negative value—but of one positive value weighted against another, are understood and their necessity realized only with the very greatest of difficulty by the German people. This fact can only be properly understood if it is seen in the context of our experience with National Socialism and of a conscious attempt at anticipating what may well become abuse.

"Obviously critical—indeed, highly undesirable—phenomena are bound to be part of the picture and there are circumstances in which the cumulative effect of these might well result in a situation of real danger. The totalitarian state of National Socialism exploited the readiness of the population for devoted service and self-sacrifice, made such excessive demands on the stoicism of the people and placed the connotation of state and government in such a dubious context that the call for sacrifice and devotion to the fatherland frequently encountered almost uncontrollable distrust—as, in fact, it still does even today in Germany. It is not only the one-time pathos of the so-called 'national style' that has become impossible today but its ethos or ethical aspect is no longer a matter of course and is no longer automatically respected without prejudice.

"The confusion of the situation is seen from the fact that, coupled to the symptoms of a totally unjustified resentment of state interference on the one hand, we have, at the same time, an ever-wilder demand for a state system, for increased state welfare activity affecting all aspects of life and it is a fact that in the free part of Germany these state services are increasing in proportion as state competences increase despite the fact that the Federal Government tends to control rather than to promote this feature. Of course the same situation exists to a certain extent in other countries as well but in Germany it casts deep shadows and perhaps it takes on something of the nature of a crisis because it is against the background of the ruin of a state without parallel in our history—a ruin that we ourselves have experienced in our lifetime.

"In comparison with the difficulties and dangers in this sphere I would assess the dangers that beset German democracy as such as relatively slight. There are, of course, anxious people even in a strong government who tend to exaggerate the danger but if we cast our minds back to the days of the Weimar Republic we realize that a head of government with authority does not necessarily constitute a danger for democracy and, in fact, the danger is far greater where the government is weak. In any case it is not as a result of having Reichs-Chancellors wielding personal power that the Weimar Republic fell but because none of its democratic chancellors opposed Hitler with sufficient determination. No, what German democracy needs are strong governments, and parliaments that are able to cope with them. The constructive vote of 'no confidence' against the Federal Chancellor that was incorporated in the Basic Law of the Federal Republic in conscious rectification of the constitution as it existed in the Weimar Republic has proved to be right.

"A further contribution to the internal stabilization of democracy in Germany was the reduction of the number of political parties as called for by a well-thought-out election law. In 1949 there were no less than ten parties in the Bundestag and in 1961 there were only three. There is no doubt at all that this situation brings considerable problems for the parties concerned. They must be far more wide-ranging in their mental attitude, in their political programme and in their social stratification than ever before in Germany. But however openminded they may be they must always have an image clearly indicative of their character. The practical consequence of all this is that although the three great parties of Germany, with their historical and ideological backgrounds, are still endeavouring, with varying degrees of emphasis, to point out the differences that are between them, they are still at the same time at pains to present all strata and groups of people in our pluralistic society with a more or less attractive programme. The result of this, in turn, is that in their programmes—and to a considerable extent in political practice as well—there is really considerably less difference between them than there used to be; a major factor contributing to this universal tendency was the Social-Democrat opposition to Adenauer's foreign policy made in the middle of 1960 in the Bundestag. The crucial problem facing the present-day political parties is that of integrating as smoothly as possible as many groups and levels of consciousness in themselves whilst at the same time leaving as unaffected as possible their capacity for independent action.

"Despite the special efforts that the parties are obliged to make—in view of the continuance of election campaigns in Germany if for no other reason—the attitude of the German public towards the parties remains decidedly reserved. In other words, the parties as such are still not popular in the true sense of the word. This does not automatically mean that there are still traces of National Socialism in Germany but the situations and personal attitudes which were always a neutral feature of everyday life in Germany must not be left out of account. Many intellectuals, for instance, have an exaggerated sense of objectivity and feel unable to plunge into the jungle warfare of political practice and thus at the same time of political party life at the expense of their intellectual integrity. Of course, this indicates a certain objection to having parliamentary democracy as the form of liberal constitutional state prescribed for us.

" I make this distinction deliberately because there are many critics of our parties to whom it appears unfair for their objections to the parties to be interpreted or described as an objection to the liberal constitutional state as such. Nevertheless in the reservations that these people have about the parties there is inevitably an element objection to parliamentary democracy. It is based in the first place on a dislike for certain less attractive forms of political dispute and on an instinctive disapproval of political wrangles in which not infrequently the essentials of a situation are obscured. In the second place these objections are kept alive by deep-rooted dissatisfaction dating back to the days of the Weimar Republic. I well remember a hotly-contested debate taking place among us half-starved political prisoners when in February 1945 we were taken by coal barge on the Brandenburg Waterways to be either taken on further or sunk on the spot, whichever seemed more expedient. The curses that we uttered then and even before that time were not directed against the Nazis alone but against the Weimar democracy because it had not destroyed Hitler in time. But these feelings of resentment are not directed solely at the small group of incorrigible Nazis but extend to the many who either had very little or nothing at all to do with National Socialism.

"And this brings us to the third point—i.e., the residue of National Socialism in Germany. I am well aware that the essential factor about it is not the part that can be proved either by organizations or by the police but that part of it (if anything at all) that can still be found in the public mind in Germany. But the picture would be incomplete without carefully considering whatever may remain of National Socialism at organizational and political levels. The Ministry of the Interior has recently issued a documentary report on this subject. The result of this investigation, which was carried out by the so-called Departments for the Preservation of the Constitution (which expression practically boils down to a political secret police) has shown that there are no less than 90 extreme rightist organizations and associations—and that means organizations more or less openly sympathizing with National Socialism within the German Federal Republic. The report shows that during the last two years these organizations have lost approximately 35% of their supporters. On December 31st, 1961 these 90 organizations had a total of 12,300 members. It is reported that the extreme rightist youth organizations have decreased in numbers to 2,100 members—out of the 4.5 million total of Germans in democratic youth organizations.

"An interesting—and at the same time a dangerous—fact emerging from the incontrovertible documentation of the report of the Ministry of the Interior is that the further rightist extremism recedes the more support it receives from outside. It is reported, for instance, that in May 1961 the Ministry of State Security in Ulbricht's East Berlin printed anti-Semitic leaflets and smuggled them into West Germany during the Eichmann trial in Jerusalem in order to create the impression that there was an SS underground organization at work in the Federal Republic. The report states that something like 450 foreign parties and organizations are known to the Ministry of the Interior in Bonn—all of them concerned with the reviving of Fascism in the Federal Republic.

"I do not think that these agitators will have any greater success in the years to come than they had in the past—and this is emphatically the case with regard to anti-Semitism. In this respect the memory of the crimes of National Socialism has also led to legal action and the imposition of increasingly severe penalties, which brought home even to the most incorrigible the desirability of caution. At all events, anti-Semitic activities have become a rarity in Germany. One could even generalize still further and say that a sober and serious philo-Semitic movement has taken the place of the anti-Semitism of yesterday. This philo-Semitic movement is not without its problems for the simple reason that it would probably be more desirable for the situation to develop naturally in such a way that racial feelings, resentments and taboos were automatically dismissed as absurd. The younger generation will, of course, find it so but whether this enlightenment will one day come naturally to the older generations seems to me to be doubtful. Not before we have got far enough away from Hitler's Reich on the time scale to obtain a true perspective view of it —and not before Hitler's crimes have been finally settled can we expect any further progress in this direction. The tormenting burden of guilt that we are bound to carry is too great for our generation to be free of embarrassment. Time and again we are brought face-to-face with the tormenting questions: 'How could it happen? How could we have let it happen? Did we really know nothing about it?'

"These same questions are posed again and again at every war crimes trial and they call for heart-searching throughout an entire German generation. I cannot deny that all this sooner or later begins to impose an excessive strain on one's own conscience and not only does the light of reason shine as a result of this heart-searching but there also appear dark shadows—shadows brought into being by the reflection that even the most severe form of penitence will be unable to make up for this monstrous guilt. It is not unnatural therefore that there should be quite a number of people who feel that it is time to put an end to all this and to abandon any further idea of punishment. At the same time, I do not think that this latter idea will gain a permanent footing in German parliamentary proceedings and so the system of penalty and penitence will remain.

"If we attempt to gain an insight into the workings of the German mentality of today we can see that much of it lies in the shadow of doubt and much of it is enshrouded in the rolling mists of unsatisfied enquiry. Any one who knows Germany realizes, of course, that there are Germans who are inspired and rational in their outlook—one only needs to pause and consider the aptly demonstrated rational aspects of economic, technical and political life. Possibly this could also be said of other spheres of thought as well, including those of religious devotion and intellectual and cultural activity. These reconcile faith and reason in more or less convincing mental and documentary forms.

"Nietzsche prophesied of the 20th century that it would become an era of nihilism. I shall not take the liberty of passing judgment on the mental and spiritual orientation of the world of our day but I think it would be wrong for the vacuum existing at present in the beliefs of many Germans to be taken for mere nihilism. There is, of course, no doubt that nihilism does exist in Germany even today—and a ruinous nihilism at that. But the vacuum about which I am speaking is a different thing altogether. It results from inner uncertainty and lack of orientation which appear in the form of mental dissociation and indecisiveness. These people do not have the strength to undertake any true personal form of engagement which goes beyond their own ego. This mental dissociation and inner feebleness, however, is devoid of that brutal egoism and presumptuous cynicism that is normally so characteristic of nihilism. Where this feebleness gives way to the adversities of the times the tendency is for 'the will to self-destruction' to supervene; this process has been dealt with by a discriminating German writer. On the whole, however, this vacuum in the prevailing outlook-patterns of the present-day German seems to me to be more like a wavering receptiveness for whatever may come along than mere cynical nihilism.

"Indeed, a story recently told by a well-known German university professor lends some support to this idea: He relates how his students in Tuebingen one day said to him that they would be very glad to have the opportunity of organizing one of these torch-light marches that were traditional in German universities in former days. But they did not know to whom they would be thus be paying tribute, what cause, what idea, what system of values it would be serving! The professor intended the story to illustrate—as, in my view it did—the fact that today's German youth simply do not want to live on the strength of insight into rational processes alone but from the depths of their souls they are seeking something for which it is worth sacrificing their purely subjective aspect of their existence. His story thus went some way to describing the vacuum of which I have been speaking here. One of the largest of the daily newspapers gave its answer to the story in the headline: 'We need no torchlight procession for our values', because—as the writer of this 'answer' went on—'the sole—but at the same time the fundamental—difference' between us and the communist East is 'the frankness, the variety and unregimented multifariousness of our combined thinking.'

"This answer is not entirely wrong. At the same time, however, it is certain that a great many Germans—and in particular German youth—will not accept this as the only difference between the communist coercion state and the free world. What they are seeking—in fact yearning for—are morally-acceptable, great and tangible causes and ideas, figures and images for which they are encouraged to engage themselves without, by doing so, running the risk of again being exploited for evil ends as they were in the days of Hitler. Their path to progress is blocked by the incubus of the past—not merely by the simple everyday things connected with money and with leisure. At all events the vast majority of Germans are well aware, even in this situation, that the East-West conflict is anything but a conventional struggle for power between nations—it is a confrontation of ideas and systems of values. As the corporate consciousness of the German people sees it, it is not the actual physical existence of humanity but humanity's future mental and spiritual existence that is at stake. That this should be the aspect of world conflict that is allocated first place—even taking precedence over quite justified claims on a purely national level such as the claim for living in one united state—is part of the stock-in-trade system of political ethics that is demanded of the Germans as a matter of course nowadays.

"Then again it is on the basis of this kind of understanding that the switch in loyalties, of which I have already spoken in a different context, is taking place. Law is superior to purpose. The cause of freedom must take precedence over any other human claims at purely national level. And this, incidentally, is the basic precept which sustained German resistance to Hitler, at least in as much as it found its natural expression in the attempted coup d'état of 20th July, 1944. I cannot claim that the German resistance movement constitutes anything of a model for the political and national life of present-day Germany. It developed under circumstances too extraordinary and had to make sacrifices that were too costly in blood and toil. And again the Western occupying powers, in taking over the initial reorganization of the state after 1945, relied too casually on the motivating forces and ideas of the Weimar days. But even in the Germany of today there is widespread acceptance at various levels of that basic precept of the German resistance movement. But again, even today, we still encounter various forms of objection to individual engagement for a cause or an ideal. These objections are typical of that vacuum which, at best, can be termed open-mindedness. At the same time, however, it is open-mindedness that can admit the utterly outrageous—with the probable exception, that is, of Communism and Fascism.

"But this picture would not be complete if I were to omit reference to that realm of the German mentality which is connected with religious energies and the strength that comes through faith, a glorious spiritual tradition coupled with fresh ideals. Even in the days of National Socialism—but, of course, to a greater extent immediately afterwards—devotion to the Church and the various faiths was a thing that touched millions of lives. It is not to be explained in terms of the moral incubus resulting from National Socialism, war and its catastrophic aftermath. Again, it is not to be explained in terms of the need to seek comfort in the Church after the collapse of the state. All these were contributory factors of course. But in the movement of the times and in its judgment there were countless numbers that experienced in themselves something like the truth Job felt: 'I had heard of these by hearing of the ear; but now mine eye seeth thee, wherefore I abhor myself, and repent in dust and ashes'.

"Something of the intensity of this confession has been removed by the normalizing effect of everyday life. At the same time, however, I do not believe that the feeling has disappeared altogether. One can see this in the public impact of religious forces on the day-to-day life of Germany and in the soul-searching of the German people. Abuse of these forces by the clergy is prevented by the provisions of the constitution. It guarantees in equal measure freedom before the law and freedom of faith. Thus it not only prevents the formation of a 'Christian state' but it also prevents the structure and the actual values that go to make up the secular state from being misused by the clergy or any anti-religious forces.

"Change in attitude and outlook of Germans? What is it, after all? Let me answer this question by summing up the essentials:

"1. It lies in the fact of a complete change in the German conception of politics. The movement of the German politics of our day away from the sovereign policy of a national state and the integration of the free part of Germany within the overall structure of the European and Atlantic communities is a truth that is graven in history in exactly the same way as the spiritual and religious transformation that has taken place in Germany. It has not only changed the conception of a state but has penetrated to the depths of the national consciousness and transformed it. It has not only focused National Socialism in the critical perspective of time but has led to its rejection through conscience. It has not only called in question the whole accepted pattern of German history but has also remoulded the historical thinking of the Germans.

"2. The aim of this German transformation, as expressed in the will of all parties, forces and groups represented in the German Bundestag today, is none other than the consolidation of this liberal constitutional state that has been obtained at such great cost. It is prepared to use all the force that it can command to accept whatever responsibility it is capable of for the burdens and obligations of history that it has to carry. As it devotes itself to the task of realizing the national unity of Germany it is also conscious of its human obligations towards 17 million fellow-Germans to whom has been denied the human right of self-determination. It is our express aim to live in the lasting union of the free world side by side with them and to be a trustworthy partner to every right-thinking man and woman there.

"3. The danger to which the Germans are subject is neither that of resurgent National Socialism in one form or another nor that of turning to Communism or to the doctrine of revenge-seeking. The internal danger for Germany stems rather from a still largely unfilled mental and spiritual vacuum and the widespread illusion that it is possible to fill this vacuum by concentrating on the full satisfaction of purely material needs. The external danger of Germany is the refusal of an ethically-acceptable compensation from the Soviet side.

"This view of Germany has been given with considerable misgivings and presented in full awareness of the fact that it is only possible to refer to and deal with individual aspects, in almost all of which it has been necessary to venture upon statements that are open to doubt or rejection. But perhaps it is permissible to show how a by no means infallible but at the same time conscientious German seeker after the truth sees Germany today.

"I am well aware of the fact that doubt can be cast on almost everything that I have said. Nobody need to convince me by searching for examples of limited imagination, thoughtlessness—indeed, even for malicious insistence on everything in this speech that they feel was wrong. All the things I have referred to are still to be found in places, even today. But they are by no means typical, in fact, it would be truer to say that it is atypical. At all events, there it is. We have the confirmation that the Germans have never been a homogeneous entity either in the good or the bad sense. The picture that I have portrayed here on Israeli soil is made up of the dealings that a German national has had with his own people in the many and various aspects of their objective and subjective existence. It may be that the light in which it is presented has its origin more in hope and in faith than I myself am aware of.

"Whenever I come to realize where I am speaking and before whom, I am reminded with terrible force and clarity of some of the pictures and documents that are not merely a matter between you and the Germans but between a large part of the world and my people. These pictures of the past are sufficient in themselves to silence us Germans and this silence is the silence of shame and the poignant fellow-feeling of countless numbers of my people in thinking of the people of Israel."

The final phase in the process of establishing diplomatic relations

Even at the beginning of the sixties, the talks on the establishment of diplomatic relations between Israel and the Federal Republic of Germany were attended with a number of difficulties. Public opinion in Israel was bound to be subjectively affected in the first place by the fact that German scientists were collaborating in the development of Egyptian rocket weapons. Then again, the problem of the threatened application of the statute of limitations to bar the National Socialist capital war crimes trials was being hotly discussed in Israel and in Jewish circles in all countries. Finally, the Arab states were spoiling the atmosphere between Israel and the Federal Republic when, after years of tacitly accepting the situation, they suddenly began to protest against the Federal Republic's supplying Israel with weapons.

German arms supplies to Israel

In June 1964 Ludwig Erhard, the German Federal Chancellor, flew to America on a private visit to President Johnson. In the course of the conversations that took place at the President's Texas ranch the President asked Erhard to make a special arrangement in connection with the American M 48 tanks discarded by the Federal Armed Forces and instead of giving them back to the USA send them on to Naples so that after a short period for re-fitting they could subsequently be forwarded to Israel. The USA had supplied these tanks to the Federal Armed Forces within their overall plan of equipment aid and they were, strictly speaking, German property. Thus it was up to the Federal Government to decide, if they wished, what was going to be done with them. Ludwig Erhard agreed with Johnson's proposal and in consequence the arms supplies to Israel were not American but German.

It is necessary to mention this point because both Franz Josef Strauss and Konrad Adenauer had been supplying nothing but defence weapons to Israel. The Arab states, for their part, certainly knew about these arms supplies during Strauss's period of office as Minister of Defence but made no protest since they were quite definitely defence weapons. But now there was a storm of protest leading to those reactionary movements which the Federal Government, with Ludwig Erhard at their head, started: We must put an end to supply arms to Israel, we must send the CDU Bundestag member Kurt Birrenbach to negotiate with the Israeli Government.

Impediments to the establishment of diplomatic relations

One of the subjects with which Chancellor Adenauer managed to occupy himself during the last year of his period of office was the matter of establishing full diplomatic relations with Israel. This was to be the final achievement of his work of reconciliation with the Jewish people and the culmination was to be his assumption of final responsibility for it while still occupying the post of Chancellor. On 10th September, 1963 the American Ambassador in Bonn, McGhee, informed a high official of the Chancellory of the American view on the question of establishing diplomatic relations between the Federal Republic and Israel. McGhee said that the Government of the United States would not presume to intervene in what was, in the strictest sense of the term, a purely German matter but in the capacity of ally and personal friend he would be frank enough to give his impression of the matter at the special request of the Federal Chancellor. McGhee pointed out that the Western powers, and in particular the USA, had very little influence on the Arab states, Jordan being, for all practical purposes, closely linked to the Soviet Union, despite the arms supplied by the West and Egypt, despite American food supplies, being pro-East in attitude; the situation in Iraq was obscure and Syria was part of the Arab Republic. McGhee said the Federal Republic should be alive to the danger of the Arab states' affording recognition to the East Zone or at the very least breaking off relations with Bonn. It would be in the interest of the USA for the Federal Republic of Germany to retain its influence in the Arab states in order to prevent even further weakening of the Western camp in the Arab area. For this reason the United States, whilst expressing full understanding of the attitude of Germany towards Israel wished to express its own misgivings about the situation but would refrain from either speaking for or against the establishment of diplomatic relations with Israel.

Konrad Adenauer was deeply impressed by this statement made by the American Ambassador on behalf of the State Department. In a talk that he had with the leader of the Israeli Mission, Felix Shinnar, Adenauer conveyed the feelings of the US Government but Shinnar could not believe it and the Chancellor asked him to go to State Secretary Hans Globke and verify the details of the records, which Shinnar did and was duly convinced—and at the same time deeply shocked.

At the press conference of 3rd December, 1963 Ludwig Erhard who, in the meantime had taken over the Chancellorship, for the first time expressed his views on the subject of Israel and the Middle East. Two questions were asked by the correspondent of the 'Yedioth Achronoth', Alfred Wolfmann: "Do you intend, Mr. Chancellor, to table, in the foreseeable future, the question of the establishment of diplomatic relations between the Federal Republic and Israel in the Cabinet agenda? Are you personally in favour of the establishment of normal diplomatic relations with Israel, on the desirability of which public statements have recently been made by your predecessor Dr. Adenauer and by prominent politicians of all three parties represented in the Bundestag?" In answer to these questions, Erhard made the following statement:

"Our relations with Israel are expressed not so much in the establishment of diplomatic relations as in the obligation of the German people and in the aid being given in respect of the debt owed by Germany to the Jewish people. I think the whole world recognizes the fact that we are completely open-minded on the subject and with due feeling of responsibility and great personal heart-searching have made the greatest possible contribution to the discharge of this debt. This seems to me to be the primary feature and it is indeed the keynote—it is the spirit that links Israel to Germany and has genuinely created a friendly relationship. The question of diplomatic relations as such rather seems to me to be of less immediate importance. It is not really a matter of *whether* we are to establish them but *when*. If we think back to the year 1952 and remember that Israel had misgivings about establishing diplomatic relations with Germany—an

Erich Ollenhauer visiting a chemical plant in Haifa, Israel. Conversation with a worker. Centre, David Hacohen, the director of the works (1957)

Eugen Gerstenmaier visiting
Martin Buber in Jerusalem (1962)

Franz Josef Strauss with General Jaffé
on the Israeli-Syrian border (1964)

attitude for which we had every understanding at that time—then we have to realize that we are today in a situation in which the establishment of diplomatic relations with Israel should not be allowed to bring about a revival of the question of recognizing the G.D.R. and I think that Israel will understand this attitude. We shall continue to maintain friendly contact with Israel, on the basis of mutual understanding of each other's problems but if you ask me straight out whether I intend at this time to table a motion of this kind in the Cabinet then I am bound to answer, not for the moment."

At the same time, the German Associations for Christian-Jewish Collaboration and the German Trade Union Movement had appealed to the people to collect signatures in order to petition for the establishment of diplomatic relations with Israel. These lobbying operations gave expression to the many voices raised by the German public—voices which were reflected in a number of newspaper articles and radio commentaries and which repeatedly put the question: Why does the Federal Republic of Germany not establish diplomatic relations with Israel?

The atmosphere for negotiations of this kind was not improved in 1964 by the discussions on the limitation statute and by the activities of German scientists in Egypt. Israel felt that she was being subjected to increasing pressure as a result of the steadily-increasing re-armament of the Arab states and particularly of the plain Arab threats that they would intercept and divert the water of the river Jordan. On October 12th, 1964, Levi Eshkol, speaking in the Knesseth, made a statement about German scientists in Egypt. This was another of the problems on which the German Bundestag had also been busily occupied. The situation is best summed up in the statement made by Ludwig Erhard on December 3rd, 1963, and which was now quoted in the Israeli Parliament by the Israeli Premier. In his speech Levi Eshkol said: "… and I am now going to give you the background to the situation which has prompted me to make my statement: I would refer to the answer that Chancellor Erhard gave to the question raised by a journalist on the position with regard to the recall of German scientists that have been engaged in the manufacture of weapons in Egypt. Owing to the fact that the somewhat sensational press reports did not reflect the exact wording of the statements made by Professor Erhard it seems only right for me to begin by quoting, for the benefit of the Assembly, the exact text of the statement:

"'If I could see any practical and efficacious method of resolving the situation the question would be easy to answer. But it is a fact that legal authorities have been much perplexed by the difficulties connected with this matter—indeed, they have gone so far as to make enquiries in other countries to find out what other avenues of approach to the problem might be available there. There is no finally-effective solution and it is an awkward and unsatisfactory business to pass a law just for purposes of show. It goes without saying, of course, that we regret such activities inasmuch as they are taking place in a sphere that may be liable to upset the peace of the world and this is a point that I want to make very clear. But that is the *other* side of the picture; the possibility of a direct approach is still being examined. A motion has been tabled by the SPD but the technicalities of the legal situation are such that we are unable to give any assurance that the mere passing of a law would automatically result in having the scientists withdrawn or recalled, so to speak.'

"These were the words of the Head of the German Government.

"We can assume from these words that there had been no change in the uncompromising attitude of Ludwig Erhard in respect of the matter of the scientists in Egypt. Meanwhile Erhard expressed doubts as to the efficacy of the legislative measures proposed. Again, if we examine the statements made by Erhard himself and his predecessor at the Chancellory, Adenauer, when they expressesd disapproval of the scientists' work and promised to do something about the situation, we find that they allow of no other interpretation.

"Before leaving this matter of the attitude of the Federal Government it is perhaps worth while to point out one or two relevant facts. The fact that German scientists were engaged in the manufacture of war materials in Egypt, first came to light some two years ago. A few months later Mrs. Golda Meir, our Foreign Minister, brought the matter to the attention of the Knesseth. The speaker of the Federal Government said that the Government disapproved of the activities of these scientists and had a) brought its influence to bear to get them to return and b) will continue its efforts in this direction.

"A similar statement, made jointly by all the parliamentary groups in the Bundestag, was made public a few days later. The statement carried a rider to the effect that the three parties in the Bundestag would do everything in their power to put the necessary legislative measures into effect. A further statement, again to the same effect, was made by the Speaker of the Federal Government at the end of 1963. At that time the Federal Government thought that the best way would be the extension of the passport laws to cover these eventualities. But nothing came of it. German television, German radio and the majority of German newspapers showed, and are still showing, disapproval of the activities of the German scientists and clearly wish to have nothing to do with it. Time and again, people in public life, leading figures in the various parties and trade unions have expressed their disapproval. At the same time, however—and to our great regret— there has been no change in the position. I should like to add right here and now that a few weeks ago I myself wrote a personal letter to the Federal Chancellor on the subject.

"When a short time ago the first voices were raised in protest against the nature of Ludwig Erhard's answer at the press conference already referred to, the speaker of our Ministry of Foreign Affairs added his statement; it ran as follows:

"'The bitterness and disillusionment with which we are filled as a result of the activities of German scientists who are supporting the aims of the Egyptian war machine is of two-fold origin. In the first place, we cannot help being deeply shocked by those ineradicable historical associations of the word *Germans* with the expression *The use of force directed against us*. The destruction of European Jewry by Germany in those unhappy days when the German people were going through its own dark age will for ever remain a component part of our collective and personal consciousness. I take the opportunity of voicing, from my place in this Assembly, the hope that the best elements of the German people and of their government will show understanding for these, the feelings, that we are bound to have. We have the right, indeed, to express in all confidence the hope that the idea of Germans no longer doing anything to harm the Jewish people—either directly or indirectly—will have become deeply-rooted in the minds and consciences of the entire German people. And let me also express the urgent hope that our understandable disgust at the work that is being done by the German scientists should not be conveniently dismissed as illogical prejudice. Surely a people that has suffered as much as our people has suffered has the right to expect special consideration in these matters? If the attempt is made to comfort us with the false assurance that we are exaggerating the extent of the danger, the answer is that if in the thirties anyone had warned us of even a fraction of the catastrophe that was visited upon European Jewry during World War II, even the best of our friends would have gone further than merely to accuse us of exaggerating the danger—they would have said that we were completely out of our senses.

No man has the right to reproach a people with a historical experience behind it such as we have either with the suggestion that its fears are exaggerated or that it is being irrational. We are told that the number of German scientists serving the Egyptian war machine is very low at present. Let us suppose that this is so—but it may increase. Again, we are told that the Germans working in Egypt are by no means the cream of German science. But would anyone be prepared to give us—and those who say things like this *with the best intentions in the world*—the guarantee that perhaps more important figures in the world of science will not follow? There were also the know-alls who were anxious to persuade us that the work of the German scientists was to our advantage— and wiseacres of this kind were to be found outside Germany as well. We need only point to the similarity between the exponents of the blind Arab hatred and the murderous executives of terror from the Hitler days in order to obtain a true view of the situation. And this applies, by the way, to scientists and technicians of this kind from any country— and of course with still greater force to those coming from Germany.'

"Now I come to the second reason for our anxiety and our sense of shock. This is the actual physical danger that must necessarily arise out of their activities particularly if we bear in mind the stress laid on long-term planning by those controlling the Arab war machine—directed, as it is, against us. I have already spoken to the Knesseth of the matter—both before the last Parliament went into recess and on other occasions—and told them that we are not in agreement with many of our friends in other countries on the importance of the work of these scientists. We have been told that there is no great immediate danger but under no circumstances can we close our eyes to the build-up and encouragement of Nasser's ever-growing war machine—a machine that is being created for the expressly-stated purpose of attacking Israel. It is quite true to say that our own forces are by no means puny and we are certainly not without friends in the world. Those contemplating attacking Israel and harbouring thoughts of revenge would be well advised to pause and consider the consequences. We ourselves are not anxious to indulge in a trial of strength, although we know that we should come out of it well.

"We have no illusions about the brutal political realities of our day; we are well aware of the fact that the expression 'local conflicts' should not be lightly used—indeed, such talk is even dangerous. Any war that might be started as a result of Arab aggression against Israel may spread beyond our region and become a major conflagration. This consideration lends weight to our argument, to our demand in particular that the activities of German scientists serving the Egyptian war machine should be stopped and our demand in general that the arms race should be halted and a situation created in which the principle of settling international disputes by peaceful means becomes of universal application; I repeat the expression, 'of universal application', without excepting Israel—an exception which the Egyptian President allows to his own country. Israel supports, with the entire force at its command, the attempt that is being made to reduce the tensions of the cold war throughout the entire world and particularly the tensions in our own area. The great powers must cease to deliver to our area weapons of aggression, to a state that threatens another state with aggression and that refuses to maintain peaceful relations with its neighbours. The arms race must be ended by mutual arrangement and agreement and the same applies to any furthering of the aims of an aggressor—and, of course, particularly to the aid that is being given to an aggressor by the German scientists, scientists who are continuing to stain their fingers with the blood which the best elements of their people are endeavouring to wash away.

"It would appear that there is a very considerable measure of agreement in the

Knesseth about the assessment of the work of the German scientists in Egypt and about the demand that this work be brought to a halt. But at the same time, it remains my duty to present details of the difference between Germany and ourselves in this most distressing business in the correct light—i.e., to present them against the general background of political security that so vitally affects our people. We are particularly concerned to retain our political orientation—our feeling of where things are heading. The origin of the hostile intentions is Cairo. In an attempt to establish permanent hegemony over the Arab states Cairo is openly displaying the banners of war; its emissaries are travelling through the Arab capitals and attempting, by enticement and threat, to enlist them in the cause of war planning against Israel. As I have already said the Egyptians are preaching the doctrine of so-called 'moderation', not in order to obtain a peaceful settlement but in order to furnish better conditions under which to wage war. The moral and practical assistance that has been given to the Egyptian President by great powers strengthens him in his desire for domination and his hopes for the fulfilment of his ambitions. We must again draw attention to the fact that the mouthpiece for expressing the ideas of the civilized world is the 'United Nations' and the world has not yet clearly and unequivocally stated that it will not tolerate such evil conspiracy and machinations in its midst.

"But no matter how many high-sounding speeches may be made on strengthening the cause of peace in the world we cannot afford to be put off by vague assurances; such speeches must therefore be accompanied by a definite, unmistakable condemnation of openly declared aggression, of war-like intentions and political or other vandalism. We cannot, on the one hand, pay tribute to the principles laid down in the Charter of the UN and at the same time allow member states of the UN to continue openly to conduct their intrigues without let or hindrance. It is a dangerously paradoxical situation for a state to be a member of the Plenary Council and the World Security Council and at the same time to be jeopardizing security by war-like acts of all kinds. We must appeal with all emphasis of which we are capable to those who, either in words or deed, are giving assistance to the Egyptian war machine to put an end to this immediately. We do not deny that many of the states that associated themselves with statements that were made purely by way of demonstration—such as, for example, the neutralist conference in Cairo and similar ones before that—privately disagreed with the statements. Although half-heartedly, and with a feeling of personal revulsion, they were compelled to subscribe to these statements as the result of the Egyptian pressure but we must now ask them to refrain from paying further lip-service to the aggressor.

"And finally I should like to mention another point in connection with the special system of relations existing between us and Germany. We do not wish the idea to become public that this chapter of history is closed on a note of bitterness, arising between us because of the activities of a handful of unprincipled and unscrupulous scientists. In our attempts to bring about closer relations and friendship with the new Europe, its social institutions and the organs of its economic union—those which are either already in existence or which still have to be built up—Germany as one of the most important factors calls for special mention. The economic and political importance of the Federal Republic of Germany is growing steadily. We are interested in the strengthening of our relations with all the countries of Europe and we do not stand to gain any advantage from tensions that may arise between us and Western Europe, of which the recreated Federal Republic of Germany is a part. These relations are of very great importance to our progress in all fields; consequently the mission that Federal Germany has in the Western world and in Europe makes it incumbent upon us to make a comprehensive assessment of the situation and maintain a strictly objective and effective watch over all the problems arising out of the situation. Above all, we must realize that we are here concerned with a people of millions, from whom rejuvenative forces spring forth—a people generating its own motivating power, the power to slough off the recent past: It is a people that has chapters in its past that are closely linked with similar chapters of our own, and we can confidently anticipate that there are immense latent forces that will be found to be available—forces that can be put to good use for the benefit of all concerned. The German people have nothing to gain from an increase in tension between themselves and Jewish people throughout the whole world."

The answer to the above statement was given by Ludwig Erhard, just three days later, in the budget debate in the German Bundestag on Ocotber 15th, 1964. He said:

"The tensions in the Middle East are now, as before, a source of potential danger for world peace and our Middle-East policy therefore calls for the exercise of particular care and attention. We have no political interests of great moment in this area and all we want is to maintain uniformly good relations with its peoples and that they may be able to make social and economic progress within an integrated system of peace and order.

"Our relations with the State of Israel are dictated not only by considerations of politics. We have endeavoured to put right whatever can be put right by human effort but we know that however much goodwill there will be, the things that have happened in the past cannot be forgotten. The Federal Republic sincerely regrets that there have been certain events taking place that have upset the progressive improvement of German-Israeli relations and have given rise to feelings of anxiety in Israel. This is all the more reason for me to welcome the latest statement of the Israeli Premier in the Knesseth. I note with gratitude that the Israeli Premier is making every effort to enlist sympathy and understanding for the situation in which Germany finds herself.

"We realize that the fact that the scientists working in countries whose relationships with Israel are strained are of German nationality is the cause of bitterness and heightened emotions. Prime Minister Eshkol has recognized that activities of this kind have been widely condemned throughout Germany, and the Federal Government regrets and actively disapproves of any activities of Germans in other countries that may constitute a danger to peace. I should like to add that we shall leave no stone unturned to eliminate the possibility of the Israeli people feeling threatened by Germans."

As the matter of German scientists in Egypt was raised it was inevitable that the subject of German arms supplies to Israel should also attract more and more public attention. On December 15th, 1964 Chancellor Erhard was questioned in detail about this matter at a press conference. The problem of the Palestine refugees had once again come to the fore as a result of the recent visit of King Hussein to Bonn and in consequence, the German-Israeli situation gained increasing currency in discussions in Germany and Israel. At the 149th session of the Bundestag on December 3rd, 1964, the Minister of Foreign Affairs, Gerhard Schröder, was questioned by the SPD member of Parliament, Karl Mommer, about the establishment of diplomatic relations. The texts of the question and answer were as follows:

Mommer: "Will the Minister be good enough to give consideration to the subject of the further relations between our country and Israel when the Reparation Treaty expires and the unilateral relations provided for by this Treaty are terminated?"

Schröder: "I imagine that it should be obvious that we shall give this matter consideration. I do not wish to prejudice any future action unduly at present but I am firmly convinced that we shall be able to find a solution satisfactory to both parties. We must remember that political arrangements do not necessarily have to be arrangements of a hundred per cent efficacy. There are other arrangements of less than a hundred per cent efficacy that may nevertheless be satisfactory. I am quite convinced that we shall arrive at a satisfactory solution."

The dicussions continued until the spring of 1965, becoming more and more intense, and the parties concerned becoming less inclined for compromise. The Soviet-Zone Head-of-Government, Walter Ulbricht, flew to Cairo on February 24th, at the invitation of the Egyptian Head-of-State Nasser. Bonn interpreted this as provocation and a challenge to its Middle-East policy. This visit of Ulbricht's to Cairo must be seen in the context of the visit of the Russian Deputy Minister President Shelyepin who, with his visit to Cairo in the autumn of 1964, had clearly ushered in a new phase of East-Bloc influence in the Arab states. Moscow had promised President Nasser well over a thousand million DM in credits and on the strength of this had not only laid the foundation for Nasser's "satellite" status vis-à-vis the East Bloc, but on this particular occasion was obviously at the same time attempting to give the East-Zone Government some semblance of diplomatic status. It was at this same time that the Soviets recommenced their substantial deliveries of weapons to the Arab states and one would probably not be far out in supposing that the visit of Shelyepin was also at the back of the visit of Ulbricht to Cairo.

Up to this point the Egyptians had not taken any particular note of the German arms supplies to Israel. In conformity with the Federal Government's system of "uniformity in Middle-East policy" the President of the Bundestag, Gerstenmaier, had been to Cairo and at this point mention must be made of the fact that although this visit was of a "purely private nature" Eugen Gerstenmaier did everything possible, in the course of his conversations over there, to convince the Egyptians of the friendly attitude of the Federal Government towards the Arab states.

There is no doubt that in his visit to Cairo Eugen Gerstenmaier also mentioned the stopping of arms supplies to Israel. Thus even at this early stage, i.e., before the visit of Ulbricht on February 24th, 1965, the government had done everything possible to keep the Arab states from drifting into the sphere of influence of Moscow—and especially of the Soviet-Zone Government. On February 26th, two days after Ulbricht's visit to Cairo, the Federal Government stopped all further economic aid to Egypt. As Under-Secretary Karl-Günther von Hase stated to the Press, the Federal Republic reserves the right to take whatever political action it may deem necessary. It may be that this action will take time, since it has to be considered very carefully and not to be taken immediately by way of emotional reaction following on Ulbricht's visit to Cairo.

Kurt Birrenbach's special mission to Israel

In the first few days of March 1965 Kurt Birrenbach was prematurely recalled from an informatory trip to the USA. After various conversations at which the Minister of Foreign Affairs, Gerhard Schröder, the Minister of Defence, von Hassel, Minister Heinrich Krone and Under-Secretaries Carstens and von Hase, were present. Chancellor Ludwig Erhard sent him, on March 7th, to Israel for talks on the cessation of arms supplies and the opening up of diplomatic relations. On the eve of Birrenbach's departure, the Leader of the CDU/CSU party group, Rainer Barzel, also joined in the dicussions.

When he was in the United States, Kurt Birrenbach had already had some informatory conversations with political personalities on the subject of the Middle East at the State Department, the White House and Congress and also with repretatives of American Jewish organizations. On the morning of his arrival he was visited by the Deputy Minister of Defence of Israel, Shimon Peres, and the former head of the Israeli Mission, Felix E. Shinnar; both were anxious to hear from him what were the terms of his instructions and what he hoped to achieve in the negotiations. No conversation of any note developed because Kurt Birrenbach's commission was concerned directly with the Israeli Prime Minister Levi Eshkol.

The two officials accompanied him to Jerusalem on his journey to see the Israeli Prime Minister. The Israeli politicians had a short separate conversation, after which Birrenbach was invited to enter and handed in the written authority that the Federal Chancellor had given him. It contained nothing more than the agrément in respect of his mission.

Those present on the Israel side were the Israeli Prime Minister, Levi Eshkol, the Minister of Foreign Affairs, Mrs. Golda Meir, Shimon Peres, the General Secretary Levavi, the Head of the Department for Western Europe of the Israeli Ministry of Foreign Affairs, Zeev Sheck, and the Ambassador Shinnar.

Birrenbach gave a survey of the main terms of his mission. These included: liquidation of the arms agreement and the taking up of diplomatic relations with Israel, the first stage to be the establishment of a Consulate-General. Birrenbach explained the course of the Middle-East policy of the Government in recent months—a policy that had often been misinterpreted in Israel. He referred to the decision of the Bundestag not to send weapons to any centres of military tension outside NATO. He did his best to make clear to the others that if the Federal Republic were to continue giving military aid to Israel it would be running the risk of having a number of Arab states, together with other states of the uncommitted world, recognize the Soviet Zone of Germany, thus threatening a "breach in the dam" which might undermine the development of any further diplomatic policy centring on Germany. The consequences of such events could not be in the interests of Israel—interests with which Federal Germany is quite familiar. The three great powers in the West were quite definite about not wanting the Federal Republic to be thrust out of the diplomatic picture in the Middle East.

Birrenbach's exposé of the situation encountered lively resistance. The Israeli side stated that this policy favoured the Arab states at the expense of Israel. The atmosphere of the negotiations became stiffer and the Israelis rejected the proposal to terminate the military-aid agreement—particularly since the Israeli Government had already committed itself to this decision in the Knesseth.

In the course of the negotiations about taking up diplomatic relations Kurt Birrenbach stated that his Government hoped that after a Consulate-General had been established in Israel a previously-agreed period, pending the establishment of full diplomatic relations, would be used to negotiate with the Arabs so that they would understand the position and would not be swept up into the camp of the East-Bloc states and the Soviet Zone.

During the negotiations, one of the Israeli officials suddenly gave the German negotiator a telegram that had been sent on to him by the German Ministry of Foreign Affairs. It contained a statement that had been officially put on record as early as Sunday, March 7th, 1965 in the name of the Federal Government. After Kurt Birrenbach's departure the Chancellor had conferred with the Leader of the CDU/CSU Party Group, Rainer Barzel, who now gave a different idea of the American attitude on this matter and, above all, of that of the representatives of Jewish organizations in the United States—

different, that is, from the report that Kurt Birrenbach had brought with him from the USA. The Government statement ran as follows:

"The Near East situation has been examined by the Federal Government in a number of sessions. The floor leaders of all the parties represented in the German Bundestag were informed. In view of their special responsibility as regards Germany as a whole, the United States, Great Britain and France were consulted.

"The Federal Government notes that the invitation of Ulbricht to the United Arab Republic and the circumstance that the reception given him there was provocative for every German has severely strained the relations between the Federal Republic of Germany and the U.A.R. Following the visit of Ulbricht, all Arab states must know that President Nasser's policy is conducive to disturbing or indeed destroying the proved and traditional friendship between the whole Arab world and Germany. The Federal Government deplores the development initiated by President Nasser—a development that increasingly gives scope to the Communist influence in the Arab world.

All Free Nations Involved

"The German people on both sides of the demarcation line expect their vital interests to be respected. Ulbricht is the representative of a Communist minority that only with the help of a foreign power is able to suppress 17 million of our compatriots. This fact is not unknown to the Government of the U.A.R. Still, this Government has countenanced that wrong, for all those nations to see that have attained their independence through the right of self-determination.

"There is only one German people. By its will, the Government of the Federal Republic of Germany is the entire German people's sole trustee. This claim is given emphatic support by all our allies, a fact convincingly demonstrated by our diplomatic relations to 97 sovereign states that on their part do not maintain diplomatic relations to the Soviet-occupied zone of Germany.

What Germany Will Do

"After careful examination of the situation as a whole and thorough consideration of all possible developments, not only in connection with Germany's immediate interests in the Near East, the Federal Chancellor has made the following decisions:

"1. The Federal Government's answer to the United Arab Republic's invitation and reception of Ulbricht has been to stop economic-aid payments. This means that the Federal Republic will not participate in the second Egyptian Five-Year Plan; nor will it take part in the preparatory negotiations. The Federal Republic will grant the U.A.R. no further capital aid, and declines to make arrangements for a new ceiling in long-term government-guaranteed loans. Current projects will be subjected to examination, naturally within the scope of the tenets of international law.

"2. The self-evident right of any people to self-determination is withheld from the part of the German people living in the Soviet-occupied zone by a dictatorial regime. Any recognition of this tyranny is regarded by the Federal Republic of Germany as an unfriendly act, and will be answered by measures appropriate to each individual case.

"3. The Federal Government seeks to establish diplomatic relations with Israel. This step would be conducive to a normalisation of relations. It is not directed against any Arab state.

"4. By its decision to deliver no more arms to areas of tension, and in agreement with Israel to transform the final part of the obligation to that country, the Federal Government has made an important contribution towards a clarified policy as regards the Near East. The Federal Government considers it important to declare in this connection that it will not countenance any attempt to influence its policies in that area, in particular the shaping of its relations to Israel, by whatever participant in the Near Eastern controversy.

"5. Together with its allies, who have repeatedly called on the Federal Republic of Germany to be coresponsible for peace and order in the Near East, the Federal Government will, by its diplomatic presence, continue its efforts to lessen the tensions in that area."

Bonn Favours "Equilibrium"

"The Federal Government's spokesman, State Secretary Karl-Günther von Hase, subsequently analysed the significance of the decisions as follows: 'The Federal Government has regained full freedom of action in an important political sphere, and is in a position to help maintain stability and equilibrium in the area (of the Near East).'

"The Chancellor's step was hailed in the parties of the government coalition, the Christian Democratic Union and the Free Democratic Party. The chairman of the Christian Social Union, Franz Joseph Strauss, said that the Chancellor had clearly marked the borderline that cannot be overstepped by any country which really values friendship with the entire German nation."

The crucial point was Point 3: "The Federal Government seeks to establish diplomatic relations with Israel. This step would be conducive to a normalisation of relations. It is not directed against any Arab state."

Kurt Birrenbach asked for the discussions to be interrupted for him to telephone direct to Under-Secretary Carstens, who then confirm edthe telegram. There was now nothing in the way of offering full diplomatic relations. The negotiations were then extended beyond the subject of the original mission to cover matters generally affecting the relations between the Federal Republic and Israel. This involved in particular the questions of prolonging the statute-of-limitation period for war crimes and the work of German scientists on rocket development in Egypt. Two days later, on March 10th, Kurt Birrenbach flew back to Bonn to report.

While Birrenbach was still waiting in Bonn after his first round of talks the Prime Minister of Israel, Levi Eschkol, made a statement in the Israeli Parliament on the establishment of diplomatic relations with the Federal Republic of Germany and recommended the approval of such relations. There were 66 votes in favour of the establishment of diplomatic relations and 29 against. Prior to this there had been a motion, tabled by the group of the Right Opposition Heruth, that the question of the establishment of diplomatic relations with the Federal Republic should be the subject of a plebiscite. 83 members had voted against and 16 for the motion. The statement made to the Israeli Parliament by Eschkol ran as follows:

"On March 7th, the Federal Republic of Germany made known its decision to take up diplomatic relations with Israel. On the same day Chancellor Erhard sent a special envoy to Jerusalem to discuss with us certain of the still outstanding problems existing between us and the Federal Republic of Germany. On March 14th, the Government decided to accept the offer of the Federal Republic of Germany to lose no time in establishing diplomatic relations with Israel.

"I have the honour to acquaint the Knesseth with this decision. The decision on the part of the Federal Republic of Germany was preceded by a very difficult trend of events which sharply brought home to us the problem of relations between Germany and Israel. At a time when we are still very much at loggerheads over the question of the scientists and are doing everything in our power to prevent the passing on of the scientific techniques of war-making to the enemies of Israel—and at the time when there was considerable contention between the Jewish people and Germany on the question of Nazi war crimes and the statute of limitation, it came as something of a shock to us when the German Government decided to terminate the obligations that it had taken on in a number of security matters.

"The catastrophe that overtook the Jewish people in the days of Nazism invests any action or neglect on the part of Germany likely to adversely affect the position of the State of Israel or the feelings of the Jewish people with a very special significance. We have not withheld our criticism whenever we were faced with a situation of this kind. On the other hand, we have never abandoned the hope that Germany will make it clear to the whole world that she is shaking off the terrible heritage of the past and is prepared to place her relationships with Israel and the Jewish people on an entirely new footing.

"All our relations with Germany in the past few years have necessarily been coloured by recent history which, in addition to obliging us to be particularly uncompromising in our outlook, imposes upon us the duty of looking forward to and preparing for a future that bears no comparison at all to that so terrible past. This considered policy has been the order of the day. Obviously, of course, the far-ranging discussion between the Israeli and German peoples is not being carried on in a vacuum without reference to other environmental factors. The relationship is influenced particularly by considerations and thought-patterns which can arise only in the Middle East.

"At the very time when we in Germany were able to detect the presence of influential forces seeking a way to atone for the terrible tragedy that haunts the memories of the two peoples and that have necessitated, amongst other things, the addition of the components of rapport and moral rapprochement with Israel to the prevailing pattern of historical responsibility—just at a time like this the Arab states governments have increased their pressure on Germany with the object of preventing the fulfilment of the duty that Germany owed to Israel and to the Jewish people; Germany did not always succeed in summoning up the political and moral courage to offer the necessary resistance to this pressure. Even before Germany gave way to the Arab moral blackmail in the matter of national security assurances, she allowed the pressure exercised by the Arabs to affect her attitude in the matter of diplomatic relations with Israel.

"This was the result of yielding to the moral blackmail and threats used by the Egyptian President to intimidate the Federal Republic. The Government, the Knesseth and the Israeli people refused to accept this and expressed their protest with deliberate and considered dignity and emphasis to the German people and to the peoples of the entire world. We were unwilling to accept the proposal: neither were we willing to accept any compensation that did not take due account of the fundamental problem which so vitally concerns every aspect of the situation. We saw Germany confronted with a historic test situation in which she has to accept the moral obligation to demonstrate her strength of will and to emerge from the dark, enveloping shadows of the Nazi régime. It was against the background of these circumstances that I made the following statement in the Knesseth on February 15th: 'All those intelligent and perceptive people making up the enlightened body of mankind will—quite rightly—incline to judge Germany by the measure in which her actions in connection with her relations with Israel and the Jewish people enable her to successfully throw off the heavy burden of the past. In consequence, it is natural for Germany's policy towards Israel to be taken as the criterion of Germany's desire to join the family of nations as an element promoting stability, security and world peace'.

"Honourable members of this Assembly, on several occasions the Government has had the opportunity of explaining its policy towards Germany. This policy is necessarily influenced by bitter and distressing memories of the past. On December 21st, 1964, in an interview that was broadcast on German TV, I said: 'I assume the Germans will understand that in view of the vast gulf that has come into being between Germany and Israel as a result of the murder of a people the question of relations between us is a matter in which interference from the Arabs cannot be tolerated. There is no doubt that in recent years the excessive consideration that has been shown to the Arabs, despite their evil attitude, has kept the German Government from proposing the establishment of diplomatic relations with Israel. Over the past ten years or so there have been quite a number of occasions on which the Bonn Government has occupied itself with this matter and has shrunk from making a decision because of the undue consideration mentioned. The attitude of the Israeli Government has been clear-cut and straightforward. We have said: It is up to Germany to take the initiative in the matter of establishing diplomatic relations with Israel and it is Israel's business to give careful consideration to this matter as soon as it is brought up.'

"The proposal that the envoy of the Federal Chancellor Erhard laid before us has a twofold value. It is an important political proposal that carries great weight. Under the prevailing conditions of time and place it is a significant example of resistance to the extortionate pressure of our neighbours who, in their impertinence, are trying to infect other states with their feeling of malicious hostility to Israel. As we now prepare to evaluate the German proposal and to decide on our attitude to it, we cannot neglect any of the regional and international factors of the situation under which the proposal was made. We must neither ignore the situation nor postpone the decision.

"And here I should like to refer to the amount of effort that we have put into forging and strengthening the links that we have with the new Europe an effort that gives us an idea of the amount that Germany has achieved in moving into such an important position within the European Community. We are doing all that we can to reinforce the position of Israel in the fabric of the new Europe. At the same time, the necessity of appealing for firmness in resisting the extortionate pressure of our neighbours calls for a clear and positive decision on our part.

"Tomorrow, Dr. Birrenbach, the special envoy of Federal Chancellor Erhard, will be returning back to Israel in order to bring to an end the negotiations which were begun ten days ago. In addition to the question of diplomatic relations, the envoy will have discussions with us about the other problems which the Governments have already expressed their wish to see solved in mutual agreement. There are grounds for hoping that we shall be successful in reaching a negotiated solution of these problems.

"I am well aware that the decision we have to make today is no ordinary one. It differs from the decision that normally has to be made on the establishment of diplomatic relations with any other state. We are all of us torn between reasoning and feeling. The balance that is drawn up between conscience and history and that is inevitably interwoven with the catastrophe of the Jews and has nothing whatever to do with politics as such—this situation, that is without parallel in its inherent pathos, cannot relieve us of the urgent and fateful mission with which we are charged in this generation—that of maintaining and fortifying the State of Israel.

"The past of the people, its present and its future—all these demand from us that we should support and strengthen the state, both materially and spiritually, so that it will be able to stand up to the trials that it will be facing in the future. We also have the sacred duty of ensuring a place for the state within the family of nations. Indeed, it is just the memories that we have of the powerlessness of those days in our history when all the destruction and suffering that now spur us on to take advantage of every opportunity of weakening our enemies and of building a firm foundation for the continued existence of the Jewish people within their own homeland. I am sure that in the decision that we must make—a decision which springs from our deliberation on the one hand and our sincerity of emotion on the other—the scale will be turned by the irresistible desire to strengthen, to consolidate and to fortify the State of Israel."

On March 17th, Birrenbach returned to Jerusalem, this time accompanied by a secretary and a cipher clerk. The main question to be discussed in the second round of talks was the termination of the arms agreement and the negotiating of the individual conditions for the establishment of diplomatic relations. The main feature of this latter discussion was whether the future German Embassy should be located in Jerusalem or Tel Aviv.

The question of German scientists in Egypt and the prolongation of the statute of limitation for war crimes were also contested subjects. A surprise was the raising of a new point by the Israeli side in the course of the negotiations: the question of economic help from the Federal Republic for Israel. The Federal Republic did not want this question to be discussed in Jerusalem but in Bonn, at some future time, well separated from the time of the present negotiations. But the Israeli delegation, this time led by the Deputy Prime Minister and the present Israeli Minister of Foreign Affairs, Abba Eban, insisted on discussing certain outline conditions in connection with this aid. As in the case of the previous round, this present round of talks was conducted very unyieldingly by the Israeli side and the third week of negotiations ended on March 23rd, without any final progress having been made. It was the economic demands of the Israeli Government that were pressed with the greatest emphasis. At the end of this second round of negotiations the Israeli Government delegation presented the German representative with a paper to sign in which all the points discussed were set forth in the form of an aide-mémoire. After protracted negotiations about this document, Birrenbach saw no possibility of meeting the wishes of the Israeli Government. The conversation about the final termination of arms aid had become a whole sheet of subjects for discussion.

For the second time Kurt Birrenbach flew back to Bonn to report again on the position with regard to the negotiations, that had become more and more difficult in the meantime. After consultations with the Federal Government, a conversation took place between Kurt Birrenbach, supported by the Head of the Political Department in the Ministry of Foreign Affairs, Ministerialdirektor Meyer-Lindenberg and the official of the Israeli Mission, Arbel, at the Ministry in Bonn. Here, the German point of view on all relevant questions was put down in writing. Arbel presented this document to his government in Jerusalem.

On April 6th, Kurt Birrenbach flew to Israel for the third and last time on this mission. This time Under-Secretary of State Karl Carstens sent Ministerialdirigent (Assistant Director) Rolf Pauls, Head of the Sub-Section of Development Aid in the Ministry of Foreign Affairs, along with him to give him support.

On his return to Israel Kurt Birrenbach at first found the atmosphere of the discussions somewhat different. The Israeli Government showed its disappointment on the result of the statute of limitations debate that had in the meantime taken place in the German Bundestag and which, in its opinion, had arranged for no more than a postponement of the date of four to five years but not a total abolition of statute-bar period. Moreover, the Israeli Government expressed its displeasure on the document that had been handed over to Arbel in Bonn. Again, all ideas of any direct intervention on the part of the Federal Government on the question of the German scientists in Egypt had to be abandoned for reasons directly concerned with the matter of constitutional rights. This was another thing that was not exactly calculated to produce favourable reaction in Israel. But despite all this, it finally became possible, after a protracted and wearisome period of uncompromising discussions, to find a formula for agreement. In the negotiations about economic aid it was possible to reach agreement on certain procedural questions, such as the negotiating procedure to be used in the future and the date on which such negotiations were to begin in Bonn.

On April 14th, Birrenbach was able to leave Israel with the feeling of having at least managed to deal with all those problems that were amenable to solution at all in discussions in Israel. At that time he had already promised Israel an extension of the trade exchange with the EEC states as understood by the Federal Republic. But again, in the third round of talks, the question of written documentation of the results of the discussions was constantly being raised by the Israeli side. This was not accepted by the German delegation.

The documented result of the very difficult but, on the other hand not unfruitful, negotiations, which had helped to get rid of a good deal of distrust, took the form of two letters which were exchanged, on May 12th, 1965, between Felix E. Shinnar, Head of the Israeli Mission in Cologne, and Federal Chancellor Ludwig Erhard in the Palais Schaumburg. They confirmed the results that had been achieved. Under-Secretary of State Lahr and Kurt Birrenbach took part in the conversations concerned. Shinnar gave the Federal Chancellor the note from the Israeli Prime Minister. The contents were made public on May 13th, when the note was published in the form of a joint communiqué at 16.00 hours in Jerusalem and Bonn. The communiqué ran as follows:

"Acting on the authority given them by the Federal President, the Government of the Federal Republic of Germany and the Israeli Government have agreed to establish diplomatic relations between the two countries."

The note of Federal Chancellor Ludwig Erhard to the Israeli Prime Minister Levi Eshkol ran as follows:

"Bonn, May 12th, 1965

My dear Prime Minister,

"The attitude of the Federal Republic of Germany in the past has shown that it is well aware of the situation in which the Germans find themselves in respect of the Jews of the entire world. It is a source of deep satisfaction to me that an agreement has been reached to bring about the establishment of full diplomatic relations between our two countries.

"And it is a further source of satisfaction to me to note that the question of modification of the outstanding consignments of weapons arising out of an earlier agreement with Israel on arms supplies has been negotiated to the satisfaction of both parties.

"In the near future—i.e. in some two to three months—the Federal Government is prepared to enter into conversations with the Israeli Government on the question of future economic aid.

"With regard to the matter of the activities of German specialists outside the Federal Republic, many of the German scientists, technicians and experts who have been engaged in the military field in countries outside the sphere of NATO have returned to Germany during the last few months. The Federal Government has reason to believe that of those experts that still remain a further number will shortly be returning to Germany; this applies particularly to those engaged in rocket construction. The German authorities are making use of the appropriate legal machinery to take proceedings against such persons as are attempting, without permission, to lure away German citizens for scientific, technical or expert work in the military field beyond the borders of the Federal Republic.

"I hope that the decision taken by the two governments to establish full diplomatic relations will prepare the way for a happier future in the relationships existing between our two peoples.

"I conclude with the expression of my most cordial esteem,

Ludwig Erhard."

The note from the Israeli Prime Minister Levi Eshkol to Federal Chancellor Ludwig Erhard runs as follows:

"Jerusalem, May 12th, 1965

My dear Federal Chancellor,

"I thank you for your letter of May 12th, 1965, in which you review the negotiations conducted in the past few weeks. You have already been informed about the decision of the Israeli Government to accept the offer presented on March 8th, 1965 by your special envoy Dr. Kurt Birrenbach, to establish full diplomatic relations between our two countries. It is against a sinister historical and a stormy political background that our two governments have made their decision. I share your hope that our joint decision will prove to be an important step forward towards a better future. I also share your assessment of the importance of finding a solution to the problems mentioned in your letter as still remaining to be settled.

"I have taken note of the passages in your letter dealing with the question of the scientists and would like to express the hope that the attitude and the intentions expressed, taken in conjunction with the statements made by you on an earlier occasion, will now allow the matter to be speedily settled.

"It will certainly be clear to you from our previous correspondence how much importance I still attach to the matter of lifting the statute of limitations time limit, this being quite understandably a matter of the utmost anxiety to us.

"I am well aware, my dear Federal Chancellor, that it is due to your personal initiative and firmness that at this significant point in the relations between our two countries, we have succeeded in finding a satisfactory solution.

"I conclude with the expression of my most cordial esteem,

Levi Eshkol."

Exchange of ambassadors

The Federal Government asked Jerusalem for Rolf Pauls' credentials to be accepted. The Israeli Government appointed Asher Ben Natan, the current Director-General of Affairs of the Israeli Ministry of Defence, who had on many previous occasions conducted negotiations with Franz Joseph Strauss and other German politicians, particularly in matters of military collaboration.

On August 11th, 1965 Rolf Pauls arrived in Israel. On August 19th, amid the sharp protests of radical groups, he presented his credentials to the Israeli President, Zalman Shazar in the latter's official residence in Jerusalem. On this occassion Rolf Pauls made the following speech:

"It is a great honour for me today, to present to your Excellency the credentials confirming that the President of the Federal Republic of Germany has entrusted to me the duties of ambassador extraordinary and plenipotentiary to your Government. The establishment of diplomatic relations between our two countries is regarded as of the greatest importance by the entire German people. It is with sorrow and revulsion that the new Germany looks back upon the ghastly crimes of the National-Socialist régime, crimes which brought such a heavy burden of suffering to the Jewish race in particular. Since that time there have been many people of good will on both sides who have worked with patience and perseverance to prepare the way for this fresh start that we are making in the relations between our two peoples. We hope that the exchange of ambassadors will help us to continue successfully to tread this same path of progress. I have no illusions about the difficulties that lie in wait for me in my capacity of first ambassador of the Federal Republic of Germany in your country and I am aware of the importance of the task before me. If, in my efforts to promote and foster these mutual relations, I may count upon the benevolent support of your Excellency and of your Excellency's officials and associates this will be a source of very considerable encouragement to me in my work. Finally, your Excellency, allow me, in the name of the President of the Federal Republic of Germany, to pass on to your Excellency and the Israeli people our very best wishes, in the cordial expression of which I beg to be allowed to join."

President Zalman Shazar replied:

"We are all very conscious of the particular significance of this political act. In the proposal made by the Federal Republic of Germany to establish full diplomatic relations with Israel and in the Israeli acceptance of this proposal, there is conclusive proof of the radical changes, which have ensued since the time, which Your Excellency justly described as a 'time of horrible crimes'. Twenty years have now passed by since the remnants of my people, those who survived, were rescued from the concentration camps and the furnaces, devised by the Nazi regime to exterminate the Jews in all those countries under their yoke.

"The memory of these horrors and their victims is alive in the thoughts of our generation and will never be forgotten by us nor disappear from the consciences of decent people as long as the inviolability of life and the principle of justice continue to be recognised by mankind. Even in the most evil days of annihilation, those of my people who suffered and were tormented, never lost their spirit of human dignity and their unshakeable belief in the future. From these roots grew up that heroism, which manifested itself in the death camps, in the ghetto revolts and in the struggle to obtain Jewish independence in our old fatherland. The words composed by a poet years before have been confirmed. He said: 'I have saved my God and my God saved me ...'

"The presentation of these credentials today in Jerusalem, the capital of the state of Israel, shows that chaos does not last for ever and that even the darkest of nights must end with the coming of the dawn. And because of the teachings of the bitter past, we are obliged to concentrate our energies on the future, so that those who spread their hate can be reduced to silence and the spirit of that period of horror can never be reawakened.

"Through you, Mr. Ambassador, I would like to return the best wishes which your president had conveyed to me and assure him that you will find the support you need for your task. May the representatives of our two peoples be so endowed that they may make a significant contribution in the laying of those principles, upon which alone relations of understanding and cooperation between our two peoples can be established."

As the German Ambassador, accompanied by the Chef-de-Protocol and the personal adjutant of the Israeli President, left the building an Israeli military band played the German national anthem in accordance with local diplomatic custom.

A few days after this, Asher Ben Natan, the first Ambassador of the State of Israel, was at the Villa Hammerschmidt to present his credentials to President of the German Bundesrat Georg August Zinn, who was representing Heinrich Lübke, the Federal President, at this time. This constituted the final procedure in the establishment of diplomatic relations between the two states.

Negotiations on the question of German economic aid

It was not until January 1966 that it was possible to start negotiations on the question of German economic aid to Israel for which preparations had already been made in correspondence passing between the two Heads of Governments. In these discussions the Israeli delegation started off by stating its view that the system of financial credit aid to Israel, that had been put into operation since the conversation between David Ben Gurion and Konrad Adenauer in the Waldorf-Astoria Hotel in New York, should continue to be paid in addition to any German economic aid which might now be made available. In the course of these conversations Kurt Birrenbach was consulted in order to ascertain what had really been negotiated up to now. On May 12th, 1966 the consultations ended with the promulgation of the agreement and the issue of a communiqué setting forth the details of this economic aid:

"The Government of the State of Israel

and

the Government of the Federal Republic of Germany

in the desire to strengthen and expand the relations already existing between their two countries, namely to promote their economic relations by means of continuous cooperation, in the consciousness that the maintenance of these relations forms the basis of this agreement, have agreed as follows:

Article 1

"The Government of the Federal Republic of Germany shall make it possible for the government of the State of Israel and/or others chosen jointly by both governments to take out credits with the Kreditanstalt für Wiederaufbau, Frankfurt on Main for projects, the promotive worthiness of which has been jointly ascertained, and these credits shall total as much as 160 (in words: one hundred and sixty) million German marks.

Article 2

"(1) The utilisation of these loans as well as the conditions, according to which they are granted, including the matter of asking for tenders, shall be determined by the agreements concluded between those taking out the credits and the Kreditanstalt für Wiederaufbau, which is bound by the legal stipulations in force in the Federal Republic of Germany.

"(2) Parity of view also prevails on the fact that the government of the State of Israel is responsible for guaranteeing all payments and the transfers, which ensue therefrom in fulfilment of the commitments taken on by the party to whom the credit has been granted on the basis of the loan agreements concluded with the Kreditanstalt für Wiederaufbau, in so far as loans are taken out by parties other than the Government of the State of Israel.

"(3) The Government of the State of Israel shall make every effort to ensure that consignments and services, for which the payments as described in Paragraph (1) are to be utilised, shall as far as possible be reserved for German firms (for firms with their headquarters in the Federal Republic of Germany).

Article 3

"The Government of the State of Israel shall relieve the Kreditanstalt für Wiederaufbau from all taxes and other public dues imposed in Israel by dint of the conclusion and/or implementation of the loan agreements mentioned in Article 2.

Article 4

"The Government of the State of Israel shall leave to the passengers and suppliers a free choice of transport media, due consideration paid to Article 5, for the transportation of persons and goods in sea and air traffic ensuing from the granting of the loans. Moreover, it shall take no measures to exclude or make difficult the participation of German transport firms, and where necessary shall grant the requisite permits.

Article 5

"Consignments and services from countries and areas to be fixed separately by the Government of the Federal Republic of Germany and of which Israel will be duly informed shall not be financed by the loans. This also includes consignments which have their origin in one of these countries or areas. The same applies to the transport media of these countries or areas, which may not be used for carrying the supplies financed by the loans.

Article 6

"The Government of the Federal Republic of Germany attaches special importance to the products of the industry of the Land of Berlin receiving preferential treatment in the consignments ensuing from the granting of the loans.

Article 7

"With the exception of the stipulations made in Article 4 with regard to air traffic, this agreement shall also apply to the Land Berlin, in so far as the government of the Federal Republic of Germany shall not make to the government of the State of Israel a statement to the contrary within three months of the coming into force of the agreement.

Article 8

"This agreement shall come into force on the day on which it is signed.

Compiled in Bonn on May 12th, 1966

in four original documents, two of which are in Hebrew and two in German, the text equally binding in both cases.

For the Government of the	For the Government of the
State of Israel	Federal Republic of Germany
The Ambassador,	State Secretary
Asher Ben Natan	Rolf Lahr"

Joint German-Israeli Press Communiqué:

"The German-Israeli economic negotiations, which began on February 23rd, 1966 and were conducted on behalf of the Government of the State of Israel by the Israeli Ambassador in the Federal Republic of Germany, Mr. Asher Ben Natan, and for the Government of the Federal Republic of Germany by the State Secretary in the Foreign Ministry, Herr Rolf Lahr, were brought to a close today with the signing of an agreement on economic aid for the year 1966.

"With the agreement, Germany will grant Israel loans amounting to 160 million German marks for infra-structural projects envisaged by the State of Israel, the promotive worthiness of which was ascertained jointly during the negotiations. The conditions on which the credits are based vary considerably, have their roots in the usual credit terms and are determined by the type of projects involved.

"The German loans are intended to finance Israeli projects for home building and for tele-communications as well as the plans of the Israeli industrial bank for the promotion of smaller and medium-sized Israeli economic concerns. Loan agreements on the amounts involved between Israeli borrowers and the Kreditanstalt für Wiederaufbau in Frankfurt for the financing of the projects are to be signed in Frankfurt during the next few days.

"The agreement concluded today can be regarded as an essential element of German policy in the sphere of economic cooperation, through which the Federal Republic of Germany supports other countries in the build-up of their economies and is in keeping with the bilateral desire to strengthen the economic relations between Germany and Israel and promote continuous cooperation between the two countries.

"The agreement signed today is to be published."

As in all the agreements on economic aid hitherto concluded the Kreditanstalt für Wiederaufbau (Reconstruction Credit Bank) in Frankfurt am Main was entrusted with the practical transaction in connection with the 160 million DM that Israel received for 1966. The majority of the 160 million DM granted in this agreement was intended for housing projects in Israel, which meant that the Frankfurt Credit Bank, for its part, had to conclude a separate contract with Israel which, for its part, passed the money on to the builders. The second project, which accounted for approximately 25 to 30 per cent of the total sum, was for the long term financing of the smaller and medium Israeli business enterprises. These amounts were handled in the intermediate stage by the Industrial Development Bank of Israel Ltd. A third agreement was made to cover the part of the money that was earmarked for the extension of the telephone service of the Negev area.

These conditions, providing repayment over 25 years—beginning after 7 years free of repayment with an interest rate not to exceed three per cent—clearly show that in practice the economic aid agreement is to be regarded as an extension of the project financing scheme introduced at the Waldorf-Astoria conversations and within the framework of the Negev development plan. A further 75 million DM for the year 1965 had been transferred by the end of December of that year by Under-Secreatry of State Rolf Lahr, who headed the discussions on German economic aid (the representatives from Jerusalem being Zeer Sheck, Head of the West European Department, and the Director-General of the Israeli Ministry of Finance who had made the journey to Bonn in order to give support to the Israeli Ambassador Asher Ben Natan).

On October 4th, 1967, on the eve of the Jewish New Year, the economic aid treaty for 1967, covering the same sum of 160 million DM, was renewed in the Ministry of Foreign Affairs without any protracted discussion. Again, as laid down in the present Treaty, these sums were for use in the same projects as the advances for 1966. Thus these matters have returned to normal, as a speaker of the Federal Government stressed when he was giving reasons for the text of the Agreement not being made public.

Konrad Adenauer in Israel

On May 2nd, 1966, the late Federal Chancellor, Konrad Adenauer, arrived on a visit in Israel at the invitation of the Israeli Government. The time of his visit constituted a certain element of tragedy. It was not to be till after his retirement from the office of Federal Chancellor that this man, who had been the most active of all in preparing the German approach to Israel for his people, was able to accept the honour which on the occasion of his visit was given him in the Weizmann Institute—i.e. after the expiration of the Luxembourg Agreement and after the establishment of diplomatic relations between the two countries. But the invitation of Israel had already been given during his period of office. The personal tribute paid to Konrad Adenauer in Israel was in recognition of his work in connection with German-Israeli understanding.

On the first day of his sojourn in Israel the Weizmann Institute conferred an "Honorary Fellowship" on him. Some 25 million DM had been received by this Institute from the VW Foundation and from Federal funds for their research work. In the interior court of the new Ullmann Institute, Konrad Adenauer stood in front of a memorial bearing the following inscription in Hebrew and English:

"This Institute is a living monument to

> Fritz Haber (1868—1934)
> Richard Willstaetter (1872—1942)
> Carl Neuberg (1877—1956)
> Otto Meyerhof (1884—1951)
> Max Bergmann (1886—1944)
> Rudolf Schoenheimer (1898—1941)

and to the German Jewish research workers who had become victims of Nazi tyranny. The creation of this Institute was encouraged and supported by Federal Chancellor Konrad Adenauer and the Max-Planck Institute."

When the Honorary Doctorate was conferred the budget expert of the German Bundestag and the Bundestag delegate Heinrich Georg Ritzel, who had previously been accorded an academic honour, was present; he had been a member of the Budget Committee of Parliament and, in supporting the policy of Adenauer, had played an important part in promoting the Weizmann-Institute project. Nahum Goldmann, the President of the Jewish World Congress, himself an Honorary Doctor of the Weizmann Institute, welcomed the German statesman with the following words:

"... We pay tribute to one of the greatest statesmen and personalities of our generation. There is not one among the leaders of post-war Germany who has shown so much understanding—for the difficulties involved and for the importance of the attempt that is being made, now that the Hitler days are over, to normalize the relations between the Jewish people and the new Germany—as has Dr. Adenauer. He was always aware of the vital moral importance of Germany's efforts to restore normal relations both with the Jewish people and with the State of Israel; the unique system of legislation enabling compensation to be made to the victims of Nazism would never have been possible without the courageous stand that he took in this matter, in respect of which he had so many internal difficulties to overcome. For many years Dr. Adenauer has shown his intense interest in the Weizmann Institute as one of the outward expressions of Israel's contribution to world civilization and science. He has been of assistance to the Institute in a great many respects. He is worthy of every form of recognition that can be shown him—as indeed, Israel is now showing him on the occasion of this visit—and the privilege of being the first to give him an official welcome is one that the Weizmann Institute has richly deserved."

Israel's Foreign Minister Abba Eban, the President of the Weizmann Institute gave a speech in English which runs as follows:

"We welcome Dr. Adenauer as one of the greatest political personalities in Europe and all over the world. Today, we are thinking of his philosophy and his actions with regard to the Jewish people. He has always adopted a clear and unequivocal attitude in this matter. He realised the need of responsibility for this people. The most effective way to fulfil this responsibility, the way of logic and of morals, is the strengthening of the State of Israel. Only a strong Israel, firmly rooted in the family of nations, can constitute the salvation of the Jewish people from its helplessness, which was its lot throughout history. This was the view taken by Dr. Adenauer during his term in office and he still takes it today ... You, Dr. Adenauer, count among our friends, among those who understand our ideas, our memories and our strivings."

Meyer W. Weisgal, the chairman of the Executive Committee of the Weizmann Institute, was responsible for the actual award of the Honorary Fellowship to Dr. Adenauer. This is what he said:

"We are grateful to Dr. Adenauer for accepting our invitation to come here personally to receive the Honorary Fellowship, the highest honour which we can bestow upon him. The award was made unanimously by the Scientific Committee and the Executive of the Weizmann Institute. We admire him for his faithfulness to democratic ideals, which he has continuously maintained and for which he was obliged to suffer during the years of the Hitler regime. The Jews of the world will not forget that. We welcome him as the initiator and patron of the cooperation between scientists from his country with those of the Weizmann Institute. During the years of his chancellorship, Konrad Adenauer encouraged the important connections between the Max-Planck Institute and our research institute at Rehovoth. It was he personally, who overcame all the bureaucratic difficulties and made possible useful academic relations. Dr. Adenauer's unshakably benevolent attitude towards the Weizmann Institute was always determined by the desire to promote the wellbeing of humanity by means of knowledge. We greet him as a true friend of Israel and of the Jewish people, and we are most deeply grateful to him."

After this address, Professor Talmi walked up to the dais and read out the citation, upon which Dr. Adenauer's Honorary Fellowship of the Weizmann Institute was based. It is phrased in both Hebrew and in English, and the text runs as follows:

"On the application of the Scientific Committee of the Weizmann Institute, the Executive of the above-named Institute herewith appoints Konrad Adenauer as an Honorary Fellow of the Weizmann Institute. In recognition of his courageous activities on behalf of promoting democratic ideals in Germany, his support of the development of the Weizmann Institute and his initiative in the establishment of fruitful bilateral relations between research scientists in his country and those of the Institute. Rehovoth, Israel, May 3rd, 1966."

Dr. Adenauer was helped into his robe and tremendous applause accompanied him, as he made his way to the microphone to deliver his speech of thanks:

"Mr. Chairman and, as I may now take the liberty of saying, my dear colleagues and friends. Believe me when I say that I am deeply moved by this journey to Israel and this acceptance into your circle, which has become mine in such a dignified and fine manner. I am most deeply moved, because my mind's eye sees moving past quite naturally those pictures of past years, which at the time filled me with horror. I am also deeply moved because I have been singled out to contribute towards reconciliation. That was the goal of my activities from that moment when I first became Chancellor of the Federal Republic of Germany: To bring about reconciliation with Israel and with Jews all over the world. That was my greatest concern out of a feeling of deep, inner obligation and also out of the feeling that humanity is indebted to the Jews for so much particularly in the spheres of the human intellect and in the field of religion. An impression, which I shall never forget, is the one I experienced when the agreement was signed in Luxembourg, my dear listeners, and I might add that that which ensued would not have ensued, if it had not been for the work done by two men on your side. One of them was Mr. Nahum Goldmann, who made it his duty right from the start to contribute towards creating a better atmosphere between Germans and Israelis. I must also mention your representative in the Federal Republic over many years, Mr. Shinnar. You can rest assured that you could not have chosen a better representative and interpreter of your wishes than Mr. Shinnar. I well remember the cooperation with him and shall always think about it with gratitude.

"And now, ladies and gentlemen, I am in Israel at last. If you had experienced those whole periods, first of all the terrible period of the war, and then the postwar period, then you would be able to feel with me what it means to be standing on Israeli territory as a welcome guest, in the way you have just described me, and participating in this ceremony here in the Weizmann Institute.

"As you well know, I arrived yesterday evening and saw the whole panorama of the city of Tel Aviv from the air. This morning, I was taken on a tour of the Weizmann Institute by your chairman. I have seen and heard what has been done here with desert soil with an almost overpowering energy and with almost a prophetic gaze into the future. When I say that, I am also thinking of Weizmann. It was a monstrous risk for him too, as it was for everyone, this making a start here. And he was only able to do that by casting his prophetic gaze into the future. I feel obliged to pay tribute here today to him and the memory of him, and I do it from the bottom of my heart. I had earlier meetings with him and I too was a member of the Zionist movement. But, I would never have thought that this creation, this State of Israel, which was brought into being, would have been possible on such dry and parched ground. It could only be transformed into such a verdure and into such magnificence by the hard work of man and by the belief of men in the future.

"Ladies and gentlemen! I would like to avail myself of this hour and particularly warmly recall the memory of my friend of so many years, Dannie Heinemann. We were linked by strong ties of friendship for many decades. And I believe that I was best acquainted with his generosity, his insight and his goodness, yes his goodness, ladies and gentlemen. Today, when I was conducted round the institute, which bears his name, a work of peace and of progress, it was as if he was standing in front of me, just in the way he stood beside me in difficult days and helped me in difficult hours. I would like to remember him and I would like to express the wish that every country might see in the State of Israel a prototype, a model of confidence in a blessed and good future for all mankind. Indeed, the State of Israel with its energy, with its zeal, with its organised planning, with the pointer to the future which an institute like this one has, is certainly a model for all peoples. That is what it has to be and deserves to be. I wish you from the bottom of my heart and all those who are immediately concerned with projects at the moment much much success for the future, for a long future, richly blessed."

On the afternoon of this eventful day, Dr. Adenauer left for a two day visit to Jerusalem, the Israeli capital and the holy city for the Jewish, Christian and Islamic religions. His journey took him directly into the office of the premier, Mr. Levi Eshkol. Here, there were ten minutes for the photographers and the cameras and then the two politicians, followed by the German ambassador, Dr. Pauls, sat down for talks. The meeting lasted more than an hour and was concerned with the problems facing Israel and Dr. Adenauer had a large number of questions to ask. The German-Israeli problem and the 500 million dollar question were not touched upon by Mr. Eshkol.

In the evening, Dr. Adenauer was a guest of the Israeli premier in his home. Invitations had also been extended to Dr. Nahum Goldmann and the former head of the Israel Mission in Cologne, Dr. Felix Shinnar. The toasts were made public afterwards. The speech made by Mr. Eshkol ran as follows:

"Dr. Adenauer, first German chancellor after the terror of the Nazi era; Dr. Pauls and Frau Pauls; Frau Multhaupt! I have the honour of welcoming you in Jerusalem. Countless personalities come here to visit us from all four parts of the globe. Your visit is nevertheless singular, just as is also true of the relations between Israel and Germany. I do not need to tell you about the disaster, which has befallen my people in this generation, a tragedy which is without parallel even in the blood-soaked history of the Jewish people, filled as it is with torment and persecution, or in the history of mankind for that matter. The Nazi regime in Germany exterminated about a third of the Jewish people with means so barbaric that they defy imagination. But then a miracle occurred. Out of the ruins of destruction and of the greatest humiliation, the Jewish people became resurrected and through the heroic courage of their sons and daughters, their sovereignty was restored in this country, the land of their fathers since time immemorial. You can now see with your own eyes the beginnings of this fulfilment, which was prophesied by the prophets thousands of years ago. We have not forgotten. We have lost six million of our people. We cannot forget the terrible mass murder. As intellectual and historical unit, we have been through a terrible blood-letting and who can say when the wounds will be finally healed. Great achievements of science, of culture, of creative genius, synthesised by generations through the spirit and intellect of our people, have sunk into oblivion. In their suffering, the Jewish people seeks consolation in their resurrection here in their homeland, in accordance with the saying of the prophet: 'Thou shalt live in thine own blood'. And we are reminded of the words of the Book of Job, Chapter 29: 'And so I thought: I would die in my nest; I lived as many years as the Phoenix'. In the return of our sons to their earth, in the return of their independence in the historical homeland, the will of our tormented people to live has found its expression once again.

"Many people in the world regard you, Dr. Adenauer, as a man who paved the way (for the Jewish people). We see in you a man, who has reflected deeply about the peculiar spiritual character of Israel, about the significance of the survival of our people across millennia, from decline to resurrection, from servitude to independence. Your place is among those, who are trying to efface the shame of the Nazi era. You understand that the Reparations Agreement, which you signed in the name of your people, is not atonement, there is no atonement for the horrors, no atonement for the annihilation. You know about the contribution of the Jewish people to Christianity and about the obligation of the Christian peoples to render their aid in the consolidation of Israel's independence. Your visit to our country at the beginning of the nineteenth year of the reinstatement of Israeli sovereignty will give you an opportunity to see the achievements and the problems of our country, in agriculture and industry, in the field of nutrition sphere, in science and culture, in pioneering constructional determination and the readiness to make sacrifices, in the sincere efforts in the cause of peace and the imperative striving to forge a deterrent defence power, in order to uphold the peace.

"On Mount Zion, which looks across over the remains of our temple; on the mountains of Galilee and the expanses of the Negev; in Massada, eternal symbol of heroism; all over the country, in all its regions, its towns and villages, you will detect everywhere the breath of the eternal spirit, which made the strings of David's harp begin to play and they are now becoming audible again. On behalf of all those present, I wish you, Dr. Adenauer, a long life and good health."

This was Dr. Adenauer's reply:

"It is difficult, Mr. Prime Minister, to make a reply to your speech. I think, you can feel how strongly I feel responsible, as do so many Germans, for what the National Socialists did in our name.

"The National Socialists killed off many Germans and many Jews. I have no single word of excuse for them; I saw and heard many things which the man-in-the-street did not see or hear. I can only say that we have done everything possible to show our striving to overcome this time of horror, which none can ever undo. But we should now leave it to the past.

"I know how difficult it is for the Jewish people to accept that. But if goodwill is not recognised, nothing good can come of it.

"My neighbour asked me prior to this, whether National Socialism could not rise up in Germany anew. I expressed my conviction that there was no danger of this happening. I would like to outline for you the intellectual attitudes of the German people: there is the group from 40—65, who made the most difficult sacrifices, and the group from 25—45, who are in part very restless. Only some of them experienced the war and do not remember all the details. Finally, there is another group, those below the age of 25.

"Thank goodness that I agree with a large number of Germans; we find in this group a rejection of every form of dictatorial inclination—the expression, 'National Socialism' may not even be mentioned in the presence of members of this group.

"You are a young state; I have already said today that you are faced with a great task, a wonderful task, to show all countries how exemplary results can be achieved, in making your land anew, so that all those who want to can and should return to it.

"Could you not see a consolation in this new task, which has been imposed upon you, for all that which has been done to you and which neither I nor anyone else would want to excuse. The facts should never be forgotten and the same applies to the terrifying phenomenon of human beings becoming beasts. Please forgive this hard expression, particularly when we know that man was created in the image of God.

"Let us help by trying together to master this phenomenon and the powers of terror.

"I shall not drink to this, for it seems to me banal (to do so) in view of the seriousness of this question.

"It is my wish that you will be able to master the task facing you to the best of your ability."

The speech made by Mr. Levi Eshkol came as a complete surprise to Konrad Adenauer. He was justified in thinking that the themes, which can be summed up in the expression "German-Israeli thematics", would not be touched upon until his meeting with the Prime Minister in his office during the afternoon. The private dinner at Levi Eshkol's was not the right setting for such discussion as far as the former chancellor was concerned.

The Prime Minister's speech was loudly criticised in Israel. Many voices asserted that Levi Eshkol was trying to pacify the opposition parties. At the desire of the Israeli Prime Minister, however, before Adenauer left Israel a conciliatory conversation took place at the Avia Hotel near the airport. Levi Eshkol presented to the Federal Chancellor the Papal Medal in gold, as bestowed on Paul VI at the time of his visit to Israel.

Dr. Nahum Goldmann, the president of the Jewish Claims Conference, had sent out invitations to a lunch in the King David Hotel. There were about eighty men and women present, all of them people who had worked closely with the Conference across the years. In his words of welcome for Konrad Adenauer, Dr. Nahum Goldmann had the following to say, in particular about the reparations which had been made by the Federal Republic of Germany:

"We have long awaited the opportunity, Dr. Adenauer, to express to you the deep recognition of Jews all over the world for the role you have played in solving our problems. The legislation reparations and compensations is indeed remarkable. There is practically no precedent for a government paying indemnities to the victims of a former regime, to those who are not even citizens of that country. This singular legislation has created new international concepts of law and established an important precedent.

"The financial extent of this legislation and the costs, which have accrued for Germany go far beyond the confines of those estimates which were made at the beginning of the negotiations and when they are complete will total some nine to ten thousand million dollars, of which the greater part has gone and is going to Nazi victims in Israel. The contribution of these payments to the development of the economy and in particular the industry of Israel—in addition to the direct supplies of goods to the Israeli Government, amounting to 823 million dollars—cannot be overestimated. Any discussion as to whether the payments have been of benefit to the Israeli economy is pointless. In addition to their decisive importance for the economy of the State of Israel, the reparations sums have enabled hundreds of thousands of Jews in many countries to begin a new life.

"Naturally, there were and still are weaknesses in this legislation, but that is inevitable in such an extensive enterprise, involving millions of applications. On the whole, however, I can say after fourteen years of experience with the Claims Conference on their behalf that Germany has shown a great deal of goodwill in fulfilling the law, despite the fact that the costs are considerably higher than the German government and the Claims Conference ever expected, when they embarked on the negotiations.

"We are gathered here today to pay tribute to the man without whose vision, courage and conscience all this would have been impossible. I know from personal experience how many difficulties Dr. Adenauer has had to overcome, if not actually concerned with the principle of reparations, certainly about its extent. He would not have used his authority and power to such an extent for the agreement in Luxembourg, had it not been his deep moral conviction that the new Germany must strive earnestly to at least make good materially the damage caused by the Hitler regime for hundreds of thousands of Jews. We owe him the greatest recognition for what he did—just as the German people should be grateful to him for creating the atmosphere for the rehabilitation of the new Germany and its readmission into the family of peoples as a great power with equal rights.

"With the Luxembourg Agreement, the way was opened for a normalisation of relations between the Jewish people and the Federal Republic. It goes without saying that this can only be a slow and gradual process, particularly during the lifetime of that generation which experienced the Nazi horrors and during the lifetime of hundreds of thousands of victims of Nazism, who survived the concentration camps. With the establishment of relations between Germany and the State of Israel and with the implementation of the reparations legislation, great progress has already been made in the way of normalisation. I am convinced that it is in the urgent interest of both peoples to continue along this path. It would be unwise for the Jewish people and for Israel to ignore the existence of Germany, which is today one of the great powers of Europe, and it is in the interest of the German people to show to the world that not only a new regime but a new spirit is ruling the country, and that the Federal Republic is firmly determined to combat immediately every attempt to revive Nazi and nationalist tendencies. The example, which Dr. Adenauer has given his people, in his attitude to the problems of Israel and the question of reparations for Nazi victims, must serve the whole of Germany as a guideline. He is not only the great leader, who, after a devastating defeat, restored the position of Germany as a great power within the shortest possible time, but he has also made every effort to fill his people with a new spirit of democracy and deep respect for moral and spiritual values, which alone constitute an effective guarantee against a revival of the horrors of the past. For all this, Dr. Adenauer deserves both our admiration and our thanks."

The visit to Afikim Kibbutz in the Jordan valley was a special item on the programme of Adenauer's journey. The leader of the Kibbutz made a remarkable speech of welcome, which closed with the words:

"We welcome every individual and every people with understanding for the great human value of our efforts and with a desire to help with heart and hand. In you, Dr. Adenauer, we recognise one of the great men, who have both a hand and understanding in helping us. May you be blessed by God and humanity for this."

Very obviously moved, Dr. Adenauer listened intently to the greeting of these socialistically organised workers. Before he climbed back into the car again, after inspecting the plywood factory, he said how very impressed he was with the hard work and the order and the life of this community.

Nevertheless anxious questions posed to the German statesman overshadowed all the conversations and visits on his schedule during those days. The Israeli president, Zalman Shazar, expressed his fear that radical rightist groups in Germany might regain the field particularly amongst youth. Konrad Adenauer firmly dismissed this anxiety. It was no use talking National Socialist ideas to German youth any more, he replied. He answered himself for the fact that youth was immune to any revival of the idea. The radical rightist NPD, he said, was a small party.

On 9 May, the last day of his stay in Israel, Konrad Adenauer went to see Ben Gurion at his Sde Boker Kibbutz. Two questions Ben Gurion had always asked the editor on his visits to Israel: How is Adenauer and when is he coming? What is German youth doing? Now these two men stood face to face at the Kibbutz in the middle of the Negev Desert, two men who had laboured with great mutual confidence at the political tasks of their states.

Lunch was held in the communal dining-room of the Kibbutz within the group of settlement members. Mr. Ben Gurion made a speech, in which he said:

"The greatness of our guest: his will for peace. During the past two centuries, hatred between the German and the French peoples existed in Europe. Despite this, Dr. Adenauer together with Charles de Gaulle has created a future of peace for Europe. Few people have done so much as Dr. Adenauer for the peace of the world ... Despite his advanced age, Dr. Adenauer still has a great historical mission to fulfil."

This speech was made in Hebrew and the Adenauer reply to it went as follows:

"Dear friends, I have now spent a week in Israel and have been full of amazement and admiration at the zeal of the Israeli people in building up this state. I have always regretted most deeply what Germans inflicted upon Germans and non-Germans. You will understand that I shall go away from here, from this country with the impression and with the intention of telling people that every people has its duties before its own conscience and to do what it can to achieve the freedom and the life of other peoples. I have been very moved to be here with you and that is why I want to be brief. I have been received with great cordiality here in Israel, particularly in this house. What the newspapers printed and were obliged to print about demonstrations is ridiculous and petty in comparison with the great things I have seen here and what I hope has been your impression of my visit to your country. The Israeli people have a long past and it is almost like a miracle that they are now called upon again as a people to raise their voice in the circle of peoples. I believe that the world is not left to its own designs, but that we are all in God's hand, and that it was his will that the Israeli people should rise up again so strongly and powerfully, in the way that any visitor to your country can see for himself with amazement and with admiration. I shall be having a further discussion with Mr. Ben Gurion, in the way that such things happen between politicians and people, who have experienced a great deal. I am particularly looking forward to this. Here in Israel, I have been more deeply moved than at many stages of my life. I hope and trust that the Israeli people will maintain their strength and strength of will, and that it may always have the kind of leaders of the type of Ben Gurion, who are wellknown and honoured and celebrated all over the world. I shall never forget this day."

Rolf Pauls's first speech in Israel

In June 1966, a few weeks after the visit of Konrad Adenauer, the Federal Republic of Germany had its own pavilion at the Israeli Industrial Fair for the first time. On the occasion of the "Deutsche Tag" ("German Day") at this Fair, the Ambassador of the Federal Republic of Germany to Israel, Rolf Pauls, appeared in public and gave a speech on the subject of German-Israeli relations; the speech was very well received by the audience. The text was as follows:

"In my first public speech after almost a year in Israel, I should like to express two things, which I regard as particularly important. I should like to thank all those Israelis, who have during these months encouraged me with demonstrations of understanding, of friendliness and, I am pleased to say, of friendship. I know how to cherish the value of such sentiments.

"When I express my concern about German-Israeli relations, I cannot begin without indicating my great respect for the work of peaceful construction which I have become acquainted with during my year here. I am very impressed. When you are today dealing with the economic problems of the present and are working to overcome an economic crisis, which is partly commercial and partly structural, then I am firmly convinced that the difficulties are those of growth and nothing more, and that your genius, your strength of will and a sure feeling for essentials will assist you in overcoming these difficulties successfully.

"We Germans are in a special position with regard to you. That is how we see it. We have reiterated this and are doing everything practically possible to conform to this state of affairs. Agreements concluded between Germany and Israel and the implementation of German laws, which apply directly to your country, testify to this. What we have already done and are doing contributes effectively, to our satisfaction, towards promoting your work of construction.

"We understand that you cannot forget, what has happened. We are convinced that we may not be allowed to forget. We have had relations since 1952. They were reparations relations. In accordance with the nature of reparations, your gaze had to be directed backwards to those terrible things, which lie behind us and for which, as far as that is humanly possible, reparations should be paid. A Jewish statesman paid tribute to this on May 5th in words, which deserve to be remembered. Nahum Goldmann said: 'The legislation of compensation and reparations is a quite singular phenomenon. There is practically no precedent for a government paying out indemnities to the victims of a former regime, to those who are not even citizens of that country. This singular legislation has created new international legal concepts and constituted an important precedent.'

"For a year now, we have been making every effort to built up relations of the kind which exist between other governments and other states. They are foreign political relations. Foreign policy does of necessity look forwards. Its task is to win from the present that which will guarantee the path into the future. And that is predominantly the task of Germans and Jews in our time. I said this on the day I arrived and underline it again after a year of experience. Against the gloomiest backcloth and despite what has happened, we have to cooperate and will be able to do things together again. We need infinite patience. We should not be in too much of a hurry. It is not important at all whether success comes quickly. It is alone important that we build on solid foundations, which are not exposed to setbacks.

"We have every understanding for genuine feelings of disinclination, for deep, sincere resentment. We respect them and cannot do otherwise. With deep emotion and with gratitude, we pay tribute to the efforts at reconciliation made by those, who themselves have suffered terribly, and out of the conviction that hate must be overcome in order to prevent further catastrophe suppress their suffering and serve the cause of reconciliation.

"There is an infinite amount to be done in German-Israeli relations for decades to come. If during the past few years, it has proved possible to achieve a great deal despite everything detrimental to these relations, then a special tribute should go to the good will deeds of those Israelis, who despite much controversy have done so much to make relations possible.

"It is inevitable that in our relations the past overshadows the present much more than anywhere else. We do not want however to deprive ourselves of confidence in the future. I am thinking of the words said by your president in Jersualem on August 18th, 1965: 'But the conclusion we should draw from the bitter past is the following: we must utilise our energies for the future, so that the preachers of hate fade away and the spirit of that terrible epoch is never revived.'

"It is only with great concern that we can note how the sufferings of the past are continually stirred up for political and other reasons and for egoistic motives, in order to disrupt the present, so that it cannot serve the future. These forces, which are hostile to present-day Germany for political reasons are also rendering a bad service to their own country with the agitation they are perpetrating. I am reminded of the words spoken by Konrad Adenauer in all seriousness on May 3rd in Jerusalem: 'When good will goes unrecognised, then nothing good can come of it.'

"That also applies to reporting on events in Germany. It is a vain attempt to want to portray the Germany of 1966 on Nazi lines. Such a Germany does not exist and never will exist again. Fiction is no good to anyone. It is both bad and dangerous to want to turn ancillary phenomena into symptoms and to report as if they were. Only seeing reality clearly can lead to progress. Characteristic reality is not that a radical splinter party gained one percent more votes in Hamburg, but that a Jewish citizen was elected to the position of mayor of the city with a majority higher than his party had ever achieved in Hamburg. It is ridiculous to want to turn Karl Orff into a Nazi in 1966.

"Important people have said repeatedly during the last few weeks that the Jewish people expect deeds from Germany, so that she can take her place again in the family of peoples. I should like to say in that respect: Germany already has a respected place in the family of peoples again. She no longer needs permission for this. Since the establishment of the Federal Republic, Germany has been constantly making a constructive contribution to the community of peoples and tribute has been paid to this generally. That is known only too well here. Had this not been the case, then Israel would certainly not have desired recognition by such a Germany. Remarks, which have a discriminating tendency and only serve to be insulting, have never held a happy place in the relations between states.

"It seems opportune for me in this connection to remind my listeners that Germany in recognising Israel consciously underwent the risk of losing her in part normal, in part good relations with 10 states. They severed diplomatic ties. As regards deeds, that is a decision, for which there is no like example in the history of diplomacy and foreign politics.

"German foreign policy has no specific interests of its own to pursue in the Near East. It attaches importance to having a part in consolidating and ensuring the peaceful development of this part of the world, for it sees in this its most necessary contribution towards peace. Such efforts are in the interest of all the powers in the Near East, and they are in our own interest. For a disturbance of the peace in the Near East must have a directly devastating effect upon the situation in the Mediterranean and in Europe. Nothing in our activity is directed against anyone. The Arab states, which broke off diplomatic relations with us a year ago, because we embarked on diplomatic ties with Israel, were not justified in doing what they did. There is just as little reason for disagreeable reactions in Israel, when we express the desire to revert our relations with the Arab states to normal. Such a renormalization lies in the interests of the states concerned. They are in the German interest, they are in the interest of Israel. It must be important for Israel that we and no one else has the German say in the Near East. All our relations with the powers of the Near East area accord with legitimate interests and are not in rivalry with one another.

"In the past weeks, one problem, which is divorced from this area and about which we could do nothing, suddenly played a role in German-Israeli relations. The public has again been approached by Israel about this matter of recent date. For that reason, I am obliged to say a word about it. The treatment of German interests by Israel is of basic significance for the quality of German-Israeli relations.

"The question of the German Eastern frontier is a problem of politics and international law, whereby our attitude has its basis in the Potsdam Agreement. The powers concerned will have to find a settlement for this, when a German peace treaty is concluded. Views will differ until then. Ours can only be evaluated in connection with Germany's unconditional and final renunciation of force, which we have stated irrevocably. I can only underline again that the German attitude to the frontier question can never constitute a threat to peace, and that no one who refutes it can base his arguments on the necessity of serving peace. Until a peace treaty is concluded, we are just as interested in our position as any other government, which has to guide its country through the rocky paths of foreign policy. We react to any undermining of our position with the same sensitive attention displayed by any other government in a similar position. It is hardly conceivable that such an attitude is difficult to understand.

"Careful consideration for the interests of the other can only be of service to the quality of our future relations. German-Israeli trade has demonstrated favourable developments. Difficulties which exist require a settlement between the organisation of the European Common Market and Israel. They are not exclusively of a German-Israeli nature. We are aware of your wishes and requirements and have shown a large measure of understanding and practical support for them in the past. The latest financial aid agreement concluded in Bonn gives also effective expression to our attitude. We wish you every success in your economic efforts in the future as well, and would like to assist you, as far as it lies in our power to do so.

"One of your predominant aims lies in increasing Israeli exports in such a manner and through the expansion of your industrial production that the balance of payments gap between imports and exports, which continues to cause such great economic worries, may be closed. We would like to help you in this industrial build-up. We are not concerned here with securing positions. In view of the size of the market, the difficulties of engagement are greater than its advantages. But we do believe that we can be of assistance in a technical and economic capacity, and we believe that practical cooperation is the most important and the most useful aspect of relations between Germans and Israelis today. Cooperation should ensue in particular where emotions are least involved, for example in the economic sphere. If we succeed in making progress there, then we shall be rendering an important service to the overall quality of our relations, and in the future will be able to draw closer in fields, which are more difficult and more painful to open up, the spheres of the intellect and of art.

"Relations with Germany will improve in the measure that policies are not only conceived in the past, but also with an eye to the future.

"Nothing should be allowed to shake our firm determination to put our relations on the right path into the future."

Asher Ben Natan and Abba Eban on German-Jewish relations

The echo that the address of Rolf Pauls found in the Israeli Press had been very critical: it became clear that there were certain groups of opinion in Israel that did not yet wish to see a normalization of relations at this time. Subsequently, two Israeli politicians made public speeches on this subject: They were Ambassador Asher Ben Natan and Foreign Minister Abba Eban.

Ambassador Asher Ben Natan, Israel's representative in the Federal Republic of Germany, had been for many years Director-General of the Israeli Ministry of Defence and had had constant conversations with German politicians and military men. His frequent visits to the Federal Republic, even before he was made Ambassador, had given him considerable insight into many aspects of political life. On July 12th, 1966 he was interviewed by the journalist Amos Elon for the Israeli newspaper "Haaretz" and the conversation ran as follows:

Question: "After a year in Germany, are you in a position to answer the question as to whether the Germans have still to produce evidence, in order to be counted among the cultural peoples?"

Answer: "I would like to answer you in a different way. Have the cultural peoples empowered us to speak in their name? The truth is that the Germans want to prove to themselves and to others that they have changed. It is their strong desire to show that they are a free and democratic people. In the education for democracy, the main effort is directed towards young people. This youth, from what I have seen, heard and read, gave me the impression that it is a good youth, no different from the youth of other countries in Europe.

"The Germans cannot free themselves from their past. Not only because the others do not allow them to do so. They cannot free themselves, even those who say that they have already heard enough and that people should stop talking about the past. They are oppressed by it and concerned with it."

Question: "Is there more democracy or less in Germany than in Israel?"

Answer: "Judging from the outward signs of democracy, there is no less democracy in Germany than in Israel."

Question: "Are there more or fewer civic freedoms?"

Answer: "It would seem to me that there were even more civic freedoms."

Question: "Were the Germans, whom you encountered, less or more tolerant than the Israelis, whom you know, tolerant with regard to other views, other beliefs, other races?"

Answer: "Those, whom I encountered, were both tolerant and balanced. I wouldn't say that they all are. The great question is, how deeply the new democracy has penetrated and how far a crisis or a sudden devastating blow would imperil that which has been achieved. That is a question, with regard to which the Germans themselves are very much on the alert. They are trying through the education of young people to make up for that which was lost during the period of National Socialist rule."

Mr. Ben Natan spoke with great bitterness about the refusal of Israeli students to receive a group from Heidelberg. That is a university where there have even been pro-Israeli demonstrations. The students of this university are known for their tolerance and liberal-mindedness. When you tell them that they cannot go to Israel because they are Germans, that is something which they cannot understand. He said further with regard to the lack of contacts between the students of the two countries: that is short-sightedness, which contains the nucleus of the same negative phenomenon, which we display everywhere—I do not want to give it a name.

Question: "The students hear that the Prime Minister said that the Germans must expressly prove etc. etc. I suppose that at least in this case you tell the Germans that they must first show that they have changed and then contacts will be established with them."

Answer: "German students are always asking me how to demonstrate this. What has that got to do with the fact that I may not speak to a young Israeli student, they ask. What does he demonstrate to me, when he says that he is not prepared to talk to me?"

Question: "How do you respond to such questions?"

Answer: "I try to explain the psychological situation and that is not always easy. I stress the emotional aspects, but it is difficult to explain that thousands of Israeli students live on their feelings only."

Question: "But why are they only complaining about the students? The government itself hinders performances of a German film of the post-war period, called 'Wir Wunderkinder', which constitutes self-criticism of Germany."

Answer: "That is one of the absurdities. I hope that it will soon be changed. I do not support the idea of showing films with former National Socialist actors and actresses. I do not however understand the ban on films simply because they are German. I am all for a minimum of State intervention in this sphere. I believe in the freedom of the individual in the sphere of cultural exchange. The existing State limitations of a bilateral cultural exchange must be removed. We are interested in connections which are as broad as possible. There can be no limitations in the sphere of the mind. We must not restrict by means of artificial bans or a giving in to public pressure which is not always representative."

In referring to the question of Germany's Eastern frontiers, Mr. Ben Natan said that "present-day Germany, just like any other State has its own interests ... its reactions are no different from those of other states. 60 percent of the youth were born or brought up after the Nazi period. These young people play an ever more significant role. If we adopt a negative attitude to every matter which concerns them—only because it is a question of Germany—when only they are to be in the right, who counter the Germans and insult them, then they cannot understand us ... Under no circumstances, will they reconcile themselves to a line which says that they are prohibited from having their own interests. That must be comprehensible. That is a quite normal reaction."

Finally, Mr. Ben Natan said that we depended on goodwill in Germany, just as everywhere else in the world and from different points of view more than in other countries.

Ten days later, on 22nd. July 1966, the Israeli foreign minister said in an interview with "Yediot Achronot":

Question: "Do you believe in the existence of another Germany?"

Answer: "It is my view that this is simply a play on words. No normal human being could allege that Hitler's Germany with its extermination camps, its conquests and its Nazi atrocities was the same Germany as that of today. Of course there is a difference between the Germany of today and that prior to 1945. This difference is a fact and not an evaluation. If we did not recognise this fact, then the defeat and downfall of Hitler would have no significance for us and this is of course absurd."

Question: "That is a formalist explanation. It is very clear that the Germany of today is not the Germany of Hitler. The question is whether there is a new spirit in the Germany of today or whether there is not perhaps the danger that a Nazi spirit could rise up again."

Answer: "There may be circles in Germany today, which are yearning for a dictatorship or which are still polluted with anti-semitism. That is a serious sideline, but not, as was the case during the Nazi period, the central point of the German spirit. In this respect, I agree entirely with our ambassador in Germany."

Question: "Are you also of the same opinion as the ambassador, when he touched on the question as to whether the cultured peoples had authorised us to accept their opinion about a relinquishment of the exclusion of Germany from their circle?"

Answer: "The whole family of peoples has to determine who belongs to it and who doesn't. As far as Israel is concerned, we attempted as early as ten years ago to assume diplomatic relations with Germany. This fact would indeed make it difficult for us not to recognise Germany as a state, which is worthy of maintaining its relations with the rest of the family of peoples. I can understand those who do not want to have any relations at all with Western Germany, but I cannot understand others, who take the view that Germany should uphold its diplomatic and economic relations with Israel and should support Israel's admittance to the EEC, but at the same time allege that Germany does not belong in the family of peoples. We have indeed to come to terms with Germany, but that is a different matter."

Question: "Do you share the disgust of the ambassador, Mr. Ben Natan, at the rejection of Israeli students of all contact with German students?"

Answer: "The word applicable here is not disgust, but shock. It is morally unjustified to hold the young people, who were born after the breakdown of the Nazi dictatorship, responsible for the Nazi crimes. A seventeen year old German boy is no more responsible for these crimes than my own son, who is almost the same age. Both of them were not born at that time. It is a matter of knowing how to distinguish between the good and the bad, between the positive and the negative in Germany."

Question: "What is your view of the decision of the Israeli Doctors' Association to boycott medical congresses in Israel, where German is recognised as one of the official languages?"

Answer: "The German language existed long before National Socialism and after it, continues to exist. It is not only the language of murderers, but also the language of many of those, who were murdered—Jews and non-Jews—and also of non-German people. As far as I know, the circulation of German-language newspapers in Israel has never been a bone of contention. We cannot refuse at international level, what we regard as our good right at home. The waiting rooms of many doctors contain Israeli newspapers, which are printed in German. I once had talks and correspondence with Einstein in German and I did not have the feeling that this was detrimental to the high level of the exchange. Einstein never used any other language but German. I do not know what Einstein's opinion of the decision of the Doctors' Association would have been."

Question: "Isn't it ridiculous to take German guests to Yad Washem and to pin the Yiskor needle on them?"

Answer: "Nothing is ridiculous, if it is sincerely intended. I have seen Germans, who were deeply perturbed by their visit to Yad Washem. Konrad Adenauer, whom I spoke to briefly after his visit there, was one of them. It is of educational significance for anyone to be confronted with the heinous atrocities of the Nazi period. I myself was very impressed by the school-children, who made organised visits to Auschwitz and Birkenau."

Question: "But a distinction has to be made between Polish schoolchildren and Germans."

Answer: "It is important for every human being regardless of who he is to be conscious of the summit of human dignity and the abyss of depravity. This is no less important for Germans than for others."

Question: "Do you advocate a lifting of the boycott against performances of the music of Wagner and Strauss?"

Answer: "There are Jews, who can listen to music without thinking about the political orientation or the moral horizon of the composer. There are also many Jews who cannot do that. I think that we ought to be tolerant and spare them painful experiences, particularly in view of the fact that we have sufficient works, which do not conjure up such painful memories. These feelings should be respected, as long as they are not detrimental to others. But just as music as such cannot be condemned because Wagner was a composer, the German language cannot be rejected because it was also spoken by bad people."

Question: "Do you think that the time has come to establish cultural relations with Germany?"

Answer: "Four years ago in the Knesseth, I suggested limitations for cultural relations with Germany and my proposal was accepted. I said then that not everything is permissible, but that not everything is banned either. It is my view that that is still generally applicable today, although this problem can always be reviewed in the light of the constantly changing situation."

Question: "What then are the limits to cultural relations between the two states?"

Answer: "It is not easy to define that exactly. It is something which cannot be changed but some time must pass, before logic can assert itself. I told the German ambassador, when he took up his work in Israel that no logical and consequent attitude could be expected from the Israeli people nor a unanimous evaluation of that which is permissible or prohibited between the two peoples."

Question: "Hasn't the economic agreement with Germany impeded our political freedom of action with regard to Germany?

Answer: "The agreement has not weakened us at all. It was not after all a new agreement, but simply a continuation. First of all, there was the loan, which was agreed upon at the meeting in the Waldorf-Astoria Hotel. After the establishment of diplomatic relations, this was replaced by a new agreement. The difference between the old agreement and the new one is that the new one is more comprehensive, contains better conditions and functions completely above board on a legal basis. I think that these are improvements. I can understand those who are against loans from Germany, but I cannot understand those who were jubilant about the Waldorf-Astoria agreement and now despise a better one."

Question: "But, don't you think that despite all the advantages we have sold ourselves too cheaply?"

Answer: "We have sold ourselves? I decisively reject this allegation. We have neither sold ourselves too cheaply nor too expensively, for there can be no question of our having sold ourselves at all. The agreement is to the advantage and for the benefit of both sides and does not limit our political freedom of action in any way at all."

Germans and Jews – Discussion during the 5th Plenary Assembly of the Jewish World Congress

Nahum Goldmann, the president of the World Jewish Congress, who had made it clear as early as Konrad Adenauer's visit to Israel that he intended to continue, among Jewish circles the world over, with efforts to normalise the relationship to the German people, had put upon the agenda of the Fifth Plenary Assembly of the World Jewish Congress the theme, "Germans and Jews". From the beginning of his conversations with post-war German political figures, Nahum Goldmann had intended through frank discussion to evolve a realistic policy, so far as possible keeping the feelings of the Jewish people out of substantive decisions. During those years Nahum Goldmann was often confronted with bitter criticism in the Jewish organisations. Only through his powerful personality could he get people to follow him. The fact that his open-minded and personal attitude toward today's Germany had proved itself right encouraged him in drawing up the agenda. It was an act of enormous daring to let the subject of Germans and Jews be discussed in an open assembly of more than 500 delegates.

Abba Eban's speech

In the debate on the agenda on 31 July 1966, a number of delegates rejected the subject; the Israeli foreign minister, Abba Eban, took the floor and delivered an epoch-making speech on the matter. Abba Eban said:

"I rejoice that my presence in Europe makes it possible for me to bring the government of Israel's sincere and fraternal greeting to this assembly of the World Jewish Congress. We meet in the very heart and centre of Europe, on the soil of the valiant Belgian nation with which Israel maintains solid links of friendship and cooperation.

"In thanking the Deputy Prime Minister for his words of greetings—let me express, in Israel's name, a fervent wish for the peace and welfare of Belgium, and for the continued progress of the European community as a whole.

"This gathering is an authentic reflection of the Jewish reality of our times. As we look around this hall we see that reality in a dual aspect. We know what we have—and what we lack. On the one hand we see here the broad range and unceasing vitality of Jewish communities across the world, drawn together here in a profound emotion of solidarity. On the other hand we are poignantly aware of the millions who were engulfed in the wave of catastrophe, of other millions who live elsewhere on this continent cut off from the main stream of Jewish life in the past and the present, and of many in free communities who feel no impulse to associate themselves with the particular and intimate values of Jewish civilization. These are the three organic weaknesses in the Jewish body-politic: the havoc wrought by Nazism; the remoteness imposed on Soviet Jewry; and the weakening of Jewish consciousness and responsibility in Western communities.

"Tragedy is the difference between what is—and what might have been. We cannot bring the past to life. Much of what we have lost is gone forever—beyond consolation or recall. But our other two deficiencies are within the scope of human repair. We do not despair of an affirmative reunion of Soviet Jewry with the other Jewries of Europe and the world. This would symbolize and promote the contemporary tendency towards co-existence and contact. The separation of a large Jewish community from the main body of the Jewish people is historically an organic part of the cold war. It has no place in the emerging concept of a new Europe in which the stream of ideas and commerce will flow between East and West, breaking down the so-called iron curtain, in a new wave of continental solidarity.

"Similarly, there is no need for us to be resigned to the corrosion of Jewish identity. As Europe and the Americas advance to higher forms of social organization and technical power, they become increasingly responsive to voices from their past, telling them of the forces and values which shaped their life and thought. The Jewish element is a part of the balance of world culture. Its disappearance would bring nothing but impoverishment. It would be a thoughtless tragedy if Jewish identity were surrendered by those who have every freedom to conserve it. The greatest injuries that nations do to themselves are often self-inflicted. The danger lies close to our door. It requires your assembly's deepest preoccupation.

"But there is no cause for us to dwell uniquely on what we have lost through tragedy—and what we stand to lose by inadvertence. Let us recall what it is that we have gained, since the dark years when your organization began its task. We have gained the incomparable pride and opportunity of Israel's sovereignty. By this gain we have transformed the spirit and structure of our nation's life. We have changed the very order of Jewish existence and in so doing we have created a new dimension in universal history. For Israel's rebirth does not signify a flight from the larger world into an intimate national enclosure. On the contrary, our aim has been to rescue Jewish history from its isolation and cause it to flow into the broader currents of world culture. Recognised statehood within the international family gives the Jewish people not only a national personality but an international opportunity.

"Some philosophers of our times have predicted that mankind has a deadline of a few decades, until the end of the century, to choose between a world state and annihilation. It seems to me that a third path appears. History has more imagination than historians have. It has thus far refused to choose between collective suicide and the abdication of states. It seeks a system of relations which will reconcile national sovereignty with the claims of international order.

"Israel's rebirth occurred at a time when national freedom has celebrated its greatest triumph. More than fifty states have been added to the organised international community since Israel's admission to membership in the United Nations seventeen years ago. It is vital that world opinion should grasp the truth about Israel's deep roots in the region of which she forms a part. Sometimes our adversaries try to portray us as an expression of colonialism. There is no state in the world to which this definition is more incongruous. No state anywhere expresses the concept of nationhood more intensely than Israel. It is the only state which bears the same name, speaks the same tongue, upholds the same faith, inhabits the same land as it did three thousand years ago. Israel is thus not alien to the Middle East but an organic part of its texture and memory. Take Israel and all that has emanated from Israel out of Middle Eastern history—and you evacuate that history of its central experience. The Arab political and intellectual leaders have never made a serious effort to understand, even reluctantly, the tenacity and authenticity of Israel as a national reality, deeply rooted in the Middle East. They would surely do well to ponder Ernest Renan's definition of nationhood: 'a nation has a soul, a spiritual principle to share, a common glory in the past, a common will in the present, to have done great things together, to wish to do them again—these are the essential conditions of being a nation'.

"This assembly of Jewish leaders, drawn from many continents, may well see our state as the supreme expression of Jewish resilience. No people in history has ever emerged from so deep a darkness into a new epoch of vitality. Israel's Jewish aspect is a crucial part of her international identity. The essence of Jewish history can be summed up in a single phrase—the few against the many. Thus it was in the past, so it is today. Yet the few are not as few as Israel's limited population might indicate. Let the word go forth from here that there are millions of Jews across the world for whom Israel's security, welfare and honour are goals worthy of every effort and every sacrifice. Those who do not grasp this fact underestimate the power of the Israeli reality and the Israeli idea in the history of our times. These three national goals—our security, our welfare and our honour—stand in the centre of Israel's foreign relations. They can only be won at the price of constant struggle and in the face of the most unyielding hostility by which any modern nation has ever been assailed. The question is whether and when we can bring the Arab world to a cool and rational estimate of Israel's capacity to stand fast, struggle and endure. It is true that the map reveals a great preponderance of Arab power in relation to Israel. It shows us thirteen sovereign states with a population of a hundred million and an area of four million square miles, confronting a single sovereignty established in a small area of eight thousand square miles with a population of only two and a half million. Yet the experience of these eighteen years demonstrates that the evidence of the map is not conclusive. There are manifestly forces at work in the history of our times and in the life of our generation which deny these facts. The first of these is Israel's capacity to deter and contain the regional hostility by maintaining a balance of military strength. The commitment of two million Israelis to Israel's defence is more absolute and passionate than the commitment of a hundred million Arabs to Israel's destruction. For Israel, survival is the first and ultimate necessity. For the Arab nation, with its own survival assured in thirteen states, Israel's submergence is at best optional. To this crucial issue of morale, we must add the reinforcement of technology. In modern strategy, the value of numbers tends to decline in comparison with the value of technical and scientific skills. As military technology develops, the quantitative element loses its decisive importance, the possibility of a small community holding its own against heavy demographic odds becomes increasingly tangible. This is not to say that it is preferable to be small, but it is at least a tolerable destiny. In Israel's national memory, the victory of David over Goliath was a result not of his smallness but of his compensating agility and talent for improvisation. Whatever has enabled Israel to succeed in deterrence and containment during the past decade seems certain to be operative for the next decade and beyond.

"The maintenance of a local equilibrium of security in the Middle East is not only Israel's concern. It also responds to broad international interests. The crises of the last few years have usually had their origin in small nations which lack either international stability or a local equilibrium of strength. The present tragic conflict in Viet-Nam, as well as recent eruptions in the Congo, Cyprus and the Yemen, illustrate this truth. In each case a vacuum or unbalance of security in a small country draws external forces into perilous involvement. A local tension becomes an international peril. This experience helps to explain why there is more overt and effective support today than formerly for the maintenance of a prudent security equilibrium in the Arab-Israel area. Israel's policy on the arms race is clear. We should like to see it halted or slowed down. But, if, through the actions and attitudes of other governments, near and far, the race goes on, then we are resolved never to lose it, we dare not tempt our adversaries by our weakness.

"But while we accept the inexorable necessities of increasing our defensive, we cannot fail to reflect at the revolution which would come over our region if its resources were consecrated to the peaceful challenge of development. If the Arab states, as seems to be the case, are themselves afflicted by the burdens and anxieties of the Middle Eastern armaments race, then we would willingly take this as the first point in the peaceful and direct dialogue that we seek with them. Let the race in armaments give way to a new race, a race in development. Let us exchange commodities and ideas instead of exchanging words of abuse and acts of enmity. Israel's strength, in which we do not conceal our pride, stands in the exclusive service of our security and our peace. Those who respect Israel's independence, integrity and legitimate interests, will encounter a reciprocal respect from us. My thoughts in this context are riveted on our frontier with Syria, which has lately been the scene of grave events. For our part, we should like to see this tension brought to a close. If the Israeli border regions are safe for us, the Syrian border regions will be safe for them. The United Nations' contribution to this cause is more likely to lie in local conciliation than in acrimonious debate. The United Nations was meant to be an instrument for solving conflicts, not an arena for waging them. The highest international organs do not exhaust their duty by reacting like a Greek chorus—expressing organised consternation at conflicts which they do little to allay.

"Israel's reliance on her independent deterrent strength does not mean that we are blind to the potential effects of external influence. For good or ill the policies of states outside our region will affect the Middle Eastern destiny. There is no such thing as an Arab-Israel map. Cut off from the currents of thought and action in the wider world, there is nothing to be gained for Israel by restricting the play of forces to that of the two containing adversaries. It is outside our region that we must look for elements of strength to offset our deficiencies within its borders. An active international policy is an important dictate of Israel's national security. Here the central question is whether international policies in favour of existing political and territorial structures and against irredentist violence can be clarified and brought to expression.

"I am convinced that all powers with interests in our region are animated in their international policies by opposition to the use of force for the settlement of territorial dispute between sovereign states. And these sovereign states and the small nations which are the bulk of the international community have a manifest interest in the integrity of existing frontiers everywhere. With ninety-eight per cent of the human race now living for the first time under sovereign flags, the doctrines of territorial expansion have lost their appeal. Every state, and especially those which have primary responsibility for international peace and security, can help the Middle East in its torment and contention by expressing, each in its own way and form, an unyielding resistance to any change of the status quo by force. Those who uphold this doctrine in Europe and in the Far East should be the first to apply it rigidly in the Middle East as well. You cannot have peace, coexistence and respect for existing frontiers in this continent of Europe, if you allow those principles to be set aside in Europe's background.

"It may be that our neighbours see Israel as menaced in her prospects of existence by what they call our regional solitude. The effects of Israel's isolation from the Arab environment are regrettable and serious, but they touch the atmosphere of the life rather than her prospect of survival. In the new age of swift communications, nations are less dependent on their regional context than in former times. Israel's markets, friendships, scientific contacts and intellectual links can, if necessary, be found in Europe, the Western hemisphere and amongst the friendly states of Africa and the Middle East that lie beyond the Arab fence. The modern world is assuming the character of a close-knit, urban society, whose several parts are mutually accessible. Affinity is now more important than vicinity as the guiding force of international relationships. Moreover, Israel, since the dawn of history, has received and exercised her major influences across the Mediterranean world in which she is far from being isolated.

"Israel's network of diplomatic and commercial relations is not yet complete, but it is already of impressive scope. It includes friendly ties with all the governments and peoples of the Western hemisphere. Our President's arrival in Washington this week, after an enthusiastic welcome in Latin America, testifies to the cordiality of these friendships. In my conversations with President Johnson and his leading associates earlier this year, I felt how far the United States has moved towards a deeper understanding of Israel's security needs. This friendship, so fruitful for Israel in so many ordeals, is enriched by a vigilant and ardent public sympathy. Further south, we find ourselves linked with nations whose revolutionary epoch is not yet ended. The revolution no longer affects the attainment of sovereignty which is everywhere assured. It concerns the pursuit of economic progress against the background of a vast demographic increase, far outstripping the more modest growth of production. It hardly seemed possible a few years ago that Israel's experience could have much to teach to nations so solidly established in international life. It now appears that there are problems, vital for the Latin American future, in which Israel's achievements are of burning relevance. Our technical cooperation agreements with the Organization of American States and with individual governments assure a friendly and constructive Israeli presence in the hemisphere.

"As our glance moves eastward, it brings us face to face with crucial areas of relationship with Europe. Israelis are profoundly impressed by the speed and scope of the European recovery. In all that was said and written about Europe at the end of the Second World War, there is not a single recorded prediction that the European scene would be as it is today. An exceptional self-confidence and zest for the future now inflame the energies of the old world. Yet less than two decades have passed since the most eloquent European voice proclaimed: 'But what is Europe now? It is a rubble heap, a charnel house, a breeding ground of pestilence and hate; ancient nationalistic feuds and modern ideological factions distract and infuriate the unhappy, hungry populations'.

"Well, the populations are not unhappy or hungry now. Their progress is expressed in living institutions whose operation closely affects the destiny of all Mediterranean lands. Israel is on the eve of a new attempt, which may be long, to reach a satisfactory association with this European community. It is not only a question of safeguarding our export trade, which is adversely affected by the customs provisions of the Treaty of Rome. Beyond this there looms a whole complex of larger issues. How can Israel achieve a high technical standard in production if she is thrown back on herself, cut off from the large markets and expanding skills of European industry? As the influence of the EEC expands southward and eastward, beyond Greece and Turkey to North and West Africa, how can Israel fail to be injured if she is excluded from widening integration? Is there not a special link of history, culture—yes, and of tragic memory between Europe and the Jewish nation? What was European unity except a reaction, after the war, to the weakness and humiliation bequeathed by the Nazi decade? When we probe the deeper preoccupations of European culture, can we go far without encountering some of the origins of that culture in Hebrew thought? Should not all these affinities of thought and action, of interest and ideals, of material concern and spiritual ambitions, find their proper institutional expression?

"These considerations imply an ever closer link of Israel with the European destiny. We seek those closer links with all members of the European community, without exception. Israel and France do not need a common adversary in order that their friendship should flourish. If we go hand in hand today, it is not because we had a common foe in the past, but because we have common interests and ideals for the present and future. There are other nations of Europe, both within and beyond EEC, whose recent memory comprises a community of experience with the Jewish people in its anguish and renewed hope.

"The sombre story of Israel's encounter with Germany is a special case. In proposing to the Knesseth that we respond to the offer of diplomatic relations, I said last year that we did not aim to end the acute and searching dialogue, but to establish a new framework for conducting it. We must somehow manage both to preserve the past and to remain capable of the future. Above all, we must understand that we can do no higher reverence to the memory of our martyred millions than to ensure that Israel shall be strong, so that never, never again shall the Jewish people be afflicted by the weakness and inferiority which made its tragedy possible. We do not honour our past by renouncing any possibility for strengthening our future.

"When we speak of Europe, we do not mean Western Europe alone. In 1947 a great power which had until then refused to acknowledge our national rights, joined with those whom it considered as its adversaries in a concerted international attempt to solve the central issue of Jewish history. This moment of convergence in the policies of the powers was brief. There is no assurance that it will soon come again. But if all the powers could be brought to give convincing expression of a desire to support the independence and integrity of Middle Eastern states, a new revolutionary period might be inaugurated. There is no virtue in a general doctrine of peaceful coexistence, if it is upheld in some areas and set aside in others.

"It seems to me that it is Israel's duty to explore all possibilities for revealing common ground in her relations with East European states. On my recent visit to Warsaw I had occasion to make a detailed review of our relations with East European states. We have diplomatic relations with all, commercial relations with most, cultural relations with some. Our support to the integrity of their existing frontiers is not in doubt. It is vital that we move to consolidate and strengthen these bonds. Europe will not forever be divided into two ideological camps, hermetically sealed one against the other. Indeed, the search for a unified system of continental relationship has already begun.

"Of the ninety-six countries with whom Israel has diplomatic relations, nearly a third are African states. Israel's presence in the arena of African development will be steadily expanded, in the measure that African governments continue to attach importance to this work. Some people expected that Africa would pass from revolution to stability overnight. History does not teach us that Europe or America made so great a transition in so short a time. The present difficulties affecting many African states cannot eclipse the brilliant success of African emancipation, as one of the most positive developments in twentieth century life.

"Israel is proud of her intimate association with this process. We do not exaggerate our capacity, we know what we are and what we are not. But when all is said, Israel's role in the great drama of African development is seriously conceived, widely respected—and full of honour.

"While we cannot be expected to become involved in Asia's conflicts, we for our part welcome the opportunity of expanding our links with the developing states of the Asian continent.

"The special challenge to Israel's diplomacy arises in the Middle East. Something is at last astir in Arab minds. The old dogmas no longer go unchallenged. There are Arabs who understand that history and geography have brought these two peoples together in a common future. The call to war and boycott is increasingly discordant with the spirit and necessities of our times. Whether the Arab nations and Israel can reach an understanding of each other depends on how they conceive the nature and destination of the Middle East. For president Nasser and the main body of Arab nationalism, the dominant theme of the region's destiny is Arab unity. Much of Arab history is concerned with the tension between unity and regionalism. Union has been the exception, not the rule. There is, of course, a unifying energy in the Arab world, which draws all men of Arab tongue together in a common identity. But there is also a strong tendency of Arab states to maintain their separate sovereignties against a claim to centralized hegemony from Cairo. Baghdad, Beirut, Damascus, and the North African states have never voluntarily acknowledged the political ukase of the Nile valley.

"For twelve years, the efforts to impose a uniform control on the restless, varied stream of Arab life has led to uninterrupted crises. Nothing has divided the Arab world more than the effort to unite it. Syria, Lebanon, Iraq, Jordan, Sudan, Saudi Arabia, Tunisia and now Yemen have been successive arenas in which Nasserism has come to grips with the desire of Arab states to be independent not only of foreign control but of each other. Today, diversity, pluralism and polycentrism are everywhere undermining the pretensions of monolithic blocs—from the Atlantic world to the communist system, as well as across Africa and Latin America. It is doubtful if the Arab world with its deep-rooted diversities will tolerate a centralized control. A Middle East in which separate Arab states could pursue their separate destiny, in a mood of tolerant variety, could more easily accommodate an Arab-Israel understanding than a homogenized Middle East convulse by an Egyptian bid for centralized control. The Middle East is not an exclusive Arab domain. Its destiny lies in a pluralistic interaction of Asia, Europe and Africa. There are nearly as many non-Arabs in the Middle East as there are Arabs (the combined population of Israel, Iran, Ethiopia, Somalia, Turkey and Cyprus is 70 million), and the dream of a united Arab domain, from the Atlantic to the Persian gulf, offends the region's essential diversity.

"There is a lesson to be learned from experiments in regional cooperation in other continents. In Western Europe, the unity movement began from common interests, proceeding from coal and steel toward broader economic integration and free communications. Existing sovereignties are respected and the sensitive issue of political coordination is left until economic mutuality has been longer at work.

"In the American republics, the continental organization avoids racial or linguistic exclusiveness. It comprises every sovereignty within the defined region. Similarly, the new Organization of African Unity avoids centralization and hegemony, Neither in

Europe, Latin America nor Africa has the federal principle yet won any notable victory. The formula is one of growing integration and harmony in relations between separate sovereign states.

"The world has generously come to terms with Arab nationalism. The question is whether Arab nationalism can now come to terms with regional and international concepts broader than itself.

"The most fruitful and natural regional concept is that of Mediterranean cooperation. The Mediterranean spirit, with the currents of thought and action which it has generated or evoked, lies at the origin of the technical and cultural transformation which has largely determined the cultural history of mankind. Egypt, Israel, Lebanon, Syria, Libya, Tunisia, Algeria and Morocco are Mediterranean nations, while Jordan is oriented by trade and history toward the Mediterranean world. The Hellenic and Latin worlds, Turkey and the island republics of Cyprus and Malta, are washed by the same waters. Every point in this littoral is swiftly accessible to every other. Three continents, Europe, Africa and Asia, look out upon it with all their diversity of fate and outlook. Five great civilizations were born here—Judaism, Christianity, Hellenism, Rom and Islam. It is a central compact world, congenial to the free interaction of commerce and ideas and alien to exclusiveness. In no other part of the globe does a similar variety of conditions exist in such close proximity or in such intensity of mutual influence. It is here that man first considered himself in the light of eternity. It is here that science broke loose from empirism in search of broad unifying explanations of the natural order. And it is here, amidst all the conditions for a new emergence of human vitality, that we find statesmanship held down in implacable conflict.

"The issue is whether the Arab and Jewish nations, which have been primary agents in the Mediterranean adventure, can transcend their conflict in dedication to a new Mediterranean future, in concert with a renascent Europe and an emerging Africa. A new impulse of thought in the Middle East, similar to that which inaugurated the European new unity 15 years ago, could open up a new era for the whole region.

"I have spoken to you, as is inevitable, in the name and service of the Israeli government alone. It is legitimate to doubt whether there is such a thing as a Jewish policy, outside the frontiers of a sovereign state. Yet it seems to me that the special memories and impulses of our history give the Jewish people everywhere a certain unifying shape of thought on central, universal issues. First there is a passion for peace—born of ancient prophecy and of recent tragedy. Then there is support of freedom. Only those societies are creative and tolerant which are open to new and conflicting ideas. As Jews we are commanded everywhere to resist every form of discrimination, whether practiced against ourselves or against others. In view of Israel's emergence to freedom, we are all better able to comprehend the struggles of other peoples for liberation from colonial rule. In the light of our experience, we are particularly sensitive to the need for international action in support of human rights and fundamental freedoms. Our people's cultural history gives it a special understanding of the healing effects of intellectual and scientific cooperation in the service of human welfare. All these elements of Israel's policy reflect the humanistic legacy that we have derived from our specifically Jewish origins. It is imperative that we maintain these links. We must not live within the confines of our small geography, but against the back-drop of our large history and our deep roots in a continuous spiritual tradition. We must banish all Canaanite heresies from Israeli thought. You cannot take Israel out of its universal Jewish context, without stunting its image and dwarfing its reality. Similarly, Israel does not aspire to draw strength from Jewish adversity. Whatever weakens the security and dignity of Diaspora Jewry must, in the final resort, weaken Israel as well. We seek accession to Israel of Jews from other lands—not because they are driven by fear, but because they are drawn by hope and touched by the creative exhilaration of a new society. We cannot maintain our achievement, still less expand it, without an infusion of man-power from the free Jewish communities of the world.

"Distinguished assembly: "Twenty years ago, we could hardly have conceived this moving encounter between a sovereign Israel and Jewish communities of the world. The lesson of this hour is that our proud and ancient people has not exhausted its vocation. The years to come will be turbulent, challenging, restless, with energies flying off in all directions. I know, better than some of you, that much in Israel is still incomplete, lacking in inner form and outer harmony. But ours is still a young society, with all its future intact before it, for the first time in two millennia the Jewish people has recaptured an autonomous control of its destiny. The forces represented in this room are summoned to a new enactment of the national experience. If we stand together—we may find that a new story, never known before, will yet unfold, and that the climax to the long record of Jewish creativity is yet to come."

Nahum Goldmann opens the Plenary Session

The result of the vote was that the controversial item remained on the agenda. Thus there ensued on 4 August 1966 the momentous Plenary Session in which Eugen Gerstenmaier, president of the German Federal Diet, Professor Golo Mann, Professor Sholem of the Hebrew University in Jerusalem, and Professor Salo W. Baron of Columbia University in New York addressed the delegates to the Congress.

Nahum Goldmann introduced the Plenary Session:

"I open this session of the Assembly which, as you know, will be devoted to a discussion of the problem of German-Jewish relations.

"Now, as it is well-known, members of three groups—groups as such don't exist at Congress, because the WJC is based on territorial delegations—but delegates belonging to three ideological groups, have opposed the putting of this problem on the agenda and, as a majority of the Executive and the Plenary Session have decided to leave it on the agenda, they will not attend this meeting. They are perfectly entitled to do so, there is no obligation in the Constitution of the World Jewish Congress for any delegate to be present at every session. But these groups have asked, and the Presidium has granted them the right that a member of each group will make a short statement at the beginning to explain why they oppose the putting on the subject on the agenda and why, because it was decided otherwise, they will not attend. And therefore, before I open the real discussion, when I will have to say a few words, and in order not to force these three friends to remain here before they have made their statement and will leave us, I will first of all give the floor to the three representatives."

Isaac Remba on behalf of the Heruth-Hatzoar

"In our generation the German people annihilated a third of the Jews, having first willingly accepted Hitler and chosen him their leader. This is the generation of Germans that slaughtered 6 million—6 million!— Jews, burnt them and killed them in a thousand other ways. And it still lives amongst us. And aside from those sentenced by courts, all the rest went free. Innumerable murderers are living free and unpunished everywhere in Germany, and their hands are defiled with Jewish blood.

"In thousands of German homes one still finds the Sabbath candlestick of our mothers; uncounted German women today are wearing the jewellery that Jewish parents give to their children on solemn occasions. Thousands of Germans are the beneficiaries of Jewish property, and feel no remorse—otherwise they would have returned it. It is the property their parents or their children took from millions of Jews when they sent them to the gas chambers and crematories. They planned and organised the destruction of the whole Jewish people—the destruction of us all. They succeeded with only a third of us, including a million Jewish children, our pride and hope for the future, who died at their hands.

"Germany also committed numerous crimes against other nations. But none can compare with the one this nation committed against the Jews. The observation of the former German Chancellor, Dr. Adenauer, during a visit to Israel, that 5 million Germans too perished in Hitler's war, is a shameful disservice to the memory of our martyrs and a glaring example of how even the so-called righteous in Sodom make light of the enormities committed against the Jewish people. One cannot compare the millions of Jewish victims with the toll of blood demanded of other nations by German vandalism. Those were fought against; the millions of Jews in Europe, however, were done to death when they were utterly defenceless. Only the ghetto fighters, the Jewish partisans in the forests, and the Jewish Brigade of Erez Israel had a chance to defend our honour with arms and to pay back the murderers for our blood; unfortunately only to a very small extent.

"These fearful crimes, to describe which human speech is unadequate, rest upon the entire German people. All are responsible. Every German bears the mark of Cain upon his brow. Not one of them can wash himself clean. Not one of them can say: My hands did not shed this blood. It is incredible, but nonetheless a fact: many Germans believe they have already settled their score with us. In fact they are offended if we call their attention to the fact that the books are not yet closed. They act as if they were conferring a great boon upon us by paying restitution and indemnity. They seem to forget that the money paid by the post-war German government to the State of Israel and to individual survivors is our money. And it is not even a fraction of what they robbed us of.

"The dark instincts are already taking possession again of the German people, not even subconsciously but on the surface—the instinct of hatred for Jews. Neo-Nazism is on the rise. The attitude of the German government towards the State of Israel, the heir and successor to the millions of martyrs, is repellent and arouses profound disgust in the Jews the world over. The German government seems to regard itself as cleansed of all its sins. The Bonn ambassador in Israel even had the effrontery to state this in public.

"It is painful to have to confess that some of us have confirmed the Germans in their belief that they are rehabilitated and free of responsibility. The impression in the world is widespread that the Jews—and of course Israel above all—have attested the moral rehabilitation of Germany. Dr. Adenauer stated this openly during his visit to Israel, and his words were like a dagger in our flesh when he thanked the president of the WJC,

Dr. Goldmann, for his contribution to this 'hechsher', which Germany so urgently needed. We would like to emphasize here that the personal reputation of individual Germans is irrelevant. Every German is a representative of his people and bears a share of responsibility for its enormities. There will never be a reconciliation—there can never be a reconciliation—between us and the German people, at least not so long as the murderers are still amongst us. Between us and the German people rises a high mountain that cannot be scaled—a hill of 6 million martyrs.

"In a minute or two a representative of Germany will come to this lectern, and when he does, he will be confronted with the spirits of millions of human beings who died a thousand dreadful deaths at the hands of his people. They will rise to bear witness that they cannot forgive. And we who live have no right to forgive in their name. This forum has no right—particularly on this occasion—to speak in the name of the whole Jewish people. The blood of our brethren cries to heaven: no dialogue; remembrance of what Amalek has done to you. It is our duty, our sacred moral duty, and it is vital for the preservation of our people and our future, to remember this constantly.

"We shall honour the commandment to preserve the memory of Amalek, so that it may never happen again."

Statement of MAPAM

"The members of MAPAM from Israel, the United States, South America, France, England and other countries, who are delegates to the Fifth Plenary Assembly of the World Jewish Congress as well as many other delegates who are partners, to our heartfelt concern have from the very start opposed the proposal to hold a Jewish-German dialogue in this forum.

"The World Jewish Congress has placed the problem of the future of the Jewish people at the center of its deliberations at this plenary meeting. There is no doubt that when we speak about the future it is necessary to recall that the survival of the Jewish people depends on its capacity to remember and to learn from the past.

"Our generation is the generation of the ghettos and the concentration camps, of the holocaust and the ghetto uprisings. Before us, there still stands the generation which marched to the sounds of the 'Horst Wessel', the generation of the S. S. and the Gestapo. The time for mutual exchanges has not arrived. Six million Jews are unable to participate in this discussion. Their absence obligates us to forego the attempt to arrange a confrontation which can be interpreted as the beginning of reconciliation.

"In order to be faithful to the memory of the Nazi victims and to the lesson which must be drawn from the destruction, it would have been necessary to set up a court of judgement here which would judge the statute of limitations on Nazi war crimes and its legislators. Such a court would surely have nullified the sentence in which the German judges at the Frankfurt trial freed the murderers of Auschwitz.

"By boycotting the dialogue with the representative of the German Federal Republic, we wish to warn the German people and the Government of the Federal Republic of Germany of the Nazi and neo-Nazi dangers still contained in the Germany of today.

"The German people and their government must know of these dangers. They must reject from their midst the Nazis of yesterday and today. They must remove the Nazis from official positions and from the cultural life, economy, civil service and the judiciary.

They must give up the dreams of a *revanchist*, great power Germany armed with atomic weapons.

"Only then will we be able to examine again our position and only then will we be able to open a dialogue and there will no longer hover over us the betrayal of those who were destroyed by the Nazis, those who fell for the honour of Israel and the defence of the life and survival of the Jewish people.

Statement of the Achdut Ha'avodah—Poale-Zion

"We consider it our duty to explain from this platform our position with regard to the symposium taking place here with German representatives in attendance. We reject any kind of racial valuation that distinguishes among peoples and assigns them to higher or lower categories. This was the German attitude under Hitler, as it had been in a veiled form the attitude of the Nazi fascists before Hitler, when Germany echoed with the tones of the arrogant hymn, 'Deutschland, Deutschland über alles'.

"We are against an encounter with German representatives at a World Jewish Congress because we are profoundly convinced that it carries the germ of palliation and appeasement, even if that be not intended, because it violates the feelings of pain and anger that the Jewish people hold, and that must never grow cold or be varnished over or displaced.

"Settlement with Germany embraces not only the past and the terrors of the catastrophe. It also includes events in today's Germany. It applies to the growing signs of anti-Semitism in various movements and the rising Neo-Nazism with its sinister instincts and its desire to revive the Hitler cult, and the policy of forgiveness practiced by Bonn judges in war crimes.

"The president of the World Jewish Congress that has organised this encounter did rightly when he submitted the proposal to the Congress and received the approval of the majority. We regret this initiative, but we must not put the president in the precarious position of evading responsibilities once undertaken. We therefore proposed converting this symposium into a frank and fundamental discussion of the dangers of anti-Semitism and Nazism in Germany—in the presence of German representatives. This might lead them to conduct an unyielding fight against a policy calculated to prepare the ground for a revival of Fascism in Germany. Our proposal was not accepted, and we therefore feel unable to take part in this symposium."

Nahum Goldmann's introductory words to the reports

"Ladies and gentlemen, although I am very keen to save every minute of this evening, I am forced to take a few minutes to make it clear, in order to avoid distortions and misunderstandings, in the interest of the World Jewish Congress, why I suggested to the Executive of the Congress to put this subject on the agenda and why the majority approved it.

"The problem of German-Jewish relations exists, it is unresolved, and it is, both historically—as you will hear from many more competent speakers than I am—and realistically, one of the most complex and important problems of our Jewish generation of today. There is no people in modern Europe which has influenced modern Jewish civilization in Eastern and Central Europe as Germany has done. The modern Hebrew and Yiddish literature has learned about modern Western civilization from Schiller and Lessing, and there is no country where Jews have occupied a similar influential position as Jews in the pre-Nazi Weimar Germany. On the other hand, there is no people which has committed such crimes against us, unspeakable crimes, as the German people in the Nazi period. This constitutes the complexity of the problem.

"There are three possibilities to deal with it:

"You could either try to annihilate Germany, which would neither be in the tradition of Jewish ethics nor would it be in any way a realistic proposal.

"You could ignore Germany, and many of my friends took this position fifteen years ago, when I advised the Jewish people to enter into the first dialogue with Germany; because this is not the first dialogue. The dialogue has been going on for fourteen years, day in day out, by representatives of the Jewish people, by representatives of Israel; delegations from Israel participate in congresses in Germany, teams of Germans come to Israel, German invitees are coming to Israel, rabbis and Jewish leaders from America and other countries visit Germany, not to speak of the formal negotiations which the leaders of the Claims Conference, and I among them, and representatives of Israel, have been conducting for many years with German representatives. And therefore I say, the advice to ignore Germany, which I could understand emotionally—and I understand even the emotions of those who made these statements here—is unrealistic, is unpractical. It may have been valid for Jews in former centuries living in the ghetto, where they couldn't determine their own destiny and fate, they could only react by being 'broiges'—angry—with enemies, trying to ignore them, it was a psychological escape of great importance. But today, we represent a generation which has created the Jewish State, and which, even before the Jewish State was established, decided—and the World Jewish Congress is one of the expressions of this—to take our destiny into our hands, not to rely for our future and for our destiny either on the good-will of our friends or on the bad-will of our enemies, but try—as far as a people can do it in this complex world—to determine our own fate, to be the master of our destiny. Such a people cannot be dominated by emotions alone, although I am glad that these emotions exist. But it has finally to be guided by what is best in the interests of the Jewish people, and just as I am sure that the big majority of those who, fifteen years ago, when we had the big fight regarding my suggestion that we should start negotiating with the Germans in order to get indemnifications and reparations, just as I am convinced that the big majority of those who opposed it at the time are today very happy that this was done and glad that we achieved what we have achieved, and enabled hundreds of thousands of Jews to start another life, not to speak about what these reparations have done for the upbuilding of the Jewish State of Israel, so I am convinced that, on real consideration of the problem and overcoming our emotions which must exist but which could not be the determining factor, we cannot allow ourselves to ignore Germany as if it does not exist. It is a big power, it is becoming a bigger power. For all kinds of interests of Israel and of the Jewish people, Germany of today and of tomorrow will play an important role and we cannot conduct world Jewish policies in ignoring Germany.

"Now, once the problem exists, I belong to those who believe in an open discussion. I don't believe in the methods of not allowing complex, delicate emotional problems to be discussed and aired openly. I know there are many Germans who would like to forget that the problem exists, and we will not allow them to do so; and I am sure the greatest, the best leaders of Germany will not allow them to do so. There are also Jews who would like to forget it. I remember, years ago, when the Claims Conference wanted to spend money on young Jewish scholars to deal with the period of the Nazi war crimes and we couldn't find the young people, I asked one of the great historians of the Hebrew University who told me that our young people don't want to be reminded of this shameful period where Jews were slaughtered without resistance. I don't accept the whole approach. There is also a certain tendency with Jews to forget this terrible period in Jewish history but, my friends, peoples cannot afford the luxury of forgetting any period, neither their glory nor their shame, neither their heroic nor their tragic periods. At that time, when I had the discussion with this great historian, I published an article under the title 'Amor Fati', the famous expression of Nietzsche where he says that a man and a people has to accept his whole destiny. Otherwise an individual ends up on a psychoanalytical couch and a people ends in frustration and bitterness and hatred. It is much easier not to acknowledge the existence of this problem, but I think it requires more psychological and moral courage of a people to bring complex and embarrassing problems into the open and discuss them. We shall not find a solution tonight, I am not so naive as to believe it; but I think it is much better for the problem to be discussed by people on both sides, men in Germany whose record is perfect, men in Germany who opposed Hitler, and by Jewish historians and scholars who can give us the historical background of this problem. Therefore I came to the Executive of the World Jewish Congress a year and a half ago and suggested this discussion, and it was approved. Then opposition developed, which is perfectly legitimate, and these three groups had a right to say what they expressed today, but I am glad that the majority of those who belong to the World Jewish Congress felt that my approach is in the long run the better one.

"One more word: all these words used in these statements tonight—reconcile, forget, forgive—have nothing to do with this discussion. Our people will never forget what happened in the Hitler period; I said it many years ago and I repeat, I would be ashamed to be a Jew if Jews forgot it. What people can forget such tragedies—do other peoples forget similar tragedies? What is this talk of forgetting, and who speaks of forgiveness? such crimes maybe God can forgive, if He wants to. But relations between peoples are not love stories or sentimental relations, they are relations between groups who fight for their existence, who sometimes have alliances and sometimes are opponents, and all these words of forgiveness are out of place: who can allow anyone to forgive? It never enters the mind of any one of us to do it, and it is a plain distortion of the facts by the opposition; they may say the dialogue is premature from their point of view, but they should not distort our motives. What is on the agenda here tonight is to find a way of co-existence between Jews and Germans in a world in which the Germans exist and are growing in importance, and in which—thank God—the Jewish people exists despite the Nazi attempt to annihilate it, to find the way for co-existence between two peoples who, in the light of the realities and whatever happened, must find means to deal with one another. All the sentiments behind it are a matter for the individual. It is not a matter for the World Jewish Congress or the State of Israel or the Knesseth of Israel to determine the emotional and sentimental aspects behind this. That is left to the individual. We have to deal collectively with the hard realities. For years we have been negotiating with Germany, and I am not speaking only of the billions which Germany has paid, but also of the political position of Germany, in what measure an anti-Semitic Germany could do harm to Israel and to the Jewish people, and how much, on the other hand, a friendly Germany could help us in our fight for our survival. That is the only point which is on the agenda, and not these distortions and misstatements, as if I were preparing an orgy of forgiveness.

"We have to find ways of co-existence, a very difficult task, especially for this generation which has among it still hundreds of thousands of survivors of the camps, for this generation which has witnessed the destruction of millions of its people. It will require great patience. What is involved is a psychological process. We can sign agreements, as we did in Luxembourg, Israel can sign agreements any time with Germany, but what we are speaking of now concerns a complex psychological process which will take I don't know how long. All that is necessary is patience, good-will and the conscience of collective responsibility on the part of the German people. Not every German is guilty; young Germans who have not lived in the Nazi period, what guilt could they have? But a people, and this is the basis of peoplehood for every people, is responsible for its whole history. It may glory in its great days, and must accept responsiblity for its shameful periods. Therefore I stress that especially the German people must have good-will and patience. If the Germans get impatient with war-crime trials, and the Jews remind them of their crimes, they must understand that. If anyone has the right to be oversensitive it is we, and not the Germans. We were the sufferers, we were the victims. We may sometimes have exaggerated our sensitivity, and we have a right to do it. It is a very mild reaction to what has been done to this generation, which lost a third of its sons and daughters.

"This I wanted to say here. I think it is useful also for the German people, if two morally and intellectually important German leaders participate in this debate. Dr. Gerstenmaier does not speak here as President of the parliament, but as a man who has fought Nazism, who has helped Israel, whose position on our common problems I have known for fourteen years; and Prof. Golo Mann is one of the great German intellectual and moral authorities. They will discuss the problem with Jewish representatives in the light of the historical background and the reality of today.

"Now one word about the procedure: We will hear first the four speakers. As I calculate it, it will take about an hour and three quarters, because all of them have agreed to shorten the speeches which will later be distributed in full. Then we will have a short discussion. Two of the participants in the discussion were named on the programme—Dr Prinz and Dr. Van Dam; a few others have asked for the floor, and if there will be any possibility I will give it to some of them, I cannot promise the floor to all of them. There will also be the possibility to ask questions, practical questions, realistic questions, and I am sure that Dr. Gerstenmaier, who is the most competent to answer them, will be ready to do so—he told me this before. I warn you that the meeting will last till midnight at least, and those who are interested enough I hope will remain, and those who are too tired, if they want to leave sometime, should leave very silently and not disturb the others.

"One last remark about the language. We will allow every speaker to speak in his own language. Some will speak English, some will speak German. Before I call on the first speaker, Prof. Gershom Sholem, who is a professor of the Hebrew University and one of the leading Jewish scholars and intellectuals of our time, I want to explain that he could easily speak in Hebrew, but he wants to be understood and especially by his German counterparts, and so you will have to bear with him if he speaks in German. Prof. Baron will speak in English, Prof. Golo Mann will speak in English, Prof. Gerstenmaier will speak in German. The discutants will speak in the language which they want to use, and I ask you to accept this freedom of language which is done for practical purposes in order to be best understood by all.

"I will call now on our first speaker, who is Prof. Gershom Sholem of the Hebrew University of Jerusalem."

Gershom Sholem's speech

"Ladies and gentlemen,

"To talk about Jews and Germans and their relationship to one another in these last two hundred years is, in the year of 1966 a melancholy enterprise. The burden of the emotions is still so great that an objective consideration or analysis seems almost impossible, and all of us are still so deeply influenced by the experience of this generation, that objectivity can hardly be expected. There are many Jews today who consider the German people a 'hopeless case' or, at most, a people with whom they would not like to have anything to do, either affirmatively or negatively. I am not one of them, for I simply do not believe that there ought to be a permanent state of war among nations. I deem it right and even important that Jews talk to Germans as Jews, in full consciousness of what has happened, and without any attempt to obliterate the differences between them. To many of us, the German language, our mother-tongue, has given unforgettable experiences which have determined the landscape of our youth, and has given it its own expression. Now that we hear a call from there, out of the realm of history and particularly from a new young generation, although this call is still unsure, undetermined and even shy, there is something in it from which some of us cannot possibly dare escape.

"Of course there are great difficulties in generalization. When we talk about 'the Germans' and 'the Jews', we frighten the objective observer. In times of conflict, it is easy to handle such categories. However questionable such general categories are, they were used quite vocally and audibly. However it is necessary to introduce some differentiation here. For the Germans are not all Germans, and the Jews are not all Jews. With the one unthinkable exception perhaps: when those Germans who really meant all the Jews had all possible power in their hands, they used it as much as they could in order to exterminate all of them. Since that time the survivors of the mass murder, or those who by accident of history escaped being victims, find it difficult to differentiate. The traps which render every generalization dangerous are clear: arbitrariness, contradiction and lack of context; the circumstances are too manifold and individual so that every generalizing statement could be easily contradicted by an equally valid opposite contention. Nevertheless, knowing all these dangers. I am ready to address myself to this topic, certainly one of the most exciting topics in the Jewish world since more than 150 years.

"Alfred Döblin, a Jewish writer who, in his latter days, became a convert to Catholicism, wrote in 1948 to another Jew that he should take great care not to use the word Jews when writing to a German. In Germany, he said, the word Jew has remained a derogatory term, and using it one could only do the bidding of the anti-Semites. For anti-Semitism is deeply rooted in the Germans and—in 1948—was even more evil than before 1933. As a matter of fact, I myself have often experienced that many Germans, in order to dissociate themselves from the Nazis (at times belatedly) still vindicate Döblin's observation by refusing to call Jews, Jews. After the Jews had been murdered, they are now being posthumously and triumphantly proclaimed as Germans, and it is said that to emphasize their Jewishness would mean to yield to anti-Semitic theories. What perversion in the name of progress, which evades every possibility of facing facts! And it is exactly this which I consider to be our task, and we cannot possibly speak of the Jews more emphatically than when we talk about their fate among the Germans. The atmosphere between the Jews and the Germans can only be cleansed if we approach these conditions with reckless criticism. This is difficult. For the *Germans* it is difficult because the mass murder of the Jews has become the greatest nightmare of their moral existence as a people; for the *Jews* because such clarification presupposes a critical evaluation of the most important phenomenon of their own history. Where love, in as far as it existed, was suffocated in blood, historical understanding and clarity of concepts are the prerequisites for any future dialogue between Jews and Germans. Such dialogue, if it is conducted in earnest, can only be approached beyond the political and economical factors and interests which exist between the State of Israel and the German Federal Republic. I have no competence in this area, and in no way will I refer to them. I am not even certain that, by including such consideration, we gain anything for either the question or the answer to it which is before us. We have heard a great deal about it, and I must say that particularly we Jews did not always like what we heard.

"Up to the second half of the 18th century and partly even beyond that, the Jews in Germany existed as Jews did everywhere. They were clearly discernible as a nation, possessed an unmistakable identity and a history of many thousands of years, whatever they themselves or other people may have thought of it. They had a clearly defined consciousness of themselves and lived within a religious constitution which permeated their life and their culture in an extremely intensive manner. In as far as the influences of the German surrounding world penetrated into the ghetto, and such influences existed, it did not occur in a manner of conscious acceptance of such elements but mostly in a hardly conscious process of osmosis. Of course, often enough German cultural values underwent a transformation into Jewish values and linguistically even into Yiddish. The conscious relationship between both societies was of a delicate nature and particularly so in the two centuries preceding the period of emancipation. The religious culture of its representative groups rested within itself and remained foreign to the German world. But the economically strongest elements, for instance in the phenomenon of Jewish court factors, and the socially lowest group, which had communications with the German underworld, had a relationship with the Germans which in both cases was dangerous. They moved, each in its particular way, among the Germans and paid the price for it when the slightest changes in political and social conditions occured. Nothing is more foolish than to speak of the Jews in Germany in those centuries as though they had been deeply rooted in Germany. For such deep integration there existed no real condition, either in the Germans or in the Jews. Everybody knew that the Jews were in exile and, however this exile was valued, there was no doubt of its tremendous importance for the human condition of the Jews.

"The overwhelming majority of those Jews who did not belong to either of the two camps which we mentioned, and therefore were not touched by the changing conditions, had their own traditional image which was determined by history and spirituality, an image which had been moulded during the long centuries of their exile. At the same time it must be admitted that, in the second half of the 18th century, there appeared a profound weakness in their Jewish existence. It is as though a phase of their historic existence had reached a law and that nobody knew where it would end. When Moses Mendelssohn began his career as some sort of conservative reformer in German Jewry, its weakness was evident. With him and particularly his disciples began that process of Jewish approaches to the Germans as a conscious phenomenon which was favoured by important historic factors. There began the propaganda for the determined alliance of the Jews with the German culture, and not long after that even with the German people. There began also that battle of the Jews for their rights which lasted three or four generations and which they won (let us not delude ourselves) because there was a decisive and victorious group among the non-Jews who fought for them. It is with these battles, during which the German enlightenment and in no smaller measure the French Revolution helped, that an important change took place which had its consequences for the Jews in the German society.

"First this change was hesitating and very unsure of itself, as indeed Judaism itself is often unsure. They were still aware of their Jewish nationhood, although they were often uncertain of its meaning which was about to get lost. To say it quite clearly, there began that yearning for the German historic consciousness which was supposed to substitute for the Jewish one, something which is so characteristic for more than hundred years of the relationship between the Jews and Germans. The groups within German Jewry which participated in this process with great hesitation were mostly the numerically still strong circles of the traditional pious Jews. But they were almost always strangely silent and only seldom do we hear their warning voices as though they had been afraid of their own pathos. Till approximately 1820 it was general usage to speak of the Jewish nation and their members in Germany. In the next two generations this usage disappears almost completely and, favoured by both sides, they now spoke of the Jewish denomination and similar phrases.

"The changes and distortions which were the natural consequences of this yearning for the Germans and which later, as it progressed, led to such bitter problems, were considerable. The emancipation brought in its wake the determined denial of the Jewish nationality, a denial which was demanded by the Germans as well as by the avantgarde of the Jews. The mere yearning for German historic consciousness became a determined participation in it, and the objects of enlightened toleration were often articulated by prophets who now spoke in the name of the Germans. The attentive reader of the German reaction to this acrobatic process will be struck by a tone of amazement and benevolent or malicious irony. What to many of us today seems to be the wrong beginning in the relationship between Germans and Jews, but what, in the conditions of 1800, seemed to have been logical, led to the denial of the totality of a Jewish existence in Germany. The most determined fighters for the cause of the Jews among the non-Jews were those who counted articulately and most consciously on the disappearance of the Jews as Jews. As a matter of fact, the disintegration of the Jewish national group as a group was considered a perequisite of their advocacy for the cause of the Jews, such as is the case with Wilhelm von Humboldt. The liberals hoped for a determined and progressive self-liquidation of the Jews. The conservatives assumed a more reserved attitude towards these new approaches; they began to accuse the Jews of an all too great readiness to deny their own consciousness. The self-liquidation of the Jews on the one hand is welcomed and at times demanded, yet at the same time it serves as an argument to prove their lack of substance. We have witnesses who confirm that the contempt with which so many Germans looked at the Jews was stimulated by the easy readiness with which the cultivated group among the Jews denied their own traditions. How valuable could indeed be a heritage whose carriers and particularly whose élite were so eager to deny it? Thus a weird and dangerous dialectic came into being. Important circles of the German élite demanded that the Jews deny their heritage and were ready to honour such denial; but at the same time many expressed their contempt for the Jews for this very readiness of self-denial. The Socialists, whose total lack of seriousness and equally total ignorance in the discussion of the Jewish question was determined by the contemptible invectives in Karl Marx's essay 'On the Jewish question', proved to be completely helpless in view of the new changes. They could only demand the dissolution of the Jewish people and its historic consciousness, which would end in the rebellion of the masses and the final victory of the revolution. They could not find any meaning in welcoming the Jews as active partners in any kind of debate. I spoke of the dangerous dialectic in this process. The Jews conducted the battle for their emancipation (and this is the tragedy of this battle which moves us today so deeply), not in the name of their rights as a nation but on behalf of their integration into the nations among whom they lived. Admitting that they were ready to give up their nationhood or at least to deny it, they did not end their misery but opened a new source of their suffering. For the assimilation in Germany did not eliminate the Jewish problem, as their advocates had hoped, but rendered the situation even more acute, albeit in a changed position. The more common areas of communication between the two groups were created, the greater became the possibilities for growing frictions. The adventure of assimilation into which they threw themselves so passionately and so understandably was bound to increase the dangers which stemmed from growing tensions. In addition to that, something happened to the Jews who were now exposed to this new encounter with the Germans, which Arnold Zweig called 'undermining'. And this in a dual sense: in their existence under imposed undignified conditions, and the consequences for them personally and socially. It also originated in their own profound sense of insecurity, which became quite visible at the moment when they left the ghetto in order to become Germans, the great goal of the times. This dual destruction of the German Jews is part of the factors which, in the beginning process, worked as a retarding and often destructive moment. The refusal of so many German Jews to understand the effectiveness of these factors, and the beginning dialectic which is attached to them, is one of the most depressing experiences of those who read these disputations. The emotional turmoil of the German Jews between 1820 and 1920 is an important stepping stone for the understanding of themselves. I refer to that 'German Jewishness' (Deutschjudentum) as we know it from our youth and which, in our own circles, led to so much rejection.

"At the same time something else happened within this lack of security: with it some of the creativity of the Jews, which had lain dormant, was strangely liberated. It is true that with the entry into the new and eagerly accepted world, the sense of security which was once theirs through the Jewish tradition, was lost. But, on the other hand, the Jews who had thrown themselves into this exciting experience developed new talents which in the old order, had been hidden or buried. These things are deeply connected with one another. It is important for us to pause briefly in order to clarify the positive elements which became so important in this process, particularly for the Jews, even those outside the borders of Germany. The intimate character of the relationship between Jews and Germany, as it appeared to the Jews, was dependent upon the specific historic hour during which it was created. When the Jews, having left their Middle Ages, turned in large numbers towards the new era of enlightenment and revolution, it was the German civilisation which they first encountered, in Germany, Austria-Hungary and the Eastern

European countries, practically four-fifths of the Jewish population of the time. This happened, and it is decisive, at one of the most creative turning points, the climax of their period as citizens. It can be said that it was a happy hour in which the newly awakened productivity of the Jews coincided with the great productivity of the German people. It was destined to become important after 1750. This coincidence created the image of the Germans which, before 1940, in spite of the many bitter experiences, could not be shattered among many of our people. This amalgamation of a great historic hour, characterized for the Jews by the names of Lessing and Schiller, has in its intensity no parallel in the encounter of Jews with any other European nation. It is because of this encounter, the first one of the way towards the West, that everything German was considered in its light. Even today, after so much blood and so many tears, it is impossible for us to say that it was merely an illusion. It was not merely that. It contained elements of great creativity and the beginning of important developments.

"It is difficult to measure the important role which Friedrich Schiller played for the relationship of Jews and Germans. This has very rarely been appreciated by the Germans. Schiller, the spokesman of pure humanitarianism, the German classic, the proclaimer of the highest ideals of mankind, has for many generations of Jews within and even more without Germany represented that which they considered to be German. This they did even in the last third of the 19th century, when in Germany itself Schiller's world was already considered hollow and meaningless. The encounter with Friedrich Schiller was, for many Jews, much more real than that with the actual Germans. Here they found what they sought most passionately. German romanticism meant a great deal to many Jews, but Schiller was near to all of them. He was a factor in the Jewish belief in humanity. Schiller was the most eloquent, the most impressive, the most resounding cause of their idealistic illusions, which established the relationship between the Jews and the Germans. Here was the program which seemed to promise everything to the Jew who had lost his self-assurance as a Jew. Here he found what he sought, and thus for him there was no false tone in it, because it was the music which appealed to him in depth. It was to Schiller, who never spoke to the Jews immediately, that the Jews responded. It is in the failure of this dialogue that we might discover the secret of the failure of the whole relationship. Because Schiller, to whom they attached their love with so much passion, was not just anybody. He was really the national poet of the Germans and, in the time between 1800 and 1900, the Germans considered him as such, so that the Jews did not make the mistake of which they were often guilty, to have addressed themselves to the wrong person.

"The unbelievable passion which caused the Russian Jews who had looked for a road to humanity within their own people to adopt the name of Schiller (one of the noblest figures in the Zionist movement, Solomon Schiller, is an example of this), tried to build a real bridge to the Germans. But this bridge building, alas, was undertaken only by Jews. The enthusiasm of the Jews for Schiller impressed the later Germans as touching but comical. Very rarely was there any feeling that here could have been really at long last a common ground for many things.

"The first half of the 19th century was a period of the most determined approaches. It was at that time that the Jews found an amazing amount of help among the Germans. Many individuals found much understanding of their passionate yearning for education. It cannot be said that there was no good-will at that time and he who reads the biographies of the Jewish elite of that time, meets up again and again with such understanding among devout Christians, such as the Herrnhuter. But the dynamics of this process demanded more than yearning for education. We find here the radical transformation of the Jews from the old traditional attitudes, which were still the way of life of their majority, to a Germanism which proclaimed that 'the German national education of the Jews and their participation in the general human and civil institutions is the main essential task to which everyone must dedicate himself', as Moritz Lazarus said. He was a representative of this tendency which accomplished the transformation from a pure Talmudic Judaism to this new German Jewish way of life within a mere five years. The yearning to *come* home changed soon into the illusion that they *were* at home. It is well-known and understandable that the pace at which the transformation took place, the speed with which the Jews undertook it, provoked equally rapid reaction on the part of the Germans. They did not know how deep the process of the disappearance of Jewish tradition was and the self-consciousness of the Jews with which they had to deal, and this process frightened them. However much they would have welcomed the final result of this process, (at least the Liberals would have done so), however much it corresponded even to the conservative ideology, they were poorly prepared for the rapidity of what was happening. In their eyes it indicated an aggressiveness which called for self-defense. All this allied them sooner or later with those who, from the very beginning, had watched this whole process with displeasure. There were articulate spokesmen in the post-Mendelssohn period.

"The term 'host-nation' (Wirtsvolk) who tolerated us as guests made sense. Even in the best of cases, it was the reception of a guest in the family. Hospitality could be revoked if the conditions were not properly met. This is often particularly clear in the utterances of the liberals. We sometimes hear nowadays something about a process of amalgamation of the two groups, which allegedly would have come about, had the process not been interrupted by National Socialism. But this is belatedly wishful thinking. Of course the complete dedication of so many human beings to the German people which can be seen in the numerous autobiographies of those who designate themselves as 'of Jewish descent', are among the most moving phenomena of this process of estrangement. They had indeed nothing in common with the Jewish tradition and certainly not with the Jewish people. The list of Jews who disappeared among the Germans is infinitely large. It is a list of great and often amazing talent and productivity, which was offered to the Germans. Who can read their history without being deeply moved? That of Otto Lipmann of Hamburg, for instance, who, until the moment when he committed suicide, maintained to have been a better German than those who drove him to death. It is no wonder that, now that everything is past, there are many who would acknowledge his assumption as justified. These people have chosen and we shall not deny them to the Germans. But nevertheless we do not like it, for what we feel points to the inner conflict which can be found even in these biographies. Even in their complete estrangement from everything Jewish, we can notice in many of them what Germans and Jews alike would have considered Jewish substance. This is true of so many important people, from Karl Marx and Lassalle, to Karl Kraus, Gustav Mahler and Georg Simmel.

"Nobody has described more deeply this process of the exodus of the Jew from himself than Charles Péguy. Very rarely has a non-Jew achieved greater insight into the Jewish situation. It is he who coined the sentence 'être ailleurs—le grand vice de cette race, la grande vertu secrète, la grande vocation de ce peuple'. It was this 'being somewhere else' which was combined with the desperate desire to be at home. This desire was intense, fruitful and destructive at the same time. It is the key to the understanding of the relationship between Jews and Germans. What in those days seemed disquieting and was undertaken under false pretences and therefore provoked opposition, seems today symbolical, attractive, deeply moving and in an important sense positive. The Jews and Germans did not profit from what today, under changed circumstances, gives them a particularly positive importance. Today the Jew is valid as a classical representative of the phenomenon of man's estrangement from society. The estrangement of the Jew from his own soil which nourished him, from his history and tradition, and even more his estrangement in the growing society of citizens, caused displeasure. That he was not really at home, however much and emphatically he insisted, has now become a symbol of the 'condition humaine'. It now accrues to his credit and glory, as much as formerly estrangement was a curseword and an accusation. It is in keeping with this protracted and complex situation that the Jews in their vast majority shared the evaluation of their fellow-men. In their great consciousness, they strove to be rooted, to be at home with the Germans and in Germany, but they maintained that the vast majority of their fellow-men did not really believe them. The phenomenon of the so-called national Jews in the 20's evoked derision and laughter, which is very characteristic. Thus from the very beginning these conditions contained something which had to lead to a dangerous conflagration. The process of the entry of the Jews into the German society had various aspects. The important fact that the Jews had lost their own elite, mainly through conversion and mixed marriage, points to differentiations of great consequences. Large groups among the German Jews were ready to liquidate their own nationhood. Yet at the same time they wanted to preserve their Judaism, either as heritage or a religious entity or God knows what. At any rate, something intangible yet clearly discernible in their consciousness. They were, and it is often forgotten, really not ready to disintegrate totally, while their elite was prepared to pay for their assimilation by disappearing completely. In their emotions they were unsure and confused. And the spectacle of their own avant-garde, which ran away from them, was too much for them. This incessant bloodletting, through which the Jews lost the majority of their most advanced people to the Germans, forms an important aspect of the so-called German-Jewish symbiosis, of which many speak so glibly. To the Jews it is a melancholy aspect. The petty bourgeois formed the majority of the Jews, when their so-called advance in the course of the 19th century began. For them it was necessary to create in every generation a brand-new group of leaders. It is the rare exception to see in the 20th century Jewish descendants of those families who were still Jews after 1800, when they began their assimilation with German civilization. The lower classes remained steadfastly Jewish, although Judaism itself had become diluted, watered down and emptied of its old meaning. It had suddenly become a strange mixture of a religion of reason and certain emotions which were often denied but remained effective. The attitude of the Jews to their own traitors was not at all clear. A good exemple of this is the phenomenon of Heinrich Heine. This attitude changes from deep emotional rejection to partly approving indifference. Of course Heine was a border case. He was able to say of himself that he had not returned to Judaism since he had never left it.

"For all that, we must not leave unconsidered the inner tensions within the Jewish society. They influenced the relationship to Germany considerably. After all Germany was the stage for the bitter disputations between the pious Jews of the old school, the country Jews and their leaders on the one hand, and the neologians who won out, socially and politically, if not numerically. The term 'assimilation' was used by the defenders in terms of an ideal. It was only later that the Zionists degraded the word through derision and contempt, and only then did the assimilationists refuse to be called that. This tendency to assimilation, which varied greatly, was certainly an important factor. But it is not quite clear to what extent the advocates of this tendency were ready to accept the consequences. Generalizations here are dangerous. At any rate, the Jews themselves were critical of the Jews and of the old Judaism, and it is well known that some people indulged in extremism such as Jewish anti-Semitism. After all, it was a German Jew who had left Judaism, knowing that that was hardly possible, who wrote those merciless exposures of the Berliner Jewish bourgeoisie; I am referring to Kurt Tucholsky's essays on 'Herr Wendriner', a weird document of a certain German Jewish phenomenon. The Anti-Semites tried to malign the Jews as much as they could, but what they wrote is clearly exaggerated and hollow. There is hatred to be sure, but no knowledge and no real understanding. Thus it is small wonder that it was one of the most talented and most despicable Jewish Anti-Semites who lifted anti-Semitism to a level of which the Anti-Semites themselves were hardly capable.

"Often we find in the same family representatives of extreme examples. This is true, for instance, of the brothers Jacob and Michael Bernays, whose niece was married to Sigmund Freud. One of them, a classical philologist of highest rank, remained almost neurotically faithful to the strictest Jewish Orthodoxy. The other one left Judaism in order to begin a more glittering career as German philologist and interpreter of Goethe. The brothers never again talked to each other. This is equally true for Georg Herrmann, who hail from the family of Borchardt and succeeded in depicting the Berlin Jewish bourgeoisie with much sarcasm and irony as well as love, something unequalled in literature, and on the other hand. his incredibly intelligent cousin Rudolf Borchardt, who believing to have destroyed everything Jewish within himself, became the most articulate spokesman of a conservative German traditionalism. It is frightening in its sheer paradoxical form for everyone who heard or read him. But it did not frighten *him*. The majority, however, was not ready to go to the very end of the road, and many of them were looking for a compromise. Their great talent very rarely benefited the cause of the Jews. Such was the case with important and, at the same time, problematic figures such as Leopold Zunz, the founder of the 'Wissenschaft vom Judentum', Ludwig Steinheim and Hermann Cohen. These were the best religious and philosophical minds. We must also mention Abraham Geiger and Samson Raphael Hirsch, the two most significant figures of the Jewish Rabbinate in Germany. The majority of the most talented Jewish minds, however, has benefited the German society to an amazingly great degree in economics, literature and art.

"The great American sociologist Thorstein Veblen wrote in his essay about the intellectual 'pre-eminence of Jews in modern Europe'. It is hardly this pre-eminence which caused the downfall of the German Jews. When the Jews had fulfilled their economic function in the developing Germany of the 19th century, and when they were no longer needed, they assumed a cultural function in the 20th century. From the very beginning, it awakened unrest and opposition and it did not benefit them. That the Germans needed the Jews and their intellectual world is being noticed now, when they are no longer there, and many mourn the loss. But when they were in Germany they were willy-nilly an irritant and the vast majority watched, with scepticism and with many reservations, the onslaught of the Jewish intelligentsia, which to them was a symbol of the Jewish penetrations into the German society. We have already said that they were not prepared for the rapid advances. The political emancipation, to which they had declared their consent in the middle of the 19th century, was not paralleled by equal readiness to accept without reservations the Jews into the cultural and active society. The Jews however, with their long intellectual tradition, found that they were particularly well prepared for such an active role. But it was exactly this that caused an opposition which became active and virulent before the completion of the process. Looking at the whole of it, the love affair of the Jews with the Germans remained one-sided and unreturned and awakened in the best case something like sentimental sympathy, as in Theodor Fontane, or maybe gratitude. It was not rare that the Jews found gratitude, but the love which they sought so much they found hardly ever.

"There was many a genius among the Jews who was not always recognized, and prophets who were not popular. These were people of intellect who fought for justice and not a few men who fought for the great minds among the Germans. The latter happened to an amazing degree and needs no documentation. It is no coincidence that almost all of the important interpreters of Goethe were Jews. But none among the Germans went out of his way to do anything for any of the Jews of this group which we mentioned. Here is the difference between the French and the Germans. Nothing in all German literature can be quoted, resembling those unforgettable pages in which the Catholic Frenchman Charles Péguy depicted the portrait of Bernard Lazare, a Jewish anarchist, as one of the true prophets of Israel. And this happened at a time when the French Jews knew nothing better than to deny the existence of him who was one of their great men, either because of malice or stupidity. At least here was a process of give and take. Here a Frenchman actually saw a Jew as the Jews themselves refused to see him. Would that a single such phenomenon of seeing us would ever have existed among the Germans! This would have vindicated much. But I know of no such case. Would that a single German writer would have recognized and acknowledged the greatness of Moses Hess, as the Jews remained silent about him or even mocked him! But Moses Hess was the German Jewish equivalent of what Bernard Lazare, the first French Zionist, was to the French Jews. Such phenomena would have proven that the Jews had made a dent among the Germans, and that the echo was not merely that of the Germans among the Jews. Péguy has proven that a French-Jewish dialogue is possible in the truest sense. He understood that particular Jew as a Jew, and he understood him better than any Jew. There is no justification for the oft-proclaimed German-Jewish dialogue which has never taken place and is still wanting. No German has understood and recognized Kafka, Simmel, Freud or Walter Benjamin when they were unknown and certainly not recognized them as Jews. The belated activity of the busybodies does not change my judgement.

"Only very few Germans, certainly some of their noblest spirits, possessed the naiveté of true humanity to see the Jew as a Jew, as we find in Johann Peter Hebel.

"The Liberals had particular reservations. Fritz Reuter, one of the most characteristic minds of the North German intelligentsia, delivering his speech in 1870 at the celebration of the German Reunification, had nothing better to do than to attack 'those miserable Jew-boys like for instance Heinrich Heine 'who lacked patriotism. The notion that the Liberalism of the Jews was of a more radical nature, bordering on subversion, was widely believed. The share which the Jews had in the hundred years of their activities in public affairs in Germany is quite evident. It is counterbalanced by the conservative tendencies which were particularly impressive in converted Jews such as Friedrich Julius Stahl or Rudolf Borchardt. It was as a reaction to this critical attitude which was rooted in the history of the Jews and their social situation, that the phenomenon of anti-Semitism began to grow. In the increasingly critical relationship between Jews and Germans, it assumed an unproductive and even destructive importance. It is not necessary for me to emphasize that specific social and political conditions caused anti-Semitism in its most radical forms to dominate Germany. But nothing is more foolish than the notion that National Socialism came out of the blue sky and was exclusively a product of conditions after the First World War. That it did become virulent in its most murderous consequences is the result of a long history. Some of the writings against the Jews of the nineteenth century read like documents of the later Nazis. Nothing makes weirder reading than Bruno Bauer's 'Das Judentum in der Fremde', written in 1869. There one can read everything and in not less radical formulation what was preached later in the thousand-year Reich. And this was written by a leader of the former Hegelian Left. Of course there were more subtle forms of Anti-Semitism, for instance the ambivalent formulation, hovering between hate and admiration, in Hans Blücher's 'Secessio Judaica' shortly after the First World War. Here the already discredited metaphysics, masquerading as Anti-Semitism, provided the Nazis with their slogans. And nothing is more depressing to us today perhaps than the wavering of many Germans during the dark days, among them some of their most important minds.

"Max Brod spoke of the 'Distanzliebe' (love at distance) which he considered the ideal relationship between Germans and Jews. This is a dialectic concept where the consciousness of distance prevents too great intimacy but where also the sense of distance creates the desire to bridge the gap. If both parts would have agreed, this might have been the solution for the period with which we have been dealing here. But Brod himself understood that where there is love, the sense of distance disappears. This is true of the Jews. But where there is distance, love can not prosper, and this is valid for the majority of the Germans. The love of the Jews for Germany was echoed by the emphasized distance with which the Germans approached them. It is true that in this love at distance the two partners could have mustered more tenderness, readiness and understanding. But historic assumptions are always illegitimate. The Zionist response to the inevitably growing crisis between Jews and Germans came too late. The German Jews who had established themselves as critics and had become famous because of it were, at the same time, getting on the Germans' nerves. In all this, during the generations preceeding the catastrophe, they showed an amazing lack of critical understanding of their own situation. The apologetic attitude, the lack of critical frankness, spoils almost everything which has been said by the Jews about their situation in the German world of literature, politics and economy.

"The readiness of many Jews to invent a theory for the sacrifice of their Jewish existence is an astonishing phenomenon, which has expressed itself in a great variety of thought.

"Where do we stand now, after the indescribable horrors of those twelve years? The Jews and the Germans have taken very different roads after the war. In their most vital part, the Jews have tried to build their own society in their own country. Nobody can say whether they will succeed, but everybody knows that the case of Israel is vital to the Jews of the world. The dialectic of the enterprise is evident. They live on a volcano. This great upsurge, which is based upon the experiences of the mass murder of the Jews by the Germans, and with the indifference of the world at large, has now given way to deep exhaustion. But they are still motivated by their original insight into their true situation. The Germans have paid for their catastrophe with the partition of their country but, on the other hand, experienced material prosperity which overshadows preceding years. Will there be a bridge between the two mountains which owe their existence to a volcanic eruption?

"The abyss which exists between them and which was caused by what has happened cannot be measured or even understood. I do not believe that only the complete acceptance of this abyss into our consciousness will make it possible to overcome it. This is an opinion which is often heard in Israel. It is a prognosis without comfort which really consists only of words. In reality such a possibility does not exist. We cannot fully understand what has happened, for, because it is unique, it is incomprehensible and thus it cannot become part of our consciousness. It is unnatural to accept such a solution. Whether we can recognize ourselves in this abyss I do not know. And whether the abyss itself, which was caused by these indescribable and truly unthinkable happenings, can ever be closed, who dares to say? Abysses are created by events, but bridges are built by sheer will-power. Bridges are necessary to permit us to cross over the abyss. They are being constructed because they are the product of conscious thinking and desire. Moral bridges, I repeat, are products of pure will-power. They must be anchored firmly from both sides if they are to endure. Israel shares the frightening experience with almost all the European nations. The bridges on which we meet other nations are sufficiently shaky, even if they are not burdened by the memory of Auschwitz. But is this memory not also an opportunity? Is it not true that there is light in the darkness? Is it the light of contrition? To say it differently—productive relations between Jews and Germans, in which there is preserved an important and also horrible past, which has to be approached anew, must be prepared quietly if we expect them to become a reality. In such new activities lies the only guarantee that the relations between our nations will not be poisoned by false goals or demands. Where love is no longer possible, a new understanding must be built with different ingredients: distance, respect, honesty and open mind and, above all, good will.

"A young German wrote to me that it was his hope that the Jews thinking of Germany, may remember the words spoken by the prophet Isaiah, 'Think never of what was and do not remember the past'. Whether the Messianic era will also present the Jews with the gift of forgetting, I do not know. It is a delicate point of theology. But of us who live without illusions in a time without a Messias, nobody can demand the impossible. However sublime it may be, we are not able to do it. Only in burying the past, the meaning of which our mind will never be able to penetrate, can there be a new hope for the restitution of a newly found dialogue between Germans and Jews, that is for the reconciliation of those who are now separated."

Golo Mann's speech

"Let me begin with a brief 'confession'. I accepted Dr. Nahum Goldmann's invitation not light-heartedly, and I speak to you with a sense of shame, doubting whether I may speak at all and whether one may discuss the subject calmly, objectively and scientifically, as if it were just one historical theme among others. I could perhaps claim that I personally may feel 'absolved', since my mother comes from a Jewish or largely Jewish family; since, among the victims of Nazism, there were also relatives of mine; since my father left Germany forever in 1933 in protest, and because I also emigrated as a young man at the time. But I cannot do so. In my view, a German is a German, a German writer is a German writer, and what has been called 'collective shame'—but, I am afraid, is not very 'collective' in Germany today—also applies to him. This would perhaps be my position, too, if both my parents were of Jewish extraction. For—and I shall try to give the reasons for my thesis at a later stage—I have always considered the large majority of German

Jews to be Germans, and could not have considered them differently, on the basis of my observations and experience.

"My second 'confession' is the following: I do not know whether I was destined to enjoy life very much; but I do know that the extent of my enjoyment of life was greatly reduced, and will always remain reduced by the experience of the '30s and '40s, in particular by the murder of the Jews; by other cruel and mad acts as well, perpetrated by others than the Germans and those committed against the Germans—but above all by the murder of the Jews. I cannot get rid of this burden on my life. I can never fully trust my compatriots, the Germans; I can never fully trust human beings, as the Germans are also human beings, highly civilised Europeans. Whatever we may do and may strive for—the shadows of Auschwitz, Treblinka and the Warsaw ghetto are upon us. If we want to act and hope at all, and believe in the good and the beautiful, we have to force ourselves to look away from these things as if they had not existed. That is the way one must act; for, after all, life claims its rights. It is as though we were to grow fruit at the foot of a volcano which had just had a murderous eruption. But grief will always remain with us, as well as fear of a new volcanic eruption. Where *that* was possible, anything can always happen.

"But now to the subject matter. I want to make a few basic points which, I know, differ from the views that are represented among you.

"American Jews are Americans, very good and very typical Americans. Within a century, often within much less than a hundred years, they have acquired American characteristics, physically and psychologically.

"They have the virtues which one may describe as 'specifically American'; they often also have the weaknesses which one describes as 'specifically American'. French Jews—authors like André Maurois, politicians like Léon Blum or Mendés-France—are Frenchmen. The German Jews were Germans. To what extent they were accepted as such by their non-Jewish compatriots is another question, which I shall have to deal with later. For a start I merely ask: what were they considered to be objectively, what did they feel they were subjectively? To this question there is only one answer: in their overwhelming majority they were Germans and considered themselves to be Germans.

"I have known many German Jews in my youth. Firstly because, in my school and student years, one could not help knowing them; secondly, through my mother's family; thirdly, because my father was a writer and there were many Jews among his friends and colleagues in the sphere of literature.

"A German Jew was the director of my boarding school. He was a fervent patriot and the close collaborator of a German prince who had, for a short time, been Chancellor. We had many Jewish fellow-pupils. We would not have dreamed of considering them anything else but compatriots. The same applies to the boy scout group to which I belonged.

"While I studied in Heidelberg, one of my teachers was Friedrich Gundolf, the professor of German literature, one of the most respected and most popular figures of the academic community; he was of Jewish origin. Gundolf belonged to the circle around the poet Stefan George, a decidedly conservative, anti-democratic, esoteric, slightly arrogant but nationally minded group, to which belonged, in addition to such aristocrats as Count Stauffenberg—who in 1944 made the attempt on Hitler's life—such Jews as the poet Wolfskehl and the historian Kantorowicz. The students never showed Gundolf any enmity because of his Jewish origin. It did not surprise me that he had written a book on 'Shakespeare and the German Spirit'. I knew enough German Jews with distinctly national, sometimes nationalistic, attitudes. One of them, Peter Cossmann, the editor in chief of the leading daily of my hometown Munich, had put into the world, or at least done much to spread, the false slogan of the 'stab in the back of the German front', implying the guilt of the Left for the German defeat in 1918. Another Jew, Ernst Lissauer, had during the First World War written his 'Songs of Hate against England', which the Supreme Army Command had had distributed among the soldiers. The generals had not objected at the fact that the author of these poems was a Jew.

"A distant relative of mine was Secretary of State for the Colonies under Emperor Wilhelm II. My Jewish grandfather, who was professor of mathematics at Munich University, was a highly respected citizen of this town, a sponsor of the arts, a friend of Richard Wagner in his youth, to the financing of whose festival theatre in Bayreuth he had rendered assistance. His sons were commissioned officers in the Bavarian army. Like most Jews, he was a patriot and conservatively minded. A long time before the Nazis robbed him of the rest of his property, he had already lost much of it by subscribing to patriotic war loans. Like Gundolf, he was a highly popular and successful teacher. To state that he was not a German would have appeared utterly ridiculous to himself as well as to his many non-Jewish friends. For accuracy's sake, I wish to add that he had left the Jewish faith, but had refused baptism, notwithstanding the advice of the academic bureaucracy. This somewhat slowed down his career without essentially impeding it.

"From among the many authors with a Jewish background who were regular guests in my father's home, I should like to refer to three in particular: Wassermann, Hofmannsthal, Bruno Frank. Jakob Wassermann, in former times a highly celebrated, today regrettably forgotten novelist, wrote a personal statement under the title 'My Way as a German and a Jew'. He was, therefore, aware of the tensions between these two entities. His early and best novels—'Kaspar Hauser', 'Das Gänsemännchen'—are however closely connected with his country of origin, Franconia. Later on, he tended to be 'up to date', and won a powerful position in the United States, but this was not his best period. Hugo von Hofmannsthal's father was an ennobled Jewish banker. I do not know whether his mother was of Jewish origin as well. Since he also married a Jewish lady, one may well consider him to be a Jewish figure. But has anybody ever doubted that the poetical works of Hofmannsthal are the late and most exquisite flowering of a specifically Austrian, Habsburg culture? Who would consider them to be 'Jewish'? When, after the collapse of the Habsburg Empire, someone asked the poet what Austrian writers should do now, Hofmannsthal replied: 'Die'. But life had to go on, and he wanted it to, after all. After Austria ceased to exist, Hofmannsthal actually stressed the German aspect of his work. In 1928, he delivered at Munich University a lecture, which was to become famous, on 'Literature as the Spiritual Area of the Nation'. He now felt that he belonged to the German nation, and no longer to the domain of specifically Habsburg culture. For whoever knows the nuances of the German language, the title of his address 'Schrifttum' (for 'literature') and 'geistiger Raum' for ('spiritual area') sounds somewhat sinister, as well as the fact that Hofmannsthal coined in this lecture the term which later on gained an unpleasant popularity: 'conservative revolution'. Not the actual Nazis but their spiritual and political pioneers played much mischief with these two words.

"I should like to mention a third very close friend of my father, the writer Bruno Frank. He came from an old-established Württemberg family. His adopted home town was Munich. But his love was for Prussia and, to be more precise, for the Prussian King Frederick the Great, to whom he dedicated no fewer than three books: a collection of short stories, a novel and a play, 'Twelve Thousand', in which the noble king appears as a deus ex machina to save twelve thousand subjects of a wicked German prince from being sold to America. The play was a tremendous success, as were Frank's plays generally, and he personally as well. He belonged to the most popular personalities of Munich, and was always made use of when foreign guests were to be honoured, particularly Frenchmen, since Frank was a brilliant conversationalist and spoke French well. He had been an officer in the First World War, but had not forgotten the lyre for the sword. He wrote patriotic war poems, very simple ones, in the Swabian popular tradition, and they came from his heart. In 1933 one had to let him go, with regret of course, but without daring to express this openly. Frank was neither happy nor very successful in the United States—a German writer whose soul and art slowly withered away, far from his home country.

"These are personal reminiscences of my youth, from the period of World War I and the '20s. And I could carry them on far into the Hitler era. I then spent a year in Prague and again I maintain: the Jews of Prague whose language was German were Germans, felt as Germans, and made an essential contribution to what remained of German culture in Bohemia. I think, for instance, of my old friend, the philosopher of history Erich von Kahler (who has now for many years been living in Princeton, New Jersey) and of his monumental, 800-page work on 'The German Character in the History of Europe'—good heavens, how German it is, with its bold ambitions, its speculations and meditations, its pride in the uniqueness of the nation—even when he was critical, and this he had to be and sharply, in the '30s. The German Prague daily 'Bohemia', a decidedly conservative and distinctly national paper, had a Jewish editor-in-chief. Sometimes—let me speak frankly—the rich Jews of Prague, who formed a kind of aristocracy, showed a certain haughtiness towards the Czech democracy. It was not the arrogance of the rich or of the Jews—it was German arrogance. You may doubt this; it may appear unbelievable to you, in the year 1936. But I cannot doubt it, for I experienced and observed it.

"One could object: all these personal impressions do not prove much. They are impressions from the academic world, the world of higher literature, impressions from a cultured upper-class milieu. There, German anti-Semitism did not exist, or hardly existed. It existed among 'the people'; it was stirred up by those who wanted to bend the masses to their will. I would not dismiss this argument offhand, but it is only half true. The world in which the German Jews lived was not a fictitious no-man's land: it consisted not of the whole of Germany, but was a part of it. Not only the bourgeois upper class but the middle class, too, listened to the symphonies of Gustav Mahler, saw Max Reinhardt's productions, read the historical novels of Lion Feuchtwanger. On the bookshelves of the middle class, too, one could find Heine's 'Book of Songs' and in their living-rooms lay the German newspapers founded and edited by Jews: Frankfurter Zeitung, Vossische, Berliner Tageblatt. The majority of the German Jews themselves belonged to the middle class: they were merchants, doctors, opticians, jewellers, lawyers and so on, down to the cattle dealers in the country, who were by no means hated by the peasants. It was a matter of course that their sons volunteered for the army in 1914, in numbers at least in proportion to their share of the population. They were not only Germans, they were extremely deeply rooted in the soil of their provinces of origin—Munich Jews, Swabians, Franconian, Rhenish, Berlin Jews. It is well known that this deep attachment to their homeland, their belief in the security of their political rights, contributed to their catastrophe. They simply did not sense what threatened them, even after Hitler's accession to power, and therefore most of them failed to leave Germany while they still could, though with great difficulties and financial sacrifices. In retrospect this feeling of security was tragic and terrible, but we have no reason to deride it. How could the citizen of a civilized country, a chief medical officer of the Prussian army, an officer who had lost a leg in the war and had been given high military distinction—how could they ever fear to end in Auschwitz?

"One will object however: German anti-Semitism had a long past. Of course it had, but the situation was different from that in other countries in which, as one knows, anti-Semitism also existed. I would not dare to decide where it was strongest in the 19th and early 20th century. Such things are difficult to measure, for the very reason that the situation was different everywhere. Was it stronger in Poland than in Germany or in Russia or in France? I do not know. I should have thought that, about 1900, it was strongest in France. 'Vive l'Armée, à bas les Juifs' was a shout by millions not then heard in Germany. On the other hand, neither did there exist in Germany idealistic and courageous 'Dreyfusards'. Passionate political struggles, inspired by ideas, did not exist at all in the Reich of the Hohenzollern, but only turgid conflicts of interests.

"What were the specific characteristics of German anti-Semitism in the era of Bismarck and the Kaiser? It was no doubt its connection with rumbling protests against the modern world, against industrialization and urbanization, against the whole social process which cost much suffering and uprooting. The demagogues maintained that it was the fault of the Jews. The Prussian conservatives, who felt themselves and their outdated privileges threatened, did not refuse from time to time to make use of this slogan. I should, however, warn against exaggerating the importance of the German anti-Semitism of the '80s and '90s of the last century. We are inclined to such exaggeration because we know the outcome and believe that the end was already part of the plan of German history. This is precisely what I resist. Nothing falls from heaven, it is true, and Hitler had predecessors, but this does not by any means amount to the inevitability of Hitler's triumph.

"As a historian, I know the names of the itinerant preachers of anti-Semitism in the Bismarck era: Boeckel, Ahlwardt and Liebermann and whatever their names were. If, however, you ask a German today, even if you had asked a German 40 years ago, who were Boeckel, Ahlwardt and Liebermann, not one in a thousand could have given you an answer. They had not made an impression on people's minds. They never enjoyed the popularity of the anti-Semitic mayor of Vienna, Lueger, they were never able to organize mass movements or parties. And if no 'Dreyfusards' rose against them in Germany, there were at least the Social-Democrats. They fought, in the '90s, a courageous battle against what they called the 'cultural disgrace' of anti-Semitism; at a time when they had only a small following themselves, they used to attend anti-Semitic meetings and often succeeded in winning over the audience. One can read about these things in the memoirs of Philipp Scheidemann. The Social-Democrats also knew a thing or two about 'the people' and demagogy, and they felt no need to make use of anti-Semitism. They were by far the strongest party in Germany since 1912, at a time when the 'German Socialist Party' of Boeckel and Liebermann was long forgotten.

"I shall not and must not give an idealized picture of the past. There was always anti-Semitism in Germany, partly loud and aggressive and partly of a more discreet and—if the expression may be used in this context—civilized character. German Jews, and particularly German patriots of a more sensitive character, have always suffered on account of it. As far as I know it did not cause any suffering to the Colonial Secretary whom I mentioned before, because he was of a robust nature. The political writer Maximilian Harden did not suffer either, or his views would not have been so bellicose and nationalistic, his style not so aggressive. But it caused bitter suffering to Walther Rathenau, and to Friedrich Nietzsche, who was not a Jew, but felt disgusted at and tortured by it. There has never been a lack of tensions, of the experience of loving and wooing and of rejection.

"However, that particular German anti-Semitism which we are considering tonight and which ended in the most horrid crimes in European history, started only with the German defeat in 1918. The existence of predecessors does not disprove this thesis. There are always bacilli in the air. The question is when did the body become prone to infection and when did the illness become apparent? It became virulent only in 1919. The colossal moral confusion and brutalization as a symptom of the defeat, the subsequent total pauperization and loss of social status of many millions by the inflation—events which far surpassed the understanding of most people—provided for the first time a powerful sounding-board for the slogan 'The Jews are our misfortune'. I would dare to state that anti-Semitic passion in Germany was never more rabid than in the years 1919 to 1923, much more so than in 1930—1933 or 1933—1945.

"It was the time of the first great success of the National-Socialists. The movement declined as soon as, with the end of the inflation, new hope for a decent human life rose for the masses. In the Parliament of 1924, the Nazis were left with only 24 seats, in 1928, at the height of the boom, they had only 12. But already in the following year the big economic crisis started and, a year later, in 1930, they increased their mandates from 12 to 107. One would have to be blind not to see the causal connection.

"Yet—and this is a question which I consider to be of utmost importance—do not believe that all these petty bourgeois and unemployed people, ruined or threatened by ruin, who voted for Hitler, did so primarily because he was an anti-Semite. This played a very small part in the period 1930—1933.

"One can distinguish three stages in the history of Hitler's hatred of the Jews, as far as it came into the open. As long as he saw no serious chance to rise to power, he gave full expression to his obscene instincts in his speeches and writings, as for instance in his book 'Mein Kampf', written in 1924. When the economic crisis began to drive the masses into his camp, he became much more cautious. He knew that one could make small-scale political gains by Jew-baiting, but not the 'big business' deal which he now saw within his reach. Let us, for instance, have a look at his 'Manifesto' for the elections in 1930, which suddenly made the Nazis the leading party. This 'Manifesto' which is extremely efficient from a demagogic point of view, consists of thirteen closely printed pages. How many of these many thousand words are devoted to the 'Jewish question'? Not one! It enumerates and insults one after another the opponents and enemies, scoundrels to be chucked out and traitors to be punished, but says not one word about the Jews. This applies, with a few insignificant exceptions, to all speeches and pronouncements of Hitler between 1930 and 1933. It is truly astonishing that this fact has never yet been noted, but the conclusiions to be drawn from this silence on 'the Jewish question', particularly in the very decisive years of the struggle for power, in the years of accomplished mass propaganda, seem clear to me.

"German anti-Semitism had its peculiarities in contrast with Polish, Hungarian or French anti-Semitism. But it was not basically different. Different, however, was the obscene hatred of Jews which the young Hitler had acquired in Vienna—the only genuine deep emotion of his black heart. It was his one peculiarity and that of his most intimate supporters. This peculiarity materialized to the same extent as Hitler consolidated his power over the Germans. His dictatorship reached completion only in the summer of 1934. It was not until a year later, in 1935, that he proclaimed the Nuremberg Laws. And when did the real first pogrom, the so-called 'Crystal Night' occur? Five weeks after the Munich Agreement, that unprecedented triumph which made Hitler complete master of the whole of Central Europe. Only then could he give free rein to his own devilish passion without inhibitions.

"But did not the Germans who voted for Hitler—35% of the electorate at the last free elections—know that he hated the Jews? This they knew indeed, but they did not hold it against him. 'This would pass ... it would not have serious consequences ...' I was in Germany in 1933, I listened to hundreds of conversations in third-class railway carriages, at the tables in inns reserved for 'regulars'. The words which I heard most often were the German saying 'Things are not eaten as hot as they were cooked'. Things would calm down again.

"The fate of the Jews did not greatly interest most Germans. But they should have been interested in their own destiny. They should have been interested in whether there would be peace or war, and it is well-known that they did not want Hitler's war. They still bore too heavily the experience of the first World War. Yet they ought to have known that Hitler would wage war. They ought to have known it from 'Mein Kampf', in which this was explicitly stated; they ought to have felt it, from the appearance of the monster. But they did not take seriously what they knew—if they knew anything at all, if they had read 'Mein Kampf'—and they lacked any perception whatsoever. Believe me, anyone who knew or perceived anything in Germany at that time was very isolated. Hitler was 'national' minded; this the Germans were too; Hitler was so only a little too much. He was anti-Semitic; so were they; Hitler was so only a little too much. But this 'too much', this exaggeration, which was a remnant of the years of struggle for power, would diminish and disappear with governmental responsibility. This is what Hitler's voters thought, and the majority of German Jews thought so at the beginning.

"But nothing diminished nor disappeared. The implementation of Jew-hatred went on step by step. So did also the nationalistic aggression against Europe, but both were applied in doses. It is likely that the German Army would have intervened, had Hitler's Storm Troops murdered all the German Jews in 1933. It took no action against the pogrom of 1938, corrupted as it already was by then. Had Hitler attacked Austria in 1933, the French would have intervened. They did not do so any longer in 1938.

"The implementation of Hitler's hatred of the Jews was never popular in Germany. It constituted an unpleasant blot on the picture, which appeared to most people to be very bright until 1939 or 1941: the abolishment of unemployment, internal order after years on the brink of civil war, the triumphs in the sphere of foreign policy, regained national honour, pride and glory. The Jews? This one had to accept, since the authorities had ordered it. One accepted it still more easily, because many non-Jews profited by it. They could from the first move into the positions in State offices, from which Jews had been expelled. They could take over later the aryanized businesses, private banks, etc. This was by no means unpleasant. It would have been likewise if the plundered victims had not been Jews. This I know from personal experience, for the confiscated property of my father, who was not a Jew, was taken over by strangers as gladly as Jewish-owned property.

"For the sake of truth I must add that this was the attitude of the majority but not of all. There were Germans too—and it is impossible to count them—who pined away in loneliness and disgust in the years of the Third Reich. In Germany too, Jews were saved by non-Jews who hid them in their homes, endangering their own lives. In Germany such rescue operations never reached the extent they did in Holland, Denmark and Italy. There are many reasons for this, which I need not go into and which you can guess. One of the reasons is that it is easier, from a moral point-of-view, to resist a foreign conqueror and oppressor, than one's own government, which is backed by the mass of the population.

"In pointing this out, I do not want to put up a defence for my compatriots. I only want to tell you the truth as I see it. And the truth would make for a very doubtful defence. It would have been very bad if a wave of barbaric superstition, in the style of the 15th century, had swept over Germany in the '30s and '40s, but it might have been better than the obtuse obedience, the turn-coat opportunism, the cynicism which actually prevailed. Everything was ordered; everything was carried out, without spontaneity, without hysterics, without belief or disbelief. This was the situation at the beginning, as well as when things reached their climax. One single devil in human shape made the over-all decisions, but an industrious bureaucracy planned the details, as efficiently and preciseley as it would have planned the implementation of any other order. The executioners, the immediate murderers, were just as easy to find. Sometimes they were actual sadists, more often brutal mercenaries or rather humdrum people. Rolf Hochhuth gave a terrifyingly lifelike portrait of one of them—the officer who takes the Jews of Rome prisoners—in his play 'The Deputy'. Hermann Göring, the second in command of the Nazi State, stated before the Nuremberg Tribunal: 'I have never been an anti-Semite—ask Bernheimer'. (Bernheimer was an important art dealer in Munich, from whom Göring had bought a great deal). You may think that Göring was a liar. I do not think so. He followed suit out of sheer opportunism, ranking as the second highest official in the State, just as millions of little people followed suit in millions of smaller positions.

"One observed the laws, irrespective of their content. I can illustrate this by a sad example out of my own life. In 1936, my Jewish grandfather had his passport revoked. His only daughter, my mother, lived at the time in exile in Switzerland. He would have loved very much to see her once more. He had been told that German citizens could, at the Swiss-German border, obtain a permit valid for one day even without a passport. He therefore travelled to Konstanz. The German frontier officials just laughed at him when he put forward his request. All he could do was to phone my mother from the border. The poor old man was heart-broken, but he said on the phone: 'If these are the orders...'. If these are the orders... These sad words, which are terrifying if one thinks more closely about them, could serve as caption to the whole catastrophe of the German Jews.

"When the yellow badge appeared and goods trains to Poland filled up and Jewish neighbours disappeared on all sides, the reaction of the people consisted of some pity, some shame, a little contempt and a lot of indifference. These were about the same feelings one had for the victims of the German resistance against Hitler, of 20 July 1944. Heinrich Himmler decided, in 1943 or 1944, on the murder of all German princes and all members of the formerly ruling dynasties, because they were just as much 'aliens by blood', just as 'international and treacherous' as the Jews. He had already thought out a plan for their ignominious public execution in Berlin. This story has been told by Felix Kersten, Himmler's private physician, whose memoirs have been proved to be highly reliable. Kersten had influence over Himmler, because he was able to assuage his stomach ailments. He could persuade him to postpone the murder of the princes, and we know that nothing came of it. If, however, fifty or a hundred German princes had been taken through two long lines of SS-men in Berlin, had been spat upon by them and had been finally hanged, the people would have accepted this just in the same way as they accepted what happened to the Jews. Perhaps with a little more pity and shame, maybe with a little less contempt and indifference. But they would have accepted it. And the famous teacher of Constitutional Law, Carl Schmitt, who saw in the Jew-baiting of Gauleiter Streicher a magnificent manifestation of the German spirit, would no doubt also have proved that there was something magnificent in the murder of the princes.

"The catastrophe of the German Jews and of the European Jews was not destined by German history. While the legal emancipation took place somewhat later than in England, Holland and France, while anti-Semitism in Germany was perhaps somewhat more intense in the 19th century in Germany than elsewhere, the relation between Jews and Germans was also closer, the influence of the Jews on German spiritual and cultural life stronger than elsewhere. The assimilation of the German Jews was almost completed before 1914, irrespective of whether they remained faithful to their religion or not. In order to bring about the catastrophe it required a combination of circumstances which could not possibly have been foreseen. Had World War I ended with a peace based on reconciliation instead of the defeat and the break-down of the old order; had Chancellor Brüning not tried to cure a wild deflation by a 'superdeflation'; had he not conducted at the same time a cold war against France and the Treaty of Versailles, thereby bringing the economic crisis to a climax—the Nazis would not have become a mass party and would never have come to power. Had not a few scheming bunglers, a few bankers and members of the landed Squirearchy belonging to the circle of President Hindenburg concluded a pact with Hitler at a moment when the Nazi movement was already declining, they would not have come to power inspite of the economic crisis. But Brüning was certainly no anti-Semite; nor were, as far as I know, Herr von Papen, the banker von Schröder or Colonel Hindenburg, at least not as a main occupation. They had quite different ideas in their stupid heads. And finally, had there not existed that technician of power, that fascinating demagogue, that devil gifted with immense energy and cunning, that monster Adolf Hitler—something similar to the Nazi party might have resulted, but not with such success. Of course, Hitler manipulated existing forces and instincts; of course he was not, in this respect, accidental. But it required this one individual to unite these forces and instincts, to mobilize them, to lead them to this end.

"The fact that the catastrophe was not inevitable and that it lacked any historical meaning, does not, in my opinion, make it any better. It would make it even worse if this were possible. It makes the German people as a whole no less responsible. It makes leading strata of the nation as they were at the time—industry, the universities, bureaucracy and administration of justice—no less guilty and no less contemptible. Since then, many things have changed in Germany; I dare not say, how deep reaching this change is. In the area which I know, the universities, I consider it to be deep and good. I wish torepeat, in conclusion, what I stated as an introduction: whoever has lived as a German through the '30s and '40s, can never fully trust his nation, can have no greater trust in democracy than in any other form of government, cannot trust men in general nor can he trust what used to be called by optimists 'the meaning of history'. He will, however much he may or even should strive, remain in the innermost of his soul a sad man until he dies."

Salo W. Baron's speech

"Perhaps it is still too early to discuss a normalization of relations between Germans and Jews. The Bible tells us that it took the Israelites forty years of wandering in the desert—forty years may be a biblical round number for a generation—before they could discard their Egyptian experience and start afresh. Nor did they ever really forget it, not only negatively with respect to their sufferings, but also positively in regard to Egypt's 'fleshpots' and culture which long thereafter continued to influence that of Israel. Possibly it will require forty years for a completely new generation of Jews again not to forget, but to submerge in their consciousness, the tragic experiences of the Nazi era. Similarly, it may take forty years, or the rise of an entirely new generation of Germans, before the last vestiges of the Nazi ideology and methods will be relegated into a corner of German national consciousness. At the moment, no one who lived through that period of great aberrations of the human mind can quite approach the consideration of the future relationships between the two peoples without a tinge of horror at the recollection of what happened in so recent a past.

"At the same time, one cannot suppress the sense of wonder of how the world has been able to carry on in its customary ways after the stark tragedies of a quarter century ago. After the First World War a German writer concluded his story of four German soldiers fighting on the Western Front with the bitter exclamation, 'Life proceeds at its usual pace over the ten million dead bodies!' Yet one cannot help feeling that the murder of six million Jews, in addition to millions of non-Jews as well as the death of other millions of active combatants on the various fronts had left a deep dent in the vast body of humanity which no amount of the population explosion, nor man's usual desire to return to normalcy, can wholly obliterate. Certainly, in historical reality, as in the physical world, no energy, particularly of such dimension, is ever totally lost.

"It may well be that one of the main explanations of the great tragedy was the peculiar nature of the uninterrupted Judeo-German symbiosis over more than a millennium. A brief recital of some elements of that ancient heritage may, therefore, be in order here. Possibly it was a blessing in disguise for the West-European Jews that their ancestors had been eliminated from England in 1290, from France and the Low Countries in the fourteenth and fifteenth centuries, so that when the Resettlement started in the modern period there was a definitive break with the past. The United States, having itself emerged as a western nation from recent colonizers, naturally had but dim recollections of what had happened in Europe centuries before. True, these medieval animosities and misunderstandings have not completely disappeared from the memories of these western peoples. In this beautiful city of Brussels, annual church processions have been commemorating the 'Miracle of the Holy Sacrament' at the church of St. Gudule, a miracle associated with the alleged desecration of a host by Jews in 1370 which ended in the burning of the small Jewish community then living here. Every fifty years thereafter, until 1820, the jubilee of that event was celebrated as a major international festival, attracting hosts of pilgrims from many parts of Europe. Nonetheless, with the nearly total absence of living Jews from Belgian soil for many generations, this event remained as a pale literary reminiscence, rather than as a living reality.

"In contrast, similar celebrations, for instance, in Bavarian Deggendorf have eversince 1338 served to inflame the popular passions against the few Jews living in the vicinity whom the populace considered direct heirs of the desecrators of the holy relic which for several centuries was reputed to have great healing qualities. Constantly shown to pilgrims, it appeared as an unmistakable testimony of the allegedly innate Jewish hostility to the Christian faith and its rituals. Even in recent years many of the one hundred thousand annual visitors who have come to that small town to admire this vestige of a medieval miracle—incidentally, an important source of revenue to both the church and the town—cannot help viewing the stained glass windows of the small church depicting in graphic detail that Jewish 'crime' purportedly committed more than six hundred years ago.

"Nor has the German people been able to forget that only a few generations ago all Jews appearing on the streets of any German city wore distinguishing yellow wheels on their garments. Only an informed minority realised that the badge had been first imposed upon the Jews by a decision of an ecumenical council of 1215 only for the purpose of preventing *too intimate* relationships between Jews and Gentiles. More or less effective as an instrument of segregation, which in essence both parties desired, this symbol became in Germany more than anywhere else also a sign of degradation, and came rightfully to be designated the 'badge of shame'. The gullible masses were quite ready to believe even such fanciful explanations as that offered by a seventeenth-century scholar who stated:

'There is, my dear friend, a well-known question: Why does the Jew carry an O on his clothes? it is to serve as a permanent reminder of the painful O! for he is rightly subject to eternal sufferings in Hell. Also because we thus express naught in ciphers, for he ought to consider himself as nothing among men. Perhaps also because he lives from usury and, through the addition of this cipher, every number is multiplied (by ten).'

"Similarly forgotten was the origin of the ghetto. At first merely a natural growth arising from the religio-cultural separation of the Jewish community from the rest of the urban population, it became another instrument of discrimination and degradation. Outside of scholarly circles it was no longer remembered that the bishop of Speyer, the first recorded founder of a German-Jewish ghetto, had done it in 1094 as a favour to Jews, in order to attract them to his city and thus to 'enhance the dignity' of his bishopric. Few men realised that in most older German localities the original Jewish quarters were living testimonies to the antiquity of Jewish settlement there because they were as a rule located in the very centres of these cities, that is, in the sectors reaching back to their very foundations. In Cologne, the city council had to pass in 1341 a resolution that, because the city hall was located in the midst of the Jewish quarter, its gates should not be closed at night when the city elders were in session. As time went on, however, Jews were often forcibly relegated into new, less attractive sections. With the increase in their population even originally desirable quarters turned into regular slums, unsanitary and ugly to behold. To the early modern Germans, these Jewish habitations served as another permanent reminder of Jewish inferiority, and they equated their inhabitants with outcasts from general society.

"Even more significantly, behind these ghetto walls Jews seemed to be living an uncanny, mysterious life. The more segregated the Jewish community became, the less knowledge their neighbours had about the daily life in that suspect quarter, the more readily were the people prepared to believe the most incredible rumours about these strange neighbours. Ancient folklore was magnified into a general conviction that, because Jews had repudiated Christ, they must have sided with his counterparts, both Antichrist and Satan. The old New Testament phrase of the 'synagogue of satan' (Rev 2:9, 3:9) seemed to bear out suspicions that the Jews were the permanent allies of the demonic underworld, Even a scholar of some standing like the fifteenth-century professor of the University of Vienna, Heinrich von Langenstein, could claim to see in 'the rise of Jewry' portents for the advent of Antichrist and figure out that, with the help of Jewish money, Antichrist would conquer the world in two and a half years.

"If, despite many prohibitions, many a Christian patient repaired to a Jewish doctor because of his reputation as a great healer, the latter's successes were often attributed to the doctor's compact with the devil. Similarly, quick accumulation of riches by Jewish bankers could easily be explained by such an alliance with demons. That these patients and borrowers voluntarily co-operated with the Jewish doctors and moneylenders by no means diminished their sense of guilt. Nor did it prevent them from believing that, out of their innate hostility to all Christians, Jewish physicians often administered their patients deadly poisons, rather than curative medicines. Did not even Martin Luther contend that 'If they (the Jews) could kill us all, they would gladly do so; aye, and often do it, especially those who profess to be physicians. They know all that is known about medicine in Germany; they can give poison to a man of which he will die in an hour, or in ten or twenty years; they thoroughly understand this art.'

"It is small wonder then, that the popular mind was ready to lend credence to the general assumption that the purported Jews' body odour stemmed from their association with the devil. Because of their relations to goats resembling the devil, moreover, the goat cry of 'Hepp' was readily applied to them—this seems to be the origin of the 'Hepp Hepp' slogan (rather than the frequently assumed derivation from an abbreviation of *Hierosolyma est perdita*) which resounded through the length and breadth of Germany in 1819 as an accompaniment to the anti-Jewish riots—and that the old Teuton designation for gnome, Gütchen or Grietel could be quickly translated into Jüdel. Nor did the populace disbelieve a story like that told by Johann Fischart in his *Wunderzeitung von einer schwangeren Jüdin zu Binswangen*, graphically describing a Jewess purportedly giving birth to two piglets, a story underscored by a woodcut depicting that incredible scene.

"Such folkloristic preconceptions, repeated in untold variations over several centuries, deeply sank into the psyche of the German people. They could not readily be eradicated by a few generations of official enlightenment which often failed to reach down to the uneducated masses. It was the very irrationality of these preconceptions which played into the hands of Nazi propagandists claiming to revive the good old days of the Germanic Middle Ages. At first they seemed merely to wish to restore the old ghetto and badge and to resuscitate the numerous discriminatory provisions of the medieval decrees. In fact, to superficial observers the Nuremberg Laws of 1935 appeared merely to exclude Jews from certain occupations, to prohibit them from employing Christian servants, and to re-establish other long-accepted medieval institutions. This system meant, of course, the revocation of Jewish Emancipation which anti-Jewish spokesmen had long postulated; partly under the excuse that Jews had not kept their part of the bargain of becoming fully assimilated to the German people. (This 'contract myth' has long ago been effectively exploded by Harry Sacher and others.) The battle-cry that Nazism meant a return to the Middle Ages now resounded among both friends and foes of the new regime.

"In fact, however, this comparison was tantamount to maligning the medieval civilisation. With all their numerous shortcomings the Middle Ages basically represented a system of law and order, seeking within its framework the establishment of some permanent, more or less equitable, relationships with the Jewish dissenters. Very rarely, indeed, did a medieval king, prince or bishop encourage violent extermination of Jews. For the most part they tried to stave off massacres with all the power at their disposal, taking seriously their primary obligation of maintaining public order. If they wished to eliminate Jews they did it by way of a formal decree of expulsion. In contrast, the Nazis from the outset staged governmentally sponsored attacks on Jews, controverting what even such a racist as Count Ernst von Reventlow has emphasised in 1932 'that separation (of Jews from Germans) will of course be accomplished in humane forms. National Socialism plans no programme, nor does it wish to furnish the Jews with a fine vehicle for world-wide propaganda'. However, the inherent trend in Nazism pointed toward the ultimate sanguinary 'final solution'. By October 1943, Heinrich Himmler in his well-known address to the SS generals delivered in Posnan at a time when he must have known that the tide of war had already turned against the Reich, spoke of the mass extermination of European Jews, which to a large extent had already been accomplished, as of 'a page of glory in our history about which nothing has been written nor is it ever to be written'.

"This successful Nazi appeal to a return to the hallowed Middle Ages, however distorted the picture of the medieval conditions may have been, was particularly tragic because it brought back the most vivid memories of the medieval persecutions of Jews, although these dated in the main from the time of the breakdown of medieval civilization under the blows of the dissolution of feudalism and its replacement by the nascent capitalistic, secularist, and particularly nationalist forces. The fourteenth to the sixteenth centuries were much better remembered than the earlier periods, because they had been perpetuated in a mass of writings still extant and widely read in the subsequent centuries. Unfortunately, those three centuries were the scenes of an unprecendented series of massacres and expulsions, particulary during the Black Death era, which eliminated the Jews from most areeas of the Holy Roman Empire. What made these developments doubly portentous for modern secular anti-Semitism was their increasingly secular character and their transformation of the earlier religious frenzy into a lay-dominated primarily socio-economic hostility. Even the Passion plays, often performed on public squares during several days before the majority of the local population, now presented the ancient Jews of Jerusalem in medieval garb, talking in impossible gibberish, and bent upon usurious gains. Deep into the modern age did these newer plays help to envenom the outlook of the German peasantry on Jews and Judaism.

"All this was but a manifestation of the new spirit of nationalism which increasingly dominated the European scene. German nationalism, to be sure, still was far from crystallized; it was subject to a variety of meanings, ranging from tribal and regional solidarity to that of an all-German unity. Nonetheless, it mattered little to the masses that the accomplishment of the nationalist aims through the modern German states was effectively supported by the presence of Jews. The distinguished historian, Karl Lamprecht, has long ago pointed out, on the example of the archbishopric of Trier, that the capital and know-how placed by several Jewish financiers at the disposal of the archbishop-elector, helped to stem the process of feudal dissolution and to preserve the unity of the territorial state. Later on, according to Werner Sombart's well-known dictum, the German prince *(Landesherr)*, marching arm in arm with his court Jew, built the modern German territorial state, the nucleus for the nineteenth century German Reich. But to outsiders, particularly those whose vested interests were affected by the great economic and socio-political transformations, this alliance of prince and Jew appeared as but a selfish endeavour at self-aggrandisement and profits. The majority of the people shared the opinion of the Hessian clergy which, in trying to persuade Landgrave Philip in 1538 to restrict Jewish rights, argued that the sole reason for the toleration of such infidels in the country had been their usefulness to the Treasury. In this connection, the Hessian churchmen coined a simile, which has ever since been often repeated in the polemical and apologetic literature. They contended that Jews had been used by the respective governments 'as a sponge. No sooner did they suck up the money (from the population through their usury), than the overlords proceeded to squeeze it out of them into their own pockets'.

"These spokesmen of the nascent Protestant Churches well reflected the impact of the new secularist and nationalist forces replacing the old medieval rationales. With all its attempts at sharp segregation of Jews from Christians and at keeping them on a low social level, the Catholic Church has since ancient times insisted on the need of preserving the Jewish people to the end of days or, as it called it, the second coming of Christ. Whether, to speak in Pauline terms, as the 'root' from which Christianity sprang, or as the formerly chosen people though subsequently repudiated by God because of its rejection of Christ, or as a living witness to the truth of the Christian tradition attested by the Old Testament 'Testimonies', or else for the sake of fulfilling the ancient prophecies about Israel's return to its ancestral land in the Messianic age—the Jewish people was to be kept as part and parcel of Christian society for all time.

"An ancient legend going back to the second century jurist Tertullian and repeated by Augustine and other Church Fathers well described this basis ecclesiastical outlook. With the aid of typical patristic hermeneutics, the biblical narrative of Cain and Abel was transformed into an historic lesson for all future times. The two sons of the first man were supposed to be but an adumbration of the rise of Christianity. Cain, the older brother stood for ancient Israel, Abel for Jesus. Reading the Bible in this light one could see that what was foretold was that both Israel and Christianity would ultimately bring their offerings to the Lord and that that of the older brother was to be rejected, while that brought by Jesus would be fully accepted. Thereupon Cain-Israel would rise up in arms and slay his younger brother, Abel-Jesus. As a punishment, we are told, Cain was to 'be a fugitive and a wanderer on the earth', but at the same time he was to be guarded against hostile assailants. 'Therefore whosoever slayeth Cain, vengeance shall be taken on him sevenfold.' This combination of homelessness and perpetual wandering on the one hand, and the safeguarding of life and limb on the other hand, was indeed to remain the keynote of the Church and state policies towards Jews throughout the Middle Ages.

"Ultimately, this picture of the wandering Jew likewise underwent secularisation. Particularlary in the form presented in a German booklet published in 1602, it attracted wide attention and induced even such great poets as Goethe and Shelley to compose poems on that theme. It has been found that between 1774, when Goethe wrote his unfinished fragment on the 'Wandering Jew', and 1930 no less than 460 different versions of that tale have appeared in many European languages. While in its modern secularized form this story carried with it many intriguing humanitarian aspects, and even pretenders impersonating Ahasver in practice were often hospitably received by German peasants, its most pervasive effect was to bring home to the German and other peopels the image of the Jew as a perennial outcast and gypse-like wanderer.

"Such 'outsiders' began to be increasingly resented by ardent German nationalists. Originally such spokesmen of German nationalism as Herder or Fichte were dreaming that their nation, united in one country and pursuing its great cultural role of a nationa of poets and thinkers, would become the true *Menschheitsnation*, a nation in the service of humanity at large. In fact, the enthusiastic patriot Fichte saw in the phenomenon of the German people living without what he considered a political history and without a single state of its own the great challenge for Germans to build an unprecedented, humanitarian nation. Inescapably, the similarity with the fate of the Jewish people intruded upon any observer; here was the most typical example of a dispersed and stateless people without any political history for some two thousand years. Yet it was characteristic that not Fichte nor other German nationalist thinkers, but rather the Pole,

Adam Hickiewicz, and the Italian, Giuseppe Manzini, fully drew that parallel between their own and Israel's messianic nation.

"With the progress of expansive nationalism, the success of German unification, and the building of the Bismarckian Reich, these humanitarian elements receded into the background, giving way to an increasing emphasis on the drive for unlimited imperial power. To some extremist spokesmen of the new tendencies the presence of a Jewish people adhering to its old Messianic traditions, however disguised at times among so-called assimilated Jews, was felt as a serious obstacle. More the very Judeo-Christian tradition with its stress on the brotherhood of man and ethical behaviour in relations with other nations, as well as among individuals, was deeply resented. This was indubitably one of the mainsprings in the rise of the modern variety of anti-Semitism which increasingly assumed racial characteristics. From the 1870s on, there was gradually building up that atmosphere of rejection of all both Judaism and Christianity had stood for which ultimately paved the way for the Nazi seizure of power. Long before Hitler appeared on the scene, such German voices were heard as that of one Ernst Wachler who wrote in 1909: 'Woe to the nation which behaves in a Christian fashion at a time when a battle is raging over the possession of the globe'. Another German publicist, Heinrich von Pudor, combined this imperialist drive with a demand for the annihilation of Jews because 'the Christian religion has taught fear to Siegfried the Teuton ... all Christianity is Judeo-Christianity and as such the most daring fraud perpetrated upon races and nations in world history'. Thus the ground was indeed prepared for a people, later frustrated in its high-strung ambitions by its defeat in World War I and the subsequent economic chaos, to listen to prophets of doom and the promise of regeneration only under the standard of the extreme racist ideology of the Nazi movement.

"Not that the German people were unanimous in hating Jews. In all ages there appeared personalities and groups which extended to their Jewish neighbours tolerance, even genuine friendship. Protective decrees issued by the Hohenstaufen emperors or Austrian dukes, effective measures taken by bishops and princes to protect their Jewish wards, the not infrequent actions by individual burghers to hide Jews at their homes in the face of pogromists at a risk to their own lives, all are rays of light moderating the gloom covering the Judeo-German relations throughout the ages. Martin Luther's *Von den Juden und ihren Lügen* had its counterpart in Gotthold Ephraim Lessing's *Nathan the Wise*; Eisenmenger, Rühs and Fries had their opposite numbers in Dehn and the brothers Humboldt; Treitschke, Lagarde, and Chamberlain were controverted by Mommsen, Frans Delitzsch, and Strack. But among the broad masses of the population the virus of anti-Semitism deeply affected even the workers enrolled in the powerful Socialist Party whose leader August Bebel had long condemned that ideology as a 'religion of fools'. It is certainly characteristic that, as Fritz Kynass has pointed out, 'there exist no medieval German folksongs revealing a friendly attitude to Jews'.

"On their part the Jews developed a deep attachment to the German people and their culture. The accusations of Luther and others that Jews were inveterate enemies of all Christians sounded rather hollow; they may have legitimately referred to but a few individuals reacting strongly to the environmental hatreds. But the people as a whole felt an intimate relationship with the German lands, whose Hebrew name *Ashkenaz* they used to designate all co-religionists north of the Alps and Pyrences. Friedrich Wilhelm Heinz, a former S.A. officer, despite his twisted interpretation, was not wrong in contending that 'the *metaphysical rejection* by the Germans is answered by no less a *metaphysical love* from the Jews. It is the pernicious love of the sick blood for the healthy;

we see here, in its rational distortion, the operation of the ancient myths of the primitive peoples about the healing and saving powers of the virginal blood'. Much more to the point was Hermann Cohen's *Deutschtum und Judentum* which, though inspired by the great patriotic fervour of the First World War, served nevertheless as a sort of testament of one of the greatest modern thinkers to his German and Jewish compatriots.

"Centuries ago this metaphysical love induced the Jewish exiles from Germany to transplant with them their German dialect into the vast expanses of Eastern Europe which before long embraced the majority of their people. They lovingly developed their Germanic speech long after the Christian German colonists of the Polish cities had surrendered their identity and adopted the idiom of their environment. East-European Jewry gradually transformed this dialect into a new great language which helped express its innermost feelings and which ultimately produced an extraordinarily rich and qualitatively high literature of its own. In the Enlightenment era generations of Jews were raised on poems by Schiller and Heine which became household letters in many homes, rivalling some of their ancient Hebrew classics. Russian and Polish Jewish students studying at German schools of higher learning became bearers of German culture upon their return to their homelands or wherever else they may have settled. Many of us still feel everlastingly grateful to the German-speaking universities which opened up for us vast new horizons and taught us methods of research which we are using for the rest of our lives. In short, the Jewish and the German peoples have become so deeply entwined in their historic careers that, despite all resentments and mutual suspicions, they must appear to historians as twins, almost inseparable for over a thousand years."

"What about the future?"

"In the first place we must realize that we have before us a problem of great profundity and intensity. It simply will not do glibly to pass over the experiences of the recent past and to declare the Nazi period as a great aberration of the German mind which has been rectified by the subsequent good-will shown by the German government to both Israel and the Jewish people. Admittedly, as I have been told, confirming my impressions received during the few relatively brief visits I paid to Germany in the post-war era, on the whole the governmental organs, the press, the universities, and the world of creative arts have gone a long way in trying to extirpate the vestiges of Nazism. But the German people at large seem not yet to be quite ready to draw a line under the experiences of the 1930s and 1940s and still less under its deep-rooted millennial tradition which had penetrated deeply their subconsciousness as well as consciousness.

"I do not know how reliable public opinion polls are with respect to such complex attitudes as those relating to anti-Semitic feelings when the same individuals are likely to answer the same questions differently at different times. Nor have I examined carefully any pertinent recent polls. However, it may be characteristic that a poll taken by the West German Institute of Public Opinion within five years after the fall of the Nazi regime showed that fully 13 percent still admitted to harbouring outright anti-Semitic feelings, a majority of 55 percent claimed either to have certain 'reservations' concerning Jews or at best to be 'tolerant' towards them, and 15 percent professed indifference. There is no question then that a real problem exists. True, a wise man once told me that difficult problems as a rule are never solved; they disappear. Nonetheless, we cannot simply stand by with complete passivity and let the wheels of history hopefully turn by themselves in the proper direction.

"We must also realize that there are again Jews in Germany and that probably there will be more of them in the future. I recall a discussion in May 1946 (within a year after the German surrender) with the late Dr. Maurice Liber, head of the College Rabbinique in Paris. Discussing the outlook for German Jewry which appeared utterly bleak at that moment, Dr. Liber drew a parallel with the years immediately following the Black Death. 'Would anyone have dared to predict then', he asked, 'that after the *Judenbrand* in most parts of Germany any Jews would be willing, or permitted, to settle again in that inhospitable country?' Many survivors of World War II might, indeed, have echoed the following comment by Heinrich von Diessenhofen, a contemporary of the Black Death:

'I might have thought that the end of the Hebrews has now come, if the predictions of Elijah and Enoch had been fulfilled. But since they have not been fulfilled, it is necessary that some (Hebrews) should be preserved so that the Scriptural statement concerning the hearts of the sons turning to the fathers and those of the fathers to the sons be realized. But I do not know where they would be preserved, though I assume that it is more likely that the people and the seed of Abraham will be maintained in regions beyond the sea.'

"In our post-war era the centre of gravity of the Jewish people has, indeed, moved out of Europe to the 'oversea' countries of Isreal and the Western Hemisphere. Yet it is undeniable that, as Dr. Liber and I agreed in 1946, not only did Jewish communities spring up in various German regions in the generations following 1348, but, even more significantly, that perhaps the greatest flowering of German Jewish culture was yet to come.

"It is further remarkable that after the great holocaust of the 1940s no legends have sprung up relating to any oath taken by Jews never to return to the land of their great sufferings, similar to the oath purportedly taken by the Jewish exiles from Spain in 1942. The latter oath, too, is very likely unhistorical, but it is an incontrovertible fact that for centuries thereafter no professing Jew would, or for that matter could, visit Spain without danger, and that not until the twentieth century were small organised Jewish communities formed on Iberian soil. In contrast, there are already a number of Jewish communities in various parts of Germany, trying to revive their ancestral culture. True, many Jewish individuals in other lands still have an uneasy feeling about visiting Germany. But it stands to reason that, long after the survivors and contemporaries of the holocaust will have died out, new generations of Jews, doubtless in smaller numbers than before, will again partake of the further building up of Germany's flourishing economy and civilisation. Hence, the problem of the future symbiosis of the two groups is of most direct relevance to the inhabitants of West and East Germany and other German-speaking lands. In our growingly interdependent world, moreover, some *modus vivendi* between the German nation and world Jewry, including the State of Israel, is of great significance not only to these two peoples but to humanity at large.

"Even to-day, more than two decades after the holocaust it may be too early to make any kind of optimistic predictions about their possible genuine rapprochement. Yet there are some hopeful signs on the horizon. From our earlier presentation it must have become manifest that, more than any other factor, extreme nationalism served to poison all Judeo-German relations. Whether it was the unconscious nationalism of the late Middle Ages, the fully developed nationalism of the nineteenth century, or finally the nationalism run amok in totalitarian Germany, it suspected even the smallest deviation or characterological difference between Jew and Gentile as a sign of 'separatism', if not of outright betrayal. Moreover, while the heroic nationalism of a century and a half ago recognized the supremacy of a moral order in humanity, the subsequent totalitarian nationalism knew no bounds. In fact, this was the great tragedy of the entire Western World that its early modern period was dominated by the doctrine of national sovereignty as the supreme vehicle of political evolution. If national sovereignty meant anything at all, it was that the state was the ultimate source of law and that it thus had become a law unto itself. In ancient and medieval times even the most powerful rulers were restrained by the possibility of a prophet or a priest reprimanding some of their actions as a breach of a divinely instituted moral order. In the secularized societies of the modern period there were no such restraints, and the ultimate decision rested with might rather than right. Totalitarian nationalism thus was but the logical culmination of an evolution of several centuries.

"The Second World War, however, has not only shown how greatly this extreme form of nationalism had overreached itself, but it has also demonstrated to all that national sovereignty often became a hollow principle when the chips were down. Never before has a great country like Holland, backed by a large Southeast-Asian empire, been occupied by a foreign enemy within four days. Other great countries like Czechoslovakia or Denmark surrendered without firing a shot. Clearly the national sovereignty of these countries has been a shambles. Since World War II it has become even clearer that if mankind is to survive the atomic age, each nation must forego some of its sovereignty and adhere to some supranational order by agreement, and if need be, by the force of a majority will.

"Germany, in particular, has learned that its human and natural resources are not equal to those of the super-powers of the United States, the Soviet Union and, before long, possibly of Red China, and that only by joining the Common Market, hopefully as a preliminary to a United States of Europe which may also include some or all of the Outer Seven, it has a chance to play the great historic role which its patriots envision. This new situation has indeed created a novel climate of opinion in which recognition of unity within diversity has become a real possibility. Perhaps the time is not too far off for the German nation to hearken to the words of Frederick Barbarossa, one of the heroes most exalted in its legends and poetry, written in his basic privilege for Regensburg Jewry:

'It is the duty of Our Imperial Majesty, as well as a requirement of justice and a demand of reason, that We rightly preserve his due to everyone of Our loyal subjects, not only the adherents of the Christian faith, but also to those who differ from Our faith and live in accordance with the rites of their ancestral tradition. We must provide for their persevering in their customs and secure peace for their persons and property. For this reason We announce to all faithful subjects of the Empire, present and future, that, deeply concerned with the welfare of all Jews living in our Empire who are known to belong to the imperial Chamber by virtue of a special prerogative of Our dignity, We concede to Our Regensburg Jews and confirm with Our imperial authority their good customs which their ancestors had secured through the grace and favour of Our predecessors until Our time.'

"The German people, which had long learned to transcend the differences between the Saxon, the Swabian, or the Bayuvar, and which has been able to achieve its national unity despite the great religious diversity between the Catholics and the two Protestant denominations, may indeed in time sincerely accept not only a peaceful but an amicable coexistence with the even more diverse group of Jews.

"To bring about such a whole-hearted acceptance is by no means an easy task. It will not even suffice merely to adopt a comprehensive educational programme and to pursue it relentlessly over years and decades, although, of course, such a programme is absolutely indispensable. But beyond all rational approaches one must devise some novel instrumentalities of combating what has essentially been an irrational millennial antagonism. We all realise the perennial dichotomy between the application of means and methods which of necessity are rational to the remedy of ills stemming from irrational impulses. However, mankind and human science have already advanced far enough to recognise these immense difficulties and to try to find some new ways to combine irrationality with rationality in curing deeply rooted ancient evils of this type.

"On the Jewish side, too, it will take a long time before the present resentments will subside. In time, however, there probably will emerge something which will neither resemble the 'metaphysical love' for the old German heritage, nor its sharp reversal toward the more recent German past, but rather a more subdued, customary spirit of neighbourly co-operation. If such 'hereditary enemies' as France and Germany could finally bury their hatchets and become friendly members of the European community, economically and culturally as well as politically, one may perhaps look forward to the establishment of more normal—and not only 'correct'—relationships between Germans and Jews as well. And our deeply disturbed world can indeed use every ounce of amity among peoples it can possibly secure."

Eugen Gerstenmaier's speech

"Ladies and gentlemen,

"I regard the invitation of the World Jewish Congress to speak here as a special distinction, but I gravely doubt whether it is possible for a German—who speaks not for himself but for his country—to make his voice heard across the abyss which separates Jews from Germans.

"I understand quite well those among you who opposed this initiative, and I understand why some of you might close your ears in order not to hear a German voice, whatever it may have to say.

"I only wish to suggest with these words that, despite your invitation, I have no illusions about the historic burden and the human consequences of the terrible debt of blood perpetrated in the name of Germany not solely but mostly against Jews. Today, even after more than twenty years, this debt of blood looms inescapably over us. Such a cloud of darkness and aimlessness emanates from it, that many Germans are utterly unable to face it. The curse of the unchangeable is so great, that even the most decided, the most active and the most good-willed among us are hard put to escape its paralysing effect. This is precisely the reason why this hour must have a meaning for us Germans. However great were my hesitations, however earnestly I asked myself whether the World Jewish Congress was not daring too much, I am grateful to your President, Dr. Nahum Goldmann, for the attempt to make human voices audible between Jews and Germans above this terrible abyss, at a meeting of the World Jewish Congress.

"I consider this attempt to examine the reality of history primarily important, because we must discover what we have lost, and because we must know that the racial mania of Hitler, Himmler and their asscociates was unfortunately not the craze of a demented gang of criminals. This madness had roots. We must uncover them in order to uproot them.

"If I understand this occasion correctly, it should consider not only the past and view into the abyss and what has been lost. It may be that my generation will not be allowed to see a new, free relationship between Germans and Jews. 'All this is to no avail! No one will be able to cross this mountain of corpses!' That is the voice which I hear more often from Germans than from Jews. It threatens so paralyse everything, for it leads not only to silence but also to resignation and apathy. One cannot deny that this sterile repentance is not too infrequent in the Germany of today.

"At times it is linked with a primitive thoughtlessness, but more often still with an instinctive repressiveness. Not to hear any more of the whole sorry business, not to see any more of the horrors of the abyss. O why cannot it at long last finally be finished with! Thus, more or less, is formulated the escape of many Germans from our most recent past.

"Reports on the concentration camp trials are, as far as I can judge, not popular. But it is a thoroughly erroneous interpretation, in my opinion, to deduce therefrom any noticeable remnant of National Socialism in Germany. The contrary might be the true conclusion. Because in this attitude of defence we also find sensitivity for the greatest shame which Germany ever experienced at German hands. And in it, we find a muted protest against the burden of a cursed past, which no man can overcome.

"To-day, anyway, there is no Germany that has overcome its past. But there is a Germany which is ashamed of it and which swore to itself that nothing similar will ever happen to it again. This is the strongest and greatest Germany—whatever the suspicious may say. I make this statement based on facts. They are not only the consequences of external events, such as the loss of the war, but more because of an inner change in the Germans themselves. What I said about this a few years ago at the Hebrew University of Jerusalem needs no alteration. But may I be allowed a few additional remarks regarding the relationship of Jews to Germans.

"For myself and many other Germans of my age and origin, a Jewish problem arose only when Hitler's rise to power was imminent. To us, our Jewish fellow students were quite naturally Germans. In the circle of my friends, there was no change in this attitude even later. But time and again, we reproached ourselves bitterly for having measured Hitler and his entourage too long by the standards of our own world. Hannah Arendt, in her book on Eichmann, coined the concept of the 'banality of evil'. I cannot follow her in this. It was precisely in the appearance of Hitler, Himmler, Goebbels, Eichmann and their associates that we learned together with innumerable other Germans that it was not evil that was banal but our ordinary understanding of the word. Our misfortune began with the fact that most Germans, including the German Jews, assessed Hitler and his people by the standards of their own bourgeois morality and the superficial aspects of National Socialism. That is why, for example, they were naive enough to believe, that the Nazis might be removed by the usual parliamentary methods, once their political failure became apparent. That was not evil—that was banal—and the way to catastrophe. In other words: at the emergence of what was really evil in the history of Germany, not only our sense of perception but also our moral sense of orientation failed in general. Golo Mann's story of his grandfather's attempt to cross the border is a touching example of this. Professor Mann is quite right in saying that one might have inscribed the words of the old sage, 'if such are the instructions', as a caption on the whole catastrophe of the German Jews. But one can equally apply it to the catastrophe as a whole, which was, in its entirety a German catastrophe. The saying of the old Jewish professor from Munich expressed a somewhat respectable but nevertheless unthinking sense of order and discipline—as characteristically German as anything could be. These five words negate the abstruse nonsense of Hitler's anti-Semitism about the unbridgeable difference. They also prove—forgive my bitterness—the total, partly touching, partly despicable insufficiency of that conventional morality face to face with evil. With all its qualities it simply did not have the understanding for the infernal power and diabolical force of evil, of which man is evidently capable. It did not even have an inkling of it. Golo Mann is right when he says that whoever experienced what we experienced 'cannot fully trust man again'.

"But did what was really evil come into the world only with Hitler? Did not the keen sighted, the incorruptible, glimpse it even earlier? And what did the Bible tell us about it? Far be it from me to plunge headlong into the depths of metaphysics or theological anthropology in order to conceal the share of responsibility for the catastrophe which belongs to the German people. Perhaps we Germans should admit, that the catastrophe in this form was possible only among us. And nevertheless Golo Mann is right in his statement that Hitler's rule—and William Shirer said it too—'was not foreseen in German history'. I may add that it was not anticipated either in German thought and feeling. But just because I agree with Professor Mann I regard his image of a volcano as inapposite. And in his sombre phrase 'where that was possible, everything will always be possible' one word, at least, seems to me wrongly placed. It is the word 'always'.

"Just as German Jewish emigrants to the United States in their talks with Shirer, so did Professor Mann prove, too, that Hitler could only rise to power on the crest of a wave of great economic crisis and because of inadequate action on the part of the democratic government of the Reich. I stress this situation—which is as sad as it is pitiful—not as an excuse but to destroy historical myths, such as those fabricated by Shirer. Only after Hitler came to power, only after the other Germany had been trampled on and terrorised, could there be war and murder of Jews.

"Can this be possible 'always?' I regard this pessimism as unfounded and the attempts to present it as a reality as having failed. The recent prophecies of the famous professor from Basel about the future of Germany are equally unfounded and his analysis as false as the fear roused here and there by the emergence of small groups of the radical right in the Federal Republic. This emergence is worrying and it demands firm control, but it does not indicate that National Socialism is being reborn or that a return to barbarism is 'always' possible in Germany.

"May I say a word, in this respect, about the heritage of German resistance. It is not true that it felt obliged to its own country. It arose while Hitler's Reich was still at the height of its power, as a revolt against the murder of Jews. There are witnesses and testimony for this. This German resistance against Hitler did not prevail. But it achieved something that had not existed in Germany before: it led many individuals to a new orientation of conscience, to a new personal morality and it led them thereby to break with old taboos and conventions, in the cause of justice and humanity. From the oath to the flag to an attempt on the life of the 'highest war lord'—that is a long way for a German to go. German resistance took this road consciously—and this consciousness, the daring of one's inner conviction is, what I believe, is active in Germany even today. Something of this heritage is alive among the great German parties and is consciously being cultivated by their leadership. Among the happiest experiences of my parliamentary life in the last seventeen years is the spontaneous unanimity of the parties represented in the Bundestag today, when the existence of the state based on liberty under law was at issue.

"This element of consciousness determines the world political orientation of the German Federal Republic too. Its positive response to European integration, to its changes of structure and its renunciation of sovereignty are consequences for us which we maintain even against resistance, which is more external than internal. This is why I cannot but subscribe to the sober political outlook of Professor Baron.

"Notwithstanding all this I cannot deny nor do I wish to—that there are in the Germany of today many unanswered questions and grave problems. They originate not only in the abnormal partition of our country and in unsolved issues of our time. They originate, too, and time and again, from our recent past. German national consciousness is blurred and unclear. German historical consciousness is diffuse and problematical.

"In contrast, there is little of significance in the remnants of bestial and malignant anti-Semitism and Hitlerism in today's Germany. I consider the danger of their minimisation and underestimation as smaller than the danger of their over-estimation and of exaggerated public reaction. A consequence of this is, for instance, the proven fact that swastika daubing and even the desecration of cemeteries is a favourite pastime for young rascals who do not even know what anti-Semitism is. But they know well enough that nothing can make the citizens and public opinion of Germany as nervous as provocation with an anti-Semitic tinge.

"As to Döblin's comment of 1948, that the name 'Jew' is still a derogatory term, I can only confirm it. The remnants of decaying Nazism will use it as such. But what does this prove? For the overwhelming majority in Germany, Döblin's statement does not apply. It is much more exposed to the counter peril of turning everything Jewish into taboos. Repentance, contrition, understanding of the terrible extent of brutal annihilation—all this exists. The wish for compensation as well—if this is at all possible. But what is still missing is that inner balance between Germans and Jews which, as a rule, requires normal human relations. But where shall they come from? How can we free ourselves from the traumatic inhibition laid upon us by a past of which we must still say—as Golo Mann so rightly depicted it—that it does not lie only behind but upon us. Upon all of us, on those, too, who do not wish to think of it and much less talk of it. As long as that it so, there are limits to our tongues and to our behaviour, which we Germans cannot cross, even when our heart impels us.

"A word to Gershon Sholem in this regard: there are unhappy love affairs also between Germans and Jews! I do not take into account the Weeks of Brotherhood and similar earnest insistent efforts, in which not only good will but tears of shame, of heartache, and of love, bear precious fruit, as I believe. Among these unhappy love affairs I do not count our relations with Israel. The difficulties that we encounter here are a product, in part, simply of the hard facts of politics. They must be overcome without dramatizing. The Israeli Ambassador in Germany, Mr. Ben Nathan, has recently given a noble example of this. In the background, however, will be the reflection of processes of which Mr. Van Dam, of the Zentralrat of German Jews, spoke soberly and concisely some time ago. He mentioned that the new German-Jewish symbiosis had become a 'German-Jewish, at least a German-Israeli *psychosis*, which contains all the neurotic symptoms of exaggerated expectation, unhealthy love and unhealthy hatred—in other words, an unbalanced relationship to reality".

"The danger to which Mr. van Dam referred must be recognized first of all by the young Germans, who stormily aspire to such a symbiosis. One must also understand that anti-Semitism cannot be cured by any, and however zealous, philo-Semitism. More is needed, namely a storm-resistant normalization. It can, in my opinion, be based only on the belief that 'the other' with all due respect to his individuality and historic uniqueness of his existence is finally 'like you'.

"But perhaps I am already, with this statement, overstepping the limit set me. We Germans may possibly have to accept for a long time, that patient and respectful distance, which is probably most adequate to the aver memorable catastrophe and of uniqueness of Jewish existence.

"Let me say, in conclusion, that this is why I thank the World Jewish Congress, and its President, Dr. Nahum Goldmann, all the more, for the generosity with which they allowed German voices to be heard here. I do not thank you only personally. The German Bundestag thanks the World Jewish Congress."

The message of Karl Jaspers to the Congress

Professor Karl Jaspers sent his message to the Congress in written form, being unable to come to Brussels himself. The message reads as follows:

"The mass murder of six million Jews, committed in the name of the German Reich, is condemned with disgust by almost everyone everywhere, but the question which it raises, such as how Jews and Germans can live together after it, have not come in for a clear answer. The monstrosity of what was done has interrupted the continuity of history. I cannot see a solution to the problems, which have arisen. I, as a German, can only speak for myself and say what I think without laying claim to general validity.

"The crime will remain associated with the German name, just as the more harmless pyramids of skulls are associated with the Mongols. The German name is also connected with intellectual creativeness, with great personalities of world history. That, too, remains. But it cannot erase the new and horrible.

"There are Germans who defend themselves against the accusation of mass murder. They say: we knew nothing about it. Indeed, the apparatus of murder was kept as secret as possible. The broad mass of the people knew nothing about it. Even I, who lived in Heidelberg at the time, did not learn the facts until 1945.

"A great deal was however known. Everybody saw the Jews being taken away. They never returned. Nothing more was heard of them. Non-committal cards came from certain individuals and one was told that others were dead. It was known that being taken away was synonymous with danger to life. Those who were taken away were not as a whole devoid of hope position. Rumours to the effect that the Jews were settled in the East, that they would build up their own state in Jewish areas, were regarded at times as possible or even believed, for the establishment of mass ghettos was not understood as a preparation for extermination.

"Very many Germans, most of them, refuse the idea of being murderers. They say: I murdererd nobody, I was not an accomplice, I did not want it to happen. When occasionally I heard of individual cases of murder, I did not approve of them. This is all correct. Nevertheless, indication should be made of two points.

"We stood there with half knowledge and did not do anything effective. That is why I said in 1945, in my first public speech. 'We survivors did not look for death. When our Jewish friends were taken away, we did not go out into the street, did not shout out loud, until we too were destroyed. We preferred to stay alive with the weak, but nonetheless correct reason that our deaths would not have helped at all. It is our fault that we are alive."

"Hochhuth has not only made the Germans, but also the whole of Western humanity, aware of the fact that they all stood idly by, in that he chooses the Pope as the most important example. Our standing by does, however, have a different sense from that of the other peoples and states. We were not only immediately present, but as citizens of the (German) state were responsible for the actions of the State, under which we were living as citizens. I did therefore in 1945 distinguish political liability from criminal and moral guilt. No German can escape this political liability.

"Guilt of standing idly by and political responsibility apply to us Germans without exceptions. The extent to which the leading groups and persons in National Socialist Germany were aware of what was going on and in particular, the generals, who had the highest responsibility, because they had the power of weapons in their hands—the extent to which they tolerated the situation and in part, cooperated in it and displayed consent, has become ever more apparent across the years. Only one example: Kunrat von Hammerstein reports (Spähtrupp, P. 193): on January 25th, 1944, 250 army generals from all the fronts were assembled in Posen Theatre, to hear speeches by Himmler and Goebbels. Himmler informed them of the final solution: all Jews, including women and children are to be exterminated. General Reinicke then went onto the stage after Himmler's speech and expressed respectful thanks. At the back of the theatre, a general started to count: there were five who did not clap.

"And then, the other side. We think of the many German people, whom we knew, who quite uncalled for, assisted Jews always at a risk to themselves and often in danger of their lives.???

"But that does not help very much: Apart from political liability and the passivity of standing idly by, the fact that broad sections of the leading classes were informed is reason enough for the crimes being bound up with the German name for all times.

"What has happened since then? Jews and Germans live on the same earth. After the extreme events one can think that Jews and Germans must find each other again in an unusual historically, quite singular manner. Both have an exceptional position with regard to each other, when one draws a comparison with the relations to other peoples.

"First of all, a word about the possible. Forgiving is the human act, which cannot in fact undo a deed once it has been done, but it can form the basis of a common future, as if the deed had not occurred. Forgiving is more than mere forgetting, which is usually brought about with time. It is an act, through which memory is not removed, but is deprived of practical continuance. There should be no eternal enmity.

"But now the impossible: A Jew who has survived, can perhaps forgive on his own behalf what has been done to him. But who can forgive the mass murder of six million Jews? Those who were murdered are alone entitled to do that. No one can speak on their behalf, no human being and no state and no religious organisation.

"Who would be the forgiven? The actual culprits? Their accomplices? Those who stood idly by? They will soon be extinct. Does a people still remain guilty, when none of this people is living any longer? Does the guilt continue from generation to generation? There is indeed a tremendous difference between those immediately concerned and later generations. But this sentence is also applicable: Nations do not live only of their forefathers' good deeds. They have to take over the bad deeds as well. The matter can be weighed up this way or that way. I see no proper solution.

"Politically speaking an important step has been taken, indeed without pardon, yet as a means of reconciliation in the practical sphere: the so-called reparations.

"Adenauer embarked on the path, which is the only possible one for the German side. We are grateful to him for doing this regardless of other German attitudes. He had understanding for the irreconcilability of the Jews. He suffered their noisy acts of repulsion. He countered their utterances with patience. He saw from political commonsense that assistance in material things is the minimum fulfilment of a duty. But, there was more than mere politics at play here. The Germans were at least showing a sign of their attitude.

"Under the pressure of the fact of mass murder, there was little else we could do but help the Jews in a tangible manner. Through the fact that we are helping them, we are also helping ourselves a little to ward off the pressure, which is bearing down upon us.

"Today, there are not only the Jews there, but also the State of Israel. Israel and the Federal Republic of Germany have connections with each other. As a result of reparations, not only many individual Jews, who escaped death, but were nevertheless robbed of all they had, have been freed from need, the State of Israel has also received considerable aid. This does not by any means solve the basic problem.

"Both those individual Jews, still living, who sustained damage and Israel are entitled to our help. But, despite all the help, they cannot remove that elementary disinclination with regard to the name of that people, whose state destroyed a third of their people. Something irreconcilable remains in broad circles of the Israeli population.

"The Federal Republic of Germany yearns for reconciliation. But among the Germans, there are those—we do not know how many—who are indifferent to reconciliation and who regard the assistance rendered to Israel as a burden.

"And then: What difficulties at the negotiations between Israel and the Federal Republic! When negotiations are conducted politically and juristically, then moral claims play no part either as an object of negotiations or as an argument. The moral claims, laid by the Germans as such, is a tacit prerequisite of the negotiations. If the moral claim is expressly raised by the Israelis, then it immediately becomes transformed into a legal claim. This results in a troubled atmosphere.

"Everything moral however has its power solely from the freedom to lay the claim to itself. It becomes wrong and powerless when the moral claims are laid to others. The clarity of the matter and the purity of the atmosphere will be spoiled, if morals and right are intermingled. The moral aspect, invalid as it is in claims against others, decides however the course of legal negotiations as a motive. But the moral claim of Israel expressly raised in the case of the Federal Republic simply provides food for the disgusting reactions of German nationalists.

"German Jews and Germans, in the determination to clarify the sense of this crime of mass murder and not to excuse anything, rather to seize its historical situation and its consequences, have made the distinction: This crime against the Jews is not only a crime against humanity, but also a crime against mankind.

"Crimes against humanity are all the horrors committed by men against men since time immemorial. Crimes against mankind are however the implementations of the claim to decide over the right to exist of groups of human beings, who can be defined according to their type and origin. The execution of this crime could theoretically take place without horrors by means of a mild, hardly noticeable dying out of the group, though factually the opposite occurred with unimaginable horror.

"The individual state puts the murderer on trial, even if no one submits a charge. It is in the interest of the state, that no murders shall occur. In humanity itself, there has existed hitherto no institution for the murderers of whole groups of people, one which in the name of humanity and in the interest of humanity can make these murderers account for their crimes. The motives of murder, which are to be found in the criminal code manuals, just do not apply for these quite different cases of genocide. When such a crime had occurred for the first time in history, the situation demanded that it should be dealt with as such and that a legal judgement passed by an institution of humanity should be found, or at least conceived.

"But the concept of crime against humanity had never helped the Jews previously in the slightest. They had always had to depend upon themselves. I shall report a scene, where the provisionally Utopian character of the concept, 'Crimes against humanity', became apparent. In 1949, at a Berlin mass assembly, after a talk by a German-American Jewess, the discussion turned to the destruction of Dresden by English bombers and this was described as a parallel to the murder of the Jews. Her response was passionate. When day after day the trains were moving continuously taking the Jews to the gas chambers and no one did anything to stop the transports and the murders, then the destruction of cities such as Dresden were both a reply and a demand to intervene. The horrified listeners remained silent. But the speaker had been completely mistaken. Nothing was done by the Allies to save the Jews. Protest meetings in America against the massacre were of no avail. No leaflets whatsoever were dropped in showers over the German towns and cities telling the Germans about the mass murder of the Jews and indicating that as long as they stood idly by, the bombs would rain down upon their cities; that they were permitting a crime against the Jews, which was at the same time a crime against humanity. No reference was made to the fact that mankind wanted to do everything in its power to protect the Jews against the murderers and that it was obliged to do so. Everyone is a criminal who orders murder and has a part in its execution. Everyone is equally responsible who knows and sees and does not intervene. They were not told that they had to see to it that the trains should no longer be permitted to travel, that the extermination camps should no longer be allowed to exist. That they would be destroyed by bombs, whenever they were found. But, none of that happened. No one had then thought of the concept of crime against humanity. The expression, genocide, did not contain this concept. And it should not be forgotten: the Allied governments did not dare in front of their peoples to step in expressly in support of the Jews. This was prevented by anti-Semitism in the form of indifference towards the Jews and a fear of revealing all too pro-Jewish feelings. The Jews have discovered that when it is a question of their people as a whole, then they are dependent upon themselves alone.

"Three facts: the State of Israel, the holding together of world Jewry on a Biblical basis, the individual Jews, are not the same.

"Israel, a national state, has strengthened the self-consciousness of all Jews. A catastrophe for Israel would be a catastrophe for all Jews. Today, in the mundane world of politics, a blow against Jewry would have the same devastating effect as in bygone times the destruction of the temple. Everyone agrees about that. However, the manifestation of nationalism in Israel, does not encounter the same approval from Jews and Israelis alike.

"Israel isn't Jewry. This continues to embrace the overwhelming majority of Jews in the Diaspora. Jewry has established a mundane state in Israel, looking historically to Bar Kochbar and not to the prophets. The downfall of Israel would not mean the downfall of the Jews. Jewry has not placed its destiny on that one highly dangerous card.

"The individual Jews constitute a wonderful richness of personalities, a quite singularly large number of them from such a small people. But we are not talking about them. They are unimportant in the face of the course of things on a large scale. I should however, like to mention a small, disappearing group of such individuals, the German Jews. They are the closest to us Germans.

"What has occurred and is still occurring deep down in the minds of the individual German Jews, or as one used to say of the Jewish Germans, and with them will soon have passed away and be forgotten, is of no importance to the great course of history. Publicly, they play no role. The steam roller of history moves over them. In the face of eternity, however, the individuals mean perhaps more than history, which is in any case without meaning for human cognition.

"The German Jews react so differently to the Germans and the Germans to the German Jews that one can only see: there is no solution.

"The slow exclusion of the Jews, which finally ended in mass murder, was itself synonymous with a murder of the soul. The Jews were deprived of their homes, their origin, their fatherland, their real and recognized unity with the German spirit. Now, they are nowhere, at home they can find nowhere a world, which can replace their homeland and their origin. 'It is terrible to emigrate', is something which even the most successful Jew in another country can say. All that remains for him is an unsatisfiable yearning for the irreplaceable. He never stops being an emigrant. 'When my homeland is taken away from me, there is not other that I want; there is only one', said a Jew, who freely admitted his plight. German language, German spirit, German poetry, German music and German philosophy and German friends remained the foundations of his existence, whereas Germany had expelled him. His existence in the world is shattered.

"If he returns to Germany, he does not find it again, except in a few old friends, who have survived, and in the landscape. Directly in 1945, it was a terrible realization that most Germans were still indifferent to the Jews. Previously, the Jews had been deprived of their fatherland by force (if they emigrated in good time or were saved on German soil by a happy coincidence) and now the same applied through indifference. It was quite unbearable for a German Jew at that time, when he had the free choice of remaining in Germany. No transformation in the general attitude had set in there. Time and again, there were difficult situations and underhand conversations.

"Other German Jews seem to have found their new fatherland in Israel. But for many German Jews, Israel is only an emergency solution, which they find bearable, but is no replacement for what they have lost. They remain German, yet may not remain so. Perhaps, they themselves do not admit that. Only a few of the quite frank ones actually say it. Others say that they feel not the slightest nostalgia. For now they have their own ground. They no longer need Germany. It does not even interest them.

"Jews scarcely refer to loyalty, in the way that is often the case with the Germans. In substance, however, they can feel deep down that magnificent and painful loyalty, which never abandons their own roots and origin and identity. However, such loyalty has no public and no state significance.

"There is no general answer to the question as to whether Jews and Germans can talk to each other. It is just as difficult to talk to nationalist Jews as to German nationalists. A dialogue with close affinity can take place between individual Jews and individual Germans, each aware of his 'Jewishness' and his 'Germanness'. One ought to stop talking about the Jews and the Germans in general as collectives. Infertile nationalism, which is bad for peace and common sense and human existence, ought to disappear. Nowadays, a state has as much value as the amount of justice and political freedom it upholds for its citizens. National traditions are priceless, but non-political. In a true, political state, they are to be found as a compound.

"At the beginning, I said that the problems between Jews and Germans were unsolvable. I did not want to say that they were hopeless.

"Jewry has a continuous existence of three millenia. The question of Jews and Germans is only one wave in the great river of time. Everything in history has its end, even the phenomena, in which Jewry lived in a state society, in which culture as an effective factor was at one with it, without being completely absorbed by it. That is how it once was in Spain, that is how it was for one and a half centuries in Germany. But the end is not only the permanent effect of these great phenomena on the Occident, but also the changes which came about through the terrible experiences associated with failure.

"Nothing repeats itself in history. But it can also be encouraging. Not everything was quite in vain. What followed the downfall on each occasion, cannot be known by anyone in advance. It comes from the unfolding of the ethos of the peoples, who press for pure policy of state leadership through justice and freedom for the people; they will achieve implementation in unforeseeable situations and from inforeseeable statesmen, who at the same time will educate their peoples. It is also manifested in leaps and bounds by creations of belief, of poetry, of thinking, which come to men as inspirations.

"Therefore, our unfathomable basic attitude may hope for realities, which will indeed emerge in this world. No knowledge and no direct ambition will have such results. Hope is justified, when each of us in his situation does what he can with the highest principles here and now. I am one of those, who hopes that a new and quite unimaginably deep affinity will arise again between Jews and Germans, thus completing the assimilation of German Jews which only recently had so nearly succeeded."

Comments

Following the lectures, Joachim Prinz, chairman of the Conference of Presidents of American Jewish Organisations, spoke:

"I want to indicate certain premises which form the framework in which, as I believe, our conversation has to take place.

"1. A famous German philosopher wrote a book entitled 'Beyond Good and Evil'. Our discussion can only be fruitful if it takes place beyond love and hate. Neither love nor hate are at issue.

"2. The experience of the Hitler period, from 1933 to 1945, has become an integral part of the Jewish consciousness. I want to say clearly that the human condition of the Jew of 1966 cannot be understood lest it includes the experience of that time. It is deeply imbedded into the consciousness of those Jews who are part of Jewish history. Therefore I want to say clearly that a Jew who does not remember (that is a Jew who does forget what has happened to his people) cannot be considered a Jew. Such a Jew cannot be respected either as a human being or as a Jew. This memory is not merely one of the horrors of Auschwitz. I am talking about the period before Auschwitz. To use a Dostoyevskyan term, I call it the period of degradation and humiliation. It was the period of segregated Jewish schools, of the proclamation by the German Government of second-rate Jewish citizenship, of separate Jewish benches in the parks, of the exclusion of the Jews from society, of the exposure of the Jews to mockery and ridicule, not merely by the political leaders but by the German people itself. It was a time during which the Jew, who had lived in Germany for 1,600 years, was made an outcast and a pariah. This cannot and must not be forgotten, and no intellectual surgery is going to be able to extricate it from our minds, our bodies, our dreams and our nightmares.

"3. By the same token, in my opinion a German who does not remember what his own people did to the Jewish people does not command my respect. Nor should he be respected by the Germans. A German who does not remember, with genuine contrition and a profound sense of personal involvement and responsibility, has no right to any kind of consideration or respect. We will not nor can we talk to a German who does not remember, as we cannot and will not talk to a Jew who has forgotten.

"4. The Germans therefore must understand that the relationship between the Germans and the Jews of our generation can never be normalized. We can talk to each other, and indeed we must, but only for the purpose of clarifying each other's minds. But it must be understood that Germany, which was our home for so many centuries, is no longer that, nor can it ever be that. There are Jews who live in Germany today. The Jewish people has recognized the existence and the legitimate rights of the Jewish communities in Germany, but as a totality we shall not return to Germany, as we have not returned to Spain after 1492.

"5. It is very difficult to talk about an encounter of Jews and Germans if there are no Jews in Germany. It is fair to say that for all practical purposes there are no Jews in Germany today, because their number is so small and their spiritual influence so limited that the average German rarely meets a Jew. There are hundreds of German communities in which no single Jew exists. Therefore the image of the Jew, both physically and spiritually, has disappeared for Germany and it will remain so for a long time, certainly as long as our generation lives and probably much longer.

"It is important that we examine the problem of a possible return of Jews to Germany with all sincerity. I have had two such discussions. One took place during the war, with my old friend the famous theologian, the late Paul Tillich. He said in a public debate with me that the Jews ought to return to Germany, but he qualified his statement by saying that there should be a limited number of Jews to return to Germany. The Germans, he claimed, need the Jews because they provide the 'salt and pepper' which the German people lack. Such a statement was repeated by Dr. Rainer Barzel during his presence in New York. He also complained that the Germans miss the Jews sorely, because they had provided the sharpness of mind and an attitude of criticism badly needed in the political and literary life of Germany. To them I said that for my people I refuse to serve as condiment for the German nation. It is too bad for the Germans that they cannot produce the salt and pepper which they evidently need. If they cannot do without, I want to be clear in saying that there will be no Jews in Germany who will provide it. I consider this an undignified function for the Jewish people, far beneath its dignity, and we are not going to be the intellectual hand-maiden of the German people.

"6. The dialogue between Germans and Jews is possible. It is even necessary. But it will remain a dialogue. It will lead to no concrete consequences either, within the necessary establishment of an attitude of mutual respect. While I repeat that a conversation between the German people and the Jewish people is both necessary and possible, the only area in which such a dialogue can lead to any concrete results is the relationship between Germany and Israel. I emphasize the term 'concrete'. For between two nations, each of which is sovereign, and between two governments, the relationship must be different than that between a people scattered over the globe of the earth and the German people, residing in its own country. In the relationship between Germany and Israel, the Jew now living in his own country and thus constituting a radically new phenomenon, the Jew freed from the shackles of ghetto and galut, will meet the German who lives in the post-Hitler period and will hopefully develop into a new type of German.

"I consider it important that we analyze and clarify the place of German restitution and indemnification in their proper historic context and particularly in terms of the topic which we are discussing here. I am not one of those who consider the whole problem a moral question. We have long decided that those who have murdered us should not also inherit, according to the biblical admonition. But it has blurred the issue. I believe that Israel and the Jewish people were entitled to the money that was paid. But I also believe that it was much more for the sake of the Germans that the payments should have been made. If I were a German, I would shudder to think what would have happened to the soul of the German people if the Germans would not have made the attempt to 'make good', where in fact every monetary indemnification must remain a feeble response to the crime of murder. I know that there are Germans who say, and say clearly and officially, that no money can pay for a life lost. But that, I am afraid, is no longer the accepted and deeply acknowledged view of a majority of the German people. But the Germans cannot have it both ways. They cannot say, on the one hand, that money cannot really make restitution for the loss of millions of human beings, and at the same time emphasize again and again how much they have done for the Jewish people. I do not minimize the effect of the German reparations, both for the State of Israel, thousands of Jewish individuals and Jewish life itself. But nobody has the right to be satisfied with what has been done, for not a single murdered life has been revived and resurrected by the billions of dollars which have been paid.

"I believe this to be of greater importance for the German people than for the Jews. Any German who really believes that the payment of money to the Jewish people constitutes a proper and sufficient response to the horrors of Auschwitz and Bergen-Belsen does not have my respect. He does not understand the problem. He has no concept of the moral issue which is one for the German people. He does not understand that the miracle of a new Germany cannot possibly consist of mere prosperity, but that a moral renewal and intellectual honesty are the only acceptable symbols of a new Germany. A relationship of decency and honesty which should exist between Germans and Jews will be for ever prevented if this is not clearly understood by the German people and if those in authority do not make a serious attempt of teaching their own people what is the only real lesson of the past.

"7. It is for all these reasons that the relationship between Germany and Israel cannot be normal and must not be normal, and whatever political exigencies and practical considerations there may be, the principle of a unique relationship must not be relinquished. If this is done, the basis even for a discussion and for a collective dialogue is totally removed."

Next, the Secretary General of the Central Council of the Jews in Germany, Hendrik van Dam, took the floor:

"The relationship between Germans and Jews cannot be discussed without dealing with the fact that a Jewish community in Germany has existed for nearly 2,000 years.

"In 1933, the number of Jews living in the German Reich was about 540,000. The German Reich at that time included not only the present Federal Republic and the G.D.R. but also Silesia, which included the traditionally-important community at Breslau and others in Upper Silesia.

"The brutal persecution of the Jews under the Third Reich resulted in the reduction of the Jewish population of Germany to a mere fraction of its original size.

"After the end of the Second World War and the collapse of the National Socialist regime, there were in Berlin and the area which afterwards became the Federal Republic almost 200,000 Jews. This estimate is based on figures of 1946. The composition of this Jewish population was, however, very different from that of the Jews, who had been living there when the persecution commenced. Those who survived in Germany at the end of the war were mainly Jews, who had been interned in concentration camps and who had been saved at the very last moment by the Allied armies, American, British and particulary Russian—when they opened the gates of the concentration camps and liberated the victims. By far the greater number of these Jews had come from the East—from Poland, Russia, Hungary, Rumania and elsewhere. They also included a number of German Jews, though the percentage of these was relatively small. In the years immediately following the war, large numbers of emigrants streamed into Western Germany—people who saw no possibility of settling down again in their countries of origin, such as Poland. These persons, having searched in vain for their relations or dependents, had no desire to remain in the country where they had first met with persecution. In the succeeding years up to 1949 all efforts were concentrated on the provision of opportunities for emigration for any Jews who were willing.

"The pressure which came from this source was one of the factors responsible for the foundation of the State of Israel, because Great Britain (the mandatory power) was not in a position to allow unrestricted immigration into this area. It can therefore be stated, that the years 1945 to 1948, roughly up to the date when the Federal Republic was created, were marked by the emigration of Jews from Germany. It can be said that by 1949 emigration had practically come to an end and that the period that followed was one of consolidation. In subsequent years, until about 1960, the number of Jews who returned to Germany was greater than those who left it. The Jewish communities in the Federal Republic and West Berlin now have about 26,000 registered members.

"In the Federal Republic there are more than 70 Jewish communities. The Jewish community of West Berlin has about 6,000 members, Frankfort-on-Main and Munich about 4,000 each, Hamburg 1,500, Cologne 1,250 and Düsseldorf 1,500. The remaining Jews are distributed amongst various other communities, which include those at Stuttgart, Karlsruhe, Essen, Nuremberg and Fuerth, Regensburg, Aachen, Bremen, Hanover and Dortmund. Since 1945 rabbis and teachers have been active amongst the Jewish communities. At the present time there are rabbis in Frankfort-on-Main, Stuttgart, Düsseldorf, Dortmund, Cologne, Hamburg, Berlin, Regensburg, Muenster, Mannheim, Munich and Aachen. The rabbis are associated in a Conference of Rabbis which has its headquarters in Frankfurt-on-Main. There are at present about 50 teachers of Jewish religion and history in the Federal Republic and Berlin.

In East Berlin a rabbi from Hungary holds office for East Berlin and all East Germany (GDR). This rabbi also looks after the large Jewish cemetery at Berlin-Weissensee. In many Jewish communities cantors are employed; some of them also act as teachers and as secretaries of the communities. There is a Jewish University Extension School in Berlin and Jewish Professors deliver lectures at various universities.

"The age distribution has changed in the course of time. At one time the average age was 59, now it has fallen to about 45.5. This reduction is due partly to the immigration of families with young children and partly to births in Germany. There are various

Jewish Youth Centres, for instance in Berlin, Duesseldorf, Cologne, Frankfort-on-Main and Munich. The Jewish Communities are anxious to bring up their children in the Jewish tradition. The average age of the community, even at 45.5, is undoubtedly too high. Its social and economic structure was also completely changed as compared with former times. It is true that, thanks to the effects of restitution, indemnification and other factors, the number of Jews who are in want has been reduced.

At the present time it is no longer possible to say that the Jews in Germany are on the average more prosperous than the Germans as a whole. There are, of course, a number of Jews who have become prosperous, but the Jews as a whole have no outstanding financial influence in Germany, such as they had formerly.

There are certain private banks which are under Jewish influence, but Jews no longer play any part in the control of the leading banks, even though some of them, such as the Deutsche Bank, the Dresdner Bank and the Berliner Handelsgesellschaft were originally founded by Jews.

"There are no well known Jewish industrialists. In the post-war period Jews achieved greater success in the film industry, although this is now suffering from the competition of television. Jews no longer play the important part in the P. C. which they once did, although there are a few Jewish editors.

"The Jewish community has in effect derived only an indirect advantage from the economic miracle or the trade boom, in the sense that, without it, it would not have been possible for Germany to pay reparations to the Jews. Jewish doctors have always been very successful and still enjoy great popularity. Some of them developed a practice, the size of which can be described as sensational, and which puts many of the best-known specialists in the shade. There are also a number of higher officials, particularly judges, who have had highly successful careers in post-war Germany. One of the most outstanding of them was the late Dr. Rudolf Katz, son of a cantor, who was Vice-President of the Federal Constitutional Court, the highest of all German court. Various judges in Federal courts and Senate Presidents of Supreme Land Courts are also Jews. The only Jewish Minister holding office at the present time is Dr. Herbert Weichmann, who is First Mayor i.e. Prime Minister of the Land Hamburg, and a member of the Bundestag; for instance, the late Jacob Altmeier (who interested himself particularly in Jewish questions) and Frau Jeanette Wolff (who is deputy chairman of the board of directors of the Central Board of Jews in Germany). It has to be noted, that for the first time in German history a Trade Union leader of Jewish origin, Ludwig Rosenberg, who lived in England as a refugee from Nazi oppression, has been elected as president of the Federation of Trade Unions. There are a number of Jewish professors at the German universities and famous actors like Fritz Kortner, Ernst Deutsch, and others appear on the stage or produce plays.

"Jewish members of the Laender parliaments include one in North Rhine-Westphalia who belongs to the board of directors at the Central Council, and one in the Bavarian Senate.

"It is, however, not possible to turn back the clock. For these and other reasons, the Central Council of Jews in Germany has never encouraged people to return there.

"It is only logical that the existence of a Jewish community in Germany should be a matter of special importance for German democracy. The former American High Commissioner, John McCloy was quite right when he remarked that the attitude of the Germans to their Jewish fellowcitizens was the criterion which showed whether they had turned their backs on the past. It may not be a matter of great importance whether Jews will still be living in Germany in fifty years' time, but their presence there in the period following the collapse of the Nazi regime, is an important factor.

"The question arises whether the Jewish community should liquidate itself, and thereby ensure the success of Nazi efforts to make Germany 'free of Jews'. Undoubtedly Jewish public opinion—and perhaps non-Jewish opinion—outside Germany has been opposed to the re-establishment of Jewish communities in Germany. The line of argument, which was inspired by history, was that after all that had happened Jews should not enter into any contacts with Germans, or at least that no Jewish communities should be established on German soil.

"In this connection reference was made to the fact that after the Jews had been expelled from Spain by the Inquisition, the Spanish Empire collapsed. Theories of this sort cannot be proved or disproved, but there is something to be said for the view that it would be a great pity to add to the 'curtains' which divide mankind—the Iron Curtain in Europe and the Bamboo Curtain in East Asia—by establishing yet another dividing line. It is surely better to pull down existing walls than to erect new ones.

"History has shown that the Jews are not interested in the isolation of peoples. The world can hardly afford any attempt to isolate the German nation. In 1952 Israel and the Jewish American organisations resolved to enter into negotiations with the Federal Republic on the subject of collective reparations, and the Federal Republic agreed to make such reparations to the State of Israel. Since that date there has been marked change of opinion. During the last ten years, a great number of Jews have visited the German Federal Republic and many Germans have been invited to visit Israel. In view of these developments it would be inconsistent to adopt a negative attitude with regard to the Jewish community in Germany.

"So far as the future of the Jewish community is concerned, it is not easy to see what will happen. The fact that the average age of the community is rather high and there is a tendency for many of the younger Jews to go abroad, suggests that there is likely to be a substantial reduction in numbers in the course of the next ten years. It is, however, quite easy to be mistaken in making forecasts of this sort, as is shown by the example of France, where the population increased instead of decreasing as expected. The situation of the millions of Jews behind the Iron Curtain and of Jews elsewhere suggests that it is by no means impossible that there will be a new wave of immigration into Germany. The Jewish authorities in Germany—as distinct from Adolf Arndt, the former Berlin Senator for Culture, and other politicians—do not encourage any such tendency. In recent years there has been an influx from certain countries into the Jewish community in Germany. The only thing that is important is that Jews should be able to live in Germany as Jews. This is not only a matter of importance to the Jewish community but it is also in accordance with the principles of a modern state based on the rule of law.

"The recent legislation of 1964 and 1965 has once again made restitution a topical subject of discussion, which in turn contributes to the revival of ever-present anti-Semitic tension. Although, as a result of the war, the Federal Republic has to bear great financial burdens, which did not, however, endanger the general prosperity, it is the compensation due, as a matter of course, for the wrong done by the State which above all causes public controversy and also played its part in many election speeches.

"Diplomatic relations with the State of Israel were, however, hardly ever mentioned during the elections and are generally accepted as an accomplished fact. An unusual amount of attention is paid to the Israel ambassador. The explanation for this lies not only in his being the first Israeli ambassador in Germany, but also in the fact that German public opinion, published and unpublished, is particulary sensitive, in both a positive and a negative way, towards the complex Jewish question.

"We may safely say that in the last few years anti-Semitism has tended to increase rather than to decline. Extremist trends in this field would, however, only assume major importance if the financial crisis were to become more acute and to result in a severe economic setback. We must, however, bear in mind the possibility of the National Democrats, a radical party of the Right, securing seats in the Laender parliaments, even though at the last election they did not succeed in sending a single deputy to the Bundestag.

"The political situation in the Federal Republic of Germany has not exactly improved since then.

"The question is often raised, whether it is psychologically possible for Jews to live in a German environment. The mind of every Jew in Germany is without doubt influenced by three events in history: the ruthless persecution of Jews by the Nazi regime, the establishment of the State of Israel—where not only a new State, but also a new image of the Jew of the twentieth century was created, and the reorganisation, often in opposition to world opinion, of Jewish communities in Germany. From these facts there is no escape for this group of people, because they are deeply rooted in its consciousness.

"The first fact demands a continual watch for any manifestation of a Nazi revival, and justifies a critical appraisal of current events. The second affords psychological and moral support of Israel, disproves numerous prejudices, and is a factor determining a positive attitude. The third fact has invalidated the National Socialist aim of making Germany free from Jews (Judenrein) and of destroying the Jewish position in Europe for ever."

Nahum Goldmann's closing speech

"I am very sorry that we cannot continue the discussion, nor can I give the floor to the various delegates who wanted to ask questions to which Dr. Gerstenmaier would have been very glad to answer. He is the one who is probably the least tired among us, but we cannot continue because of the tiredness of the audience. So allow me in a few minutes to try and sum up the discussion.

"Before I try to sum up, I only want to bring to your notice that both Chancellor Erhard and the leaders of the Social Democratic Party—Brandt, Erler and Wehner—have sent messages to this meeting which will be distributed to the delegates and which will be given to the press. I want to use this opportunity to express my deep appreciation of what the Social Democratic party has done in all these fourteen years, taking a consistent positive position, which has been of the greatest help in our sometimes difficult negotiations with the German authorities. In saying this, I do not want to diminish in any way the merits of the leaders of the majority parties, especially of Federal Chancellor Dr. Adenauer, without whose decisive support the whole agreement of Luxembourg would have been impossible. But, as the opposition sometimes feels that its achievements have not been fully appreciated, I feel it my duty to stress their great contribution to the legislation on indemnification and restitution. The attitude of the Social Democrats has had the invaluable result that most of the legislation was passed by unanimity or with an overwhelming majority.

"Now, ladies and gentlemen, I hope you will feel like me that, despite the risk and the unusual matter, it was worthwhile to have had this dicussion. It was not only important for us, it may have been more important even for the German people. You have heard here two great intellectual and moral leaders of the German people take a position which I would advise every German to take note of and study. Though our approaches to the future development of German-Jewish relations may differ—some may be more optimistic, others more pessimistic—I think we all will agree that it will be a long process, which requires patience and good-will, but that it is a problem which has to be tackled by both peoples who have to live in this world of the twentieth century. But I want to say something more, and this is my last remark.

"The initiative for such talks, to deal with the problem, to do something about it, has to come primarily from the German people. They are at the origin of the tragedy which created the abyss of which Dr. Gerstenmaier spoke and which all the other speakers mentioned and, in order to find bridges of understanding, if not of love then of mutual respect, as Joachim Prinz used the term, it will be necessary that the Germans take more and more the initiative. I, who am coming quite often to Germany, have the feeling that large parts of the German people are beginning to get tired of the whole problem. I am not referring, in saying this, particularly to the small neo-Nazi groups. I think their importance is often exaggerated, though it is a sacred task of the German people to watch and control them, as Dr. Gerstenmaier said. The German people should understand that Jews are very sensitive to such new efforts to revive anti-Semitic ideologies in Germany, especially as most of us once underestimated Hitler too and regarded the Nazi movement in its early years as of no great importance. But what I am worried about today is not so much these new relatively small neo-Nazi parties, but what is more dangerous and would be more harmful is this mood of larger groups in Germany, of trying to finish the process of paying indemnification, tired of continuing the process of warcrime trials, tired of being reminded by Jewish and German leaders, as is being done tonight, of what happened in the Nazi period. This tiredness could become a great calamity. The German people have to understand that, at least this generation of Germans and certainly the adult generation which has lived and gone through the Nazi period, has the primary moral and intellectual duty to find ways how to change the situation, to find methods of bridging the abyss. I remember that, when I started my first talks with Chancellor Adenauer, he agreed that there should be two kinds of reparations or indemnifications, one financial and one moral, educational, intellectual. And only a few months ago, in a talk with Dr. Adenauer, he said, 'We have only done or tried to do our duty in the field of material indemnification, but I am not very happy yet with what we have done in the field of moral indemnification'. And there are few Germans who understand this duty as well as he. This applies to schools, to education, to presenting the Nazi period and the crimes against the Jews to the young German generation, which may not know about it or may not want to know about it; this applies to the resistance against any attempts of new anti-Semitic and neo-Nazi movements in Germany; this applies to the necessity to give the conviction to the world and to us, that, as Dr. Gerstenmaier believes and I hope that this optimism and belief is justified, that there is a new spirit developing in Germany, which will really make impossible, once and forever, any renewal or serious attempt of renewal of this cursed Nazi period.

"This is something on which I am sure all of us, Jews and Germans who participated in the debate, will fully agree too. I hope that this debate will not be the end but the beginning of a number of other debates, in which we will try to air and clear up and analyse these very difficult problems with all their tragic, emotional background. From this tribune here we have the right to tell the German people: it is your primary duty to try to find ways to bridge the abyss and to re-establish and create new conditions for these two peoples, who are bound to live together in one world and are bound to find methods of dealing with problems common to both of them.

"With these remarks I want to thank you for your patience, I thank the speakers for whom it was not easy to come—some of them had to change or interrupt their vacation in order to come here—and it required for Jews and for Germans a certain courage to participate in this debate. I know that Dr. Gerstenmaier was criticized already in some of the nationalistic German press, he will probably be still more criticized after his speech today, I am sure that he knows it and won't mind it too much. So I thank all the speakers who participated in the debate. I thank you for your patience and for the disciplined and dignified way in which this debate was held."

After the Jewish World Congress in Brussels

When Nahum Goldmann returned to Jerusalem after the Jewish World Congress he was exposed to severe criticism from leftist and rightist groups in Israel because of the discussion in Brussels. The speeches given at the Congress were being discussed throughout the entire world; newspapers with the texts of the speeches and reports were in demand everywhere.

Conversation with Nahum Goldmann

In October 1966 Nahum Goldmann was again staying in the Federal Republic. In a conversation that took place in Frankfurt he reported to the editor of this book on the period when his first official conversations with Germans were taking place in 1950/51 and pointed out the connection between this and what was said in Brussels. The following is the text of the interview:

Question: "When you now assess the situation as it was at that time, what would you say about the German-Jewish conversation?"

Answer: "I think that in view of all the difficulties that were encountered and that were unavoidable and that are still in existence and will remain so for some time, I am bound to say that in the years that have passed since my first conversation with Dr. Adenauer in London we have made quite considerable progress. Dr. Adenauer himself once said to me: 'You know, Herr Goldmann, when I come to think that in 1951 you came in secretly through a side door of Claridge's Hotel because no one was to know about it and we had both arranged to deny that you had visited me if anyone got to know—when I now see how you have arranged this banquet in my honour, then I am bound to say that we really have made great progress in the years since then.' And he was certainly right about that. I believe that the conversation in Brussels is a further step in this direction and is bound, sooner or later to lead to a situation of normal coexistence between the two peoples. The difficulties or perhaps the opposition that has developed at the idea of this symposium which includes prominent Germans is understandable and as I have so often said, I should be ashamed if I were a Jew and if opposition had not been made—both to my suggestion at that time—namely that we should negotiate direct with the German Federal Republic—and to the idea of the symposium in Brussels. The really important thing is that, despite all the emotional difficulties and misgivings, the majority, not only of the officials of the Jewish World Congress but, as I believe (since it is a democratic plenary organization representing the Jewish people), the majority of the Jewish people have decided in favour of this discussion. I think that the so peaceful, dignified and impressive progress of the evening has shown that the risk inherent in undertakings of this kind was not so great after all. The idea of having this symposium is quite definitely useful and justified by the results. As I said recently in a Press Conference in Berlin we must have a great deal of patience in this matter and, above all, it is up to the Germans to have patience as well and not to think that the conduct of what was, on the whole, quite a generous indemnity legislation, the recognition of Israel, the economic aid that is being given to Israel—that all these things mean that the whole problem is already solved. In view of the enormity of the crime that has been committed it is quite natural that this generation of Jews who have not only lived through this tragedy and personally experienced these crimes—this generation of which there are still hundreds of thousands who were saved from the concentration camps—will have difficulty in continuing to follow this path of coexistence. It would be the worst thing possible if it were to be the Germans, of all people, who, after all, bear the responsibility for these crimes that were now to lose patience. Such are the psychological and moral processes that are taking place. The problems they raise cannot be solved overnight by resolutions and the decisions of congresses or by conferences. The fact that the World Congress has recognized the existence of the Jewish community in Germany—the Zionist World Organization has done the same thing (in both organizations the Central Council of Jews in Germany plays a part commensurate with its importance)— world Jewry has shown that it is prepared to develop and strengthen these contacts not only with the German Jews but with the German people and with the German Federal Republic. No one knows how long this process will take; we shall have setbacks and difficulties again and again; on occasion, we shall encounter protest. But that is something that we must regard as an almost unavoidable hazard and it goes without saying that we must be prepared to take the rough with the smooth. We must have mutual understanding for each other's difficulties and we must have the will to persevere on both sides, no matter how long the process may last. After the experiences of these 15 or 16 years, and particularly after the experience of the Brussels World Congress, I do not doubt for a moment that further progress will be made."

Question: "Dr. Goldmann, Brussels was a step forward. You have seen in Berlin how Axel Springer made that great donation for Jerusalem. This was a cultural event and possibly the beginning of a cultural link between our two peoples, such as we have only seen in individual cases up to now. Do you believe that with Brussels and these meetings or similar occasions we are now gradually opening up the way to closer cultural contacts and that closer ties between our peoples will be the result?"

Answer: "Cultural relations are, of course, always somewhat more delicate and difficult than purely economic, financial or formal diplomatic relations. But here again I am not pessimistic. I believe above all that it will certainly be possible to extend and intensify the relations between the younger generations—both in Israel and in Germany—which, after all, were not immediately concerned in the tragedy. I have been particularly happy to note that recently a man such as the present Prime Minister of Israel has adopted the same attitude and has declared himself in favour of promoting relations with German youth. Here again, as I have already pointed out, we must not be shocked or disappointed if we receive some setbacks; we may find that there are some youth groups in Israel who hesitate or even here and there refuse to resume relations altogether. Youth is always rather more extreme in its reactions and it is quite right, indeed, that it should be so. But I am convinced that if the necessary energy is put into this matter from the German side, influential sections of Israel opinion and, indeed, influential sections of at least a large proportion of opinion among the youth in Israel, will be ready to resume and increase contacts of this kind, provided, of course, that they are made and fostered with the necessary tact and with the necessary patience."

Question: "Dr. Goldmann, I believe that it would be relatively easy with youth, despite the emotions of which youth is capable. But do you not think that there is a certain difference between the present-day statement and those that were once made by Ben Gurion—when he said, for instance: 'The German people of today can no longer be compared with the people of the Hitler days'. When I say that, I mean—do you not believe that we have today in our generation, the mid-way generation between 40 and 50, a large number of people who, just like the young people, want to co-operate without being prejudiced—and have a sort of avant-garde attitude to the whole mass of problems connected with German-Jewish relations—and would be prepared to help but whose help would perhaps be impeded if we were to concentrate on German youth alone in our efforts?"

Answer: "I did not think that the contacts should be made only between representatives of youth in Israel and youth in Germany: Indeed, the fact that we placed this matter on the agenda in Brussels proves what I say. The Jewish World Congress is not a youth organization. There are perhaps five to ten per cent of the delegates appearing as youth representatives at the World Congress. On the Jewish side, as I said before, it is, indeed, the grown-up generation that has experienced the tragedy personally and directly, in contrast to many young people who were not born until the immediate time of the tragedy was past or were so very young that they were unconscious of it. On the other hand, of course, relations between the grown-up generations are rather more difficult because there are hundreds of thousands of them who, for their own part, will refuse to have anything to do with such contacts—a thing that I can well understand. I have already said in Israel that when a man like Herr Zuckermann, who was one of the fighters in the Warsaw ghetto, rejects the idea of coexistence with the German people and will have nothing to do with the idea of friendly and fruitful relations I understand this perfectly and I take off my hat to him. The achievements under the duress of circumstances, the heroism that they have shown has given them the right to adopt this point of view, and I acknowledge that right, even though in the light of cold reason I cannot approve of it. I believe that if the Jewish people were to accept *in toto* it would be a bad thing, seen from the purely Jewish point of view. Of course, the fact must always be taken into account that there are these people among us and as a result, the contacts between the grown-ups will perhaps be rather more difficult but I believe that there are large sections of this part of the population that would be willing. I was very interested to note that, after the attacks made on me subsequent to the Jewish World Congress in Brussels, I received, in Israel, dozens of letters—I could almost say hundreds—and telegrams accepting the point of view that I represented; this moved me very deeply—particularly the fact that some of them were from people that had previously been in concentration camps."

The death of Konrad Adenauer

When on April 19th, 1967 at noon the flags in Bonn came down to half mast to announce the death of Konrad Adenauer it immediately became clear that this was a great bereavement for Israel as well as for Jewish communities throughout the entire world. In the days preceding the funeral this feeling was expressed in many expressions of sympathy, both spoken and written, and in visits of mourners. The funeral obsequies came at the beginning of the feast of Pessach which set a limit to travelling for Jewish politicians. It was therefore a great moment when Nahum Goldmann, coming from New York on Sunday, April 23rd, appeared, shortly before four o'clock in the afternoon, at the Palais Schaumburg and passed in front of the coffin. He was alone except for his closest colleague in the Jewish Claims Conference in Bonn, Ernest Katzenstein. And it was in this way that Nahum Goldmann took leave of the man with whom he had had so many conversations and dealings on the question of German-Jewish reconciliation. Directly after this short minute of commemoration Goldmann flew straight back to New York again.

For the funeral ceremony itself a delegation had arrived from Israel such as no German had ever expected. Israel's grand old man, David Ben Gurion, came, together with Israel's Foreign Minister Abba Eban and Felix Shinnar who, as Head of the Israeli Mission was to a considerable extent responsible for the Luxembourg Agreement.

At the time when Ambassador Pauls was spending his first few days in Israel the editor of this book met Ben Gurion at his Tel Aviv home for a private conversation. Ben Gurion asked after Konrad Adenauer's health and sent his regards and said that he must certainly come back soon. I countered by asking if he would not come to Germany some time, to that Germany of which he had said that it was a new Germany, not to be compared with the Germany of Hitler's day. No, he said, he did not want to come to Germany. He was in Germany in 1946 in Jewish refugee camps, he had seen the concentration camps and he could not forget all that he had seen there.

I then asked whether he would come if Adenauer invited him, when he could travel from Rhöndorf to youth camps, which would mean that he could travel in Germany without "making a trip to Germany as such", so to speak. Yes, then, he said, he would come; if Konrad Adenauer "were to call for his presence", then he would.

Ben Gurion came; he had kept his word. According to the rules of precedence this man sat among the many foreign ministers in one of the first rows at the great state ceremony in the large assembly hall of the Bundestag. On the right and left of the Federal President in the very first row were President Johnson and President de Gaulle. It must have been a great event for the journalists that these two statesmen of the Western world had come to Bonn at an hour like this; but actually the journalists' real attention was for Ben Gurion and Abba Eban. This was made clear in many newspaper reports and there was criticism of the fact that Konrad Adenauer's efforts for reconciliation with the Jewish people were not mentioned in the commemorative addresses. This was not due to any ill will, as was found out later in many conversations that took place after this eventful day. One speaker had left it to the other to bring up this point and in the crowded timetable of the ceremonies the necessary co-ordination had not been properly carried out. Federal President Lübke wanted to leave the subject to President of the Bundestag Gerstenmaier, who, only eight short months ago in Brussels, had spoken at the Jewish World Congress. Gerstenmaier did not want to take this political subject out of the hands of the Chancellor and so it came about that it was Cardinal Frings at the requiem mass in Cologne Cathedral who paid tribute to the work that Adenauer had done to bring about a reconciliation with the Jewish people. Perhaps after all, that was the best place to commemorate these activities because as far as Adenauer was concerned the reconciliation with the Jewish people had always been a matter of moral reponsibility, to be later translated into political activity.

On the day after the funeral, Ben Gurion met Chancellor Kurt Georg Kiesinger in the Palais Schaumburg. The Chancellor invited his Israeli guest to sit down in the chair which had always previously been occupied by Konrad Adenauer, saying that it was fitting for him, the one who had shown so much trust in the Germans, to occupy this place.

At that time Israel's Foreign Minister Abba Eban conferred with the Federal Minister of Foreign Affairs, Willy Brandt; the conversation concerned the grave problems of Israel and its entry into the EEC as an associate member; the Foreign Minister also reiterated what had been made clear in many statements by the Federal Government: "The Federal Republic of Germany will support Israel's proposal in European circles and groups where it is discussed."

Among the numerous telegrams and messages of condolence from all over the world there were also messages of condolence and tributes to Konrad Adenauer from Jewish circles. Here are one or two examples typical of the many that came in those days from Jewish sources:

The Israeli Prime Minister Levi Eshkol sent the following telegram of condolence to Federal Chancellor Kiesinger:

"The passing of Konrad Adenauer deprives the world of a statesman, whose work exerted a profound influence on Europe and post-war Germany. He regarded the recognition of the crimes committed by Nazi Germany against the Jewish people and the acceptance by the German people of responsibility for the holocaust as one of the most important of his objectives in life. He laboured without respite towards this end. He saw in the State of Israel a noble expression of the aspirations of the Jewish people, and for him, the re-establishment of Israel on native soil was the surest guarantee of its continued existence."

The Israeli ambassador in the Federal Republic of Germany, Asher Ben Natan, said on the occasion of the death of Konrad Adenauer:

"Konrad Adenauer will go down in the history of mankind as one of the greatest statesmen of our time, because he led his country out of the chaos of tyranny into the camp of democracy. His courage, foresight and his high humanitarian standard established the moral conditions, which made possible a positive dialogue between the Federal Republic and Israel."

A handwritten letter from the ambassador to Konrad Adenauer junior in Rhöndorf ends with the sentence:

"The trees in the Adenauer Wood in Israel have taken root and will grow and flourish. May they be the symbol of Konrad Adenauer's legacy."

Before his departure by air to Bonn, where he laid a wreath on Konrad Adenauer's coffin, Nahum Goldmann said the following in New York:

"In Chancellor Dr. Adenauer, the Jewish people and Israel have lost one of their great friends. In the 16 years that I have known him and during which I met him very frequently, he has proved again and again his inflexible determination to make good as far as possible—at least on the material plane—crimes committed by the National Socialists against the Jews; this attitude he maintained in the face of much opposition. The unique work of indemnification and restoration of property for the victims of National Socialism, that found its reflection in the Luxembourg Agreement and a large number of German laws, would not have been possible to achieve in its present form without his unwavering pertinacity and good will.

"I have met a large number of the leading statesmen of my generation. I considered Konrad Adenauer one of the greatest figures of the post-war era, indeed, as a man uniting in one person admirable human qualities and remarkable political and statesmanlike talent.

"The Jewish people will never forget his attitude and his achievements in the work of indemnification for the crimes of National Socialism and also his most effective cooperation and support in many other most important of the problems arising in connection with Israel and the Jewish people. His memory will always be held in reverence by this and future generations."

The Central Council of the Jews in Germany sent a telegram of condolence to the President of the German Bundestag, Eugen Gerstenmaier:

"The Central Council of Jews in Germany wishes to express to you and the German Bundestag their most sincere condolences on the sad occasion of the loss of that most irreplaceable of delegates, the retired Federal Chancellor Dr. Konrad Adenauer. His death was a source of great shock and deep sorrow to us. The eminent German and European statesman, Konrad Adenauer, had great contempt for the National-Socialist régime of injustice and offered all possible resistance to it at every opportunity. After the collapse of this régime he played an active part in the reconstruction of an economic and independent and powerful democratic constitutional state. He was fully conscious of the difficulties of his mission—namely, to restore the misused German honour—not merely the political honour but, in particular, the moral and ethical honour of Germany. In this connection, it was a matter of great importance to him to restore the healthy relationships that once existed between Germany and the Jewish community in the Federal Republic and also to ensure the best of relations with Israel. He always had a ready ear for the suggestions of the Central Council of Jews in Germany because the existence of the Jewish community in Germany seemed to him to be a most important social and political factor in the life of the country. The re-establishment of the rights of the community in this country was to him a logical consequence of the existence of a constitutional state. The achievements of Adenauer are ineradicably engraved in the annals of history. The unforgettable factors in the life and work of Adenauer are not merely his achievements as a statesman but his achievements as a personality."

The development of cultural relations

Increasing cooperation in the sphere of science

"The cultural relations between the Federal Republic of Germany and Israel have developed very considerably during the last few years but I should like to emphasize that they have, in fact, been in existence for quite a number of years."

These words were spoken in May 1966 by the Head of the State and University Library of Jerusalem, Prof. Woermann, some-time Head of the Berlin Municipal Libraries.

"As far back as the year 1952 we had made a start on preliminary talks with German libraries and with the Stock Exchange of Publishers and Booksellers. To me it seems a matter of the utmost importance for us in Israel to have an ever-increasing supply of German books and periodicals. The students can in any case obtain a much better and more genuine idea of life in Germany and of its cultural and spiritual values if they, themselves can make use of these books in the libraries—and particularly in our library, which is at the same time a national and university library. I would be very happy to see these contacts duly fostered. I am sure that the necessary good will is present on both sides."

This is only one of the spheres in which cultural relations have developed. Many contacts have been established with the Federal Republic by Israeli artists, scientists, authors and journalists who lecture at German universities, in evening classes, at various cultural events and community organizations.

Collaboration with the Weizmann Institute and Israeli scientists

But in addition to all these contacts, which are supplemented by articles in newspapers and periodicals, in TV broadcasts and in radio reports, there is close collaboration between German science institutes and Israeli institutes—particularly the Weizmann Institute in Rehovot in Israel. Indeed, quite a number of years ago, a mixed German-Israeli commission was formed under the chairmanship of the Heidelberg professor of nuclear physics, Professor Wolfgang Gentner. This commission lays down the schedules of scientific operations in its annual meetings, schedules which apply particularly to joint operations carried out by the Max-Planck Institute in the Federal Republic and the various research groups of the Weizmann Institute in Israel. Since 1960 six different funds have been allowed for this research work in the budget of the German Ministry of Scientific Research. These amounts are shared out as follows:

1960	General expenses of the Institute	3.0 million DM
1961—63	Research programme in molecular biology	3.0 million DM
1962/63	Purchase and installation of a 10 Megavolt tandem particle accelerator	5.9 million DM
1964	Specified medical and biological research projects	3.5 million DM
1965	Research as above	3.7 million DM
1965/66	Extension of the biological and medical departments of the Ullmann Institute	2.5 million DM
1966	Research as above	4,0 million DM
	Total	25.6 million DM

Four million DM have been earmarked in the 1967 budget of the Federal Ministry of Scientific Research for research projects in medicine and biology at the Weizmann Institute. The same amount has been noted for the continuation of the individual research projects for 1968.

In addition to these grants from the Federal budget there is a programme of the Volkswagen Foundation. The following note appears in the annual report of the Volkswagen Foundation for 1963:

"In addition, in October 1963, the Volkswagenwerk Foundation made available a grant of 2 million DM for studies in the academic schedules of the Weizmann Institute at Rehovot (Israel). The funds are intended to be used for technical equipment and for the salaries of scientists engaged upon basic research in physics and what has come to be known as bio-science.

"There are approximately 350 scientists at present working in the Weizmann Institute, which is a private foundation. In the world of science it is regarded as one of the leading research institutes. Further funds are to be made available with the object of facilitating the exchange of scientists and exhibitioners studying in similar fields, between the Weizmann Institute and German science institutes. It is hoped to achieve a profitable exchange of experience in the fields concerned. In the Federal Republic, scientists from the Max-Planck Institute and a number of universities have been to Israel on an exchange basis; these include the Nobel Prizewinner Prof. Jensen, Prof. Gentner, Prof. Lynen, Prof. Weber and Prof. Westphal, who have helped to make a success of this exchange with the Weizmann Institute which, in turn, has already accepted a number of young German scientists for intermittent post-graduate courses. The funds made available by the Volkswagenwerk Foundation will enable contacts of this kind to be usefully augmented."

In addition to the 2 million DM mentioned, there are 200,000 DM for the exchange of scientists between the Weizmann Institute and German science institutes, again for the year 1963.

The annual report of the Volkswagen Foundation for 1965 gives the following records on contacts with the Weizmann Institute:

"In the year covered by the report, the Weizmann Institute of Science, Rehovot, one of the world's leading natural science research institutes, received approximately 1.5 million DM to be used for the improvement of its equipment. The Institute is cooperating with other research institutions in Germany by virtue of an exchange programme of exhibitioners—also made possible by the funds of the Foundation—and this grant also benefits the German scientists working in Rehovot."

Up to the present time, the exchange programme for scientists has included 31 exhibitioners (half of them Israelis and half of them Germans), either by way of financing their studies or financing an educational tour. The total funds available for this purpose are approximately 500,000 DM. There were 10 German exhibitioners out of a total of 14 taking advantage of the long-term study facilities involving periods of a year or more and the Germans were thus in the majority. The scientists of the Weizmann Institute, on the other hand, have, up to now, made more use of short-term visits of not more than a few weeks (though sometimes as much as a few months) but, in many cases, have made up for this by visiting a number of German institutes during their stay. All those concerned have stated that they have profited considerably from the exchange programme, both from the scientific and human points of view. There is now very close co-operation between German institutes and certain of the departments of the Weizmann Institute.

The programme of scientific research and projects undertaken jointly by the Max-Planck Institutes and the Weizmann Institute are discussed by a mixed German-Israeli commission of scientists who meet alternately in Germany and Israel. At the first session in 1967 the German commission consisted of the following members:

Chairman: Prof. Wolfgang Gentner, Professor of Nuclear Physics in Heidelberg; Nobel Prizewinner Prof. Hans Jensen, Director of the Institute of Theoretical Physics at the University of Heidelberg; Prof. Hans Friedrich Freska, Director of the Department of Bio-Science at the Max-Planck Institute for Virus Research in Tübingen; Prof. Hans Hermann Weber, Scientific Adviser, Istitute of Phyiology of the Max-Planck Institute for Medical Research, Heidelberg; Prof. Heinz Staab, Director of the Institute of Organic Chemistry of the University of Heidelberg. Also present as a guest was the scientific adviser of the Volkswagen Foundation, Frau Dr. Marie-Luise Zarnitz, Tübingen.

On the Israeli side, members of the commission included: Prof. Amos de Shalit, Director-General of the Weizmann Institute; Prof. Shneior Liffson, Director of Studies of the Weizmann Institute; Prof. Michael Feldmann, Professor at the Weizmann Institute; Prof. Gerhard Schmidt, Professor at the Weizmann Institute. In addition to the professors of the Weizmann Institute from Rehovot, the Head of the European Office of the Weizmann Institute in Zurich, Dr. Josef Cohn, was present at the session of the commission.

At these sessions detailed discussions are held on the programmes and the use to which the funds made available by the German Ministry of Scientific Research or the Volkswagen Foundation for joint German-Israeli scientific work are to be put.

Honorary Fellowship for Ludwig Erhard

On November 7, 1967 the Weizmann Institute made Professor Erhard one of its honorary fellows, as a way of paying tribute to the services rendered by him in the field of cooperation with Israeli science. The text of the citation was as follows:

"As proposed by the Scientific Council of the Weizmann Institute for the Sciences, the Committe of the Institute herewith elects Ludwig Erhard to honorary fellowship, as a tribute to his untiring efforts to forge and to maintain a new and important link between the Jewish people and Germany and to his support for scientific research in Israel as well as to his great contribution towards promoting Israeli economic growth and economic development."

The laudatio in connection with the award of the honorary doctorate was given by the former Minister of Justice and present member of the Knesseth, Pinhas Rosen, after a review of the life of Ludwig Erhard given by Dr. Shinnar, the former head of the Israel Mission. Mr. Rosen said in his address:

"A large number of personalities from public life in the Federal Republic of Germany, statesmen and scientists, artists and writers have visited Israel during the last few years. The names of the deceased Federal President, Prof. Heuss, the deceased Federal Chancellor, Dr. Adenauer, such leading politicians as the Speaker of the Bundestag, Dr. Gerstenmaier, the Foreign Minister, Herr Brandt, Professor Carlo Schmid and Professor Franz Böhm stand for many, who have been the guests of Israel and whom we have also received in the Weizmann Institute. Since the capitulation of 1945, the Federal Republic has indeed embarked on the path of freedom, leading to a new democratic life, and we are happy about such visits, because we see in them signs of the determination of the past into a better future. We agree with such German guests about one thing, namely that the past should not and cannot be extinguished. Historical memories separate our two peoples and at the same time chain them together, and both of them are required, each in its own way, to get to grips with this burden of the past. All that has often been said and written and may thus sound like a common platitude. However, neither we, who have built for ourselves here amid toil and strain a new home of our own, nor the German people have the right to evade the repetition of such historical truths. This repetition is more natural, self-evident and purposeful than ever an embarrassed or shameful silence could be.

"We all know full well what you, Professor Erhard, through your personal initiative in the first place as Minister of Economic Affairs and later as Federal Chancellor have done towards improving relations between your state and the State of Israel, and with that I do not only mean the exchange of ambassadors, which is to be attributed to you. The envoys of the Jewish people and of the State of Israel, who had to discuss with you the questions of principles and all those countless individual matters, and to settle them, are full of unstinted praise for your truly understanding and commonsense attitude. Your office entailed not only stating abstractly the will to reparations, as far as that is possible, but also transforming this will into deeds, which you did in a practical and, if I may say so, incredibly tangible form … You are both an economic theoretician and practician. Weizmann was an outstanding chemist. If I may use the distinction made by Wilhelm von Humboldt, Weizmann was more a man of the academy than a man of the university. In our days of advanced technology, which prevails over everything, the differentiation made by Humboldt has indeed lost a great deal of its weight, but at this ceremonious gathering, one may at least quote him and at the same time indicate that in his view the academy, and this applies to a high degree to the Weizmann Institute, was the supreme and last free haven of science and a corporation which must remain utterly independent of the State. The Weizmann Institute is without doubt a 'supreme', if not the last free haven of science in Israel. We are pleased to say that we have several institutions of such a kind. At the same time, the Weizmann Institute is a modern university sui generis in Israel. Weizmann not only gave it his name, but also imbued it with its specific character for all time. But to continue in the same vein, we have a special tertium comparationis in the founder of this institution, the guest of honour at the present ceremony and Wilhelm von Humboldt. The last-named, a friend of Goethe and Schiller, was not only a scholar, but also an important statesman. University or academy—their teachers play a decisive role in the life of their peoples, if they are made of the right material and if duty calls. The Germans and the Jews know all about this.

"The Weizmann Institute has an international renommé far outside the frontiers of tiny Israel. That can be said without wanting to be superior. That which is created and thought out, experimented and discovered here is not only of importance for Israel. The laboratories of the Institute have young scholars from many peoples, they can develop here, and what they achieve in the sphere of the exact sciences is also of benefit to other states, particularly to the developing countries.

"We know that our guest is not only concerned with the economic but also with general developments in the State of Israel. He has testified to this and proved it on a number of occasions, and he may understand right here, in this institution, an honorary member of which he is becoming, that a people with all its energy and despite unfavourable circumstances is at work serving the progress of mankind and of peace.

"The Weizmann Institute, which regards it as an honour to be able from now on to count Prof. Erhard among its own, serves in its work both peace and progress, just as the great dead man, whose name it bears, desired peace all his life with every fibre of his being and devoted all his great ability and inventive genius to the cause of progress."

The next speaker was the former Head of the Israeli Mission, Felix E. Shinnar. He said:

"Mr. President, you have entrusted me with the task of presenting the retired Chancellor of the Federal Republic, Professor Erhard, to the esteemed audience gathered here today. It is a task of great honour and one which I have great pleasure in undertaking.

"The mere mention of the milestones marking the road to progress trodden by Professor Erhard is sufficient to recall the memory of his splendid contribution to the economic history of his country and his sentiments and his attitude in respect of the State of Israel.

"Erhard laid the foundation of his later successes in the intensive study he made in his student days of the theory of economics. Mention must here be made of two important encounters from those days which were destined subsequently to lead to such long and fruitful associations. In the first place there was his Nuremberg co-student, who has also studying economics, Luise Schuster, who became his life companion; in the years of study spent at the University of Frankfurt, Erhard came into close contact with Fritz Oppenheimer; we see here a relationship of close friendship. Erhard was greatly stimulated by his tutor and mentor and, indeed, remained in close and friendly contact up to the time of Oppenheimer's emigration to America, where he died in 1943 in Los Angeles.

"In the bad days Erhard headed the state Institute of Market Research but his uncompromising political attitude was such that he was compelled to leave the Institute. He subsequently continued his research work under free and independent conditions in his own private institute.

"Immediately after the end of the war in 1945, charged with the handling of economic problems by the American occupation authorities, Erhard devoted himself with great single-mindedness to the realization of his conception of a free and social market economy—his economic creed of fair competition and the maintenance of a healthy relationship between the social partners. For him, the economist who was at the same time a psychologist, it was more important to have a lively insight into the socio-economic problem-pattern and to interpret it correctly for practical use than to have an abstract discussion.

"The currency reform and the end of rationing in June 1948 were the first important constructive stages. Thus the conditions essential for the atmosphere in which Erhard's idea of the new economy could flourist were created. Erhard was so convinced of the rightness of his method that in June 1948 he announced the termination of the controlled-economy system, not only without permission but against the active protest of the American military authorities. In the conversation with the representative of the American Government, Lucius Clay—a conversation which made history—he succeeded in convincing Clay that he was right. Thus the decisive step in the execution of the Erhard pattern of a social market economy was taken.

"In September 1949, Erhard became Minister of Economics in the first Government of the Federal Republic under Adenauer. His programme, 'Social Welfare for All', made rapid progress. The phrase 'economic miracle' became a household word throughout the world but the use of this phrase, which by 1954 was already being widely quoted, was deprecated by Erhard himself as being a greatly oversimplified way of looking at it. At the 10th anniversary of the termination of the controlled economy he said that there was no such thing as a miracle of this kind. What had been achieved was simply the result of tenacity, endeavour and the unwearying devotion of all strata of society throughout the entire people.

"When in October 1963 Erhard took over from Adenauer the office of Chancellor, there were three outstanding results of his work to be seen:

"It is to this enthusiastic protagonist of his economic philosophy and to those who, by their unremitting efforts since the collapse of the régime of force and brutality, made its realization possible, that the thanks of his country were due for the rehabilitation of German economy—a process that has earned the respect of the world.

"The position of the Federal Republic in world trade is second only to that of the United States, and it ranks third among the industrial nations.

"In mid-1966 there was something of a slow-down in the economic tempo of the Federal Republic—a slow-down that was almost to be expected after the prolonged period of boom. When at the end of 1966 Erhard saw himself face to face with the decision of abandoning, against his better judgment, what were for him the indispensable principles of his whole economic conception, he gave up his office as Federal Chancellor—a natural move in the hard give and take of politics.

"It is an understandable and, indeed, a natural thing for Israel and the Jews in the world to assess statesmen and their contemporary achievements from the point of view of their view of Jewish people. Side by side and in collaboration with Adenauer Professor Erhard was in the forefront of the delicate advance towards gradually developing a new relationship between the Jewish and German peoples.

"Entrusted with the handling of all those economic problems connected with the Reparations Agreement of September 10th, 1952 (some of which were extremely complex) Professor Erhard worked unwearyingly to bring about this memorable agreement and to arrange for reasonable compensation where material compensation was possible. Erhard worked with the true statesman's sense of responsibility and it was due to his never-failing open-mindedness and constant willingness that the spirit and content of the Agreement was worked out in a way strictly appropriate to the background of the circumstances, producing a result that was almost without parallel in the history of mankind.

"In the years 1960 and 1962, there were two meetings in Brussels with the present Prime Minister Eshkol, who was Minister of Finance at that time, at which other matters were discussed that were of crucial importance to the rehabilitation of Israel; these included development plans, Israel's associate membership of the EEC and the export trade, so vital to Israel. Considerable impetus was given to the settlement of these matters by Erhard's lively interest in the success of Israeli reconstruction.

"It was Professor Erhard who put an end to the protracted and wearisome series of empty discussions on the question of establishing conventional diplomatic relations between Israel and the Federal Republic by making a decision which did him honour—and in which he stood alone—when, on March 7th, 1965, he made known the desire of his Government to establish diplomatic relations with the State of Israel—a natural decision and one that was in conformity with his views on this subject.

"When on May 12th, 1965 I was at Professor Erhard's residence in Bonn, I had the honour, on behalf of my Government, to conduct the exchange of correspondence between Chancellor Erhard and Prime Minister Eshkol about the important agreements made—agreements which guaranteed relations for the foreseeable future—Erhard gave lively expression to his feelings at the end of this memorable act of statesmanship when he said that this agreement, based as it was on understanding and good will on both sides, was the most satisfying and salutory event in all his political experience.

"The history of a people is its collective memory—in the documentation of this event, Professor Erhard's principles, as translated into action by him, and his efforts on behalf of Israel and the Jewish people are perpetuated in honoured memory."

After the presentation of the document Ludwig Erhard gave the following address of thanks to the assembly:

"Mr. Chairman, colleagues, ladies and gentlemen:

"I have regretted on many occasions that science still lacks everywhere confident integration in a particular state with its rulers. If it is incontestably correct that a never-achieved closeness to the sciences and scientists is a disadvantage for the politician, it is also true on the other hand that it is no less disastrous for the scientist, if he is not in a position to grasp fully and recognize the democratic aspect of his work and his place in the spirit of the community.

"The connection here is especially apparent in the Weizmann Institute, for the presence of so many foreign scientists testifies to the fact that you want to see your research placed on a worldwide footing, far removed from national narrowness. You will understand, if your new German honorary member is filled at this hour with the belief that the scientific links between our two states and peoples can contribute a great deal towards building a bridge leading to a good future for our youth above the abyss of terror.

"You yourselves expressed impressively this intention of fruitful cooperation, when you awarded honorary membership to the Director of the Max-Planck Institute for Nuclear Physics in Heidelberg. Prof. Gentner, I, too, will do everything in my power, to ensure that the service of science to humanity in a peaceful world brings together many scientists in Israel and in Germany to fulfil the common task.

"That connection between scientists and active life is also demonstrated by the scientific and technical aid, which the Weizmann Institute in such a fortunate manner is rendering to the countries of Asia and Africa. This goodwill with regard to cooperation creates new and hopeful indications to the effect that all people of goodwill do in fact constitute an intellectual and moral unit. I share the view of your former President, the Foreign Minister, Mr. Abba Eban, who sees in scientific community a first-rate task in the build-up to other countries.

"Because of the heavy burden of hunger and poverty all over the world on our consciences, the contribution of the individual countries towards overcoming need can only be understood in terms of helping others to help themselves. The training of an intellectual elite filled with profound ethos will make it possible for new generations across frontiers of thought and space to allow all progressive and peaceful countries to benefit from the progress made in their own community."

Scholarships of the German Academic Exchange Service

Every year since the year 1959 the German Academic Exchange Service has granted two scholarships to Israeli students studying at universities in the Federal Republic, including West Berlin; Moshe Birnbaum, the Academic Secretary of the Hebrew University in Jerusalem, acted as the liaison official from the Israeli side.

Among these scholarship-holders was Dr. Shlomo Aronson, who was thus enabled to study for four years at the Free University in Berlin and obtained his doctorate there with a thesis on the SS-Führer Heydrich. Today, Aronson holds special responsibility at Kol Israel for work in connection with the Federal Republic of Germany.

For the first time since the establishment of diplomatic relations between the Federal Republic of Germany and Israel, the German Embassy was used as a medium for arranging the scholarships of the German Academic Exchange Service. Applications were officially invited by the German Embassy through advertisements in Israeli newspapers and a mixed German-Israeli commission met in Jerusalem to produce a short list of applicants. The documents of the 23 selected applicants were sent to the German Academic Exchange Service for final selection. In 1967 14 scholarships were awarded to Israeli students. They included a student of zoology, two economics students, students of metallurgy, archaeology, veterinary medicine, architecture and engineering. In 1968, 14 more free places were awarded to Israelis. Up to 1967, there were 45 Israeli scholarship-holders studying at German universities through the offices of the German Academic Exchange Service.

In addition to these free places the German Academic Exchange Service received grants from the Federal Ministry of Economic Co-Operation for six scholarships for scientists from developing countries who are studying at the Weizmann Institute in Israel. These scientists come from India, the Argentine, Greece and the Sudan.

Alexander-von-Humboldt Foundation Scholarships

Since 1954, Israel has also been included as eligible for scholarships for scientists who are required to have been occupied for at least two to five years in teaching and research work after taking their doctorate and have distinguished themselves by scientific achievements of particular merit. These scholarships are awarded for pre-specified research projects among which the exhibitioner may make his own choice and he is also completely free in his choice of university or institute and of the university lecturer in charge of the research. He also has free access to all scientific and educational facilities in the Federal Republic, including West Berlin.

The scholarships made available by the Alexander-von-Humboldt Foundation are the best endowed of all those emanating from the Federal Republic. They usually provide for study of one to two years and never for less than six months. The exhibitioner receives DM 1.000.— to 1,400.— nett per month with an extra monthly marriage allowance of DM 180.— if his wife accompanies him and DM 50.— for each child. Fares are also included in the grants. As a result of the initiative of the Alexander-von-Humboldt Foundation 20 hostels have been built at German universities and colleges in which these exhibitioners are usually accommodated. The President of the Alexander-von-Humboldt Foundation is the Nobel Prizewinner Prof. Heisenberg. At present there are three scientists from Israel in the Federal Republic holding Alexander-von-Humboldt Foundation scholarships. These are one veterinary researcher working in Hanover on a cattle disease, one graduate in International Law, working at the Max-Planck Institute of International Law in Heidelberg and a physicist specializing in the branch of astrophysics, working at the Max-Planck Astrophysical Institute in Munich. Astrophysics is concerned with the forming of scientific conclusions arising out of combustion processes and the gas fields of stars and suns, with special reference to their use in nuclear physics.

The Friends of the Hebrew University Society

For some time now, the head office of the Friends of the Hebrew University Society, which has already formed groups of members in various university towns, has been in the Bethmannstraße in Frankfurt am Main. The President of the Society in Germany is Chairman of Directors of the Bank for Gemeinwirtschaft AG, Walter Hesselbach, city councillor in Frankfurt am Main. The secretary of this Society, Prof. Simonson, is a lecturer at the Johann-Wolfgang-von-Goethe University at Frankfurt am Main. The editor of this book spoke about the work of this Society to Max Levy, European representative of the Hebrew University, who has his office in Strasbourg but is in Frankfurt almost every week to discuss current problems with the presidium of the Society in Germany. Asked about the concrete projects that are the joint concern of the Hebrew University in Jerusalem and the Society he answered:

"The projects have been under way for a number of years but the project that the Friends of the Hebrew University took up approximately a year ago is the Martin-Buber Institute of further education and a building is to be put up at the Hebrew University for this faculty. Funds are to be collected in Germany. (The foundation stone for this Institute was laid on November 6th, 1967 in the presence of 40 German professors and the President of the Society, Walter Hesselbach.) As you know, Israel is an immigrant country of so many cultures with so many educational origins that it is essential to establish a common standard of reference. Everybody cannot, of course, go to a university but a certain cultural level can be established by the further education of adults. It is in the interests both of the state and its population for teachers to be sent out to even the smallest villages."

Difficult beginnings

The details mentioned of contacts in cultural and scientific spheres can only be appreciated by considering the conditions imposed by the Israeli Government for cultural relations with Germany and then looking back on the situation as it was only a few short years ago. The Israeli Government set up its own committee for formulating the necessary guiding principles for cultural relations with Germany. The instructions that were drawn up and ultimately issued on December 5th, 1961, were as follows:

Ludwig Erhard in Israel with the
Mayor of Jerusalem,
Teddy Kollek (1967)

Kurt Birrenbach in Israel, preparing
the way for the establishment of
diplomatic relations. From right to left:
Felix Shinnar, Shimon Peres,
Kurt Birrenbach and Ari Rath of the
"Jerusalem Post" (1965)

Rolf Pauls, the first German Ambassador in Israel, hands over his credentials to the Israeli President Zalman Shazar (1965)

Asher Ben Natan, the first Israeli Ambassador in Germany, hands over his credentials to the Representative of the Federal President, Bundespräsident (President of the Federal Council) Georg August Zinn (1965)

"1. *International programmes and events*

The participation of Israel in international programmes taking place in Germany and the participation of Germany in international programmes in Israel is approved.

"2. *Visits of German citizens to Israel*

Visits of German citizens, and particularly young people, school-boys and school-girls, students, young workers etc., to Israel shall be approved to enable them to obtain a better idea of the development of the country.

"3. *Indoctrination in Germany*

The indoctrination of Israeli citizens about the Jewish people and the State of Israel shall be encouraged. A committee consisting of authorized persons from the Ministry of Foreign Affairs, the Ministry of Culture and Education and the Ministry of Transport, will decide on the choice of candidates for this purpose. It is desirable that this committee should work in co-operation with centres of higher education (universities) in Germany.

"4. *Entertainment*

No public performances featuring German citizens will take place in Israel and no performances featuring Israeli citizens in Germany insofar as this depends on the Israeli Government.

"5. *Art*

In every case in which an Israeli body is invited to artistic performances in Germany the committee referred to in Paragraph 3 will decide on the acceptance of the invitation. This also applies to Israeli exhibitions in Germany inasmuch as they are not for commercial purposes.

"6. *Education (studies) in Germany*

a) Education for young people under the age of 20 years in Germany will not be encouraged and no foreign currency will be made available for this purpose.

b) The education of Israeli students at German universities will not be encouraged; no foreign currency will be made available for this purpose and no German scholarships will be accepted.

c) Offers of education at universities or other academic institutions will only be approved if this education is clearly to the benefit of this country. In these latter cases scholarships will be accepted.

d) The training in German enterprises of workers or technicians of the higher age brackets will only be approved if this training is necessary in order to operate machines that have been bought in Germany or if there are any particular reasons which make it imperative for the learning of the trade or professional training to take place in Germany.

"7. *Establishment of institutions with German financial assistance*

"The establishment of branch offices of German societies, institutions or associations in Israel is not permitted. This regulation does not apply to philanthropic donations, which do not give the donor the right to intervene in any way in the administration of these institutions made possible by the donations.

"8. *Visits of delegations from public associations and institutions*

"Public associations and institutions that were invited to Germany or that wish to invite a similar German body to Israel and make application to the Government for a ruling will be given a ruling in accordance with the above instructions.

"9. A permanent Committee of Ministers will be set up to decide all questions arising in connection with cultural relations with Germany that are not covered by the above instructions. Members of the Committee: Minister G. Meir (Chairman), Minister A. Eban, Minister J. Ben-Jehuda."

The great seriousness with which cultural relations with the Federal Republic of Germany are taken is shown by the speech given on January 9th, 1962 by the present Foreign Minister Abba Eban, who at that time, was Israeli Minister of Education, when he commented on these points concerning relations with the Federal Republic of Germany and made the following statement:

"... But in view of the need for a clear definition of what is allowed and of what is not allowed the Government had decided to set up a Committee of Ministers to formulate a set of rules and instructions that were to apply to all Ministries ... The Committee was faced with the need to respect those deep feelings that cannot be separated from the discussion of these matters and also to take into account the historical fact that the government of Hitler was destroyed in 1945 and that we ourselves must determine our actions in the light of the conditions of both yesterday and today; even those who are the most cautious in assessing the situation in the Germany of today cannot claim that nothing has happened since 1945 and that there have been no changes at all since then.

"The Committee of Ministers, acting in accordance with the views held by the parliamentary groups within the Government, has accepted rules which, in the meantime, have become the policy of the entire Government. I should now like to sum up these rules: Israeli participation in international programmes in Germany and German participation in international programmes in Israel are both allowed. This also applies to visits of Germans to Israel in the normal course of things and in particular to visits of German young people, schoolboys, schoolgirls, students, young workers and members of the free professions who, in this way, will have the opportunity of getting to know something of the reconstruction work that is taking place in our country.

"With regard to informative and educational work in Germany it was decided to form a committee consisting of representatives of the Ministry of Foreign Affairs, the Ministry of Education and the Ministry of Transport to choose suitable persons for this work. The choice will be made after consultation with the authorities at the higher educational level in our country.

"The Committee and the Cabinet have decided that—inasmuch as this is a matter for the Israeli Government to decide—programmes coming under the heading of light entertainment will not be presented by either side. Whenever an Israeli group is invited to appear in Germany in any artistic pursuit the decision on acceptance or non-acceptance shall be taken by the Joint Ministerial Committee referred to above. This also applies to non-commercial Israeli exhibitions in Germany.

"With regard to study in Germany the sending to Germany of young people below the age of military service shall not be encouraged. We are not making any foreign currency available for this purpose nor are we accepting any German scholarships. In the interpretation of this rule we make a distinction between those who are not old enough to make mature decisions and those who bear responsibility to state and government and adults who have a right to their own decision inasmuch as this decision does not conflict with the general principles laid down. The acceptance of offers for advanced studies at German universities or other academic and scientific institutions is declared acceptable inasmuch as the educational training is essential to the development of the country. The training of adult workers and technicians in German firms is approved where this training is concerned with the operation and maintenance of German engineering equipment.

"With regard to the German-aided establishment of institutions, the establishment of branches of German institutions, societies and organizations is not allowed in our country. This rule does not apply to contributions to philanthropic organizations inasmuch as such contributions are not connected with any share in the running of these institutions.

"Representatives of organizations and public institutions that are invited to visit Germany or those that wish to invite a similar organization or institution from Germany to visit Israel and who apply for advice to the Government will be advised in conformity with the rules quoted above.

"From these rules it can be seen—as I have already pointed out—that not everything is allowed and not everything is forbidden. We are at a point of time that lies somewhere between the past and the future. We are not free to ignore either the one or the other. The fact that certain limitations exist proves that the past is nearer to us at the moment than is the future.

"The distinctions made between past and future, and which find expression in these rules, will have to prove their worth in the time to come. Even now the overall picture is not all of one colour. In any case, the seven Ministers, coming from three parliamentary groups, who have done their work in a condition of maximum mental tension—as indeed is the case with the entire Cabinet—are convinced that these rules are an honourable and honest answer to the exigencies of the situation—a situation such as has never before confronted any country in the world."

It is only by appreciating the atmosphere reflected in the rules and opinions given here that it is possible to understand the situation which must necessarily define the cultural relations existing between Israel and Germany.

German films in Israel

Up to the beginning of 1967 it was forbidden to show films coming from the Federal Republic of Germany in Israel. The interpretation of this law was so strict that in 1960 Ben Gurion was obliged to get special permission from the Government in order to obtain the release (for showing in Israel, at least in the Hebrew language) of the full-lenght documentary film 'Paradies und Feuerofen' which was made with the co-operation and the approval of the Israeli Army in 1958. But this decision did not allow the film to be shown in the cinemas of Israel in the original German version. At the same time, however, the Israeli Government bought six copies in English and French in order to use it as public relations film about Israel for showing in African and Asiatic countries. Thus it was by no means an aversion to the film or the representation of Israel that was the motive of the censor in not releasing the film but the general attitude of rejecting films from Germany. This, as a matter of fact, led to the grotesque situation that the company that had made the film in 100 days in Israel was asked to take the film to Israel in the guise of an Austrian co-production. For years German film renters had tried the roundabout way via Austria or Switzerland to get German feature films into Israel. This is yet another obstacle that has now been overcome.

Even at this early stage it would be impossible to compile a comprehensive list of all the German films dealing with Israel. For indoctrination in national policy, for which today in Germany more than 40,000 16 mm projectors are available on the premises of youth groups, schools, associations, trade unions, police and army units and similar institutions, some German films were produced, constantly showing new and varied aspects of life in Israel. This process began in 1955 with the first film of this kind, 'Israel—Staat der Hoffnung' (Israel, a country with prospects), 250 copies of which were distributed to these users. It was also the first time that a comprehensive survey of Israel had been shown on German television; this film was followed by countless television *reportages* on all eleven stations and the Second German Television Programme, a process that is still going on at the present day.

Depiction of Jewish life

It is not only the large number of film and television shows that reflect Jewish life for the German public; there have also been two exhibitions that deserve special mention here: The 'Synagoga' shown at the turn of the year 1960 in Recklinghausen and the 'Monumenta Judaica—2,000 years of history and culture of the Jews on the Rhine' held in 1964 in Cologne. It is also worth mentioning that for the exhibition 'Monumenta Judaica' a large number of exhibits, cultural relics of earlier centuries and the precious Machsor Manuscripts, were brought specially from Jerusalem to be shown here before an extensive German and European public.

The Machsor Manuscripts are part of the valuables that the municipal keeper of archives of the town of Worms, Friedrich M. Illert, who has since died, was able, on a night in November 1938, to get away to safety together with the municipal archives before they could fall into the hands of the Gestapo and before the synagogue of the town was burned down.

Jewish antiquities of the town of Worms

The French Office of the Branche Française of the Jewish Trust Corporation for Germany has been conducting litigation for many years with the object of obtaining possession of these antiquities from the town of Worms. On October 2nd, 1956, after negotiations in the Chancellory which were conducted by (at that time) Ministerialdirektor Janz, on the German side, with the Branche Française, a settlement was arrived at by which the Machsor Manuscripts and a number of Imperial documents, Thora scrolls and the archives of the ancient Jewish municipality of Worms went to Israel and relics belonging to the municipality and of particular cultural interest remained in Worms—including, for example, the Raschi chair from the Raschi Chapel of the old synagogue. In December 1961 the synagogue, which had been reconstructed in the old style, was again consecrated in Worms. The Federal Minister of Economics and Vice-

Chancellor (at that time Ludwig Erhard) spoke the following words during the consecration ceremony:

"The newly-created ancient synagogue of Worms is a shrine of commemoration for the victims of tyranny but at the same time let it be a visible sign of the genuine will of the Federal Government and the genuine will of the whole German people not to forget the crimes that have been committed and to obtain forgiveness from their own consciences in mourning the dead. Let it announce to the generations to come what once happened on German soil and let it show how desperately mankind can err when it ignores God's commands."

Axel Springer donates nearly DM 4 million to the Jerusalem Museum

On September 27, 1966, a few days before the official opening of the new Ullstein/Axel-Springer Publishing House in Berlin, the publisher Axel Springer, in the presence of the Head of the Administration of the Israel Museum in Jerusalem, Daniel Gelmond, and the Israeli Ambassador to the Federal Republic, Asher Ben Natan, presented the deputy town mayor of Jerusalem, Dr. Nathan Chouraqui, with a note in which he promised him a gift of 3.6 million DM for the Israel Museum. A joint communiqué issued in Berlin and Jerusalem stated that the money was to be used for housing the central library for art and archaeology in a special building. The numerous students of history of art and archaeology who come here to Jerusalem from all parts of the State of Israel and from other countries will have more than 70,000 volumes available for reference. There will be a lecture theatre accommodating 430 people in the library building and there will be club rooms for the International Society of Friends of the Israel Museum and for other visitors.

The architect, Prof. A. Mansfield from Haifa and Mrs. Dora Gad were responsible for the design of the new building.

At the presentation in Berlin of the note promising the gift to the Jerusalem Museum, Springer gave the following address in the presence of the visitors from Jerusalem and the Israeli Ambassador:

"Your Excellency, Professor Chouraqui, Gentlemen, I wish to bid you a most cordial welcome and to express the great pleasure that I have in seeing you here this morning. The pleasure that I have is twofold. It stems from the fact that we are using these new rooms for the first time and it is a source of deep satisfaction that it should be you that are visiting us today. I have already presented the members of my firm to you—all of us have been looking forward to this morning.

"I now thought that I might perhaps again read out the document which lays down the substance of that event about which so much has been said. And so I have great pleasure in handing to the director of the Museum, Mr. Gelmond, this letter and in adding a few remarks that come from me personally.

"The letter I have written to my good friend, Herr Gelmond, runs as follows: 'I feel called upon to tell you, as representative of the administration of the Israel Museum in Jerusalem, that I consider it a great privilege to be concerned in the rewarding work of extending the facilities of your museum. I had made a definite statement to the Mayor, Theodore Kollek, on August 19th, confirming that I was prepared to meet the costs of the projected library, including a lecture room and the club rooms for the International Society of Friends of the Israel Museum and Jerusalem. The amount of 3.6 million DM, which I have pleasure in putting at your disposal, includes both the building costs and the foundation which is intended to cover the running expenses of the part of the museum referred to here. The amount will be transferred to you by the Axel-Springer Foundation as arranged, in two equal parts, the first in the middle of November 1966 and the second at the end of March 1967. Once more, I should like to confess how very pleased I am to have been associated with you and your colleagues in the work of building and extending this great modern cultural institution in your country. From the very outset I was perfectly aware of the difficulties that are still bound to confront any German engaging in such a project in Israel. The controversies attending the putting forward of my name in connections with our building—a thing never asked for by me, by the way—neither surprised nor in any way upset me. There could never be any question of my not understanding the implications of the situation.

"In order to eliminate any possibility of misunderstanding from the start I sent the following telegram to your mayor, Mr. Kollek, on September 21st: 'It was my sincere wish to contribute to this work but not to be named as a contributor when I saw this great and beautiful Israel Museum in your town. Please inform those of your esteemed colleagues that may at present be worrying about it that the desired anonymity does not offend me. I look forward to another trip to Israel and remain with best wishes, Yours very sincerely, Axel Springer.'

"The same day, I received from Mr. Kollek the following answer to my telegram: 'I was greatly impressed by your most praiseworthy attitude and prouder than ever to have the benefit of your understanding in this matter. My respectful admiration and my sincere good wishes, Teddy Kollek.' In conclusion may I say how happy I am that it is private initiative that is now leading to the realization of our plan. Here we have no formulated law, no formal agreement but solely and simply that best of all informal laws for which we have that most expressive word, conscience. For me it is a pleasure that I find it difficult to express in words to be able to welcome you here in our new building in the Kochstrasse, at the side of the Berlin 'Wall' in the days in which the ceremonial opening is taking place. My dear, respected and esteemed Herr Gelmond, I would ask you and your friends to interpret this coincidence of events as an obligation binding upon me and my firm. With all best wishes, yours sincerely, Axel Springer.

"In this connection I, for my part, am actually very glad that I had been somewhat remiss in setting the original invitation for you for October 6th—not remembering, of course, the fact that the 6th of October is also one of the consecutive high Jewish Holy days. I had simply thought of it in connection with the birthday of my mother—a remarkable woman, if I may be permitted the remark, en passant. Thus, it was made October 6th.

"We shall not be seeing each other on October 6th, and this gives me the privilege of being able to welcome you here on the premises of my firm; it may, perhaps, be in order for me to take the opportunity of adding a few remarks on my own personal account—remarks which would perhaps not be fitting if made at a more formal level.

"Let me be very cautious and confess that no words of mine can be in any way adequate to deal with the vast and tragic Theme and I shall not attempt it. In my view there is no compensation for what has occurred and there is no forgetting. And as for what we call forgiveness—this is a function of the Divinity where humans have little or nothing to contribute. Surely it is a matter of grace? But on the other hand, in these days in which a publishing house is being re-established in Berlin—days that are thus of such moment for us—I want to make something of a confession. I speak as a German who is one of those making such efforts to overcome the present distress of a divided country and I wish to say that I have never lost sight of the original causative factors that are at the root of our present troubles. I know that in looking at the political ruin of Germany today we are looking at something for which we must ourselves bear the responsibility. Do not be shocked when I say that the responsibility is ours. It may be that the man who is now standing before you is not a particularly guilty German but I prefer to use the 'we' for us Germans. Anybody taking over a new country must take the rough with the smooth and take over the passive as well as the active assets. In my view a man like Willy Brandt has survived the terrible days of the past with the quite justified attitude of considering the war not as a dispute between the powers but as an international civil war in which he was on the right side. We can only speak of 'we'. 'We', the new generation, have to clear up the mess and we cannot get this job done by making any great distinction between the actual weight of guilt that can be allocated to one or the other of us. That is my considered opinion and I wished to state it openly in your presence.

"On October 6th, this house will be opened and I am, my dear Heinz Ullstein—if I may express it in this way—a rather less than practical and ideal heir to the house of Ullstein. When we look back and realize that it was here that the foundations of the excellent and world-wide German Press were laid and when we conjure up the ghosts of the past and find among them so many fellow-citizens of Jewish origin, we can surely say at a time like this, when our house is being opened, that in this we have a very special kind of compensation and it is in this spirit that I should like you to accept what I hope may be seen as an eloquent gesture towards a country for which our house entertains the warmest regards and good feelings.

"And now another point: I am known outside this firm as a man who presses persistently (for many, sometimes rather too persistently!) for the settlement of German problems. It was my idea for the foundation to provide visible evidence of the fact that anyone so persistent is very well aware of the past and its inference, its aftermath and its effect on the present day and I wish to make it clear that it is just those people who are most persistent that have never for a single moment lost sight of the past—and indeed, it was just this that lay at the root of all my efforts to do something constructive—if I may take the liberty of so describing it—in Israel.

"And now, for a moment, may I address myself particularly to his Excellency, Asher Ben Natan. Your Excellency, you were kind enough to invite me to Israel and at the time I told you that I had often had occasion to be grateful for invitations to visit your country. But I had always postponed acceptance for two particular reasons: These were that on the one hand I thought it was still a little early to pay a visit to the country and on the other—perhaps the main reason—because I *know myself*. For I knew that when the day came for me to visit the State of Israel, this country that so many of my friends have seen and of which I had heard so many enthusiastic reports, I would inevitably be unable to stop myself from becoming directly and personally involved. I did not want to visit this country as a tourist and I wanted my firm to have made sufficient progress for this inevitable involvement of which I speak to be material as well as purely personal. Then I did pay a very short visit to Israel at the end of June of this year to see its Museum; I am very happy to have made this flying visit and look forward to another and longer visit to your beautiful and interesting country.

"In conclusion, may I emphasize once again the great pleasure that it has given me to have you as the first official guests in my new building in the Kochstrasse."

The Israeli Ambassador Asher Ben Natan made the following speech in reply: "Herr Springer, gentlemen,

"I myself would like to add a few words to what has been said. Since I have been in the Federal Republic there have been occasions, there have been various feelings, there have been shades of emotion that I have known, some of them very pleasant, some of them perhaps less pleasant than others. This was something I knew would happen beforehand, and there was simply nothing that anyone could do about it. This is the third time that I have been in Berlin. The first time was when I made my official visit to the city and to its Lord Mayor. On my very first visit to Berlin I was conscious of the feeling of being what I might call en rapport, and I found in the conversations I had there, there was a level of mutual understanding which appealed to me most strongly from the very start. My second visit was on the day the German-Israeli Society was founded and I knew that I was among real friends here. Today is my third visit to Berlin and this occasion is the one of the series that is of the greatest importance to me. When I spoke to you in Hamburg, Herr Springer, I quickly realized that this was one of the good—in fact one of the best—talks that I ever had with anyone in Germany. And even at that time I saw that real contact had been made, though I never realized at the time that such magnificent results would ensue from the contact. On the other hand, however, I must make a personal confession here: when I heard that you were going to Israel and that you wanted to see what Israel was like and might perhaps be doing something for Israel, I had a suspicion that after you had seen all there was to see you would decide on Jerusalem. The irresistible parallel of Jerusalem and Berlin—divided cities, if they are not divided for the same reasons—but two cities, each of which constitutes a spiritual centre, because for you Berlin is certainly the spiritual centre of Germany today. And to this must be added another point: Archaeology as a whole is a subject concerned with cultures that have already disappeared from the world but still have echoes in later ages, still have influence on the cultures of later times. But in Israel archaeology is living history; it is not only the history of the Jewish people but actually the living history of the entire occidental world. The movements and events arising out of it have affected many things, in fact, one might say that they have laid the spiritual foundation for the spiritual world of the Western lands. Even though in its practical forms and in its effects it may often have strayed onto false paths, even though it has sometimes happened in these 2,000 years that our people have had to suffer—in spite of all this the fact remains that those spiritual values that are latent in the tradition of history are still in existence today and today they represent our common cultural heritage. It is just this that gives your foundation this additional meaning, this additional value. This is something I should like to stress: not only what you still have with you, the problem of an unburied past—in this work, in this foundation I see a bridge that you have made to span the gulf of history—an achievement the importance of which cannot be overestimated, for it may be of considerably greater importance than we can possibly imagine today. There can be no possible doubt that there are such things as catalysts in the relationship between our two peoples—a relationship that has to bear the lasting burden of the past. There are, of course, catalysts that produce an undesirable effect and there are catalysts that produce a beneficial effect. This work of yours is one of these latter, the incontestably beneficial effect of which will remain unchanged for a long time. I am very sorry that we cannot be here on October 6th, but I am very glad that we now have the opportunity, in this small and intimate group, to take part, together with you, Herr Springer, in this modest ceremony in this beautiful building—itself so eloquent of culture. And as we look out over this divided city we join you in hoping that one day this gulf too will be spanned and ways will be found to achieve unity for this city again.

"But you have heard of the response that there has been to the work of your foundation in Israel. One thing is already quite clear: the lecture room in Jerusalem will be known as the Springer Auditorium; it is already known as such in Israel today—indeed not only in Israel but in the world at large. I do not know whether this was the intention of the critics but the desirable result has been achieved. It was indeed a particular pleasure for me to note the reactions of so many of the groups in Israel that usually maintain a reserved attitude; all these groups have given their approval and all of them have said what Dr. Adenauer said in Israel—i.e. that if good results are to be achieved, obvious goodwill must be recognized.

"Today that goodwill is recognized in Israel. People have now got as far as understanding this; it is something that has penetrated deeply into the public consciousness and it will certainly have its results. The great work that you are doing in Jerusalem will contribute a great deal to this. I am very pleased that we have the Deputy Mayor of Jerusalem with us here today and this visit is in itself a symbol—an important symbol. We shall have the opportunity of promulgating this visit and this ceremony at a later time so that what has taken place here today will be made known to a wide public.

"Herr Springer, we are already looking forward to your next visit to Israel, and we hope that on that occasion you will be able to say the same thing as you did last time and that you will again find new contacts when you are there. There are many people who are looking forward to your visit and having the opportunity of talking to you and we hope that that visit will lay the foundations for impeccable and lasting relationships with you and with your firm."

This event is important because it is significant of so many different things at the same time: It shows the personal spiritual involvement of a man who had no contact whatever with National Socialism and is today making a personal effort as a German to help Israel in her reconstruction and rehabilitation. The initial reaction of the Israeli public showed that even when someone is so generous and well-intentioned feelings are aroused which, despite everything that is being done in Israel by Germans, are so lively that they cannot be disregarded. The tone of the address given in reply by the Israeli Ambassador showed the direction in which—and this indeed at the very time of the Middle-East crisis—the attitude to the Federal Republic of Germany of a large proportion of the Israeli population had developed.

The foundation of the Fritz-Naphtali Institute

On October 29th, 1967, on the campus of the Tel-Aviv University, the foundation-stone of the Faculty of Social Sciences was laid in memory of the former Social-Democrat Reichstag delegate Fritz Naphtali, who later became a Minister in the Israeli Government. The German Association of Trade Unions, and trade union circles in Austria and Switzerland are contributing to the creation of the faculty. They are collecting a million dollars for a foundation, which will promote the interests of research, aid to students and scholars and international collaboration in this Institute. The Friedrich-Ebert Foundation is also contributing to this joint effort. Those taking part in laying the foundation-stone in Tel Aviv were as follows: The members of the Board and the Chairman of the German Association of Trade Unions, Ludwig Rosenberg, the Vice-President of the German Bundestag, Erwin Schoettle, the Lord Mayor of Frankfurt Willi Brundert, the member of the Presidium of the German-Israeli Society, Walter Hesselbach and the German Ambassador in Israel, Rolf Pauls.

German youth in Israel—Israeli youth in Germany

Since the end of 1959 there has been an annual increase in the number of German youth groups travelling to Israel. The education officer of Cologne, Johannes Giesberts, has done sterling service. Since that date it has been Herr Giesberts who has taken groups of Cologne schoolboys and schoolgirls of all kinds of schools, together with their teachers, to Israel. If all examples of personal initiative were to be quoted they would fill a separate book. By now, well over 50,000 young people from the Federal Republic have been in Israel and lived and worked with Israelis in the Kibbutzim (the farms) in Israel and, in exchanging ideas with this pioneer generation of the country, have got to know something of the past and the present of the Jewish people.

In the other direction, however, it was not until much later that young Israelis began to visit the Federal Republic and even today, relatively few have done so. It was not until July 1967 that the first official group of schoolboys and schoolgirls from Tel Aviv arrived in Munich and Cologne, although there had been young teachers, students, trade-union members and various mixed groups travelling to Europe and visiting the Federal Republic at the same time. This hesitancy on the part of the Israelis is a reflection of the sentiments expressed by the then Minister of Education, Abba Eban, in the extract from his speech printed above.

In recent years increasing numbers of Israeli artists have found their way to Germany. Numerous painters have been exhibiting in German towns and there were some young Israelis who have had no qualms about appearing in German theatres, on television and in films in the Federal Republic of Germany.

The activities of the German-Israeli Society

No description of the efforts made in cultural matters would be complete without reference to the foundation of the German-Israeli Society on May 19th, 1966. The aim of the Society is laid down in Article 2 of its Statutes.

"It is the task of the Society to strengthen relations between Germany and Israel in all matters of cultural and public life. The Society is for the promotion of international contacts, tolerance and mutual understanding of peoples, particularly in the Middle East."

On April 1st, 1967, the President of the German-Israeli Society, the Parliamentary Under-Secretary of State, Ernst Benda, together with its Vice-President, Heinz Westphal (member of the Bundestag), Prof. Rolf Rendtorff and Walter Sylten, a colleague of Probst Grüber in Berlin, flew to Israel on an official visit. In connection with the visit the editor of this book spoke to Under-Secretary of State, Benda, about the work of the Society, then almost at the end of its first year, and the prospective visit to Israel. The interview was as follows:

"Naturally, during this year the work of the German-Israeli Society was aimed particularly at attracting the largest possible number of members, building up the organization and providing the necessary financial and other organizational basic requirements for this work. This work is by no means at an end. In fact, it is only now that we are really getting to grips with it. But the time has come when we have to progress beyond the kind of work we have been doing up to now and go in for the real practical work of the Society as such. The activities of the German-Israeli Society are carried on in accordance with the rules for guidance that had been decided on by the Society itself. These rules stress that the chief aim of the German-Israeli Society will be to promote good human, political, cultural and economic relations between the two countries, i.e., the Federal Republic of Germany and the State of Israel. The rules go on to make clear that the relations thus created between the two countries and which we wish to be as close as possible are not directed at any other country in the Middle East, on the contrary, we aim, as far as possible, at good relations between all peoples in this area."

Question: "As individual Germans we shall always be sure of satisfactory relationships. We shall find friends, people with whom we can speak, but the real problem is the broad gulf that exists between the two countries themselves. What is the position at the moment as far as the Society is concerned?"

Answer: "There is, of course, a limit to what we can do as a private society but nevertheless we can try—and we are trying—to intensify the human contacts between people from our two countries. In fact, in the short time that we have had, we have been devoting attention to this, concentrating on the exchange of young people between the two countries. We have taken a number of youth groups to Israel and have also had the pleasure of entertaining and looking after a group of two from Israel. We have given particular attention to the cultural sphere and as you yourself know, there are still a large number of difficulties to be overcome especially in Israel. On the journalistic and public-relations side we have made a number of contacts, we have had groups here and have sent other groups over there. We shall continue and intensify the work that we are doing on these lines."

Question: "In Israel there is a society called *Dialog*. It consists of 'sabras'—i.e., people who were born and bred over there and thus do not belong to the immigrants' generation. These people are making quite considerable sacrifices; every month they pay a contribution of £ 10 (Israeli), i.e. DM 13.50. They do a lot to strengthen German-Israeli contacts from their side. What are the prospects of establishing relations with this group?"

Answer: "We are, of course, very pleased to note the activities of this *Dialog* group and we intend to lose no time in getting in touch with them. We have made the first approach in writing and we hope to be able to extend this approach to cover personal meetings."

Question: "Earlier on you said that you were concentrating on contacts between young people. Now you and I belong to a generation in between, a generation that is old enough to have had direct knowledge of the Third Reich; and there may be one or two among us in Germany who held office of some sort in those terrible days and I do not feel that this generation should deliberately stand aside because it is now the one that has to contribute to the financial aid to Israel. They are the fathers of the youth, the youth which today, tomorrow and thereafter have to maintain and to continue the contacts that are now being made. What do you feel about this?"

Answer: "It goes without saying, of course, that we are not confining our work to the young people, however important these contacts between young people may be. In our Society there are quite a large number—actually the majority—of older people who belong to the generation you have described or to even earlier generations; we are, of course, bound to regard them as of primary importance to our organization since we are particularly concerned to bring together eminently suitable personages; this means people whose professional, cultural or political positions are such that they are the most likely—and in any case much more likely than young people—to have at their disposal the necessary material, professional and other essentials for carrying out satisfactory work in collaboration with Israel and any societies over there having similar aims to ours.

"In our relations with Israel we shall not attempt to disguise what has been but we shall attempt to give the Israeli citizens a complete and undistorted—and as far as possible objective—picture of Germany past and Germany present—with all the dark aspects that we know but also the individual rays of light we can see and the existence of which, we believe, should be more clearly demonstrated in Israel than has been possible at present."

Question: "Herr Benda, you yourself will shortly be travelling to Israel with a group of the Executive Board of the German-Israeli Society. What is the object of this visit?"

Answer: "This will be the first visit of a delegation of the German-Israeli Society to Israel. All those taking part in this visit have already been in Israel in some other private or official capacity on one or more occasions and under circumstances unconnected with the Society. There are, indeed, some who have very close and regular personal contacts with people in Israel and are there very frequently. But we wish to make ourselves known officially to the authorities there and to the representatives of cultural and spiritual life. These circles and personalities are, of course, already familiar with our work and are interested in it but we want to talk to them directly and to try to get a definite idea of how we can work most fruitfully together in the future."

Question: "Can you give any definite examples of what you are planning to do?"

Answer: "As I have already mentioned, we have quite a number of plans ready for putting into operation. These include exchange of youth groups, the stepping-up of programmes for visits—particularly of those concerned with moulding public opinion in Israel (this would be the journalists, of course). You know yourself that this is where we are still likely to run into quite a lot of trouble. As far as possible we shall also try to get people from all walks of political life, in the widest sense of the word—including, for example, trade-union representatives—to come to Germany and we shall try to make it easy for them to obtain some idea of what Germany is like today."

The editor talked to Mr. Westphal, Chairman of the Society's Committee, after the party returned from their visit. Westphal said:

"The object of the conversations on the occasion of this first visit of the executive committee of the German-Israeli Society was to improve our present contacts and make new ones. This applied both to official Government authorities and private organizations and also to individual people. The list of persons and organizations with which we have been in touch during this one week in Jerusalem and Tel Aviv makes that clear. Let us for a start look at the official side—government offices etc. Here, we concentrated particularly on contact with the Ministry of Foreign Affairs. The Minister, Abba Eban, received us. We saw him twice while we were over there and had comprehensive talks on present-day political matters with the Under-Secretary of the Israeli Ministry of Foreign Affairs, Mr. Levavi. We visited the Head of the Western Europe Department of the Israeli Ministry of Foreign Affairs, Mr. Sheck, and also his Head of the Sub-Section for Germany, Mr. Dover, who gave so much help in the preparation and conduct of our visit. We talked to quite a number of other personages or former members of the Israeli Ministry of Foreign Affairs; these included Dr. Yahil, the former Secretary of State and Prof. Elath, who had been the first Israeli Ambassador to the United States, and later served in Great Britain and is now President of the Hebrew University.

"The second most important part of our visit consisted of our meetings with parliamentarians of the various party groups in the Knesseth. In these talks we probably extended the circle of people hitherto reached by German delegations. Not a lot further but a bit further. In this connection I am thinking particularly of the meeting with the National Liberals and with the Liberal Right, who are on the Opposition side and today belong to the Gachal group. Dr. Sapir, the chairman of the sub-group within the Gachal faction and former Minister of Transport, spoke to us, together with three other members of his group. We also spoke to the delegate Mr. Herari of the Independent Liberal group, belonging to the Government Coalition, and with Mr. Azania, a delegate from the Mapai group. I had a lengthy talk with the lady who used to be the Minister of Foreign Affairs and is now the Secretary-General of the Mapai, Mrs. Golda Meir. This group in turn was visiting Mr. Peres, the Secretary-General of the Rafi group. Mr. Peres is the former Defence Minister of Israel.

"You will see from this that we have spoken to a representative cross-section of all parliamentary groups and parties that are today maintaining contacts with Germans. The talks were more or less intensively conducted—I mean at different intensity-levels by the various groups concerned. Unfortunately, it was not found possible to make arrangements for a conversation with the two leftist groups Achduth Ha'avodah and Mapam. For technical reasons there was no conversation with the religious groups either. There were no other reasons—it was simply impossible to fit it into the very tight schedule."

Question: "What happens as a result of all these meetings, as far as Germany is concerned? Was the general impreesion you gained from talking to members of the Israeli Government, undersecretaries and other officials, favourable as far as German-Israeli conversations are concerned?"

Answer: "Well, it varies according to the way the discussion goes and whether it harks back to matters of the past or deals with the present day or with forward-looking political considerations affecting the two countries. In any case, these two aspects of the situation are bound to crop up in the course of a conversation. It is all a matter of the attitude of the partner in the discussion; in fact I would go so far as to say that there are people who really do concentrate on realities of present-day politics without harking back to the days of the past. But the different intensity-levels remain nevertheless. To take an example let us suppose that a member of the Rafi is compared with the representative of the National Liberals: a difference of this kind would be felt right away—and between these two extremes there are very many nuances, the Rafi people being forward-looking and concerned with the great political problems facing us today; this is immediately discernible. There is no question about the fact that this applies directly to the attitude of the Ministry of Foreign Affairs—and indeed to Israeli politics as a whole. In these matters it is obvious that the Israelis are particularly anxious for the Germans to commit themselves in favour of Israel's associate membership of the European Common Market. The extent to which the Israelis would like the Germans to commit themselves goes beyond the mere matter of assent. They expect the German attitude to be expressed as follows: We insist on this matter being put on the agenda of the Council of Ministers in Brussels as soon as the report of the EEC Commission has been completed.

"Among others, we also spoke to professors of the Hebrew University in Jerusalem, the Weizmann Institute in Rehovot and the University of Tel Aviv. And here, I should like to make special mention of our meeting with the great Judaist Professor Sholem. In addition, we have had interesting conversations with editors-in-chief and publishers of leading Israeli newspapers in Tel Aviv."

Question: "Did you have the impression that there was any change for the better in the attitude to Germany or that perhaps—to put it pessimistically—they are conducting liaison with us in terms of a sinister past, without looking to the future, as was your experience in other Israeli circles?"

Answer: "Here again, we encounter varying opinions but mental reservations are considerably greater outside parliamentary circles than in the case of those actually in day-to-day contact with political life. There was no doubt about this.

"But there is also no doubt about the fact that among the journalists we spoke to there were quite a number (especially among those who had had the opportunity of seeing Germany) that were thinking more in terms of the present-day situation than those who, even today (and admittedly for reasons that, from their point of view, might seem to be sober and well thought out), persist in retaining a sceptical attitude towards the changes that have taken place in the German *Weltanschauung*."

The Federal Republic and the Middle-East crisis

On May 16th, 1967, one day after Israel had celebrated the 19th anniversary of its foundation as a state with a military parade in Jerusalem, Egypt mobilized its forces. Syria was also making certain military preparations. These were 'justified' by the Arab Press and radio on the basis of alleged Israeli troop concentrations at the frontiers.

On May 17th, 1967, the Secretary-General of the United Nations, U Thant, stated in New York that if the withdrawal of the UN troops from the Israeli-Egyptian frontier was requested this withdrawal would be carried out. The next day, the Egyptian President, Nasser, was quick to demand the withdrawal of the UN soldiers, his motivation being that he did not want to see them involved in any Egyptian-Israeli conflict that may arise. 24 hours later U Thant complied with Nasser's request. While the United-Nations troops were withdrawing from their positions, more and more Egyptian forces moved into the Sinai area.

During the night of 21/22 May, 1967, President Nasser announced that the Gulf of Aqaba was closed to the Israelis. Egyptian troops had once again occupied the gun-positions at Sharm-el-Sheikh that had been blown up in the Sinai campaign in 1956, and thus closed the Gulf to Israeli shipping.

Increasing concern that a new armed conflict in the Middle East might develop was not confined to the capitals of the great powers. A special so-called "Middle-East Crisis Flying Squad", consisting of civil servants of the various ministries, was formed in Bonn with the object of giving aid to German citizens in the threatened areas, evacuating families and giving prompt aid to any German nationals in the area that might find themselves in difficulties.

Ever since the beginning of the steadily-increasing conflict, offers of assistance from the German people had been arriving at the Israeli Embassy in Bad Godesberg. Pro-Israeli feelings were spontaneously expressed in the form of donations of money, clothes etc. and offers of aid. The offers of aid and the feelings of the German people, as expressed in the numerous demonstrations in the Federal Republic, will be dealt with later in this book.

In the meantime, Nasser had been making statements and issuing appeals in which he repeatedly accused the Federal Republic of supplying Israel with tanks, aircraft, guns and weapons of all kinds behind the Arabs' backs. He also accused the German Press of being whole-heartedly on the side of Israel.

The following day, Conrad Ahlers, the Deputy Head of the Federal Information Service, rejected the attacks of Nasser as completely unjustified and emphasized that German arms supplies had been given at a time when supplies from another source to Egypt had reached their peak. German arms supplies were only "for purposes of defence".

The Federal Minister of Foreign Affairs, Willy Brandt, summed up the attitude of the Federal Government on the Middle-East crisis on May 31st, when he made the following statement at a conference of the Information Services:

"The attitude of the Federal Government in the Middle-East crisis is clear and unambiguous. We are just like other countries and other peoples, in that our great interest lies in the conservation of peace and we share the great anxiety that peace will be endangered. We are not one of the four powers that the French Government has been pressing for action but we are certainly taking the liberty of pointing out the enormous responsibility borne by the world powers for conserving world peace.

"We are a sovereign state and we respect the sovereignty of other states. On December 16th, 1966, I said in the Bundestag that the German policy of not intervening or interfering in the internal affairs of other states or in regional conflicts also applies in the Middle East. And I added that the Federal Government would support any efforts—particularly those of the United Nations—to assist in arriving at a just and peaceful solution of Middle-East problems. This statement still holds good.

"We are not in favour of unilateral attempts at solving these problems but of proper treaties and agreements. We are not in favour of the use of force, but of a policy of the deliberate renunciation of force; this is the very reason why the Federal Republic is strongly advocating—amongst other things—the principle of freedom of passage for ships on the high seas.

"It is against the interests of the community of peoples for programmes of peaceful reconstruction to be disturbed or—as may well happen—even destroyed. This applies to Israel in the same measure as it applies to other states. Our policy of non-intervention is not indicative of any lack of responsibility or of sympathetic understanding of the situation.

"It is common knowledge that we have again and again emphasized our sincere desire to see friendly relations obtaining between the peoples of what is geographically known as the region of Arabia. Our attitude has sometimes been attacked and inevitably comparisons have been made between us and those politically responsible in the other part of Germany. We need not fear any comparisons of this kind. We have certainly not provoked a worsening of relations between the two parts of Germany, we have poured no oil on the flames, we are not pursuing a selfish policy in the Middle East and anyone doing so is acting against the interests of our people and against the cause of peace."

On Sunday, June 3rd, two days before the outbreak of hostilities, the German Minister of Foreign Affairs, Willy Brandt, appeared on German Television and appealed to the people of the Federal Republic to assess the situation calmly and soberly:

"At a time when the thunder-clouds of crisis are gathering with their associated threat to peace in the world, I wish to say a word on the situation—particularly in view of the many letters that I have had on the subject. At the Ministry of Foreign Affairs I am, of course, kept informed of the development of the situation from hour to hour and I am bound to say that in spite of all the efforts that have been made by many countries there is no solution in sight. Let us hope that the great powers will do their utmost to arrange a settlement.

"The Federal Republic of Germany bears no responsibility for this situation. But we cannot dissociate ourselves from it and it is our duty to do everything we can whenever peace is in danger. But there is a limit to our influence. In the Diplomatic Service, I have certain facilities which can be deployed internationally and I am constantly making use of these to prevent the situation in the crisis-ridden Middle East from getting out of hand. All the forces in this world that are directed towards the conservation of peace, towards the just and peaceful settlement of disputes, find a ready response with us and

Konrad Adenauer receiving an honorary doctorate in the Weizmann Institute from the President of the Institute, Meier W. Weisgal (1966)

Opening of the Jewish World Congress in Brussels. From left to right: Golo Mann, Eugen Gerstenmaier, Nahum Goldmann (1966)

Politicians from all over the world, including several heads of government, in the German Bundestag at the state ceremony on the occasion of the death of Konrad Adenauer. In the fifth row, the Israeli delegation with David Ben Gurion, Abba Eban and Asher Ben Natan (1967)

we are loyal and reliable allies of the cause. There can be no question of passivity here. We are ready to declare which side we are on; we must not shrink from whatever peacemaking and humanitarian tasks may lie before us.

"We know what may be at stake. We ourselves are faced with problems for the solution of which we need peace, we need understanding and the reconciliation of peoples.

"Up to the present moment there is no reason for interpreting the undoubtedly menacing aspects of the situation as inevitable destiny and I am therefore asking you to remain objective and calm.

"At this moment, it seems to me highly unlikely that the Federal Republic will be drawn into the conflict in any way and you may rest assured that everything possible will be done to safeguard the position of our community."

On the same day, in response to a request by the Israeli Ambassador Asher Ben Natan, 20,000 gas masks were taken from Civil Defence stocks and sent to Israel.

When on Monday, June 5th, the confrontation in the Middle East turned to actual war, the Association of the German Trade Unions in Düsseldorf appealed to the population for demonstrations "to re-establish the state of peace and to safeguard the existence of Israel". The Association of German Trade Unions called upon its members throughout the country to take part in joint demonstrations together with the democratic parties, youth associations and church organizations.

German policy of peace in the Middle East

Statements made by both the Federal Government and the political parties

On June 7th, two days after the outbreak of hostilities in the Middle East, during the second reading of the Federal Budget Bill for 1967 in the full assembly of the German Bundestag, the question of the Middle East was brought up and Chancellor Kurt Georg Kiesinger made the following statement:

"In my Government Statement I have already pointed out that all the good work we have done in the domestic field would be jeopardized if we were not successful in maintaining the cause of peace in the world. It could not be foreseen that soon after this statement, quite irrespective of the protracted and smouldering Vietnam crisis, a new and extensive conflict—indeed, a full-scale war—would break out on the very doorstep of Europe.

"In this struggle the Government has adopted the following attitude: It has followed the development of events carefully and with the greatest of anxiety and deeply regrets that the situation has developed into war in the Middle East. The Government hopes that the Security Council of the United Nations will be successful in bringing about a cease-fire and expects the great powers to take all possible steps to bring their entire influence to bear, both inside and outside the United Nations, in order in the first place to limit the present scope of the conflict and in the second to bring it to an end as rapidly as possible.

"There is no reason for assuming that our own security is immediately threatened, but the course of the conflict will have considerable repercussions on the further course of world politics. We should have no illusions about this, and the same applies to the great powers. They should not allow themselves to fall into the temptation of endangering the larger and more important work of instituting and promoting policies of peace and the peaceful settlement of controversial issues throughout the world merely in order to snatch illusory and short-term advantages in the present.

"The Federal Government has decided upon a policy of non-intervention in order to prevent any intensification of the conflict and to leave unaffected its potentiality for settling or improving the Middle-East situation. Despite the conflict, it will do all that it can to maintain its contact with the countries in this area—and this also applies to matters of trade and economics; at the same time, the Government will remain true to its principle of non-intervention and will not supply weapons to the warring parties; it will make sure that this decision is strictly adhered to.

"On the other hand, the Government will not prevent German citizens from undertaking relief work in the area—and even in the actual theatre of operations. The Government has recommended those of its citizens living in affected areas to leave. Since May 24th, the Ministry of Foreign Affairs has put into operation plans that had already been in existence for contingencies of this kind. In collaboration with other Departments, and particularly with German airlines and shipping companies, the Ministry has taken all necessary steps to afford maximum protection for German citizens and property and to make arrangements for possible evacuation should this become necessary. The rapidly-changing situation in the areas where fighting is taking place renders it necessary to keep all planning as flexible as possible and to make rapid decisions if necessary. The Government is in constant touch with friendly and allied powers and has given the governments concerned detailed information on the way Germany sees the situation and the political decisions already made by the Government.

"At the same time, however, I still consider it necessary to add a further word in this connection before leaving the matter. Against the background of recent history of our people, it is really tragic that the authorities in the other part of Germany should be attempting to whip up the conflict by persisting in an attitude that is in every respect irresponsible. It is perfectly clear that the only reason that they are doing this is to take advantage of the misery and terror of war, when passions run high and tend to cloud thinking, in order to obtain some shred of recognition for their régime."

The Chairman of the Social Democrats, Helmut Schmidt, Hamburg, had the following to say on behalf of his party:

"For the past ten days the work of the Federal Republic—and particularly the work of the Chancellor himself and his Deputy, the Minister of Foreign Affairs—has been overshadowed, as, indeed, have the thoughts of us all, by the conflict in the Middle East. It has been quite clear for a week—possibly, indeed, for as long as ten days—that a centre of tension was forming there which, in its political implications throughout the world, was likely to reach proportions comparable with that of the Cuban crisis, although the Middle East is different from Cuba in that it is not directly on the doorstep of one of the world powers. On the other hand, however, it is certainly on the threshold of our Continent of Europe. There is danger of the conflict spreading and we Germans are also bound to allow for our own situation, for the part that we may have to play and for our own security.

"The Social-Democrat Party very much welcomes the statement on non-intervention made by the Federal Republic of Germany and just repeated for us by Herr Kiesinger. I should, however, like to add, in the name of my colleagues here in Parliament, that we Social Democrats do not interpret the term 'non-intervention' as covering moral or political indifference to the ultimate issue of this conflict—an issue that cannot yet be foreseen. We are greatly disturbed about this war, that has been being systematically prepared for months. However much our people may be linked to the Arab people by ties of traditional friendship we are bound to oppose the intention of their leaders to destroy Israel. We would remind the House that the State of Israel has been created in accordance with a decision made by the United Nations and has the full sanction of that body. A democratic system has been successfully built up by the people of this country and we have no doubt of their desire to continue to develop their country by peaceful means; we cannot simply bear mute witness to a situation menacing the existence of this state, and hear the publicly and cynically uttered threat to bring about the destruction of a people without being emotionally involved. We are convinced that all extant problems in the Middle East can be solved without the use of force. We wish to take this opportunity of expressing our sympathy with the Israeli people and at the same time of publicly announcing—and here I wish to underline what Herr Kiesinger himself said—that we have been literally shamed by the fact that the official speeches have shown not the slightest sense of the very special obligation that we Germans have towards this people.

"The members of this House will certainly be unanimous in expecting of the Federal Government of all responsible governments and in particular of the two great powers—that they will make use of all their diplomatic facilities and moral persuasive powers to obtain a cease-fire and a re-establishment of the situation in the Middle East as it was before the United Nations had prematurely withdrawn their troops.

"I also wish to make use of the present occasion to add a remark or two which will further illustrate how an extension of this crisis in the Middle East might affect Europe and the security of its peoples—and I am deliberately using the conditional 'might'! There is no doubt at all that the Soviet leaders are exploiting this crisis in the Middle East in order to start what one might refer to as a 'second front' of tension against the United States of America in order to relieve North Vietnam. If the present situation is allowed to continue it may enable the Soviet leaders to gain a threefold victory.

"In the first place, the Soviet Union might actually achieve relief of the pressure in Vietnam and thus help in accelerating a 'settlement'. I have no comments to make on this.

"In the second place, the Soviet Union might be successful, both politically and strategically, in gaining access to the main Mediterranean area by breaking through the Dardanelles and thus through the Persian Gulf to the Indian Ocean. It has become clear that in the last few days a number of Arab states have been plunged much more deeply into the vortex of Soviet policy than has hitherto been the case. Whether, and if so to what extent, this trend can be reversed is a question of time and not of the short-term settlement of the crisis per se.

"In the third place, the fact that this is a possible development might result in a most remarkable situation as far as the whole of Europe is concerned; and when I say 'most remarkable' I mean in the sense of a situation of vital or critical significance and not in the sense of something definitely good. A situation which might suggest that the United States of America is not in a position simultaneously to fulfil its obligations in more than one part of the world must not be allowed to arise. If, as a result of the deliberate policy of the Soviet leaders, it were possible to provide proof of this possibility then indeed a vital part of the structure of the balance of power throughout the world—as we know it at present—would be at stake, just as it once was at stake in Berlin in 1961 and again in Cuba in 1962. The undermining of essential psychological key positions in the policy of the Western Alliance is the real issue. I think there can be no doubt in our minds about the fact that any disturbance of the delicate balance of German interests must necessarily touch very closely on German security; in the same way there is no doubt that any disturbance of the balance to the disadvantage of the United States of America brings the danger of a kind of pernicious anaemia—or perhaps one could think of it as 'undiagnosed leukaemia'—undermining the structural homogeneity of the Western defence system. I am sure that in Washington the world-wide implications of the present Middle-East crisis are sufficiently realized. This crisis affects not only the Western system of the Pacific and Asia but in the same way, and perhaps even more, the Western system of the Atlantic and Europe. In this situation the eyes of Europeans and the eyes of Germans alike are turned expectantly, and at the same time in complete confidence, to the American Government and its President. In this connection I am assuming, of course, that regular consultations are also being held at this time of crisis in the Council of the North Atlantic Treaty Organization.

"The diplomatic facilities of the Government of the Federal Republic of Germany for assisting in settling the conflict are, of course, limited and, as I have already pointed out, full use should be made of them by you, Mr. Chancellor, and by your Government. But the fact of this limitation does not at all mean that the resources of Germany are to be regarded as of no account in the present situation. We ourselves can certainly contribute to the process of political détente. Last December, we—and when I say 'we' I am speaking to the other parties of the Grand Coalition—began our joint effort to find new ways of working for all-round relaxation of political tensions. The present emergency confirms the analysis which was the basis of our work in December in a most alarming way. This is all the more reason why every one of us should now make great efforts to demonstrate our firm and unswerving determination to pursue an active policy of détente and to support our declared intention with our deeds."

The Chairman of the Free Democratic Party, Freiherr von Kühlmann-Stumm, spoke as follows:

"This debate is taking place in an atmosphere that is oppressed by the potential dangers to world peace that arise out of the conflict in the Middle East. We had hoped that it might prove possible to avoid war in the Middle East but this hope has not been fulfilled. A shooting war is taking place and people are being wounded and killed. The efforts of all those bearing any sort of political responsibility must now be directed towards localizing this conflict and putting an end to it as rapidly as possible.

"After the grievous experiences of two world wars the German people are bound to attach crucial importance to the efforts being made to re-establish peace in the Middle East. We are exposed to the danger of an armed conflict at a time when the troops of two treaty organizations are confronting each other on German soil; the most powerful members of these organizations, the USA and the Soviet Union, are directly affected by the war in the Middle East. In addition, our capital, Berlin, is in a distressingly exposed position.

"In view of this situation our people must remain alert, as alert as perhaps no other people has ever needed to be, to prevent the conflict now spreading in the Middle East from overflowing into Europe. The Government will therefore have to observe as never before the strictest neutrality as laid down by international law and in this it can rely upon the unanimous support of the parliamentary Opposition. We shall propose to the House a resolution which will confirm this determination to be neutral and we should be very glad, ladies and gentlemen of the Coalition Government, if we could take this decision unanimously in the Bundestag with the votes of the Coalition Government. We must remain firm in our decision to prevent anything from happening that might lead to an extension of the conflict; in this hour, the watchword of our policy must be sympathetic awareness and sober appraisal of the situation. By adhering to this attitude we shall establish a firm basis on which to continue our work in this House."

Rainer Barzel, Chairman of the CDU/CSU party group, made the following remarks on the Middle-East crisis:

"The serious problem, the problem to which the Chancellor himself has given priority, is the war in the Middle East. We support the position adopted by the Government and this support holds good for all the details given. We believe that the Government's position is governed by sober assessment of facts and is the result of mature consideration and we believe that it is in accordance with our principles, our interest in respect of the whole of Germany and the resources we have at our command.

"First of all, it is with some satisfaction that I note that the speaker of the FDP, who has made reference to the subject in the House today, has definitely not repeated the protest against the humanitarian supply of gas masks for the protection of the civil population which was reported in the press and I may therefore perhaps express the hope that this House is now unanimous on this point. For a long time now, disavowal of any form of military engagement outside NATO has been not only our political opinion but our considered and practical policy. We had, in fact, to make up our minds on this point at the time of the Cyprus crisis—I see the former Chancellor Erhard in front of me—we had to make up our minds about the Far East. There is no doubt at all about our position: however emotionally involved we may be, military engagements outside NATO are not for us. In saying this, I have not the slightest intention of making excuses or trying to avoid the issue. There are questions upon which one has to make a definite decision about one's attitude and we are now faced with a situation which concerns us politically and, indeed, engages us politically; we are bound to see—and this is a point that the Chancellor and my colleague, Herr Schmidt, have quite rightly stressed—that Europeans, *qua* Europeans, no longer constitute an effective factor even in these areas; we see the obvious implications as far as the Alliance is concerned because the situation touches upon just those moral and political principles by which we are guided.

"I think that there is no doubt in the public mind about these matters. The situation has made an indifferent mental attitude impossible. At the same time it is right for the Government to pursue, soberly and deliberately, the line which it has pursued from the start. Israel is a country that is recognized by UNO. Some of the people in Israel's neighbour states—those that have perhaps been hitherto misled by the slogans of hatred—will even then be forced to consider whether, in fact, others who had issued the order to destroy had been right in allowing foreign influence to sway them; they may perhaps conclude—and I say this quite openly—that even the Arabs do not need to use force to settle their problems.

"I do not propose to read out to the House that formidable collection of quotations from the German press—the accusations and counter-accusations which date back to before the armed conflict—but at the same time make perfectly clear the sort of destructive intentions that had already been announced beforehand. If in this connection we do not propose to commit ourselves for the time being, the reason is that the time is perhaps not yet ripe for the as yet unexploited German vote to be used in such a way as to carry any real weight in this crisis.

"At the same time, my friends, I believe—and this is a question that has been raised outside this House—that we still owe our own people an answer; in other words, we have *not* forgotten the way in which France, Great Britain, the USA and the Soviet Union interpreted international law at Nuremberg. They were at considerable pains to enumerate how many actions constitute violation of the law—and we inserted an additional article (Article 220a) in our Code of Criminal Law.

"There exists an Agreement, international in nature, with which we are familiar; this Agreement is designed to prevent and to punish genocide. Ladies and gentlemen, please understand that this is only incidental to the discussion, the idea being to demonstrate that our position here is based upon international law and it therefore follows—and this I wish to stress (I put it forward only as my own personal view)—it follows that this includes the idea that no one should be coerced into using force to defend themselves."

The following is an extract from the speech of the Leader of the Regional Group of the Bavarian CSU, Richard Stücklen:

"And now a word about the war in the Middle East: I am in complete agreement with what was said by my colleague Dr. Barzel. In our opinion the Government has acted quite rightly in that it could not have done anything else in the situation in which we in Germany find ourselves—i.e., that of maintaining strict neutrality. But at the same time we also feel that it is not only common humanity but, as far as we Germans are concerned, a moral duty of the most urgent nature to help the sufferers in the affected areas by giving whatever humanitarian aid is within our power, and by giving it unsparingly."

The Minister of Foreign Affairs, Willy Brandt, added his voice to those raised in the debate on the crisis in the Middle East:

"On this matter of the Middle-East conflict, may I just add a word or two by way of emphasis to what has already been said, and perhaps also amplify one or two points. We really have summed up the situation on the basis of the Government's not having any mandate to take sides in this conflict—i.e., in the sense of intervening in the hostilities, either directly or indirectly—and I should say at once that this was our attitude before the shooting war started and not merely afterwards; on the contrary, we have made it perfectly clear, both before the outbreak of hostilities and after, that we are impelled by a desire to maintain peace in general and to re-establish it after a rupture of peaceful relations such as has now occurred over there. But even though I am speaking for the second time after this first round of the debate, I should particularly like to emphasize once more—and what I am about to say is my personal conviction, but at the same time a conviction in which I am by no means alone—that our non-intervention and, as a logical consequence, neutrality, in the international-law sense of the word, cannot by any means be interpreted as any moral diffidence or as emotional sluggishness.

"We have heard that during the night the Security Council of the United Nations has unanimously appealed to the warring parties to cease fire. The first country in the crisis area to obey this appeal was the Kingdom of Jordan. We earnestly hope that this unanimous decision of the Security Council will persuade the great powers to disregard their differences in ideology and to co-operate in the re-establishment of peace.

"Our own bitter experience has made us well enough acquainted with the horrors of war and so it is quite natural that not only the Government or the parliamentary delegates should speak on behalf of the German people but that the people itself should be able to take a lively and constructive interest in the human destiny of those caught up in the maelstrom of war; naturally, our people are filled with the whole-hearted desire to free the world from the spectre of destruction and annihilation in the Middle East. I am genuinely of the opinion that when the hostilities cease—and I hope that this may be a matter of days—our people should disregard our present economic troubles—troubles that are certainly of a temporary nature—and be prepared, and this not merely by means of budget funds, to show that we are capable of great humanitarian work, not only within Germany but beyond our borders, so that we can give whatever assistance is possible to the victims of this war. We believe that it is high time that a real attempt was made to seek a lasting solution to the problems arising in the Middle East. This solution must be such as to permit the governments and the people in this part of the world to direct the whole of their efforts, with maximum efficiency, to serving the ends of peaceful reconstruction and the welfare of mankind."

Agitation against Israel in the Soviet Zone

There is a direct connection between the failure to reply to the Israeli Note of March 12th, 1951, on the question of reparations, and the present situation. The communist rulers in the Soviet-Occupied Zone of Germany have refused again to recognize the State of Israel until this moment when, even more vehemently than the Soviet press, they branded it as an aggressor. Moreover, ever since the founding of the Federal Republic of Germany, the Propaganda Ministry of the Communist Government in Pankow has been conducting a smear campaign against the Federal Republic, alleging that it was the successor to Hitler, Himmler and Eichmann.

The material that had flowed from this propaganda machine in East Berlin since the beginning of the Middle-East crisis can only be compared with the wildest tirades of the Goebbels days. Below, the editor presents extracts from the statements made by communist politicians in the Soviet-Occupied Zone, repeating what has appeared again and again in leading articles and commentaries and so-called "resolutions" (manifestos) in the Press over there or what has been broadcast in radio and television commentaries.

The most repugnant document was the so-called "Declaration of the Jewish citizens in the DDR". There may be some who are really convinced and support the statements made in this Declaration. But not by any stretch of the imagination does it become credible that the majority of the Jews in the Soviet-Occupied Zone of Germany subscribe to it. There is evidence that the Jewish heads of the communities were summoned before the Under-Secretary of Religious Affairs, Seigewasser, to issue on their own behalf a similar Declaration and that some of them rejected the unreasonable request. The Declaration was nevertheless published in their name.

The most important passages of this Declaration, which appeared in the newspaper "Neues Deutschland" on June 23rd, 1967, are as follows:

"We, citizens of the 'Deutsche Demokratische Republik', being of Jewish origin, raise our voices in order to condemn solemnly the aggression that has been committed by those in power in Israel against the Arab neighbour-states. We feel that we are justified in raising—and, indeed, are obliged to raise—our voices, for we are citizens of the 'GDR' in which anti-Semitism is a thing of the past and in which there is no room for anti-Semites; we who suffered in the days of Hitler fascist persecution, in the same way as a large number of the citizens of Israel, have lost many of our relatives who were murdered by the German imperialists. If the Israeli Government now has the impertinence to speak in the name of Jewry let it be stated at once that the overwhelming majority of the Jews are living outside Israel and do not consider Israel to be their country at all. The plan is to misuse the feelings of sympathy towards the Jews, oppressed as they were by Hitler fascism and anti-Semitism, in order to camouflage the underlying imperialist interests.

"The tragedy of the Jewish population of Israel is that the rulers of this country are carrying out a policy that serves the strategic ends of the great imperialist powers that are interested in the Suez Canal and the Arab oil resources. Unfortunately this does not apply exclusively to the year 1967. The very founding of the State of Israel is associated with annexation and the breaking of promises. The provisions of the resolution of UNO in 1947, proposing the creation of an Arab state and a Jewish state in the area of what was at the time called Palestine, have not been honoured. Reactionary forces have ignored the resolution of UNO and in illegal military action, have occupied 80% of the territory of what was formerly Palestine. Many hundreds of thousands of Arabs were brutally driven from home and country by the leaders of the Israeli bourgeoisie. In just the same way as the USA imperialists have made of the Federal Republic a spearhead for use against the peoples of Europe, Israel was made the spearhead for use against the Arab peoples. The role that had been allocated to Israel became particularly obvious in 1956 when Israel, followed by the great powers of imperialism, attacked Egypt. The present rulers of Israel, whose foreheads are branded with the mark of the 1956 aggression, are also in charge of the aggression of 1967, as shown by the fact that it is Dayan who is the Minister of War. Dayan also took part in the aggression of USA imperialism against Vietnam and he never loses an opportunity of glorifying it in both the spoken and the printed word.

"It is the policy of aggression that is jeopardizing the existence of Israel and is jeopardizing the lives of all its citizens. Those who live on islands should not make an enemy of the sea. There will not be peace in the Near East until the Government of Israel abandons its imperialist policy and, at long last, adopts a good-neighbour policy and begins to show consideration for the interests of the Arab people.

Carlheinz von Brück
Prof. Wolfgang Frankenstein
Kurt Goldstein
Prof. Lea Grundig
Prof. Siegbert Kahn
Prof. F. K. Kaul
Dr. Franz Loeser
Dr. med. Ernst Reifenberg (medicine)
Dr. med. Elisabeth Thierfeld (medicine)
Gerry Wolf."

This statement is absolutely typical of the communist propaganda instructions of the East-Berlin Government. After the military successes of the Israelis the daily press was instructed under no circumstances to give prominence to military events in the Middle East. The Press was also instructed to give the definite impression that the USA, Great Britain and the Federal Republic of Germany were responsible for the war by virtue of their huge arms shipments to Israel. These instructions were rendered necessary by a flood of letters and queries received by the daily papers from the people of the East Zone, who suddenly began to experience doubts as to the suitability of the Middle-East policy of their Government. Then there was a further series of instructions, also published in the Soviet-Occupied Zone of Germany (German: "SBZ"). These ran as follows:

"The journalists of the SBZ (Soviet-Occupied Zone) have sent telegrams, expressing solidarity, to the Ministry of Information of the UAR and to the Egyptian Press Syndicate.

"In resolutions 'emanating from all strata of the population' constant protests must be made against the 'huge arms shipments made by the BRD (Federal Republic) to the Israeli aggressors'.

"The Afro-Asian Committee, in its capacity of solidarity organization specializing in 'solidarity work' in the SBZ (Soviet-Occupied Zone), must lose no opportunity of identifying the SBZ (Soviet-Occupied Zone) with the 'anti-imperialist struggle of the Arab peoples'.

"At major factories, solidarity demonstrations must be staged in which the workers declare themselves to be on the side of the Arabs.

"The Red Cross of the 'GDR' will immediately give all possible aid, in the way of medical supplies, to the 'victims of Israeli aggression'.

"All sanatoria suitable for accommodating foreigners will immediately make available beds for wounded Arab soldiers and civilians in need of convalescence. It must be publicly announced that, where necessary, German patients will curtail their treatments in sanatoria and nursing homes if their places should be required for 'victims of Israeli aggression'."

In the "Nationale Volksarmee" (East Zone Armed Forces) of the SBZ (Soviet-Occupied Zone) there were also many problems that had to be solved by the operational staff of the troops. The generals were not able to issue instructions as to how the Israeli victory was to be interpreted and orders were therefore given that there were to be no discussions on the victory of the Israelis in army units.

Memorandum of the Federal Republic to the Plenary Assembly of the United Nations

In order to counter all the tirades of hatred and untrue allegations of the communist world against the Federal Republic of Germany the permanent observer of the Federal Republic at the United Nations, Ambassador von Braun, addressed, on June 19th, 1967, the following memorandum to the President of the Plenary Assembly of the United Nations:

"Your Excellency, in accordance with instructions received from the Government of the Federal Republic of Germany and with reference to Point 5 of the Agenda of the 5th Emergency Session of the Plenary Assembly, I have the honour of conveying to you the opinion of my Government on the above Point of the Agenda. I am particularly grateful to the distinguished representative of the United Nations of the People's Republic of Hungary for raising the question of the policy of my Government in respect of the present situation in the Middle East and I have the honour, your Excellency, to request you to be good enough to circulate, as an official document of the Plenary Assembly, this Note and the enclosed Statement, which is a reply to the distinguished representative's Note of June 22nd, 1967 (Document a/6728).

"During the past few weeks, a dangerous situation has arisen in the Middle East, a situation which jeopardizes the cause of world peace. In response to the request of the great majority of governments of the world, a special emergency session of the United Nations has been called. The German Federal Republic is not a member of the United Nations. On the other hand, however, its policy and its membership of all the individual separate organizations of the UNO and its contributions to numerous aid programmes of the United Nations have shown its crucial interest in the maintenance of peace and in the easing of international tensions.

"The bitter experience that they have had has made the German people familiar with the horrors of war. They know that wars and the use of force are not suitable methods of fulfilling national aims or settling international disputes.

"In accordance with its policy of reflecting the desire for peace of the German people, the Government of the Federal Republic of Germany has always endeavoured to bring about the easing of international tensions, to encourage effective and world-wide disarmament and to settle disputes without the use of force. It is now 13 years since the Government made the decision not to manufacture atomic, bacteriological and chemical weapons of war.

'It is these same principles that are now governing the policy of the Government of the Federal Republic of Germany in respect of the situation in the Middle East. The Government has made every effort to maintain constant, close and friendly relations with the peoples of this part of the world. These relations were based upon respect for the self-determination of peoples and the recognition of the sovereignty of their countries. At no time in history have the Germans ever had any selfish political aims in the Middle East. There has, of course, always been a close cultural and economic exchange between the countries of this region and this has been of advantage to both sides.

'The Government of the Federal Republic of Germany refuses to give 'good advice', schoolmaster-fashion, to other sovereign states. It knows that the people of the Middle East have not obtained their independence without a struggle and that they do not want to be again subject to foreign tutelage. The sole aim of German policy is therefore to co-operate with the peoples of the Middle East on a basis of dignity, trust and mutual respect. Unfortunately, the Government of the Federal Republic of Germany has been informed that an attempt has been made by third parties to exploit the recent crisis in the Middle East in order to pursue selfish aims. References are here made to the memorandum (UN document a/6728) presented to the President of the Pleanary Assembly by the distinguished delegate of Hungary.

"There are certain people in the other part of Germany—and not only in Germany but also in a small number of other countries—who have seized this opportunity to start a smear campaign against the Federal Republic of Germany. This is a matter of regret to the Government, not only because the allegations made against us are completely devoid of foundation but—and this is far more important—because it is the view of the Government that the present situation in the Middle East—particularly in view of the great distress of the people in the fighting area—is as inappropriate as it could possibly be for propaganda campaigns of this nature. Instead, the Government believes, every effort should be made to relieve the distress caused to humanity by taking whatever humanitarian steps may be feasible and, if possible to arrive at a solution of the problems inherent in the situation by means of constructive peace proposals.

'A special appeal is made to the United Nations to assist in finding a peaceful and just settlement. The Federal Government has held this view from the time that the tensions in the Middle East began to increase and before hostilities began and would like to take the present opportunity of again stressing this fact.

'The absurd accusation has been made that the Federal Republic of Germany has contributed to both the development and the intensification of the crisis by arms supplies to Israel, supplies which were alleged to have increased in the month of March. This accusation is false and the mere fact of constant repetition will not make it true.

'It is a fact that up to the spring of 1965 the Federal Republic had supplied weapons and war material up to the value of US $ 45 million to Israel and weapons and war material up to the value of US $ 30 million to the Arab states. This amounts to less than 2 per cent. of the overall amount of arms supplies to the area over the last twelve years and which, according to international estimates, were of a total value of 4 to 5 thousand million US $, a total made up of the supplies from a large number of different countries. In view of the increasing tensions in the area, the Government of the Federal Republic of Germany decided, in the spring of 1965, to supply no more weapons or war materials to the Middle East and since that time it has adhered strictly to this decision. And here, let me at once state that it is determined to adhere to this decision in the future as well.

'It is the view of my Government that governments should refrain from allowing tensions that do not involve the Middle East to be linked with the extremely difficult problems of this area and that in particular, the problems existing there should not be burdened at the present stage with slanderous statements in line with the technique of the cold war. The Federal Republic of Germany is doing what it can to bring about an easing of the tensions inherent in the present situation. False accusations, having their origin in the European situation, might jeopardize the efforts we are making.

'It is the considered opinion of the Government of the Federal Republic of Germany that it is high time to banish for ever from the Middle East the spectre of war and destruction so that the inherent abilities, inventiveness and talent for peaceful reconstruction can be successfully deployed by the entire population of this area.

'The Government of the Federal Republic of Germany has declared its willingness, immediately after the cessation of hostilities in the Middle East, to give humanitarian aid to the afflicted people and particularly to the refugee emergency cases. The first German consignments of foodstuffs, medical supplies and clothing have already arrived; theses supplies will be continued.

'In his speech on June 24th, 1967, the Federal Chancellor appealed to all the countries of the world to set aside their rivalries and unite in joint reconstruction and rehabilitation work in the Middle East. The Government of the Federal Republic of Germany is determined that it will play its full part in any such programme'."

Kurt Georg Kiesinger on the situation after the Arab-Israeli war

On the occasion of the annual meeting of the Deutsche Gesellschaft für Auswärtige Politik (Society for the Discussion of German Foreign Policy), on June 23rd, 1967, Federal Chancellor Kurt Georg Kiesinger gave a lecture in which he explained many of the individual details of the situation of German foreign policy. An important part of this speech was that devoted to the situation in the Middle East; at the same time, Kiesinger set forth some ideas on a possible German peace and détente policy. This particular part of the speech ran as follows:

"At the moment it is not clear how a lasting system of peace can be created in the Middle East. But I would like to say a few words, both on behalf of myself and the Government. As long as this area continues to be regarded, in the conventional sense, as the sphere of interest of rival great powers it will be difficult, if not impossible, to arrive at a peaceful settlement. Again, the system of controls and guarantees—however necessary this may be in itself—can never get to the root of the trouble. And this applies in exactly the same measure to other crisis areas.

"We are firmly of the opinion that if a joint effort is made—and if large material investments are made—it ought definitely to be possible to advance the peaceful development of the entire area. Large-scale projects with the practical aim of improving living conditions, without regard to purely national frontiers, and particularly ensuring a safe livelihood for the Palestine refugees, should be an international matter—international both in conception and execution. When the passions caused by war have abated somewhat, it will, of course, be necessary for the warring parties to co-operate in peaceful reconstruction. The Federal Government would be prepared to play its part in a large-scale peace campaign and in the execution of such projects on a scale commensurate with the extent to which the scheme is to be developed.

"During the last few days a number of attempts have been made to cast doubt upon the genuineness of the peace policy of the Federal Government as far as the Middle East is concerned. The mouthpiece of this smear campaign is once again the Soviet Union. But the facts speak for themselves so eloquently that there are really very few (and those few have special motives) that feel impelled to follow the Moscow party line and support this propaganda campaign. And indeed, the Soviet accusation has hardly ever been taken seriously in the debate up to now—not even by the Arab states.

"By now it has become a cliché to account for the unstable situation in the Middle East—and also in many other parts of the world—by saying that it is due to the inherent impossibility of supplying exploding populations with the most urgent necessities of life and ensuring them an existence consistent with the dignity of man. It looks as though the increase in population will make it impossible to maintain even the present existence-level—unsatisfactory as it is—and that an even greater degree of misery is in store for many millions of human beings. The population in many parts of the world is increasing much more rapidly than the social product. We are well aware of the fact that the efforts of the industrialized nations to cope with the dramatic crisis arising out of this situation are being very severely tested.

"I also made reference to this problem in my Government statement in the Bundestag. I pointed out that we must economize in all fields of our activity. There are only two activities that I have deliberately excluded from this economy drive. One of them is the training and research programme in science and industrial engineering and allied trades and the other is development aid. We had these same principles in mind when we passed the Budget because we realized that it was obviously in our own interest to feel a sense of responsibility for the part we are called upon to play in the general advancement in the world.

"The problems arising in connection with this question of development aid are well-known. It is, of course, more than we in Germany can do to give every kind of aid wherever it may be necessary. The Government will therefore attempt to draw up a programme—at least where bilateral aid is concerned—to ensure that our resources are concentrated on projects that are particularly designed to give aid in the most efficient and the most essential way—i.e., to feed more people and to encourage the development of a reasonable degree of appropriate industrialization. We shall attempt to choose fields of activity in which our particular knowledge and experience can be used but we shall also attempt to pass on to others engaged in the same project our earnest convictions of the importance of the methods employed.

"It is regrettable that there should be some powers who often supply weapons in large quantities and at large costs but who, as far as development aid goes, are not contributing in proportion to their economic potential. It is my earnest and sober belief, without any Utopian illusions, that in our own, clearly understood mutual interest, East and West should cease to use development aid as a weapon in the struggle between two systems. Instead, they should co-ordinate their efforts and decide on a practical course of collaboration. The Middle East could be the first great task in which, under the stress of necessity, co-operation of this kind could be achieved. It would be the surest guarantee of lasting peace in that area. Here again, the Federal Government is prepared to give whatever aid it can. The highly industrialized countries of the world could make co-operation in this field an important element in their general policy of preserving peace and easing political tensions. Even now, many of the old enmities are beginning to appear illogical and outdated in view of the new and more urgent tasks that are facing us today.

"The policy of peace and political détente that we in Germany are pursuing is, indeed, directed to just this end—namely, that of settling obsolescent antagonisms and encouraging co-operation instead—however difficult this may be to carry out. Without this co-operation new divergencies of interest are bound to arise in the world: There will be a gulf between the interests of North and South, between those of rich and poor, between those of white and coloured, and all these are bound to result in tensions and conflicts in comparison with which our present-day conflicts would appear harmless. We hope that this realistic assessment will have an increasing effect on political thought and action in both East and West. Here again, we are prepared to make whatever contribution we can."

Other German activities

The public statements of the Federal Government were designed to show that it was actively interested in a lasting settlement throughout the entire Middle-East area and that this particularly includes affording practical aid to humanity in distress. One of the main tasks underlying the Government's offers of aid is that of re-settling the Arab refugees and putting an end to their near-captivity of almost 20 years in camps. It was with these points in mind that the Note was presented to the United Nations and that a speech was made by the Federal Chancellor on July 31st, 1967, and a statement made by the Federal Minister of Foreign Affairs, who in the same way, outlined the attitude of the Government to the Middle-East conflict. The text of the statement was as follows:

"The Government of the Federal Republic of Germany has followed with close attention the proceedings of the special emergency session of the United Nations dealing with the Middle-East crisis. In company with the member states of this organization, the Government fervently hopes that in the interests of world peace and a thriving system of co-operation between peoples a peaceful, just and lasting settlement of the problems in the Middle East will be found as soon as possible. The Government will support all efforts directed towards eliminating the distressing consequences of military operations and will do all in its power to eliminate at the same time any circumstances which might lead to the development of new conflicts.

"One of the most important tasks confronting us in this situation is that of helping the distressed people of this area and safeguarding their rights and privileges. The German people share with all peace-loving nations the conviction that now, at long last, the spectre of war and the terror it brings should be banished forever from the Middle East so that the inherent abilities, inventiveness and talent for peaceful reconstruction which is their heritage can be successfully deployed by the entire population in this area. The Federal Government has not intervened in the conflict. It has decided, once the hostilities are at an end, to lose no time in giving assistance and relief to war victims and it has made offers to this effect to the governments concerned. Without regard to the conflict, it is continuing its development projects in these countries. It is particularly concerned with the fate of refugees and is ready to make whatever contribution it can to the settlement of this problem. At the same time it has the desire to live in peace and friendship with all the Arab countries and would consider it a catastrophe if any further obstacles to the successful pursuit of this aim were to arise.

"As Federal Chancellor Kiesinger stated on June 23rd, the Federal Government is prepared to engage in co-ordinated efforts to provide practical and efficacious aid where needed. It believes that the present situation in the Middle East calls for co-operation between East and West and is most willing to join both in constructive planning and in the subsequent taking of practical steps, whether in collaboration with the Special Organizations of the United Nations or in some other way."

This speech, given by the Federal Minister of Foreign Affairs, must be seen in the context of the reception of the Soviet Chargé d'Affaires, Ambassador SmM. Kudriavtsev, by the Federal Minister of Foreign Affairs, Brandt, on July 27th, 1967. On this occasion the Soviet Chargé d'Affaires handed the Federal Minister of Foreign Affairs a "Statement from the Soviet Government" on its attitude in the Middle-East conflict. In an announcement made by the Ministry of Foreign Affairs it was said that this statement was made in the light of the question of the Middle-East conflict being submitted by the UN Plenary Assembly to the World Security Council on July 21st, 1967. The text of the Soviet statement is as follows:

"The Soviet Chargé d'Affaires will verbally explain that the statement of the Soviet Government is directed to all countries with which it has diplomatic relations. Although the Federal Republic of Germany is not a member of the UN the Soviet Government hopes that the Federal Government will also contribute to the cause of peace and the easing of tensions in the Middle East. The Federal Minister of Foreign Affairs has promised to examine the Soviet statement carefully."

By August 7th, the Federal Government had already published a further statement on the Soviet Note in which the following comment is made on the points raised by the Soviet Ambassador on July 27th, 1967:

"The Federal Government has examined the Soviet statement carefully and with interest. Whereas it is true that the Federal Government, not being a member country of the United Nations, did not take part in the debates of the Special Emergency Session, it nevertheless entertains in common with the member countries of this organization, the sincere desire that in the interests of world peace and a thriving system of co-operation of peoples, a peaceful, just and permanent settlement of the problems in the Middle East will be achieved as soon as possible. It notes with satisfaction that it and the Soviet Government are in agreement in this desire. Although, as is known to the Government of the Soviet Union, the opinions of the two Governments differ on the origin and the subsequent development of the Middle-East crisis we nevertheless feel the same concern for the welfare and safety of the population in this area. It is for this reason that the Federal Government included in its Statement of July 31st, 1967 a reminder that it is prepared to take part in appropriate, co-ordinated measures to be taken by both East and West for the benefit of the Middle East."

Spontaneous reactions among the German people

On June 2nd, 1967 the German-Israeli Society published an appeal written by Adolf Arndt, one of the delegates to the Bundestag, which was supported by the Presidium and the Board of Trustees of the German-Israeli Society and a large number of personalities from the world of politics and from economic life, from professional associations and from the Press.

The appeal was worded as follows:

"We appeal to you to re-establish peace in the Middle East and to save Israel from destruction. The closing of the straits of Tiran is a deadly blow to the cause of peace. Its aim is to paralyze the Israeli port of Eilat, the intention being to destroy the economic viability of Israel. Israel is to be given the bitter choice to be doomed either by the blockade in the Gulf of Aqaba and the burden of armament thus forced upon it or else to resist and thus give the false impression of being the aggressor.

"We cannot remain silent when the Israeli people is threatened with genocide. The State of Israel is the last refuge of many people coming from our country who escaped from the genocide once instituted by the Germans against the European Jews.

"We warn all those bearing public responsibility in our country—and particularly the Bundestag and the Federal Government—not to turn silently away from this state of affairs but to throw its influence for peace into the balance and, with all the moral and peaceful means at its disposal, to support the Israeli people against the threat of extermination and also to support every attempt to obtain justice and to re-establish peace.

"We appeal to all of you to show, by peaceful means, your solidarity with those threatened people who are to be burned by bomb and rocket or extinguished by starvation. If there are others who shrink timidly from action and think it is enough to save one's own skin, show them that there are many ways of voluntarily working for peace. It is in itself something to give the threatened people the strong conviction that they are not abandoned by the whole world. In that very moment when we have begun to help Israel to bear the trade losses and financial burdens of its alertness and defensive preparedness, we are already helping those in danger by this activity alone.

"We appeal to the youth of the country to show that it can see through the efforts of certain powerful forces in the world to create artificial centres of crisis. It is not by means of a game of hide-and-seek, camouflaged as diplomacy, that peace can be saved; and again, it is not by deceiving oneself that this time it is not our own fate that is being decided. The youth of both parts of Germany should join in feeling and expressing disgust and revulsion at the people of Israel being threatened with extermination. They expect an uncompromising statement of policy from those in power."

This appeal, which was published in the majority of daily German newspapers and appeared on placards in towns and villages, did more than just elicit feelings of sympathy for Israel, it produced a flood of offers of aid from everywhere throughout the land.

Reports from the various towns

It is impossible to describe all the reactions throughout the entire German nation. But the many and varied expressions of solidarity with Israel in its fight for freedom are reflected in the following reports. They bear testimony to the change of mental attitude of the entire German people.

Aachen: The Committee of the "Help for Israel" campaign makes an appeal for moral support and practical aid for humanitarian purposes in Israel. The appeal is signed by numerous well-known organizations and persons in public life.

Augsburg: The Committee of the "Humanitarian Aid for Israel" campaign appeals for financial donations, "Caritas" (Church Welfare Organization), Inner Mission and Workers' Welfare Movement open up a Donation Benefit Account.

Berlin: The Senate of Berlin allocates DM 10,0000 for humanitarian relief work. The district Berlin-Charlottenburg remits DM 10,000 to the German-Israeli Society for the "Aid to Israel" campaign. An ecumenical service of intercession at the Gedächtniskirche of Jews and Christians of all denominations is held. Rabbi Lehrmann pronounces the final benediction. The Protestant Student Community hold a meeting of solidarity with appeals by Günter Grass and Professor Helmut Gollwitzer. Appeal of the German Co-ordination Council for Christian-Jewish Co-Operation to "make practical efforts" with the object of organizing material and financial aid. Declaration of sympathy with the Israelis on the part of the Lord Mayor Heinrich Albertz. Declaration of solidarity by the Berlin Social Democrats, the Youth Circle of the Land Berlin, the Circle of Political Youth, the Youth Union and the Federal Association of German-Israeli Study Groups. Appeal from the Chairman of the Council of the Protestant Church in Germany, Bishop Dietzfelbinger, to all parishes to hold services of intercession. Appeal to support Israel made in the annual general meeting of the League of those Persecuted by the Nazi Régime. Appeal of the author Günter Grass to young Germans to undertake voluntary work in Israel (reconstruction) under his leadership, in response to which there have already been 500 applications. Distribution of a leaflet issued by the Federal Board of German-Israeli Student Groups (BDIS); the leaflet is entitled "Peace for Israel" and 20,000 copies were printed and issued to the universities and colleges of the Federal Republic and West Berlin.

On June 7th, 1967, more than 300 young Germans report at the Jewish Community Centre in Berlin for civilian service in Israel. A ceaseless flow of financial donations and declarations of solidarity from the population of Berlin reach the Jewish Community Centre. There are demonstrations by various student groups bearing placards such as "We are for Israel—In Our Hearts Burns the Flame of Solidarity" or "Berliners, help Israel!". The German-Israeli Society publishes a new appeal for donations in the Berlin daily papers. Classified advertisements "Help for Israel" are given free space by the Berlin publishers—and the same applies to the Press in West Germany. A large number of families in Berlin express their readiness to take in any Israeli children that may be left uncared for. There have been collections by the BDIS and the Friends of the Hebrew University in the streets of Berlin. The Berlin taxis that are on the hire-car radio network hold an Israel benefit-day, the proceeds to be credited to the Donations Account of the Jewish Centre. The State College of Creative Arts in Berlin wishes to be associated with the "Help for Israel" appeal. The Society of Young German Employees plans a voluntary service mission lasting three or four weeks. The proceeds of an entertainment given in the "Albert-Schweitzer Youth Hostel" have been allocated to

Israel. Declarations of solidarity are made by the PEN Club, the Association for Protection of German Authors and the Academy of Arts. In the Jewish Centre there is still a flood in donors, and also volunteers for harvesting and construction work—a flood that has been maintained ever since the hostilities began. Berlin actors, the students of the Academy of Graphic Arts and the "13th August Teamwork Group" declare their solidarity with Israel. The proceeds of a Berlin Philharmonic Concert, arranged specially for the purpose, are sent to the Red Cross for the benefit of war-victims in the Middle East. In the second joint Jewish-Protestant-Catholic service to be held since the outbreak of hostilities in the Middle East, the Protestant Bishop of the Land Berlin and Brandenburg, Kurt Scharf, appeals in the Charlottenburg synagogue, "for the right to exist of the country of Israel" and for peace in the Middle East.

Bielefeld: Silent protest march of the students of the Teachers Training College calling for peace in the Middle East. Service of prayer in the Church of Zion at Bethel. The Jewish cultural centre receives many donations and declarations of sympathy from the population.

Bochum: Associations of the Youth Circle call for a demonstration of sympathy for Israel. The District Chairman of the German Federation of Trade Unions appeals to the Bochum trade union representatives to support all measures taken by and demonstrations etc. staged by the democratic parties, associations and churches "to preserve the existence of Israel".

Bonn: Visits or telephone calls from approximately 1,000 German doctors, nurses, workers, soldiers and young people from all professions to the Israeli Embassy, offering their services for work in Israel. Appeal for help of the German-Israeli Society; opening of three "Aid for Israel" bank accounts for donations. Statement by Federal Chancellor Kurt Georg Kiesinger before the CDU party to the effect that the Government will introduce a humanitarian aid programme for the areas affected by the war. Declaration of sympathy for Israel from the SPD party. Silent protest march of approximately 2,000 students, with demonstrations in the Münsterplatz. Appeals by Günter Grass and the Bundestag delegate Adolf Arndt, calling for aid to Israel. A doctor in private practice donates a complete operating-theatre. The Association of Private Children's Homes offers the Federal Ministry of Family Affairs 150 places in their homes for any Israeli children that may have to be evacuated and 15 places for expectant mothers. Medicines, bandages and blood-bank donations from the German Red Cross, valued at DM 100,000, for the countries affected by the war. The 'German Städtetag' (Council of Municipalities) sends an express letter to its member towns and cities asking them to support the appeal made by the Bundestag delegate Adolf Arndt on behalf of Israel. Social Democrat Youth Associations declare their solidarity with Israel in a proclamation and ask young people in Germany for financial donations to aid Israel. The Workers' Welfare Organization opens two accounts and asks for donations to its Aid-to-Israel Scheme. The President of the German-Israeli Society, Under-Secretary Benda and Bundestag delegate Westphal present Asher Ben Natan, the Israeli Ambassador with two cheques of DM 500,000 each, being the first yield of the Society's collection. The Israeli Embassy has, in the meantime, received several thousand letters containing expressions of sympathy and financial donations. The Society for Christian-Jewish Collaboration, Bonn, recruits youthful volunteers for work in Israel. The League of German Catholic Youth calls upon its members for reconstruction work in Israel.

Brunswick: Publication of an "Aid-to-Israel" appeal signed by many personages of Brunswick public life. Service of prayers in all churches of the Brunswick Protestant-Lutheran Regional Church.

Bremen: Appeal for donations from the German-Israeli Society and the Society of Friends of the Hebrew University. Almost 500 families are prepared to take in children from Israel.

Darmstadt: The South Hesse Protestant Brotherhood of Michael offers the Jewish Centre prayers of intercession on behalf of Israel.

Dortmund: The Society for Christian-Jewish Collaboration, the CDU, SPD, FDP parties, the Dortmund Youth Circle and the Political Youth Circle sign a call for a demonstration; 10,000 copies of a joint resolution distributed to the citizens. Demonstrations of sympathy in the Marktplatz (market square) with addresses by the town mayor and other leading citizens. The box-office receipts from two performances in the theatre "Folklore Studio D" are allocated to the "Aid-to-Israel" campaign.

Düsseldorf: "As a visible expression of solidarity and of the trust that we have in the Israeli people" the German Federation of Trade Unions purchases Israel bonds to the value of three million DM. A working committee is set up to organize aid to Israel in collaboration with the synagogue congregation. Nine doctors start a private aid scheme for the Israeli civilian population. Processions and demonstrations by various youth organizations. The German Federation of Trade Union calls upon all its members, particularly the younger members, to take part in demonstrations "in order to re-establish peace and to preserve the existence of Israel". Large demonstration of sympathy, with a speech by Kühn, Minister President of the Land North-Rhine-Westphalia, and an appeal by Günter Grass. Presentation of 10,000 DM to the Israeli Embassy by the Society for Christian-Jewish Collaboration. Some of this money was collected after a public concert in the streets of Düsseldorf. The box-office receipts of a performance of the "Intimes Theater" are allocated to the "Aid for Israel" scheme.

Duisburg: Silent protest march of the "Junge Union" group and the other youth associations of Duisburg; signing of a general appeal "Peace in the Middle East".

Essen: Josef Neuberger, the Minister of Justice of North-Rhine-Westphalia, speaks at a demonstration of sympathy called by students and youth organizations. Processions of young people for "Peace in the Middle East" with the town mayor of Essen and the Chairman of the Jewish community of Essen. Street-collection by the Socialist Youth Group on behalf of Israel. Resolutions of students and professors of the Pedagogical College in which the attitude of the Arabic states is condemned. Religious service of the Christian communities together with the Jewish community in the Synagogue at Essen. At the invitation of the municipal youth circle and the Society for Christian-Jewish Collaboration actors and students of acting of the Folkwang School give acting and singing performances; the receipts are for the "Aid to Israel" campaign.

Esslingen: District Youth Group appeals for aid for the Middle East.

Frankfurt: Art auction "Frankfurt Artists Help Israel" campaign yields 21,000 DM, which is transferred to Israel. The town of Frankfurt donates 30,000 DM. The town council appeals to the population for donations. Silent protest march of students, members of the 'Junge Union' youth group, the Falken youth group and the young members of the Trade Unions with demonstration of sympathy with Israel on the Römerberg. The town mayor, Professor Brundert, in an address, appeals to the population of Frankfurt to show solidarity with Israel. The Bank of Social Economy (Bank für Gemeinwirtschaft) decides to buy Israeli bonds to the value of 3 million DM. The control committee of the 'Jugendring' group of Hesse appeals to all Hessian young people and youth associations that have visited Israel to make use of their contacts with Israeli friends in order to give moral and material assistance. A "Control Board for Humanitarian Aid to Israeli Citizens" is set up with the co-operation of the three major democratic parties, the Protestant and Catholic Churches, the Trade Unions, the Chamber of Industry and Commerce, the Social Economy Bank and other organizations and institutions in Frankfurt. The "Ecumenical Educational Tours Co. Ltd." company sends a pilot group of 25 young people for a three weeks' visit to work in a "kibbutz" farm. The Protestant circle "Church and Israel" appeals for monetary donations.

Freiburg: The German Caritas Organization gives 100,000 DM for the war victims in the Middle East and conducts an appeal campaign, appealing to the whole population for donations. "Group 47" appeals to all German authors for solidarity and voluntary civilian service in Israel. Frau Gertrud Luckner starts a campaign to assist distressed persons in Israel within the country itself. The "Novalis" bookshop holds an auction of works of art, the proceeds to be used for aid in Israel.

Fürth: An "Aid for Israel" Committee is founded, consisting of representatives of the Social Democratic, the Christian Democratic and the Free Democratic Parties, the Trade Unions and personages in public life; numerous messages of sympathy and offers of aid to the Israeli religious community.

Hamburg: Hamburg doctors donate medical supplies to the value of 35,000 DM. The Midnight Show "Shalom", featuring prominent artists, yields a net profit of more than 34,000 DM for the Israeli Red Cross. The Society for Christian-Jewish Collaboration, the German-Israeli Society, the Friends of the Hebrew University, the German Trade Union Association and others appeal for donations; the Protestant Bishop Wölber and the Catholic Suffragan Rudloff and other prominent personages appeal for blood donations for Israel. The Hamburg Senate gives medical supplies (antibiotics and blood plasma) for war-disabled Israeli citizens to the value of 50,000 DM. More than 100 Hamburg families state that they are prepared, within a few days, to accept refugee children from Israel. More than 1,000 Hamburg citizens donate blood. The school parliament starts a campaign for donations through all Hamburg schools. The Hamburg 'Jugendring' youth group, the Students 'Association of the University and the Protestant Students' Union identify themselves with a silent protest march demanding justice and peace for Israel. Declarations of sympathy and offers of aid to Israel from the people of Hamburg are symbolized in a mass demonstration with an address by the former Lord Mayor of Hamburg Paul Nevermann and Günter Grass.

Hanover: "Peace for Israel" demonstration staged by town 'Jugendring' youth group and by several thousands of the inhabitants and an address given by Richard Lehners, the President of the Hanover "Provincial Landtag".

Heidelberg: Demonstrations of sympathy by the students and professors of Heidelberg University, coupled with an appeal to the population; campaign for donations conducted by the Society for Christian-Jewish Collaboration.

Kassel: Campaign committee founded and poster campaign for "Help to Israel" started; volunteers distribute leaflets, appealing for donations. The town gives 10,000 DM for medical supplies.

Karlsruhe: Service of intercession for peace in the Middle East, in numerous churches throughout the town. During the days of crisis the Jewish Community in Karlsruhe constantly receives messages of sympathy and offers of aid; numerous people—the majority of them young people—report for voluntary service in Israel; within a matter of a few days the amount of more than 200,000 DM is received by the Jewish Community from all strata of the population. The Lugert bookshop conducts an auction for the benefit of Israel.

Coblence: Publishing of an appeal for aid to Israel signed by a large number of leading personages of the town with the following words: "There must be no neutrality towards injustice. It is our moral duty to commit ourselves to this cause. Declarations of sympathy alone are not enough." The Caritas organization of Coblence agrees to make available a children's nursing home for Israeli children; Caritas and the Workers' Welfare Association appeal for aid to Israel. The Protestant Women's Aid Organization in the Rhineland starts a collection during a members' meeting, half the yield of this collection to be used for Israeli war victims and half for the Arab war victims.

Cologne: The Adam Stegerwald Social Aid Society makes available its three convalescent homes for the 'Aid-to-Israel' programme for the gratuitous use of any of those evacuated, for children and old people. In the Church of the Trinity, a joint service of intercession of the Protestant and Catholic Communities takes place. The town council gives the German-Israeli Society a donation of 30,000 DM for the civil population in the war-affected areas of Israel and Jordan. Two benefit concerts for the "Aid-to-Israel" campaign are held by the town in connection with the German-American Society and the Society for Christian-Jewish Collaboration. A "Peace for Israel" demonstration and a silent protest march in which the Minister President of North-Rhine-Westphalia, Heinz Kühn, and the President of the Land Parliament, John van Nes Ziegler, and leading personages of the town takes place. Kühn addresses the Assembly, saying: "None of us must disassociate ourselves from this situation. The individual practising neutrality is guilty of moral desertion". A demonstration of solidarity is staged in the Assembly Hall of the University in the presence of Josef Neuberger, the Minister of Justice of North-Rhine-Westphalia, whose two sons are serving on the front in Israel. The Cologne Society for Christian-Jewish Collaboration appeals for "Peace for Israel", an appeal signed by Minister President Kühn, the Lord Mayor Theo Burauen, and a large number of leading citizens of Cologne. Assistant committee of the Cologne synagogue community founded for aid to Israel. A large number of donations, both of money and of goods from the people of Cologne. Appeal on behalf of bishops in Germany by the Archbishop of Cologne, Cardinal Frings for prayers for peace. The Cologne beat orchestra "G-66", in collaboration with another eleven amateur beat groups, gives a beat concert "Aid for Israel" in the Mülheim Town Hall. The receipts from this concert (over a thousand DM) were given to the Society for Christian-Jewish Collaboration, the money being earmarked for the reconstruction of Jerusalem. The beat orchestra "G-66" is composed of two Israelis, one Egyptian and a German.

Konstanz: Demonstration procession in front of the University for "Israel's right to live". Appeal by the Society for Christian-Jewish Collaboration to the people of Konstanz to take part in the demonstration. Staff and administration of the University declare their solidarity.

Mannheim: Leaflet campaign of the Social-Democrat College Union calling on people to support the Israeli people.

Marburg: Large numbers of German youths volunteer for work in Israel at the "Development Aid Group of Youth in Germany".

Mönchengladbach: "Help Israel" appeals for donations made by the Mönchengladbach Young Socialists.

Munich: "People of Germany help the people of Israel" committee formed under the sponsorship of the Lord Mayor Hans-Jochen Vogel. The committee consists of personages of public and political life, including Frau Brigitte Gerstenmaier, Bonn; Burghard Freudenfeld of the Bavarian Radio Network; Rolf Vogel, publisher of the bulletin "deutschland-berichte" (News about Germany), Bonn and a number of Munich Bank Directors. The wording of the appeal of the committee is as follows: "Show that you, as free people are acting on behalf of free democratic people and that we could only deplore the dreadful ill-treatment of an innocent people, subsequently destroyed for the most part. Israel lies encircled by aggressive forces; what we need are mobile hospitals, blood-transfusion equipment, ambulances, bandages—in short, everything for the treatment of non-combatants and for dealing with the wounded." 3,000 people demonstrate on the Königsplatz square, where the following words were spoken by the Vice-President of the Bavarian Diet, Wilhelm Högner: "I think that I am speaking in the name of all Germans in passing on to the Jewish people all our best wishes in the hour of their peril." Blood-donation centre crowded with potential donors; centre appeals for further blood donations. The joint benefit campaign of Germans and of members of the Jewish Community of Munich yields a million DM. The German-Israeli Youth Group of Cultural Education appeals for aid to Israel.

The Protestant Rural Youth in Bavaria proclaims its willingness to accept children from the Hammacabi Kibbutz at Haifa in the event of an evacuation scheme for children from Israel being carried out. From Rosenheim it is reported that a large number of families have already stated that they are willing to receive children. Twelve members of the Protestant Rural Youth group in Bavaria have volunteered for service in a kibbutz (Israeli farm). An anonymous donor has from the rural district of Munich contributes 1,000 DM to the fares of the above group. The students of the college of political sciences appeal for aid campaigns. The members of the Munich cabaret "Lach- und Schiess-gesellschaft", in conjunction with a number of German and Israeli artists, produce a charity show "Shalom" in the German Museum; the net profits, approximately 50,000 DM, are used for medical supplies for Israel. The Chairman of the German-Israeli Educational Youth Group appeals to young people to volunteer for harvesting work in Israel; the intention is to organize group travel at concessional prices with the aid of a Munich travel bureau. 10,000 DM are earmarked by way of aid to Israel by the delegates of the SPD Landtag party group and the SPD Bavarian Association. About 25 German publishing houses combine to put a large-scale classified advertisement in the "Süddeutsche Zeitung", appealing for aid to Israel. The German-Israeli Educational Youth Group contributes 20,000 DM, obtained from appeals for donations and a collection in the street, to the border-country kibbutz En-Gev. About 65,000 DM is collected from an art auction held in the Munich "Künstlerhaus" Art Centre on July 12th, by the Educational Youth Group under the aegis of the Aid-to-Israel scheme. Some 330 works of art are donated by artists and private collectors and the proceeds passed on to the Israeli Embassy.

Münster: The German-Israeli Society forms a local team appealing for "Aid-to-Israel". In addition, the town starts a special appeal under the sponsorship of the "Münster Volunteer Aid Society".

Nuremberg: "Aid-to-Israel" committee started; joint appeal made by the Church communities and the German Trade Union Association committee of Nuremberg. The Protestant, Catholic and Trade Union Youth groups declare solidarity with Israel in a "Peace-for-Israel" campaign. The district youth association "Nürnberg Stadt", and its associated youth groups make collections in the streets. The Bavarian group of Protestant Voluntary Youth Service declares its solidarity with the "Aid-to-Israel" campaign of the German-Israeli Society.

Oberhausen: The action committee of the local control board of the German-Israeli

Society plans to set up a "Kinderdorf" for the rehabilitation of Israeli children and their parents, the land being donated by a mining company.

Oldenburg: A large number of well-known personages of the town sign the "Aid-to-Israel" appeal.

Siegburg: The "Jungsozialisten", (young socialists), run a campaign "for the moral support of Israel".

Stuttgart: 30,000 DM's worth of bandages are given by the town by way of "Contribution to the relief of distressed". Collection, run by the students of the Academy of Arts. As in the case of other West German Jewish Communities, donations from all levels of the population are coming in constantly at the Israeli religious community. Appeal launched by the Society for Christian-Jewish Collaboration for voluntary harvest workers and doctors. Protestant ministers collect more than 59,000 DM in their parishes. The plenary assembly of the Land youth group Baden-Württemberg appeals for Aid-to-Israel. The tourist organization "Friends of Nature" appeals to all its members for donations. Service of intercession in the Stuttgart synagogue appealing for lasting peace. Service of intercession in the Stuttgart Collegiate Church. A first instalment of 250,000 DM is donated by the Charity Organization of the Protestant Church in Germany for emergency measures and for first aid in reconstruction work. Blankets, tents and stretchers are sent by air from the emergency store of the Charity Organization to the bases of the ecumenical aid organization in the Middle East. There are very many well-known personages behind the appeal "Aid-to-Israel" and these give their signature in proof of the fact. The students of the Stuttgart colleges identify themselves with the "Aid-to-Israel" appeal of the German-Israeli Society. The Stuttgart Technical College organizes petitions. Anonymous donations amounting to 1,000 DM are sent to the Israeli Cultural-Educational Association. On July 8th, in Stuttgart, a cheque for 150,000 DM is presented to the Press Attaché Zwi T. Shomrat of the Israeli Embassy in Bad Godesberg, the whole amount resulting from voluntary donations in response to the local Stuttgart "Aid-to-Israel" campaign.

Wiesbaden: The "Workers Samaritan League" appeals for donations for Israel. The CDU District Association, the local SPD Organization, representatives of the two Churches, the Ministers of State Strelitz and Tröscher, publishers and journalists sign a "Solidarity with Israel" declaration.

Wuppertal: Demonstrations for "Peace in the Middle East—Aid for Israel" in the town-hall square, with an address by the Minister of Justice of North-Rhine-Westphalia, Josef Neuberger. Service of intercession by Christians and Jews. "Aid-to-Israel" committee founded and appeal made to the inhabitants for donations. The Young Socialists of Wuppertal declare their solidarity with Israel.

Würzburg: The Franconia Society for Christian-Jewish Collaboration publishes an appeal for donations to help Israel, with the support of the mayors of Würzburg, Schweinfurt, Kitzingen and Aschaffenburg.

On June 14th, the Presidium of the German-Israeli Society issued a second appeal to the German people for aid to Israel:

"The war in the Middle East is over; we are now faced with the task of winning the peace. This peace is the aim for which the Israelis have so convincingly defended themselves from the neighbour countries that threatened them with extinction.

"It is now up to the United Nations, the great powers and all countries concerned to ensure once and for all Israel's right to exist and to make the necessary arrangements for a peaceful settlement which will guarantee the position of all the countries in the Middle East, including Israel.

"The time has now come for us, filled as we are with admiration for the achievements of the Israelis and with human understanding for the position in which they now find themselves, to give practical expression to the solidarity that we feel. We must make it easier for this small country in the Middle East to devote its entire energies to the work of reconstruction. The sick and wounded must be cared for, children looked after, refugees aided, ruined dwellings replaced and Jerusalem rebuilt.

"Our first appeal for aid to this Israel, threatened as it is with genocide, has produced gratifying results and our sincere thanks are due to all those who have responded to this appeal.

"The German-Israeli Society is now appealing for still more support of this work of peaceful reconstruction that has been started in the meantime and even the smallest contribution is of some help."

Young people from Germany are helping in Israel

On July 24th, a "token" group of German volunteers travelled to Israel. The group worked in collaboration with Israelis for three months in the Kibbutz Givat Hayim. The twelve participants (consisting of students, manual workers and clerical workers) were members of the German-Israeli Society which also financed the journey, and were selected from the 3,000 volunteers who sent their offers of aid to the Israeli Embassy. The Old Testament expert, Prof. Heinz Kremers, from the Teachers Training College at Kettwig/Ruhr is the head of the group.

In its letter of thanks to all those who had offered to take part in voluntary service work in Israel the Israeli Embassy pointed out that it was not possible to make use of their offers but owing to the fact that some voices had been raised in protest against this attitude in Israel itself the Embassy and the Israeli Ministry of Foreign Affairs decided that they should at least allow official "token groups" (as a token of good will of all the offers of aid that had been received) to visit Israel. Independent of these were the "unofficial" groups arranged through the private initiative of organizations or by the kibbutzim farms.

By the middle of July, 1967, a total of some 4,000 young Germans had offered German youth group associations or the Israeli Embassy their services for reconstruction work in the Middle East. The Federal Ministry of Family and Youth Affairs made a statement on this subject on July 17th, 1967 to the effect that it would make available Government funds for work in connection with the social and educational interests of youth, for campaigns to assist in the rehabilitation and reconstruction in the Middle East. Reconstruction and rehabilitation camps of this kind would be organized by youth organizations in the Federal Republic.

A pilot group of 20 volunteers earmarked for Israel by the rehabilitation organization of young people left by air for Tel Aviv on August 11th; this group stayed in Israel until the beginning of October and its chief work was in the restoration of universities, schools and dwellings damaged in the war and in creating civil defence facilities in Jerusalem.

80 young people went for four weeks to Israel, mainly in connection with harvesting

Kurt Georg Kiesinger and David Ben Gurion in front of the Palais Schaumburg (1967)

Willy Brandt receives Abba Eban in Bonn (1967)

Reception of the publisher Axel Springer (left) by the Israeli Prime Minister Levi Eshkol (1966)

Walter Hesselbach (right), member of the Board of the Bank für Gemeinwirtschaft and President of the "Society of Friends of the Hebrew University", talking to Asher Ben Natan (1965)

Demonstration proclaiming the Israeli people's right to live; summer 1967 in Munich

in kibbutzim farms. Organizers of this work included the German Organization "Kolpingwerk" and the Action Group of the German Christian Reconstruction and Rehabilitation Organization. The young people bore the major part of the expenses involved themselves.

On August 13th, the 2nd and 14th of September, three more groups left for Israel. Their last week in Israel was spent by almost all of them in an educational tour of the country.

A group of 25 young people from Berlin had been working from July 10th, to July 31st, on harvesting at Moshav Rishpon. The request for harvesting aid from Berlin came directly from the farmers' co-operative. It was passed on by letter to 100 young people, 67 of whom had declared their readiness to depart immediately. The cost of return fares was borne by the administrative department of the Berlin Senate.

The first of the groups of volunteers organized by the German Catholic Youth Association took off by air for Israel on July 9th. This group of 10, the majority being young workmen and engineers, worked in Nazareth on the building of a school for workmen.

A group of 25 students and assistants from the University of Konstanz had already been in Jerusalem since the beginning of July, engaged in war-damage repair work. A further group organized by the Association of German Student Bodies was also sent to Jerusalem at the beginning of August, its programme being to work for six weeks and spend a fortnight touring the country.

The eleventh group, belonging to what was known as the "Expiation Campaign", to be deployed for a prolonged period in Israel was given a farewell address on July 20th, in the Jewish Parish building in Berlin. This group of 22 went to work for a year in kibbutzim and to build the Alyn Home for polio-stricken children.

On August 3rd, 30 German students flew to Israel to take part in a joint seminar together with the Israeli Students Association in Tel Aviv and also to undertake practical work on the campus of the Hebrew University in Jerusalem. Funds were received by this group from the German Youth Scheme. In addition each participant was required to contribute DM 330,—.

The Trade Union of Public Utilities, Traffic and Transport Services has sent 52 members of its youth organization to Israel for relief work.

These few groups of Germans that have gone to Israel to work for the country constitute only a fraction of the volunteers that have been giving practical expression to their views over the past few months.

Asher Ben Natan on reactions among the German people

During the weeks of the crisis and afterwards many Israeli politicians expressed their thanks to the German people for their moral support. On June 8th, 1967, Asher Ben Natan had a conversation with the editor of this book, in which he said:

"After what has happened it was actually to be expected that the press in the Federal Republic would now write about our great victories and voice their satisfaction. But I noted with pleasure that even before, during the period of the great threat to Israel, the newspapers adopted a standpoint which made it quite clear that it was the very existence of Israel that was at stake, that an iron ring was being formed around Israel and that this was something that the world could not allow and could not tolerate. People were speaking of another 'Munich'. Here, the situation was seen in its true perspective and all the responsible newspapers in the Federal Republic were even then quite clear and definite in their attitude—an attitude which, of course, we were most gratified to note. The same applies to radio and TV media and I am glad to note that the German public was kept properly informed about the situation at every stage in the conflict, by radio, press and television. The truth was our best support and it is the truth that we need now that the political struggle proper begins, now that the military operation is at an end. The actions of the German public are another thing that fills me with satisfaction, the hundreds and hundreds of letters that are reaching us from the young and the older people as well who are volunteering for work—for all kinds of work—in Israel. I believe we have had more than a thousand letters up to now; and to these must be added the donations, so freely and spontaneously given that accompany these letters. Or again the donations that are anonymous. There is something very special about the anonymous donations. The letters contain many deeply moving indications of affection for our people—utterances that are completely spontaneous and from the heart. They are reaching us from all parts of Germany. All this is evidence of the fact that here our struggle for existence and for our rights is followed with great sympathy and understanding by the general public which is willing to give us all its support. Also there are very many young people that have come to us and offered their services without there being any connection whatsoever with some feeling of guilt—no, it is a thing that refers to the present, to today, to tomorrow and not merely to the past, and I should say that the feeling of these young people is one of shame rather than guilt."

Question: "Your Excellency, the large number of offers of service, of aid, of financial donations coming from the entire people and not only from German youth prompt me to ask the question whether there is not something completely new that can be developed between Israel and Germany as a result of all this. I think of the period after the war and I should like to ask whether you do not think that closer relations and more intimate human contact between our two peoples may result—in fact, those very relations for which you, and many people in Germany, are actually working every day."

Answer: "I think there are many things that will be made easier and I hope there will be many examples of rapid progress. At times when sympathy and aid is required it is easy to see the attitudes of those with whom one is in contact, it is easy to see where one has friends. It is inevitable for there to be some kind of reaction to circumstances such as these. For years there has been a trend towards improvement of relations between Germany and Israel and there can be no question about the fact that the demonstrations of sympathy and the aid that has been provided by the German people for Israel will continue this trend; I would say that the progress of improving relations between our two peoples has been definitely hastened by the attitude of the German population. It will help many people in Germany and Israel to get over some of their difficulties."

Question: "Your Excellency, in common with other states the Federal Republic of Germany is obliged to remain neutral. But there are many politicians in our country who stated quite openly that in addition to political neutrality there is such a thing as human and moral engagement and that the heart cannot remain neutral. What do you feel about this attitude?"

Answer: "In the first place I should like to stress that there have been many personages who—irrespective of rank and title—have stated their views far more strongly in private conversations than these same personages have done officially. In the second place we noted with great satisfaction before the fighting broke out that the Federal Government fully recognized the right of free navigation. That was an important statement and one that was made just at the right time. It has frequently been my privilege and my pleasure to hear it said that there can be no such thing as neutrality of the heart. This has become obvious in many pronouncements that have been made. Many a politician has had great difficulty in finding the words to express himself in a way that could sound something like neutral. One might say that they were forced to modify the trend of their thoughts because there were no other words that they could say. We have heard much about the word 'non-intervention' and possibly 'non-intervention' is even a better word to use than 'neutrality'. I followed the debate in the Bundestag and it was easy for me to note the play of nuances in a number of public statements made. The spontaneous and obvious reaction of almost all the delegates in the Bundestag was, of course, most gratifying."

315

Summing-Up

The path taken by Germany—the Federal Republic of Germany—towards Israel is by no means at an end. When this contribution to the most exciting chapter of German post-war history ended in November 1967, hardly more than two years after the first German Ambassador set foot on Israeli soil, it was at a time when a certain normalization in the relations between the two peoples had been achieved.

The communion, the approaching of Germans and Israelis is continuing. Whatever conversations, councils and negotiations take place and in collaboration of any kind between the two, we shall always be thinking back to these years that are described—and, of course, documented—in this book.

In recent times we have heard it stated often enough that it is only the youth of the two countries that will be able to tread this pathway of communion and of normalization. Indeed, we constantly hear that we have to put up with the fact that the generations of older people, of 40, 50 and 60 years of age are usually so oppressed with the sense of the past that we shall find no morally unencumbered people at all. But the path taken by the two countries up to 1967 proves the contrary. It was in those very generations that produced the murderers and the exponents of power politics that there were so many people of all professions and strata of the population that remained unaffected and that took up the matter and deliberately ran the risk of pioneering for better relations despite the tears and the tragedy of the recent past. To this older generation belonged people like Otto Küster, Franz Böhm, Fritz Erler, Kurt Birrenbach and Walter Hallstein and all those others who ought to be mentioned here as well. And in the younger middle-aged generation there are people like Franz Josef Strauss, Rolf Pauls, Rainer Barzel, Helmut Schmidt and many, many others who simply settled down to the work of conducting negotiations and making the decisions necessary for this pioneer work. The documents are proof of this.

And there is another thing that can be seen from the documents: the freedom of action of these men, a freedom that arose from the realization that the word "reparation" should convey more than the merely linguistic connotation associated with an international expression. The statements and the actions of so many politicians have made it clear that reparation involves a human and moral way of life that can only originate in the voluntary service of free men.

Index to documents

This index is intended as an aid to those readers who are interested in the originals or the complete texts of those excerpts published here. Those particular documents which are described in brackets as tape recordings, original texts or photocopies are all to be found in the Editor's archives, and are available for inspection by arrangement.

Konrad Adenauer's interview with Karl Marx on 11th November 1949 for the "Allgemeine Wochenzeitung der Juden in Deutschland", Issue 33, 1st Year of Publication, 25th November, 1949. 17

Report by Carlo Schmid on the Congress of the Inter-Parliamentary Union in Istanbul in 1950 (tape recording) 19

Report by Herbert Blankenhorn in 1965 on the first talks on reparations (tape recording). 21

Paper by Dr. Hendrik van Dam on "The Problem of Reparation and Compensation for Israel", 1st July 1950 (original text). 21

Note of the 12th March 1951 from the Israeli Government delivered to the French Foreign Minister by the Israeli Ambassador. 27

Session of the Bundestag on 27th September 1951; statements by Adenauer, Löbe, von Brentano, Schäfer, von Merkatz, Reismann, Decker, and Ehlers. (Records of the German Bundestag, Session 165, Bonn, 27th September 1951, 6697D—6700A). 32

Letter of 6th December 1951 from Konrad Adenauer to Nahum Goldmann. 36

Letter of 29th February 1952 from Konrad Adenauer to Federal Finance Minister Fritz Schäffer. 37

Conversation with Hermann Josef Abs in 1967 on the London Reparations Conference (tape recording). 39

Report in 1962 by Franz Böhm on the reparation negotiations in Wassenaar, Holland (tape recording). 42

Report in 1962 by Felix E. Shinnar on the reparation negotiations in Wassenaar, Holland (tape recording). 42

Report in 1967 by Hermann Josef Abs on the London Reparation Conference (tape recording). 42

Statement by Embassy Counsellor Keren, the Israeli Observer at the London Reparations Conference, on 29th February 1952. 43

Letter of 23rd April 1952 from Professor Franz Böhm to Federal Chancellor Konrad Adenauer. 44

Letter of 19th May 1952 from Nahum Goldmann to Konrad Adenauer. 47

Report to the Federal Chancellor on 24th May 1952 by Professor Franz Böhm on his meeting with Nahum Goldmann. 49

Communiqué on the meeting between Konrad Adenauer and Nahum Goldmann in Paris on 28th May 1952. (Konrad Adenauer, "Erinnerungen 1953—1955", Stuttgart 1956, P. 151.) 53

Report by Felix E. Shinnar in 1962 on the signing of the Reparations Agreement in Luxembourg on 10th September 1952 (tape recording). 55

Discussion with Moshe Sharett in 1962 on the Luxembourg Agreement (tape recording). 55

Agreement between the Federal Republic of Germany and the State of Israel on 10th September 1962. (German Bundestag, 1st Term of Government 1949, Publication No. 4141, Enclosure 2, Page 18 (English original text). 56

Letter of 10th September 1952 from Moshe Sharett to Konrad Adenauer. (German Bundestag, 1st Term of Government 1949, Publication No. 4141, Enclosure 2, Page 34f, Letter No. 1a.). 68

Statement by Konrad Adenauer to Parliament on the ratification of the Luxembourg Agreement on the 4th March 1953. (Records of the German Bundestag, Session 252, Bonn, 4th March 1953, 12092 C.). 69

Ratification of the German-Israeli Reparation Agreement on 18th March 1953. Summary of the discussions of the Committee for the Occupation Statute and Foreign Affairs by Count Spreti; speeches by Eugen Gerstenmaier (CDU/CSU), Carlo Schmid (SPD), Walther Hasemann (FDP), von Merkatz (DP), von Thadden (Independent), Müller (KPD), and Decker (FU). Ehlers: The result of the voting. (Records of the German Bundestag, Session 254, Bonn, 18th March 1953, 12272 B—12282 D.) 69

Felix E. Shinnar in 1962 on the acceptance of the Agreement in Israel (tape recording). 87

Felix E. Shinnar in 1962 on the celebrations aboard the "Haifa" in Bremen harbour (tape recording). 88

Felix E. Shinnar in 1962 on the significance of the Agreement and on the work of the Israeli Mission in Cologne (tape recording). 88

Report on the delivery of goods under the agreement. (Federal Minister for Economic Affairs, Bonn, March 1966. Report on the observance of the Agreement of 10th September 1952 between the Federal Republic of Germany and the State of Israel. Made available on the authority of the Chairman of the German Delegation of the German-Israeli Joint Commission by Joachim Ebeling, formerly in the Federal Bureau for Trade and Industry, Frankfurt/M.). 89

Assessment of the German-Israeli Reparation Agreement by Nahum Goldmann in 1962 (tape recording). 99

Statement by the Federal Ministry of Finance on the reparation instalments up to the end of 1966. ("deutschland-berichte", No. 2, 3rd year of publication, February 1967.) 99

Excerpt from Paragraph 2 of the statutes of the German Association for the Furtherance of Economic Relations with Israel, Incorporated. 103

Speech by Theodor Heuss at the dedication of the monument on the site of the former concentration camp at Bergen-Belsen on 30th November 1952. (Official text from the Offices of the Federal President.) 105

Speech by Heinrich Lübke at a Festival of Remembrance in Belsen on 25th April 1965 ("Bulletin issued by the Press and Information Office of the Federal Government" No. 75, 29th April 1965). 108

Concluding comments by Federal Chancellor Konrad Adenauer and Prime Minister David Ben Gurion on the meeting in the Waldorf Astoria in New York on 14th March 1960 (Radio RIAS II, 14th March 1960). 119

Conversation with Franz Josef Strauss on 19th January 1967 on military co-operation between the German Federal Government and Israel (tape recording). 122

Shimon Peres' interview with Rolf Vogel early in 1967 on military co-operation between Israel and the Federal Government (tape recording). 126

Statements by well-known Germans about the Eichmann Trial: Heinrich Lübke, Konrad Adenauer, Eugen Gerstenmaier, Carlo Schmid, Willy Brandt, Thomas Dehler, Franz Böhm, Bruno Heck, Julius, Cardinal Döpfner, Provost Heinrich Grüber ("Der Eichmann-Prozeß in der deutschen öffentlichen Meinung", a collection of documents by Hans Lamm, Frankfurt/M. 1961). 129

David Ben Gurion's interview with Rolf Vogel ("Deutsche Zeitung und Wirtschaftszeitung", August 1961). 132

Speeches by Martin Buber, Theodor Heuss and Professor Simon in the Hebrew University, Jerusalem in May 1960 ("Staat und Volk im Werden", Talks in and about Israel, Frankfurt/M. 1960). 134

Ben-Gavriêl on the visit of the President of the Bundestag to Israel ("Süddeutsche Zeitung", 4th December 1962). 144

Speech by Eugen Gerstenmaier in the Hebrew University, Jerusalem on 21st November 1962 (original text). 145

Question put by journalist Alfred Wolfmann and the answer given by Federal Chancellor Erhard at the Press Conference on 3rd December 1963 (excerpt from the shorthand report of the Federal Press Conference on 3rd December 1963). 160

Excerpt from the speech made by Levi Eshkol to the Knesseth on 12th October 1964 (official text of the Information Department of the Israeli Mission, Cologne, 12th October 1964). 161

Ludwig Erhard in the Budget debate in the German Bundestag on 15th October 1964 (records of the German Bundestag, Session 137, Bonn, 15th October 1964, 67D—87D). 165

Question put by SPD Member of Bundestag at question time in the House and the answer given by Federal Minister Schröder, on 3rd December 1964 (records of the German Bundestag, Session 149, Bonn, 3rd December 1964, 7361 C). 165

Statement by the Federal Government on 7th March 1965 ("Bulletin of the Press and Information Office of the Federal Government", No. 41, 9th March 1965). 168

Speech by Levi Eshkol to the Knesseth on 6th March 1965 ("Frankfurter Allgemeine Zeitung", 18th March 1965). 169

German-Israeli communiqué and correspondence of 12th March 1965 between Ludwig Erhard and Levi Eshkol concerning the commencement of diplomatic relations (Photocopies). 173

Addresses delivered at the presentation of credentials by the Ambassador Rolf Pauls to the Israeli Head of State, Zalman Shazar, on 19th August 1965 ("deutschland-berichte", No. 12, 1st Year of Publ., August 1965). 175

Agreement and communiqué of 12th May 1966 on economic aid to Israel (text of Foreign Ministry). 176

Nahum Goldmann's welcome to Konrad Adenauer in the Weizmann Institute on 3rd May 1966 ("deutschland-berichte", No. 5, 2nd Year of Publ., May 1966). 180

Speech by Abba Eban in the Weizmann Institute on 3rd May 1966 ("deutschland-berichte", No. 5, 2nd Year of Publ., May 1966). 181

Speech by Meier W. Weisgal in the Weizmann Institute on 3rd May 1966 ("deutschland-berichte", No. 5, 2nd Year of Publ., May 1966). 181

Document relating to the award to Konrad Adenauer of Honorary Fellowship in the Weizmann Institute on 3rd May 1966 ("deutschland-berichte", No. 5, 2nd Year of Publ., May 1966). 181

Konrad Adenauer's speech of thanks on 3rd May 1966 ("deutschland-berichte", No. 5, 2nd Year of Publ., May 1966). 182

Toast by Levi Eshkol to Konrad Adenauer on 3rd May 1966 in Jerusalem ("deutschland-berichte", No. 5, 2nd Year of Publ., May 1966). 183

Konrad Adenauer's reply to the toast on 3rd May 1966 ("deutschland-berichte", No. 5, 2nd Year of Publ., May 1966). 184

Speech by Nahum Goldmann at the luncheon of the Jewish Claims Conference in Jerusalem on 4th May 1966 ("deutschland-berichte", No. 5, 2nd Year of Publ., May 1966). 185

Speech by the Head of the Kibbutz Afikim on 8th May 1966 to welcome Konrad Adenauer ("deutschland-berichte", No. 5, 2nd Year of Publ., May 1966). 186

David Ben Gurion's after-dinner speech in Sde Boker on 9th May 1966 (excerpt) ("deutschland-berichte", No. 5, 2nd Year of Publ., May 1966). 187

Konrad Adenauer's reply ("deutschland-berichte", No. 5, 2nd Year of Publ., May 1966). 187

Speech by the Ambassador Rolf Pauls in Tel Aviv at the Israeli Industrial Fair in June 1966 (original text). 188

Excerpts from Amos Elon interview with Asher Ben Natan's in the "Haaretz" on 12th July 1966. 192

Excerpts from Abba Eban's statement in an interview by the "Jedioth Achronoth" on 22nd July 1966 194

Speeches made at the World Jewish Congress in Brussels (texts released by the "World Jewish Congress, Fifth Plenary Assembly, Bruxelles" on 4th August 1966):
Abba Eban on 31st July 1966 in the Standing Orders Debate (English original text). 197

Opening of the Plenary Meeting by Nahum Goldmann on 4th August 1966 (English original text). 205
Isaac Remba for Heruth-Hatzoar (English original text). 206
Speaker for MAPAM (English original text). 207
Speaker for the Achdut Ha'avodah — Poale-Zion (English original text). 208
Nahum Goldmann's intermediate speech on the reports at the 5th Plenary Meeting on 4th August 1966 (English original text). 208
Speech by Professor Gershom Sholem, Hebrew University Jerusalem. 212
Speech by Professor Golo Mann, Kilchberg/Zürich. 222
Speech by Professor Salo W. Baron, Columbia University, New York. 230
Speech by Eugen Gerstenmaier. 240
Written message from Professor Karl Jaspers to the Jewish World Congress. 244
Speech by Rabbi Joachim Prinz (English original text). 249
Speech by Hendrik van Dam, Secretary-General of the Central Council for Jewish Affairs in Germany. 251
Concluding speech by Nahum Goldmann (English original text). 255

Talk with Nahum Goldmann at Frankfurt/M., in October 1966 (tape recording). 258

Telegram of condolence from Levi Eshkol on the death of Konrad Adenauer (released by the Press and Information Office of the Federal Government). 262

Asher Ben Natan on the death of Konrad Adenauer ("deutschland-berichte", No. 5, 3rd Year of Publ., May 1966). 262

Handwritten letter from Asher Ben Natan to Konrad Adenauer Jr. ("deutschland-berichte", No. 5, 3rd Year of Publ., 1966). 263

Statement by Nahum Goldmann in New York before his departure to lay a wreath on the coffin of Konrad Adenauer ("deutschland-berichte", No. 5, 3rd Year of Publ. May 1966). 263

Telegram of condolence on the death of Konrad Adenauer from the Central Council for Jewish Affairs in Germany (released by the Press and Information Office of the Federal Government). 263

Talk with Professor Curt Woermann, the Director of the State and University Library in Jerusalem, May 1966 (tape recording). 264

Grants made by the Federal Ministry for Scientific Research to the Weizmann Institute, from 1960 to 1967. 265

The amounts set aside in the Volkswagen Foundation for the Weizmann Institute and for the exchange of scholars ("Jahresberichte der Volkswagen-Stiftung", 1963, 1965 and 1967). 265

Documents relating to the award of Honorary Fellowship to Ludwig Erhard at the Weizmann Institute on 7th November 1967 (English original text). 266

Speech by the former Israeli Minister of Justice, Pinhas Rosen, when Ludwig Erhard was awarded the Honorary Fellowship on 7th November 1967 (text by the Press Department of the Weizmann Institute). 267

Speech by Felix E. Shinnar, the former Head of the Israeli Mission, when Ludwig Erhard was awarded the Honorary Fellowship on 7th November 1967 (text by the Press Department of the Weizmann Institute). 268

Speech by Ludwig Erhard at the Weizmann Institute on 7th November 1967 (original text). 270

Conversation with Max Levy, the European representative of the Hebrew University in Strasbourg in 1967 (tape recording). 272

General instructions for cultural relations between Israel and the Federal Republic of Germany, 5th December 1961 (Israeli Foreign Ministry). 273

Report by Abba Eban to the Knesseth on cultural relations between Israel and the Federal Republic of Germany, 9th January 1962 (excerpt, released by the Information Department of the Israeli Mission, Cologne, 5th February 1962). 274

Ludwig Erhard at the consecration of the new synagogue in Worms, December 1961 (tape recording by IFAGE, Wiesbaden, from the film "Deutschlands Weg nach Israel"). 277

Address by Axel Springer on 27th September 1966 in Berlin to the Israeli guests at the handing over of the document confirming his donation to the Jerusalem Museum. 277

Asher Ben Natan's reply to Axel Springer on 27th September 1966. 280

Paragraph 2 of the statutes of the German-Israeli Society. 282

Interview in 1967 with Ernst Benda, Member of the Board of the German-Israeli Society (tape recording). 283

Conversation in 1967 with Heinz Westphal, Executive Board Member of the German-Israeli Society (tape recording). 285

Statement by Federal Foreign Minister Willy Brandt at the Federal Press Conference of 31st May 1967 (shorthand report of the Press and Information Office of the Federal Government). 288

Appeal by Willy Brandt on German television on 3rd June 1967. 288

Session of the Bundestag on 7th June 1967: statements by Federal Chancellor Kurt Georg Kiesinger, Helmut Schmidt (SPD), Baron von Kühlmann-Stumm (FDP), Rainer Barzel (CDU/CSU), Richard Stücklen (CSU Regional Group) and Willy Brandt (records of the German Bundestag, Session 11, Bonn, 7th June 1967, 5267D—5288D and 5303 B). 290

Excerpt from the declaration by Jewish citizens of East Germany ("Neues Deutschland", 23rd June 1967). 296

Regulations in the Soviet-Occupied Zone of Germany, 1967. 297

Memorandum from the Federal Government to the General Assembly of the United Nations, 29th June 1967 (Press and Information Office of the Federal Government, Bulletin No. 71, 5th July 1967).

Speech by Federal Chancellor Kurt Georg Kiesinger at the annual meeting of the German Society for Foreign Policy on 23rd June 1967 (text of the Press and Information Office of the Federal Government; excerpt). 300

Statement by Federal Foreign Minister Willy Brandt on 31st July 1967 on the position of the Federal Government in the Middle-East conflict ("Bulletin of the Press and Information Office of the Federal Government", No. 81, 1st August 1967). 302

Statement by the Soviet Government on 27th July 1967, delivered by the Soviet Chargé d'Affaires in Bonn, Ambassader S. M. Kudriavzev to Federal Foreign Minister Willy Brandt ("Bulletin of the Press and Information Office of the Federal Government", No. 81, 1st August 1967). 303

Statement by the Federal Government on the attitude of the Soviet Government on 7th August 1967 ("Bulletin of the Press and Information Office of the Federal Government", No. 83, 8th August 1967). 303

"Help Israel" appeal of the German-Israeli Society on 2nd June 1967. 304

Second appeal of the German-Israeli Society on 14th June 1967. 311

Conversation with Asher Ben Natan on 8th June 1967 (tape recording). 313

Index of names appearing in text

Abs, Hermann Josef 20, 39, 42-3, 45, 47-8, 49, 53, 77, 82, 118, 120
Adenauer, Konrad 17, 20-1, 32, 36ff, 47ff, 47ff, 53ff, 67ff, 115ff, 119ff, 129, 133, 146-7, 153, 159-60, 162, 176, 180ff, 195, 197, 206, 246, 255-6, 258, 261ff, 267, 269, 281
Ahlers, Conrad 287
Ahlwardt, Wilhelm 226
Albertz, Heinrich 305
Altmaier, Jakob 20, 253
Arendt, Hannah 241
Arndt, Adolf 254, 304, 306
Aronson, Shlomo 271
Avner, Gershom 51

Bakunin, Michael 137
Baron, Salo W. 205, 211, 230ff, 243
Barou, Noah 21, 45, 49, 51
Barzel, Rainer 167-8, 250, 293ff, 316
Bauer, Bruno 221
Beck, Max W. Freiherr von 139
Bebel, August 236
Bejerano, Shimon 102
Benda, Ernst 282ff, 306
Ben-Gavriêl, M. Y. 144-5
Ben Gurion, David 115, 117, 119ff, 129, 132-3, 145, 176, 186-7, 261-2, 275
Benjamin, Walter 220
Ben-Jehuda, J. 274
Ben Natan, Asher 102, 122, 175-6, 178-9, 192ff, 243, 262, 277, 279-80, 289, 306, 313ff
Ben Zvi, Jizchak 19
Bergmann, Max 180
Bernays, Jacob 219
Bernays, Michael 219
Birnbaum, Moshe 271
Birrenbach, Kurt 159, 166ff, 171ff, 316

Bismarck, Otto von 137, 226
Blankenhorn, Herbert 21
Blüher, Hans 221
Blum, Léon 223
Boeckel, Otto 226
Böhm, Franz 38, 41-2, 44ff, 49, 130-1, 134, 316
Borchardt, Rudolf 219-20
Brandt, Willy 130, 134, 255, 262, 267, 279, 287-8, 295, 303
Braun, Sigismund Freiherr von 298
Brentano, Heinrich von 19-20, 34, 75-6, 115-6, 119, 121, 123
Brod, Max 236
Brück, Carlheinz von 297
Brundert, Willi 282, 307
Brüning, Heinrich 230
Buber, Martin 134-5, 272
Burauen, Theo 309

Carstens, Karl 167, 169, 173
Caspar, Walter 102
Chamberlain, H. S. 236
Chouraqui, Nathan 277
Churchill, Winston 111
Clay, Lucius 269
Cohen, Hermann 219, 237
Cohn, Josef 266
Cossmann, Peter 224
Cues, Nicolaus von 143

Dam, Hendrik van 21, 26, 211, 243, 251ff
Dayan, Moshe 122, 128, 297
Decker, Hugo 35, 76ff, 86
Dehler, Thomas 130
Dehn 236
Delitzsch, Friedrich 236
Deutsch, Ernst 253
Diessenhofen, Heinrich von 238
Dietz, Fritz 102
Dietzfelbinger, Hermann 305
Döblin, Alfred 212, 243
Döpfner, Julius Cardinal 131
Dover, Seev 285

Eban, Abba 172, 181, 192, 197ff, 261-2, 270, 274, 282, 285
Ebeling, Joachim 89
Ebert, Friedrich 282
Ehlers, Hermann 19, 35, 86-7
Ehrenberg, Henry 102
Eichmann, Adolf 28-9, 124-5, 127, 129ff, 145, 154, 241, 296
Einstein, Albert 195
Eisenmenger, Johann A. 236
Elath, Eliahu 285
Elon, Amos 192ff
Erhard, Ludwig 21, 121, 159-60, 161-2, 165, 167, 169, 171, 173-4, 255, 266ff, 277, 294
Erler, Fritz 127, 255, 316
Eshkol, Levi 121, 161ff, 167, 169, 173-4, 183, 185, 262, 269-70

Faul, Richard 142
Feldmann, Michael 266
Feuchtwanger, Lion 225
Fichte, Johann Gottlieb 235
Fischart, Johann 233
Fontane, Theodor 220
Frank, Bruno 224-5
Frank, Hans 30
Frankenstein, Wolfgang 297
Freisler, Roland 145
Freska, Hans Friedrich 266
Freud, Sigmund 219
Fries, Jakob Friedrich 236, 309
Frings, Joseph Cardinal, 262
Frowein 85

Gaulle, Charles de 187, 261
Geibel, Emanuel 106
Geiger, Abraham 219
Gelmond, Daniel 277-8
Gentner, Wolfgang 264-5, 270
George, Stefan 223
Gerstenmaier, Brigitte 309
Gerstenmaier, Eugen 78ff, 130, 134, 144ff, 166, 205, 211, 240ff, 255ff, 262-3, 267

Giesberts, Johannes 282
Globke, Hans 160
Gobineau, Joseph Arthur Comte de 140
Goebbels, Joseph 241, 245, 296
Goethe, Johann Wolfgang von 107, 135, 219, 235, 267
Goldmann, Nahum 21, 36-7, 40, 45, 47-8, 49ff, 71-2, 99, 107, 115, 119, 180, 182-3, 185, 188, 197, 205, 207-8, 222, 240, 244, 255ff, 263
Goldstein, Kurt 297
Gollancz, Victor 15
Gollwitzer, Helmut 305
Grad, Dora 277
Grass, Günter 305ff
Grossmann, Kurt G. 26
Grüber, Heinrich 16, 131-2, 283
Grundig, Lea 297
Gundolf, Friedrich 223-4
Gutermann 142

Haber, Fritz 180
Hallgarten, Charles 143
Hallstein, Walter 38, 53, 116, 123, 316
Hammerstein, Kunrat von 245
Harden, Maximilian 226
Hase, Karl-Günther von 166-7, 169
Hasemann, Walther 81ff
Hassel, Kai Uwe von 166
Hebel, Johann Peter 220
Heck, Bruno 131
Hegel, Friedrich 137, 143
Heine, Heinrich 33, 218, 220, 237
Heinemann, Dannie 182
Heinz, Friedrich Wilhelm 236
Heisenberg, Werner 272
Herder, Johann Gottfried von 138-9, 235
Herrmann, Georg 219
Herzl, Theodor 143
Hess, Gerhard Moshe 102, 220
Hesselbach, Walter 102-3, 272, 282
Heuss, Theodor 105ff, 134ff, 145, 267
Heuss-Knapp, Elly 144
Heydrich, Reinhard 28, 271
Hickiewicz, Adam 236
Himmler, Heinrich 240-1, 245, 296
Hindenburg, Paul von 230
Hirsch, Otto 105
Hirsch, Samson Raphael 219

Hitler, Adolf 17, 19, 28-9, 55, 70, 85, 100, 106, 108, 110, 112-3, 121, 127, 129, 134-5, 138, 140, 145-6, 149, 151, 153-4, 156, 163, 180-1, 168, 194, 206, 208, 210, 223, 225-6, 236, 240ff, 245, 249, 256, 260-1, 274, 296
Högner, Wilhelm 310
Höss, Rudolf Hans Ferdinand 29
Hoffmann, Chaim 20
Hofmannsthal, Hugo von 224
Holl, Julius 42
Humboldt, Wilhelm von 214, 237, 267, 271-2

Illert, Friedrich M. 276

Jaspers, Karl 244ff
Jensen, Hans 265-6
Johnson, Lyndon Baines 159, 201, 261
Josephthal, Giora 49, 51ff, 55

Kafka, Franz 220
Kahler, Erich von 225
Kahn, Siegbert 297
Kaisen, Wilhelm 88
Kant, Immanuel 107
Kantorowicz, Ernst 223
Katz, Rudolf 253
Katzenstein, Ernest 261
Kaul, Friedrich Karl 132, 297
Kempner, Robert M. W. 26-7
Kennedy, John F. 119
Keren, Uri 26, 43, 47
Khrushchev, Nikita 137
Kiesinger, Kurt Georg 122, 262, 290-1, 293, 300ff, 306
Kollek, Theodore 277-8
Kortner, Fritz 253
Krämer (siehe Keren)
Kraus, Karl 217
Kremers, Heinz 312
Krone, Heinrich 167
Kühlmann-Stumm, Knut Freiherr von 293
Kühn, Heinz 307, 309
Küster, Otto 41, 316
Küstermeyer, Rudolf 15
Kynass, Fritz 236

Lagarde, Paul de 236
Lahr, Rolf 173, 178-9
Lamprecht, Karl 234
Langenstein, Heinrich von 232
Laskov, Chaim 123
Lassalle, Ferdinand 217

Law, Basic 32
Lazare, Bernard 220
Lazarus, Moritz 217
Lehners, Richard 308
Lehr, Robert 85
Lessing, Gotthold Ephraim 107, 209, 216
Levavi, Arye 285
Levy, Max 272
Liber, Maurice 238
Liebermann, Max Hugo von Sonnenberg 226
Liffson, Shneior 266
Lipmann, Otto 217
Lissauer, Ernst 224
Löbe, Paul 33-4, 75, 77
Lochner, Louis 15
Loeser, Franz 297
Lübke, Heinrich 108ff, 129, 176, 262
Luckner, Gertrud 15
Lüth, Erich 15
Luther, Martin 233, 236
Lynen 265

Mahler, Gustav 217, 225
Mann, Golo 205, 211, 222ff, 241-2, 243
Mansfield, A. 277
Manzini, Giuseppe 236
Marcel, Gabriel 112-3
Marx, Karl (Journalist) 15, 17, 20-1, 26, 140, 215, 217
Maurois, André 223
McCloy, John 25, 253
McGhee, George 160
Meir, Golda 162, 167, 274, 285
Mendelssohn, Felix 33
Mendelssohn, Moses 214, 217
Mendès-France, Pierre 223
Merkatz, Hans-Joachim von 34, 76, 83
Meyer-Lindenberg, Hermann 172
Meyerhof, Otto 180
Mommer, Karl 165-6
Mommsen, Theodor 236
Müller, Oskar 84ff

Naphtali, Fritz 281
Nasser, Gamal 'Abd en- 163, 166, 168, 203, 287
Naumann, Friedrich 143
Nes Ziegler, John van 309
Neuberg, Carl 180
Neuberger, Josef 307, 311
Nevermann, Paul 308

Nietzsche, Friedrich 155, 210
Nurok, Rabbi 20

Ollenhauer, Erich 134
Oppenheimer, Franz 268
Orff, Karl 189

Papen, Franz von 230
Pauls, Rolf 173, 175, 183, 188ff, 261, 282, 316
Péguy, Charles 217, 220
Peres, Shimon 119-20, 122ff, 167, 285
Pferdmenges, Robert 85
Prinz, Joachim 211, 249ff, 256
Pudor, Heinrich von 236

Rathenau, Walther 33, 226
Reichert, Karl 37
Reifenberg, Ernst 297
Reinhardt, Max 225
Reinicke 245
Reismann, Bernhard 34, 76
Remba, Isaac 206
Renan, Ernest 199
Rendtorff, Rolf 283
Reuter, Fritz 220
Reventlow, Count Ernst von 233
Riesser, Gabriel 140
Ritzel, Heinrich Georg 180
Rosen, Pinhas 267
Rosenberg, Ludwig 134, 253, 282
Rothfels, Hans 112
Rousseau, Jean-Jacques 108, 137ff
Rühs, Friedrich Chr. 236

Sacher, Harry 233
Sapir, Joseph 285
Schäfer, Hermann 34, 76
Schäffer, Fritz 37
Scharf, Kurt 306
Scheidemann, Philipp 226

Schiller, Friedrich von 107, 209, 216, 237, 267
Schmid, Carlo 19, 80-1, 130, 134, 136, 267
Schmidt, Gerhard 266
Schmidt, Helmut 291ff, 316
Schmitt, Carl 230
Schoenheimer, Rudolf 180
Schoettle, Erwin 282
Schröder, Gerhard 165-6
Schröder, Kurt von 230
Schumacher, Kurt 80
Schweizer, Albert 107
Seigewasser, Hans 296
Senarclens, Aymon de 19
Shakespeare, William 223
Shalit, Amos de 266
Sharett, Moshe 55, 67ff
Shazar, Zalman 175, 186
Sheck, Zeev 167, 179, 285
Shelley, Percy Bysshe 235
Shelypin 166
Shinnar, Felix E. 42, 45, 47-8, 49, 51ff, 55, 87-8, 116, 136, 160, 167, 173, 182ff, 261, 267-8
Shirer, William 242
Sholem, Gershom 205, 211ff, 243, 286
Simmel, Georg 217, 220
Simon, Ernst 142ff
Skorzceny, Otto 145
Sombart, Werner 234
Sommer, Margaret 15
Springer, Axel Cäsar 259, 277-8, 280-1
Staab, Heinz 266
Stahl, Friedrich Julius 220
Stauffenberg, Claus Schenk Count of 223
Steinheim, Ludwig 219
Strack, Hermann 236
Strauss, Franz Josef 119-20, 122ff, 159, 169, 175, 316

Strauss, Leo 143
Strauss, Richard 195
Streicher, Julius 230
Stücklen, Richard 294-5
Sylten, Walter 283

Talmi 181
Tanne, David 103
Thadden, Adolf von 83-4
Thierfeld, Elisabeth 297
Tillich, Paul 250
Tillmanns, Robert 19
Treitschke, Heinrich von 236
Tucholsky, Kurt 219

Ulbricht Walter 154, 166, 168
Ullstein, Heinz 279
U Thant, Sithu 287

Veblen, Thorstein 219
Vogel, Hans-Jochen 309

Wagner, Richard 146, 195, 224
Washem, Yad 195
Wassermann, Jakob 224
Weber, Hans Hermann 265-6
Wehner, Herbert 255
Weichmann, Herbert 253
Weisgal, Meyer W. 181
Westphal, Heinz 265, 282, 284
Westrick, Ludger 73
Willstaetter, Richard 180
Woermann, Curt 264
Wolf, Gerry 297
Wolff, Jeanette 253
Wolfmann, Alfred 160
Wolfskehl, Karl 223

Yahil, Chaim 117, 285

Zarnitz, Marie-Luise 266
Zinn, Georg August 176
Zunz, Leopold 219
Zweig, Arnold 215